AF838333

KAPLAN PUBLISHING

EXCITING EXTRA ONLINE RESOURCES INCLUDED

Kaplan Publishing are constantly looking for ways to make a difference to students studying for CIMA qualifications.

Understanding the Difference.... CIMA SYLLABUS CONVERSION TABLE

Syllabus until November 2009	New Syllabus
Managerial Level	**Operational Level**
Paper P1 - Performance Evaluation	Paper P1 - Performance Operations
Paper P4 - Organisational Management	Paper E1 - Enterprise Operations
Paper P7 - Financial Accounting & Tax Principles	Paper F1 - Financial Operations
	Management Level
Paper P2 - Decision Management	Paper P2 - Performance Management
Paper P5 - Integrated Management	Paper E2 - Enterprise Management
Paper P8 - Financial Analysis	Paper F2 - Financial Management
Strategic Level	**Strategic Level**
Paper P3 - Risk & Control Strategy	Paper P3 - Perfomance Strategy
Paper P6 - Business Strategy	Paper E3 - Enterprise Strategy
Paper P9 - Financial Strategy	Paper F3 - Financial Strategy

Something Different... FREE KAPLAN EN-gage ONLINE RESOURCES

FROM SEPTEMBER 2009, ACCESS THE CONTENTS OF THE TEXT IN FULL
FROM 2010, BENEFIT FROM ONLINE TESTING AND OTHER USEFUL RESOURCES

How to access your online resources

- **Kaplan Financial students** will already have a Kaplan EN-gage account and these extra resources will be available to you online. You do not need to register again, as this process was completed when you enrolled. If you are having problems accessing online materials, please ask your course administrator.
- **If you purchased through Kaplan Flexible Learning or via the Kaplan Publishing website** you will automatically receive an e-mail invitation to Kaplan EN-gage online. Please register your details using this e-mail to gain access to your content. If you do not receive the e-mail or book content, please contact Kaplan Flexible Learning.
- **If you are already a registered Kaplan EN-gage user** go to www.EN-gage.co.uk and log in. Select the 'add a book' feature and enter the ISBN number of this book and the unique pass key at the bottom of this card. Then click 'finished' or 'add another book'. You may add as many books as you have purchased from this screen.
- **If you are a new Kaplan EN-gage user** register at www.EN-gage.co.uk and click on the link contained in the e-mail we sent you to activate your account. Then select the 'add a book' feature, enter the ISBN number of this book and the unique pass key at the bottom of this card. Then click 'finished' or 'add another book'.

EN-gage

Your Code and Information

This code can only be used once for the registration of one book online. This registration will expire when the final sittings for the examinations covered by this book have taken place. Please allow one hour from the time you submitted your book details for us to process your request.

43QR-Tryu-AOoY-2eSr

CIMA

Paper P1

Performance Operations

Complete text

British library cataloguing-in-publication data

A catalogue record for this book is available from the British Library.

Published by:
Kaplan Publishing UK
Unit 2 The Business Centre
Molly Millars Lane
Wokingham
Berkshire
RG41 2QZ

ISBN 978-1-84710-884-5

Printed in the UK by CPI William Clowes, Beccles NR34 7TL.

Acknowledgements

We are grateful to the Association of Chartered Certified Accountants and the Chartered Institute of Management Accountants for permisssion to reproduce past examination questions. The answers have been prepared by Kaplan Publishing.

Contents

chapter

Intro

Paper Introduction

How to Use the Materials

These Kaplan Publishing learning materials have been carefully designed to make your learning experience as easy as possible and to give you the best chances of success in your examinations.

The product range contains a number of features to help you in the study process. They include:

(1) Detailed study guide and syllabus objectives

(2) Description of the examination

(3) Study skills and revision guidance

(4) Complete text or essential text

(5) Question practice

The sections on the study guide, the syllabus objectives, the examination and study skills should all be read before you commence your studies. They are designed to familiarise you with the nature and content of the examination and give you tips on how to best to approach your learning.

The **complete text or essential text** comprises the main learning materials and gives guidance as to the importance of topics and where other related resources can be found. Each chapter includes:

- The **learning objectives** contained in each chapter are taken directly from CIMA's own syllabus learning objectives. You should use these to check you have a clear understanding of all the topics on which you might be assessed in the examination.
- The **chapter diagram** provides a visual reference for the content in the chapter, giving an overview of the topics and how they link together.
- The **content** for each topic area commences with a brief explanation or definition to put the topic into context before covering the topic in detail. You should follow your studying of the content with a review of the illustration/s. These are worked examples which will help you to understand better how to apply the content for the topic.
- **Test your understanding** sections provide an opportunity to assess your understanding of the key topics by applying what you have learned to short questions. Answers can be found at the back of each chapter.

- **Summary diagrams** complete each chapter to show the important links between topics and the overall content of the paper. These diagrams should be used to check that you have covered and understood the core topics before moving on.
- **Question practice** is provided at the back of each chapter.

Icon Explanations

Definition - these sections explain important areas of Knowledge which must be understood and reproduced in an exam environment.

Key Point - identifies topics which are key to success and are often examined.

New - identifies topics that are brand new in papers that build on, and therefore also contain, learning covered in earlier papers.

Expandable Text - within the online version of the work book and the complete text is additional material such as more detailed explanation of key terms, further examples, additional writers' views and other background reading. These sections will help to provide a deeper understanding of core areas. Reference to this text is vital when self studying.

Test Your Understanding - following key points and definitions are exercises which give the opportunity to assess the understanding of these core areas. Within the work book the answers to these sections are left blank, explanations to the questions can be found within the online version which can be hidden or shown on screen to enable repetition of activities.

Illustration - to help develop an understanding of topics and the test your understanding exercises the illustrative examples can be used.

Exclamation Mark - this symbol signifies a topic which can be more difficult to understand, when reviewing these areas care should be taken.

PAPER BACKGROUND

Aim of paper

This paper primarily deals with the tools and techniques that generate information needed to evaluate and control present and projected performance. Thus, forecasting key variables, recognising uncertainties attached to future events, is a basis for budget construction; the budget is then used with costing systems to evaluate actual performance. Project appraisal relies similarly on future financial projections to provide the information on which managers can evaluate expected performance and actual outcomes.

Both budgeting and project appraisal emphasise the critical importance of optimising cash flow and the final section of the paper continues this theme from the perspective of managing working capital.

Students should be able to:

- apply both traditional and contemporary approaches to cost accounting in a variety of contexts and evaluate the impact of "modern" data processing and processing technologies such as MRP, ERP and JIT
- explain and apply the principles of standard costing, calculate variances in a variety of contexts and critically evaluate the worth of standard costing in the light of contemporary criticisms
- develop budgets using both traditional and contemporary techniques, evaluate both interactive and diagnostic uses of budgets in a variety of contexts
- pull together relevant cashflows for projects and assess the viability of these projects
- deal with the uncertainty that is likely to arise in project appraisal
- suggest plans for the effective management of short-term capital and manage short-term investments.

FORMAT OF PAPER

There will be a written examination paper of three hours, plus 20 minutes of pre-examination question paper reading time. The examination paper will have the following sections:

Section A – 20 marks

A variety of compulsory objective test questions, each worth between two and four marks. Mini scenarios may be given, to which a group of questions relate.

Section B – 30 marks

Six compulsory short answer questions, each worth five marks. A short scenario may be given, to which some or all questions relate.

Section C – 50 marks

One or two compulsory questions. Short scenarios may be given, to which questions relate.

Core areas of the syllabus

The Performance Evaluation Syllabus is divided into four sections.

	Topic	Study Weighting
A	Cost accounting systems	30%
B	Forecasting and budgeting techniques	10%
C	Project appraisal	25%
D	Dealing with uncertainty in analysis	15%
E	Managing short term finance	20%

THE SYLLABUS IN DETAIL

A – Cost Accounting Systems – 30%

Learning outcomes:
On completion of their studies students should be able to:

Lead	**Chapter**
(1) Discuss costing methods and their results.	2-8
Component	
(a) compare and contrast marginal (or variable), throughput and absorption accounting methods in respect of profit reporting and stock valuation;	2, 4
(b) discuss a report which reconciles budget and actual profit using absorption and/or marginal costing principles;	2
(c) discuss activity-based costing as compared with traditional marginal and absorption costing methods, including its relative advantages and disadvantages as a system of cost accounting;	5
(d) apply standard costing methods, within costing systems, including the reconciliation of budgeted and actual profit margins;	6, 8
(e) explain why and how standards are set in manufacturing and in service industries with particular reference to the maximisation of efficiency and minimisation of waste;	7
(f) interpret material, labour, variable overhead, fixed overhead and sales variances, distinguishing between planning and operational variances;	7
(g) prepare reports using a range of internal and external benchmarks and interpret the results;	7
(h) explain the impact of just-in-time manufacturing methods on cost accounting and the use of 'back-flush accounting' when work-in-progress stock is minimal.	3
Indicative syllabus content	
• Marginal (or variable), throughput and absorption accounting systems of profit reporting and stock valuation.	2
• Activity-based costing as a system of profit reporting and stock valuation.	5
• Criticisms of standard costing in general and in advanced manufacturing environments in particular.	7
• Integration of standard costing with marginal cost accounting, absorption cost accounting and throughput accounting.	4

- Manufacturing standards for material, labour, variable overhead and fixed overhead. 6
- Price/rate and usage/efficiency variances for materials, labour and variable overhead. 6
- Further subdivision of total usage/efficiency variances into mix and yield components.
  (Note: The calculation of mix variances on both individual and average valuation bases is required). 8
- Fixed overhead expenditure and volume variances. (Note: the subdivision of fixed overhead volume variance into capacity and efficiency elements will not be examined). 6
- Planning and operational variances. 8
- Standards and variances in service industries (including the phenomenon of 'McDonaldization'), public services (e.g. Health), (including the use of 'diagnostic related' or 'reference' groups), and the professions (e.g. labour mix variances in audit work). 7
- Sales price and sales revenue/margin volume variances (calculation of the latter on a unit basis related to revenue, gross margin and contribution margin). Application of these variances to all sectors, including professional services and retail analysis. 6
- Interpretation of variances: interrelationship, significance. 7
- Benchmarking. 7
- Back-flush accounting in just-in-time production environments. The benefits of just-in-time production, total quality management and theory of constraints and the possible impacts of these methods on cost accounting and performance measurement. 3

Lead	**Chapter**
(2) Explain the role of MRP and ERP systems.	3

Component

(a) explain the role of MRP and ERP systems in supporting standard costing systems, calculating variances and facilitating the posting of ledger entries.	3

Indicative syllabus content

- MRP and ERP systems for resource planning and the integration of accounting functions with other systems, such as purchase ordering and production planning. 3

Lead	**Chapter**
(3) Apply the principles of environmental costing.	5
Component	
(a) apply principles of environmental costing in identifying relevant internalised costs and externalised environmental impacts of the organisation's activities.	5
Indicative syllabus content	
• Types of internalised costs relating to the environment (e.g. emissions permits, taxes, waste disposal costs) and key externalised environmental impacts, especially carbon, energy and water usage. Principles for associating such costs and impacts with activities and output.	5

B – Forecasting and Budgeting Techniques – 10%

Learning outcomes:

On completion of their studies students should be able to:

Lead	**Chapter**
(1) Explain the purposes of forecasts, plans and budgets	9
Component	
(a) explain why organisations prepare forecasts and plans;	9
(b) explain the purposes of budgets, including planning, communication, co-ordination, motivation, authorisation, control and evaluation, and how these may conflict.	9
Indicative syllabus content	
• The role of forecasts and plans in resource allocation, performance evaluation and control.	9
• The purposes of budgets and the budgeting process, and conflicts that can arise (e.g. between budgets for realistic planning and budgets based on 'hard to achieve' targets for motivation).	9

Lead	**Chapter**
(2) Prepare forecasts of financial results	9, 11
Component	
(a) calculate projected product/service volumes employing appropriate forecasting techniques;	11
(b) calculate projected revenues and costs based on product/service volumes, pricing strategies and cost structures	9
Indicative syllabus content	
• Time series analysis including moving totals and averages, treatment of seasonality, trend analysis using regression analysis and the application of these techniques in forecasting product and service volumes.	11
• Fixed, variable, semi-variable and activity-based categorisations of cost and their application in projecting financial results.	2, 5, 9

Lead	**Chapter**
(3) Prepare budgets based on forecasts	9, 10
Component	
(a) prepare a budget for any account in the master budget, based on projections/forecasts and managerial targets;	9
(b) apply alternative approaches to budgeting.	10
Indicative syllabus content	
• Mechanics of budget construction: limiting factors, component budgets and the master budget, and their interaction.	9
• Alternative approaches to budget creation, including incremental approaches, zero-based budgeting and activity-based budgets.	10

C – Project Appraisal – 25%

Learning outcomes:

On completion of their studies students should be able to:

Lead	**Chapter**
(1) Prepare information to support project appraisal	13, 14
Component	
(a) explain the processes involved in making long-term decisions;	13
(b) apply the principles of relevant cash flow analysis to long-run projects that continue for several years;	14

(c)	calculate project cash flows, accounting for tax and inflation, and apply perpetuities to derive 'end of project' value where appropriate;	13, 14
(d)	apply activity-based costing techniques to derive approximate 'long-run' product or service costs appropriate for use in strategic decision making;	14
(e)	explain the financial consequences of dealing with long-run projects, in particular the importance of accounting for the 'time value of money';	13
(f)	apply sensitivity analysis to cash flow parameters to identify those to which net present value is particularly sensitive;	14
(g)	prepare decision support information for management, integrating financial and non-financial considerations.	14

Indicative syllabus content

•	The process of investment decision making, including origination of proposals, creation of capital budgets, go/no go decisions on individual projects (where judgements on qualitative issues interact with financial analysis), and post audit of completed projects.	13
•	Identification and calculation of relevant project cash flows taking account of inflation, tax, and 'final' project value where appropriate.	14
•	Activity-based costing to derive approximate 'long-run' costs appropriate for use in strategic decision making.	14
•	Need for and method of discounting.	13
•	Sensitivity analysis to identify the input variables that most affect the chosen measure of project worth (payback, ARR, NPV or IRR).	13, 14
•	Identifying and integrating non-financial factors in long-term decisions.	14
•	Methods of dealing with particular problems: the use of annuities in comparing projects with unequal lives and the profitability index in capital rationing situations.	13

Lead		**Chapter**
(2)	Evaluate project proposals	13

Component

(a)	evaluate project proposals using the techniques of investment appraisal;	13
(b)	compare and contrast the alternative techniques of investment appraisal;	13
(c)	prioritise projects that are mutually exclusive, involve unequal lives and/or are subject to capital rationing.	13

Indicative syllabus content

	Chapter
• The techniques of investment appraisal: payback, discounted payback, accounting rate of return, net present value and internal rate of return.	13
• Application of the techniques of investment appraisal to project cash flows and evaluation of the strengths and weaknesses of the techniques.	13

D – Dealing With Uncertainty In Analysis – 15%

Learning outcomes:
On completion of their studies students should be able to:

Lead	**Chapter**
(1) Analyse information to assess the impact on decisions of variables with uncertain values.	12
Component	
(a) analyse the impact of uncertainty and risk on decision models that may be based on relevant cash flows, learning curves, discounting techniques etc;	12
(b) apply sensitivity analysis to both short and long-run decision models to identify variables that might have significant impacts on project outcomes;	12, 13
(c) analyse risk and uncertainty by calculating expected values and standard deviations together with probability tables and histograms;	12
(d) prepare expected value tables;	12
(e) calculate the value of information;	12
(f) apply decision trees.	12
Indicative syllabus content	
• The nature of risk and uncertainty.	12
• Sensitivity analysis in decision modelling and the use of computer software for "what if" analysis.	12
• Assignment of probabilities to key variables in decision models.	12
• Analysis of probabilistic models and interpretation of distributions of project outcomes.	12
• Expected value tables and the value of information.	12
• Decision trees for multi-stage decision problems.	12

E – Managing Short Term Finance – 20%

Learning outcomes:

On completion of their studies students should be able to:

Lead	**Chapter**
(1) Analyse the working capital position and identify areas for improvement.	15 - 18
Component	
(a) explain the importance of cash flow and working capital management;	15
(b) interpret working capital ratios for business sectors;	15
(c) analyse cash-flow forecasts over a twelve-month period;	17
(d) discuss measures to improve a cash forecast situation;	17
(e) analyse trade debtor and creditor information;	18
(f) analyse the impacts of alternative debtor and creditor policies;	18
(g) analyse the impacts of alternative policies for stock management.	16
Indicative syllabus content	
• The link between cash, profit and the balance sheet.	15
• The credit cycle from receipt of customer order to cash receipt and the payment cycle from agreeing the order to making payment.	15
• Working capital ratios (e.g. debtor days, stock days, creditor days, current ratio, quick ratio) and the working capital cycle.	15
• Working capital characteristics of different businesses (e.g. supermarkets being heavily funded by creditors) and the importance of industry comparisons.	15
• Cash-flow forecasts, use of spreadsheets to assist in this in terms of changing variables (e.g. interest rates, inflation) and in consolidating forecasts.	17
• Variables that are most easily changed, delayed or brought forward in a forecast.	9, 17
• Methods for evaluating payment terms and settlement discounts	18
• Preparation and interpretation of age analyses of debtors and creditors.	18
• Establishing collection targets on an appropriate basis (e.g. motivational issues in managing credit control).	18

- Centralised versus decentralised purchasing. 16
- The relationship between purchasing and stock control. 16
- Principles of the economic order quantity (EOQ) model and criticisms thereof. 16

Lead	**Chapter**
(2) Identify short-term funding and investment opportunities.	19
Component	
(a) identify sources of short-term funding;	19
(b) identify alternatives for investment of short-term cash surpluses;	19
(c) identify appropriate methods of finance for trading internationally.	19
Indicative syllabus content	
• Use and abuse of trade creditors as a source of finance.	19
• Types and features of short-term finance: trade creditors, overdrafts, short-term loans and debt factoring.	18, 19
• The principles of investing short term (i.e. maturity, return, security, liquidity and diversification).	19
• Types of investments (e.g. interest-bearing bank accounts, negotiable instruments including certificates of deposit, short-term treasury bills, and securities).	19
• The difference between the coupon on debt and the yield to maturity.	19
• Export finance (e.g. documentary credits, bills of exchange, export factoring, forfeiting).	19

Paper-based examination tips

Spend the reading time reading the paper and planning your answers. You are allowed to annotate the question paper, so make use of this – e.g. highlighting key issues in the questions, planning calculations, brainstorming requirements – ensure that you understand the question. A key issue is to decide which questions you wish to attempt from section B – it is worth planning all three in outline before deciding.

Divide the time you spend on questions in proportion to the marks on offer. One suggestion **for this examination** is to allocate 1.8 minutes to each mark available, so a 25-mark question should be completed in approximately 45 minutes.

Stick to the question and **tailor your answer** to what you are asked. Pay particular attention to the **verbs** in the question.

Spend the last five minutes reading through your answers and making any additions or corrections.

If you **get completely stuck** with a question, leave space in your answer book and **return to it later**.

If you do not understand what a question is asking, state your assumptions. Even if you do not answer in precisely the way the examiner hoped, you should be given some credit, if your assumptions are reasonable.

You should do everything you can to make things easy for the marker. The marker will find it easier to identify the points you have made if your answers are legible.

Multiple choice questions: Read the question carefully and work through any calculations required. If you don't know the answer, eliminate those options you know are incorrect and see if the answer becomes more obvious. There is no negative marking, so at least have a guess on the remaining options as you may guess correctly.

Objective test questions: These are likely to be mini calculations on a limited set of data. Make sure you lay your answer out clearly as, even if you don't come to the correct answer, there will still be marks available for technique/workings.

Essay questions: Make a quick plan in your answer book and under each main point list all the relevant facts that you can think of. Then write out your answer, developing each point fully. Be concise. It is better to write a little about a lot of different points than a great deal about one or two points.

Computations: It is essential to include all your workings in your answers. Many computations (e.g. NPV) require the use of a standard format. Be sure you know these formats thoroughly before the examination and use the layouts given in the answers in this book. If you are asked to comment on a calculation then you must do so. Even if your computation contains mistakes, you will still gain marks if your reasoning is correct.

Reports, memos and other documents: Some questions ask you to present your answer in the format of a report, memo or other document. Use the correct format - ther could be easy marks to gain here.

Study skills and revision guidance

This section aims to give guidance on how to study for your ACCA exams and to give ideas on how to improve your existing study techniques.

Preparing to study

Set your objectives

Before starting to study decide what you want to achieve - the type of pass you wish to obtain. This will decide the level of commitment and time you need to dedicate to your studies.

Devise a study plan

Determine which times of the week you will study.

Split these times into sessions of at least one hour for study of new material. Any shorter periods could be used for revision or practice.

Put the times you plan to study onto a study plan for the weeks from now until the exam and set yourself targets for each period of study - in your sessions make sure you cover the course, course assignments and revision.

If you are studying for more than one paper at a time, try to vary your subjects as this can help you to keep interested and see subjects as part of wider knowledge.

When working through your course, compare your progress with your plan and, if necessary, re-plan your work (perhaps including extra sessions) or, if you are ahead, do some extra revision/practice questions.

Effective studying

Active reading

You are not expected to learn the text by rote, rather, you must understand what you are reading and be able to use it to pass the exam and develop good practice. A good technique to use is SQ3Rs - Survey, Question, Read, Recall, Review:

(1) **Survey the chapter** - look at the headings and read the introduction, summary and objectives, so as to get an overview of what the chapter deals with.

(2) **Question** - whilst undertaking the survey, ask yourself the questions that you hope the chapter will answer for you.

(3) **Read** through the chapter thoroughly, answering the questions and making sure you can meet the objectives. Attempt the exercises and activities in the text, and work through all the examples.

(4) **Recall** - at the end of each section and at the end of the chapter, try to recall the main ideas of the section/chapter without referring to the text. This is best done after a short break of a couple of minutes after the reading stage.

(5) **Review** - check that your recall notes are correct.

You may also find it helpful to re-read the chapter to try to see the topic(s) it deals with as a whole.

Note-taking

Taking notes is a useful way of learning, but do not simply copy out the text. The notes must:

- be in your own words
- be concise
- cover the key points
- be well-organised
- be modified as you study further chapters in this text or in related ones.

Trying to summarise a chapter without referring to the text can be a useful way of determining which areas you know and which you don't.

Three ways of taking notes:

Summarise the key points of a chapter.

Make linear notes - a list of headings, divided up with subheadings listing the key points. If you use linear notes, you can use different colours to highlight key points and keep topic areas together. Use plenty of space to make your notes easy to use.

Try a diagrammatic form - the most common of which is a mind-map. To make a mind-map, put the main heading in the centre of the paper and put a circle around it. Then draw short lines radiating from this to the main sub-headings, which again have circles around them. Then continue the process from the sub-headings to sub-sub-headings, advantages, disadvantages, etc.

Highlighting and underlining

You may find it useful to underline or highlight key points in your study text - but do be selective. You may also wish to make notes in the margins.

Revision

The best approach to revision is to revise the course as you work through it. Also try to leave four to six weeks before the exam for final revision. Make sure you cover the whole syllabus and pay special attention to those areas where your knowledge is weak. Here are some recommendations:

Read through the text and your notes again and condense your notes into key phrases. It may help to put key revision points onto index cards to look at when you have a few minutes to spare.

Review any assignments you have completed and look at where you lost marks - put more work into those areas where you were weak.

Practise exam standard questions under timed conditions. If you are short of time, list the points that you would cover in your answer and then read the model answer, but do try to complete at least a few questions under exam conditions.

Also practise producing answer plans and comparing them to the model answer.

If you are stuck on a topic find somebody (a tutor) to explain it to you.

Read good newspapers and professional journals - this can give you an advantage in the exam.

Ensure you **know the structure of the exam** - how many questions and of what type you will be expected to answer. During your revision attempt all the different styles of questions you may be asked.

Further reading

You can find further reading and technical articles under the student section of CIMA's website.

FORMULAE AND TABLES

PROBABILITY

$A \cup B$ = A or B. $A \cap B$ = A and B (overlap).

$P(B/A)$ = probability of B, given A.

Rules of addition

If A and B are mutually exclusive: $P(A \cup B) = P(A) + P(B)$

If A and B are not mutually exclusive: $P(A \cup B) = P(A) + P(B) - P(A \cap B)$

Rules of multiplication

If A and B are independent: $P(A \cap B) = P(A) * P(B)$

If A and B are not independent: $P(A \cap B) = P(A) * P(B/A)$

$E(x) = \sum$ (probability * payoff)

Quadratic equations

If $ax^2 + bx + c = 0$ is the general quadratic equation, the two solutions (roots) are given by:

$$x = \frac{-b \pm \sqrt{b^2 - 4ac}}{2a}$$

DESCRIPTIVE STATISTICS

Arithmetic mean

$$\bar{x} = \frac{x}{n} \qquad \bar{x} = \frac{fx}{f} \text{ (frequency distribution)}$$

Standard deviation

$$SD = \sqrt{\frac{(x - \bar{x})^2}{n}} \qquad SD = \sqrt{\frac{fx^2}{f} - \bar{x}^2} \text{ (frequency distribution)}$$

INDEX NUMBERS

Price relative = $100 * P_1/P_0$ Quantity relative = $100 * Q_1/Q_0$

Price: $$\frac{w * \frac{P_1}{P_0}}{w} \times 100$$

Quantity: $$\frac{w * \frac{Q_1}{Q_0}}{w} \times 100$$

TIME SERIES

Additive model: Series = Trend + Seasonal + Random

Multiplicative model: Series = Trend * Seasonal * Random

LINEAR REGRESSION AND CORRELATION

The linear regression equation of y on x is given by:

$y = a + bx$ or $y - \bar{y} = b(x - \bar{x})$

where

$$b = \frac{\text{Covariance (xy)}}{\text{Variance (x)}} = \frac{n \quad xy - (\quad x)(\quad y)}{n \quad x^2 - (\quad x)^2}$$

and

$$a = \bar{y} - b\bar{x}$$

or solve

$$\sum y = na + b \sum x$$

$$\sum xy = a \sum x + b \sum x^2$$

Coefficient of correlation

$$r = \frac{\text{Covariance (xy)}}{\sqrt{\text{Var(x).Var(y)}}} = \frac{n \quad xy - (\quad x)(\quad y)}{\sqrt{\{n \quad x^2 - (\quad x)^2\}\{n \quad y^2 - (\quad y)^2\}}}$$

R(rank) =

$$1 - \frac{6 \quad d^2}{n(n^2 - 1)}$$

FINANCIAL MATHEMATICS

Compound interest (values and sums)

Future Value S, of a sum of X, invested for n periods, compounded at r% interest

$$S = X[l + r]^n$$

Annuity

Present value of an annuity of one unit of currency per annum receivable or payable for n years, commencing in one year, discounted at r% per annum:

$$PV = \frac{1}{r} \quad 1 - \frac{1}{[1 + r]^n}$$

Perpetuity

Present value of one unit of currency per annum, payable or receivable in perpetuity, commencing in one year, discounted at r% per annum:

$$PV = \frac{1}{r}$$

PRESENT VALUE TABLE

Present value of $1 i.e. $(1 + r)^{-n}$ where r = interest rate, n = number of periods until payment or receipt.

Periods (n)	Interest rates (r) 1%	2%	3%	4%	5%	6%	7%	8%	9%	10%
1	.990	.980	.971	.962	.962	.943	.935	.926	.917	.909
2	.980	.961	.943	.925	.907	.890	.873	.857	.842	.826
3	.971	.942	.915	.889	.864	.840	.816	.794	.772	.751
4	.961	.924	.888	.855	.823	.792	.763	.735	.708	.683
5	.951	.906	.863	.822	.784	.747	.713	.681	.650	.621
6	.942	.888	.837	.790	.746	.705	.666	.630	.596	.564
7	.933	.871	.813	.760	.711	.665	.623	.583	.547	.513
8	.923	.853	.789	.731	.677	.627	.582	.540	.502	.467
9	.914	.837	.766	.703	.645	.592	.544	.500	.460	.424
10	.905	.820	.744	.676	.614	.558	.508	.463	.422	.386
11	.896	.804	.722	.650	.585	.527	.475	.429	.388	.350
12	.887	.788	.701	.625	.557	.497	.444	.397	.356	.319
13	.879	.773	.681	.601	.530	.469	.415	.368	.326	.290
14	.870	.758	.661	.577	.505	.442	.388	.340	.299	.263
15	.861	.743	.642	.555	.481	.417	.362	.315	.275	.239
16	.853	.728	.623	.534	.458	.394	.339	.292	.252	.218
17	.844	.714	.605	.513	.436	.371	.317	.270	.231	.198
18	.836	.700	.587	.494	.416	.350	.296	.250	.212	.180
19	.828	.686	.570	.475	.396	.331	.277	.232	.194	.164
20	.820	.673	.554	.456	.377	.312	.258	.215	.178	.149

Periods (n)	Interest rates (r) 11%	12%	13%	14%	15%	16%	17%	18%	19%	20%
1	.901	.893	.885	.877	.870	.862	.855	.847	.840	.833
2	.812	.797	.783	.769	.756	.743	.731	.718	.706	.694
3	.731	.712	.693	.675	.658	.641	.624	.609	.593	.579
4	.659	.636	.613	.592	.572	.552	.534	.516	.499	.482
5	.593	.567	.543	.519	.497	.476	.456	.437	.419	.402
6	.535	.507	.480	.456	.432	.410	.390	.370	.352	.335
7	.482	.452	.425	.400	.376	.354	.333	.314	.296	.279
8	.434	.404	.376	.351	.327	.305	.285	.266	.249	.233
9	.391	.361	.333	.308	.284	.263	.243	.225	.209	.194
10	.352	.322	.295	.270	.247	.227	.208	.191	.176	.162
11	.317	.287	.261	.237	.215	.195	.178	.162	.148	.135
12	.286	.257	.231	.208	.187	.168	.152	.137	.124	.112
13	.258	.229	.204	.182	.163	.145	.130	.116	.104	.093
14	.232	.205	.181	.160	.141	.125	.111	.099	.088	.078
15	.209	.183	.160	.140	.123	.108	.095	.084	.074	.065
16	.188	.163	.141	.123	.107	.093	.081	.071	.062	.054
17	.170	.146	.125	.108	.093	.080	.069	.060	.052	.045
18	.153	.130	.111	.095	.081	.069	.059	.051	.044	.038
19	.138	.116	.098	.083	.070	.060	.051	.043	.037	.031
20	.124	.104	.087	.073	.061	.051	.043	.037	.031	.026

Cumulative present value of $1 per annum, receivable or payable at the end of each year for n years $\frac{1-(1+r)^{-n}}{r}$.

Periods (n)	Interest rates (r) 1%	2%	3%	4%	5%	6%	7%	8%	9%	10%
1	0.990	0.980	0.971	0.962	0.952	0.943	0.935	0.926	0.917	0.909
2	1.970	1.942	1.913	1.886	1.859	1.833	1.808	1.783	1.759	1.736
3	2.941	2.884	2.829	2.775	2.723	2.673	2.624	2.577	2.531	2.487
4	3.902	3.808	3.717	3.630	3.546	3.465	3.387	3.312	3.240	3.170
5	4.853	4.713	4.580	4.452	4.329	4.212	4.100	3.993	3.890	3.791
6	5.795	5.601	5.417	5.242	5.076	4.917	4.767	4.623	4.486	4.355
7	6.728	6.472	6.230	6.002	5.786	5.582	5.389	5.206	5.033	4.868
8	7.652	7.325	7.020	6.733	6.463	6.210	5.971	5.747	5.535	5.335
9	8.566	8.162	7.786	7.435	7.108	6.802	6.515	6.247	5.995	5.759
10	9.471	8.983	8.530	8.111	7.722	7.360	7.024	6.710	6.418	6.145
11	10.368	9.787	9.253	8.760	8.306	7.887	7.499	7.139	6.805	8.495
12	11.255	10.575	9.954	9.385	8.863	8.384	7.943	7.536	7.161	6.814
13	12.134	11.348	10.635	9.986	9.394	8.853	8.358	7.904	7.487	7.103
14	13.004	12.106	11.296	10.563	9.899	9.295	8.745	8.244	7.786	7.367
15	13.865	12.849	11.938	11.118	10.380	9.712	9.108	8.559	8.061	7.606
16	14.718	13.578	12.561	11.652	10.838	10.106	9.447	8.851	8.313	7.824
17	15.562	14.292	13.166	12.166	11.274	10.477	9.763	9.122	8.544	8.022
18	16.398	14.992	13.754	12.659	11.690	10.828	10.059	9.372	8.756	8.201
19	17.226	15.679	14.324	13.134	12.085	11.158	10.336	9.604	8.950	8.365
20	18.046	16.351	14.878	13.590	12.462	11.470	10.594	9.818	9.129	8.514

Periods (n)	Interest rates (r) 11%	12%	13%	14%	15%	16%	17%	18%	19%	20%
1	0.901	0.893	0.885	0.877	0.870	0.862	0.685	0.847	0.840	0.833
2	1.713	1.690	1.668	1.647	1.626	1.605	1.585	1.566	1.547	1.528
3	2.444	2.402	2.361	2.322	2.283	2.246	2.210	2.174	2.140	2.106
4	3.102	3.037	2.974	2.914	2.855	2.798	2.743	2.690	2.639	2.589
5	3.696	3.605	3.517	3.433	3.352	3.274	3.199	3.127	3.058	2.991
6	4.231	4.111	3.998	3.889	3.784	3.685	3.589	3.498	3.410	3.326
7	4.712	4.564	4.423	4.288	4.160	4.039	3.922	3.812	3.706	3.605
8	5.146	4.968	4.799	4.639	4.487	4.344	4.207	4.078	3.954	3.837
9	5.537	5.328	5.132	4.946	4.772	4.607	4.451	4.303	4.163	4.031
10	5.889	5.650	5.426	5.216	5.019	4.833	4.659	4.494	4.339	4.192
11	6.207	5.938	5.687	5.453	5.234	5.029	4.836	4.656	4.486	4.327
12	6.492	6.194	5.918	5.660	5.421	5.197	4.968	4.793	4.611	4.439
13	6.750	6.424	6.122	5.842	5.583	5.342	5.118	4.910	4.715	4.533
14	6.982	6.628	6.302	6.002	5.724	5.468	5.229	5.008	4.802	4.611
15	7.191	6.811	6.462	6.142	5.847	5.575	5.324	5.092	4.876	4.675
16	7.379	6.974	6.604	6.265	5.954	5.668	5.405	5.162	4.938	4.730
17	7.549	7.120	6.729	6.373	6.047	5.749	5.475	5.222	4.990	4.775
18	7.702	7.250	6.840	6.467	6.128	5.818	5.534	5.273	5.033	4.812
19	7.839	7.366	6.938	6.550	6.198	5.877	5.584	5.316	5.070	4.843
20	7.963	7.469	7.025	6.623	6.259	5.929	5.628	5.353	5.101	4.870

chapter

1

CIMA verb hierarchy – Operational level exams

Chapter learning objectives

CIMA VERB HIERARCHY

CIMA place great importance on the choice of verbs in exam question requirements. It is thus critical that you answer the question according to the definition of the verb used.

1 Operational level verbs

In operational level exams you will meet verbs from levels 1, 2, and 3. These are as follows:

Level 1: KNOWLEDGE

What you are expected to know

VERBS USED	DEFINITION
List	Make a list of.
State	Express, fully or clearly, the details of / facts of.
Define	Give the exact meaning of.

Level 2: COMPREHENSION

What you are expected to understand

VERBS USED	DEFINITION
Describe	Communicate the key features of.
Distinguish	Highlight the differences between.
Explain	Make clear or intelligible/state the meaning or purpose of.
Identify	Recognise, establish or select after consideration.
Illustrate	Use an example to describe or explain something.

Level 3 - APPLICATION

How you are expected to apply your knowledge

VERBS USED	DEFINITION
Apply	Put to practical use.
Calculate	Ascertain or reckon mathematically.
Demonstrate	Prove with certainty or exhibit by practical means.
Prepare	Make or get ready for use.
Reconcile	Make or prove consistent/compatible.
Solve	Find an answer to.
Tabulate	Arrange in a table.

2 Further guidance on operational level verbs that cause confusion

Verbs that cause students confusion at this level are as follows:

Level 2 verbs

- **The difference between "describe" and "explain".**

  An explanation is a set of statements constructed to describe a set of facts which clarifies the **causes**, **context**, and **consequences** of those facts.

  For example, if asked to **describe** the features of activity based costing (ABC) you could talk, amoung other things, about how costs are grouped into cost pools (e.g. quality control), cost drivers identified (e.g. number of inspections) and an absorption rate calculated based on this cost driver (e.g. cost per inspection). This tells us what ABC looks like.

  However if asked to **explain** ABC, then you would have to talk about why firms were disatisfied with previous traditional costing methods and switched to ABC (causes), what types of firms it is more suitable for (context) and the implications for firms (consequences) in terms of the usefulness of such costs per unit for pricing and costing.

More simply, to describe something is to answer "what" type questions whereas to explain looks at "what" and "why" aspects.

- **The verb "to illustrate"**

  The key thing about illustrating something is that you may have to decide on a relevant example to use. This could involve drawing a diagram, performing supporting calculations or highlighting a feature or person in the scenario given. Most of the time the question will be structured so calculations performed in part (a) can be used to illustrate a concept in part (b).

  For example, you could be asked to explain and illustrate what is meant by an "adverse variance".

Level 3 verbs

- **The verb "to apply"**

  Given that all level 3 verbs involve application, the verb "apply" is rare in the real exam. Instead one of the the other more specific verbs is used instead.

- **The verb "to reconcile"**

  This is a numerical requirement and usually involves starting with one of the figures, adjusting it and ending up with the other.

  For example, in a bank reconciliation you start with the recorded cash at bank figure, adjust it for unpresented cheques, etc, and (hopefully!) end up with the stated balance in the cash "T account".

- **The verb "to demonstrate"**

  The verb "to demonstrate" can be used in two main ways.

  Firstly it could mean to prove that a given statement is true or consistent with circumstances given. For example, the Finance Director may have stated in the question that the company will not exceed its overdraft limit in the next six months. The requirement then asks you to demonstrate that the Director is wrong. You could do this by preparing a cash flow forecast for the next six months.

  Secondly you could be asked to demonstrate **how** a stated model, framework, technique or theory could be used in the particular scenario.Ensure you do not merely describe the model but use it to generate some results.

chapter

2

Traditional costing

Chapter learning objectives

Lead	Component
A1. Discuss costing methods and their results.	(a) Compare and contrast marginal (or variable), throughput and absorption accounting methods in respect of profit reporting and stock valuation. (b) Discuss a report which reconciles budget and actual profit using absorption and/or marginal costing principles.

1 Session content diagram

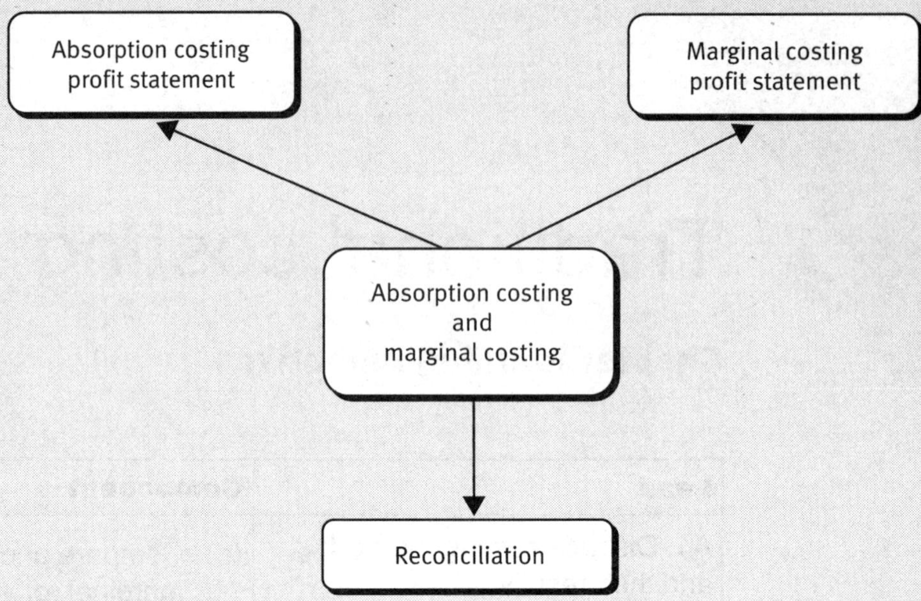

2 The purpose of costing

In the first few chapters of the syllabus we examine different techniques for determining the production cost of products. It's therefore useful to remind ourselves why we might need to know this cost.

- Inventory valuation - the cost per unit can be used to value inventory in the statement of financial position (balance sheet).
- To record costs - the costs associated with the product need to be recorded in the income statement.
- To price products - the business will use the cost per unit to assist in pricing the product. For example, if the cost per unit is \$0.30, the business may decide to price the product at \$0.50 per unit in order to make the required profit of \$0.20 per unit.
- Decision making - the business will use the cost information to make important decisions regarding which products should be made and in what quantities.

How can we calculate the cost per unit?

So we know why it's so important for the business to determine the cost of its products. We now need to consider how we can calculate this cost.

3 Absorption costing

The aim of traditional absorption costing is to determine the full production cost per unit.

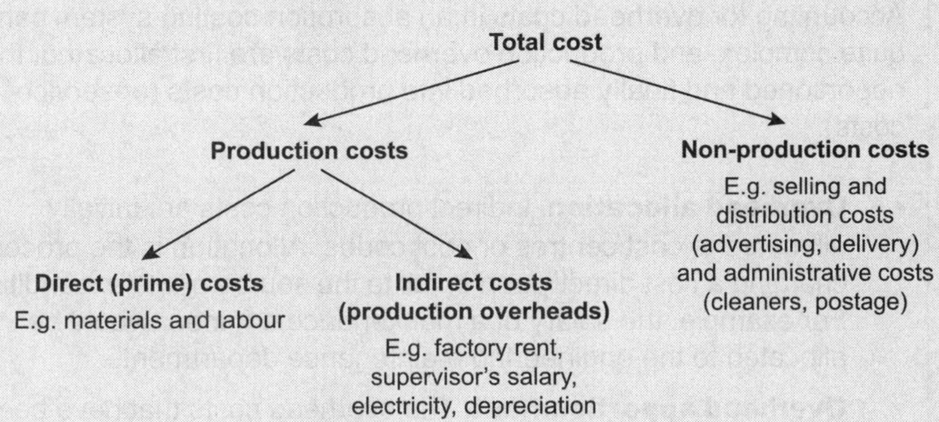

When we use absorption costing to determine the cost per unit, we focus on the production costs only. We can summarise these costs into a cost card:

	$
Direct materials per unit	X
Direct labour per unit	X
Production overhead per unit	X
Full production cost per unit	X

It is relatively easy to estimate the cost per unit for direct materials and labour. In doing so we can complete the first two lines of the cost card. However, it is much more difficult to estimate the production overhead per unit. This is an indirect cost and so, by its very nature, we do not know how much is contained in each unit. Therefore, we need a method of attributing the production overheads to each unit. All production overheads must be absorbed into units of production, using a suitable basis, e.g. units produced, labour hours or machine hours. The assumption underlying this method of absorption is that overhead expenditure is connected to the volume produced.

Calculating absorption rates

Review of overhead absorption procedure

Accounting for overhead costs in an absorption costing system can be quite complex, and production overhead costs are first allocated, then apportioned and finally absorbed into production costs (or service costs).

- **Overhead allocation**. Indirect production costs are initially allocated to cost centres or cost codes. Allocation is the process of charging a cost directly and in full to the source of the expenditure. For example, the salary of a maintenance engineer would be allocated to the engineering maintenance department.
- **Overhead apportionment**. The overhead costs that have been allocated to cost centres and cost codes other than direct production departments must next be apportioned to direct production departments. Apportionment is the process of sharing on a fair basis. For example, factory rental costs might be apportioned between the production departments on the basis of the floor area occupied by each department. Similarly, the costs of the engineering maintenance department might be apportioned between production departments on the basis of the operating machine hours in each department. At the end of the apportionment process, all the production overheads have been allocated or apportioned to the direct production departments.
- **Overhead absorption**. An absorption rate is calculated for each production department. This is the rate at which production overheads will be added to the cost of production going through the department.

  The absorption rate is calculated as:

$$\frac{\text{Total overhead cost (allocated and apportioned)}}{\text{Production volume}}$$

When the department produces a single product, production volume can be measured as the number of units produced, and the absorption rate would be a rate per unit produced.

More usually, organisations produce different products or carry out non-standard jobs for customers, and production volume is commonly measured as one of the following:

- direct labour hours worked in the department, and the absorption rate is a rate per direct labour hour worked

- machine hours worked in the department, and the absorption rate is a rate per machine hour operated
- sometimes the cost of direct labour might be used as a measure of production volume, and the absorption rate is then calculated as a percentage of direct labour cost.

Predetermined absorption rates

Although it is possible to calculate absorption rates using actual overhead costs and actual production volume, this is not the usual practice. This is because:

- It is usually inconvenient to wait until the end of an accounting period to work out what the absorption rates should be. In absorption costing systems, overhead costs are added to the cost of production as it passes through each stage in the production process, and overhead costs are absorbed when the production happens.
- A predetermined rate is required to enable a price to be estimated.
- Overhead costs may vary throughout the year. The overhead absorption rate smooths variations in overheads by applying an average overhead cost to each unit of product throughout the year.

The normal practice is therefore to absorb production overhead costs at a predetermined rate, based on budgeted overhead expenditure and budgeted production volume.

Example 1

Z Limited manufactures a single product, the budgeted selling price and variable cost details of which are as follows:

	$
Selling price	15.00
Variable costs per unit:	
Direct materials	3.50
Direct labour	4.00
Variable overhead	2.00

Budgeted fixed overhead costs are $60,000 per annum charged at a constant rate each month.

Budgeted production is 30,000 units per annum.

In a month when actual production was 2,400 units and exceeded sales by 180 units, identify the profit reported under absorption costing:

A $6,660.

B $7,570.

C $7,770.

D $8,200.

E $8,400.

4 Marginal costing

Marginal costing is a costing method which charges products with variable costs alone. The fixed costs are treated as period costs and are written off in total against the contribution of the period.

Marginal cost

Marginal cost is the extra cost arising as a result of producing one more unit, or the cost saved as a result of producing one less unit. It comprises:

- Direct material
- Direct labour
- Direct expenses
- Variable overheads

Example 2

Perry Ltd makes and sells a single product with the following information:

	$/unit
Selling price	50
Direct material	15
Direct labour	10
Variable overhead	5

Fixed overheads are $5,000. Output and sales are 1,000 units.

(a) Using absorption costing:

(i) Calculate the profi

(ii) Calculate the profit per unit

(b) Using marginal costing:

(i) Calculate the contribution per unit?

(ii) Calculate the total contribution?

(iii) Calculate the profit?

5 Contribution

Contribution is the difference between sales and the variable cost of those sales. It is useful to think of contribution as being shorthand for 'contribution towards fixed cost plus profit'.

Contribution	=	Sales	–	Variable cost
Profit	=	Contribution	–	Fixed cost
Contribution	=	Fixed cost	+	Profit

Why contribution is important

Why is contribution significant?

Contribution is an important concept in marginal costing. Changes in the volume of sales, or in sales prices, or in variable costs will all affect profit by altering the total contribution. Marginal costing techniques can be used to help management to assess the likely effect on profits of higher or lower sales volume, or the likely consequences of reducing the sales price of a product in order to increase demand, and so on. The approach to any such analysis should be to calculate the effect on total contribution.

Example 3

The details are exactly the same as for Example 2, but output and sales are now 3,000 units instead of 1,000.

Calculate the profit? Answer the question in any way that you want.

6 Contribution to sales ratios and breakeven points

Cost-Volume-Profit (CVP) analysis

CVP analysis makes use of the contribution concept in order to assess the following measures for a single product:

- contribution to sales (C/S) ratio
- breakeven point
- margin of safety

C/S ratio

The C/S ratio of a product is the proportion of the selling price that contributes to fixed overheads and profits. It is comparable to the gross profit margin. The formula for calculating the C/S ratio of a product is as follows:

$$\text{C/S ratio} = \frac{\text{Contribution per unit}}{\text{Selling price per unit}} \quad \text{or} \quad \frac{\text{Total contribution}}{\text{Total sales revenue}}$$

The C/S ratio is sometimes referred to as the P/V ratio.

Breakeven point

The breakeven point is the point at which neither a profit nor a loss is made.

- At the breakeven point the following situations occur.

  Total sales revenue = Total costs, i.e. Profit = 0

  or

  Total contribution = Fixed costs, i.e. Profit = 0

- The following formula is used to calculate the breakeven point in terms of numbers of units sold.

$$\textbf{Breakeven point (in terms of numbers of units sold)} = \frac{\textbf{Fixed costs}}{\textbf{Contribution per unit}}$$

- It is also possible to calculate the breakeven point in terms of sales revenue using the C/S ratio. The equation is as follows:

$$\text{Breakeven point (in terms of sales revenue)} = \frac{\text{Fixed costs}}{\text{C/S ratio}}$$

Margin of safety

The margin of safety is the amount by which anticipated sales (in units) can fall below budget before a business makes a loss. It can be calculated in terms of numbers of units or as a percentage of budgeted sales.

The following formulae are used to calculate the margin of safety:

$$\text{Margin of safety (in terms of units)} = \text{Budgeted sales} - \text{Breakeven point sales}$$

$$\text{Margin of safety (as a \% of budgeted sales)} = \frac{\text{Budgeted sales} - \text{Breakeven sales}}{\text{Budgeted sales}} \times 100\%$$

7 Marginal costing vs absorption costing

Marginal costing and absorption costing systems give the same profit when there is no change in stocks.

If production is greater than sales, absorption costing will show the higher profit.

If sales is greater than production, marginal costing will give the higher profit.

Absorption advantages/disadvantages

Advantages of absorption costing

The arguments used in favour of absorption costing are as follows:

- Fixed production costs can be a large proportion of the total production costs Incurred. Unless production overheads are absorbed into product costs, a large proportion of cost would be excluded from the measurement of product costs.
- Absorption costing follows the matching concept (accruals concept) by carrying forward a proportion of the production cost in the inventory valuation to be matched against the sales value when the items are sold.

- It is necessary to include fixed production overhead in inventory values for financial statements; absorption costing produces inventory values which include a share of fixed production overhead.
- Analysis of under-/over-absorbed overhead may be useful for identifying inefficient utilisation of production resources.
- There is an argument that in the longer term, all costs are variable, and it is appropriate to try to identify overhead costs with the products or services that cause them. This argument is used as a reason for activity-based costing (ABC). ABC is a form of absorption costing, and is described in a later chapter.

Disadvantages of absorption costing

There are serious disadvantages with using absorption costing to measure costs and profits.

- **The apportionment and absorption of overhead costs is arbitrary**
  There is no commercial logic or justification for the way in which overhead costs are apportioned between cost centres and absorbed into production costs. Although the process attempts to be 'fair', it is arbitrary.

  For example, suppose that a factory rental cost is apportioned between production departments on the basis of the floor area for each department. This might seem a fair way of sharing out the costs, but it does not have any commercial logic. Why not apportion the costs on the basis of the number of employees in each department? Or why not allow for the fact that some of the accommodation might be more pleasant to work in than others?In a manufacturing environment, production overheads might be absorbed on the basis of either direct labour hours or machine hours. There is no commercial logic in the choice of one instead of the other. However, choosing one instead of the other can have a significant effect on job costs or product costs.
- **Profits vary with changes in production volume**
  A second criticism of absorption costing is that profits can be increased or reduced by changes in inventory levels. For example, by increasing output, more fixed overhead is absorbed into production costs, and if the extra output is not sold, the fixed overhead costs are carried forward in the closing inventory value. This can encourage managers to over-produce in order to inflate profits.

Marginal advantages/disadvantages

Advantages of marginal costing

- It is a simpler costing system, because there is no requirement to apportion and absorb overhead costs.
- Variable production cost is a more realistic estimate of inventory value than full production cost.
- Marginal costing reflects the behaviour of costs in relation to activity. When sales increase, the cost of sales rise only by the additional variable costs. Since most decision-making problems involve changes to activity, marginal costing information is more relevant and appropriate for short-run decision-making than absorption costing.
- Marginal costing avoids the disadvantages of absorption costing, described above.

Disdvantages of marginal costing

- When fixed costs are high relative to variable costs, and when overheads are high relative to direct costs, the marginal cost of production and sales is only a small proportion of total costs. A costing system that focuses on marginal cost and contribution might therefore provide insufficient and inadequate information about costs and product profitability. Marginal costing is useful for short-term decision-making, but not for measuring product costs and profitability over the longer term.
- It could also be argued that the treatment of direct costs as a variable cost item is often unrealistic. When direct labour employees are paid a fixed wage or salary, their cost is fixed, not variable.

Example 4

When comparing the profits reported under marginal and absorption costing during a period when the level of stocks increased, identify which of the following statements would be true:

A absorption costing profits will be higher and closing stock valuations lower than those under marginal costing.

B absorption costing profits will be higher and closing stock valuations higher than those under marginal costing.

C marginal costing profits will be higher and closing stock valuations lower than those under absorption costing.

D marginal costing profits will be lower and closing stock valuations higher than those under absorption costing.

8 Absorption and marginal costing profit statements

Absorption costing format

	$	$
Sales		X
Less Cost of Sales		
Opening stock	X	
+ Production costs	X	
	—	
	X	
Less: Closing stock	(X)	
	—	(X)
		—
		X
(Under)/over absorption		±X
		—
Gross Profit		X
Less: Selling, distribution and admin. costs,		
Variable	X	
Fixed	X	
	—	
		(X)
		—
Net Profit/ (Loss)		X
		—

Marginal costing format

	$	$
Sales		X
Less: ***Variable*** *Cost of Sales*		
Opening stock	X	
+ ***Variable*** production costs	X	
	—	
	X	
Less: Closing stock	(X)	
	—	(X)
		—
		X
Less: **Variable** Selling, distribution and admin. costs		(X)
		—
Contribution		X
Less: Fixed costs		
Production	X	
Selling, distribution and admin.	X	
	—	
		(X)
		—
Profit/ (Loss)		X
		—

9 Chapter summary

CVP ANALYSIS

- B/E point $= \dfrac{\text{Fixed costs}}{\text{Contribution/unit}}$
- B/E revenue $= \dfrac{\text{Fixed costs}}{\text{C/S ratio}}$
- Margin of safety = Budgeted sales – Break even sales

Traditional costing

Absorption costing

- includes ALL production costs
- OAR $= \dfrac{\text{Total overheads}}{\text{Production volume}}$
- consistent with financial accounting
- better for long-term pricing

Reconciliation

	£
AC profit	X
(Increase)/Decrease in stock × fixed o/h per unit	(X)/X
MC profit	X

Marginal costing

- includes only VARIABLE production costs
- better for decision making
- easier
- but unsuited to capital intensive environments

10 Practice questions

Test your understanding 1

Saturn, a chocolate manufacturer, produces three products:

- The Sky Bar, a bar of solid milk chocolate.
- The Moon Egg, a fondant filled milk chocolate egg.
- The Sun Bar, a biscuit and nougat based chocolate bar.

Information relating to each of the products is as follows:

	Sky Bar	**Moon Egg**	**Sun Bar**
Direct labour cost per unit ($)	0.07	0.14	0.12
Direct material cost per unit ($)	0.17	0.19	0.16
Actual production/ sales (units)	500,000	150,000	250,000
Direct labour hours per unit	0.001	0.01	0.005
Direct machine hours per unit	0.01	0.04	0.02
Selling price per unit ($)	0.50	0.45	0.55

Annual production overhead = $80,000

Requirement:

Using traditional absorption costing, calculate the full production cost per unit and the profit per unit for each product. Explain the implications of the figures calculated.

Test your understanding 2

E plc operates a marginal costing system. For the forthcoming year, variable costs are budgeted to be 60% of sales value and fixed costs are budgeted to be 10% of sales value.

If E plc increases its selling prices by 10%, but if fixed costs, variable costs per unit and sales volume remain unchanged, identify the effect on E plc's contribution:

A a decrease of 2%.

B an increase of 5%.

C an increase of 10%.

D an increase of 25%.

Test your understanding 3

Exe Limited makes a single product whose total cost per unit is budgeted to be $45. This includes fixed cost of $8 per unit based on a volume of 10,000 units per period. In a period, sales volume was 9,000 units, and production volume was 11,500 units. The actual profit for the same period, calculated using absorption costing, was $42,000.

If the profit statement were prepared using marginal costing, identify the profit for the period:

A $10,000

B $22,000

C $50,000

D $62,000

Test your understanding 4 - KEATS PLC

Keats plc commenced business on 1 March making one product only, the standard cost of which is as follows:

	$
Direct labour	5
Direct material	8
Variable production overhead	2
Fixed production overhead	5
	—
Standard production cost	20
	—

The fixed production overhead figure has been calculated on the basis of a budgeted normal output of 36,000 units per annum.

You are to assume that actual fixed overheads were as expected and that all the budgeted fixed expenses are incurred evenly over the year. March and April are to be taken as equal period months.

Selling, distribution and administration expenses are:

Fixed	$120,000 per annum
Variable	15% of the sales value

The selling price per unit is $35 and the number of units produced and sold were:

	March (units)	April (units)
Production	2,000	3,200
Sales	1,500	3,000

You are required to:

(a) prepare profit statements for each of the months of March and April using:

(i) absorption costing, and

(ii) marginal costing

(15 marks)

(b) present a reconciliation of the profit or loss figures given in your answers to (a)(i) and (a)(ii) accompanied by a brief explanation.

(5 marks)

(Total: 20 marks)

Test your understanding 5

The following information relates to Product Alpha.

Selling price per unit $100

Variable cost per unit $56

Fixed costs $220,000

Budgeted sales are 7,500 units.

Required:

(a) Calculate the C/S ratio.

(b) Calculate the breakeven point in terms of units sold.

(c) Calculate the breakeven point in terms of sales revenue.

(d) Calculate the margin of safety (expressed as a percentage of budgeted sales.

Test your understanding 6

If inventory levels have increased during the period, identify which of the following options would be correct for the profit calculated using marginal costing when compared with that calculated using absorption costing:

A higher

B lower

C equal

D impossible to answer without further information

(2 marks)

Test your understanding 7

Identify which of the following statements would be true: fixed production overheads will always be under-absorbed when:

A actual output is lower than budgeted output

B actual overheads incurred are lower than budgeted overheads

C overheads absorbed are lower than those budgeted

D overheads absorbed are lower than those incurred

(2 marks)

Test your understanding 8

A company's summary budgeted operating statement is as follows:

	$000
Revenue	400
Variable costs	240
Fixed costs	100
Profit	60

Assuming that the sales mix does not change, identify the percentage increase in sales volume that would be needed to increase the profit to $100,000:

A 10%

B 15%

C 25%

D 40%

(2 marks)

Test your understanding 9

A company uses a standard absorption costing system. The fixed overhead absorption rate is based on labour hours.

Extracts from the company's records for last year were as follows:

	Budget	Actual
Fixed production overhead	$450,000	$475,000
Output	50,000 units	60,000 units
Labour hours	900,000	930,000

The under- or over-absorbed fixed production overheads for the year were:

A $10,000 under-absorbed

B $10,000 over-absorbed

C $15,000 over-absorbed

D $65,000 over-absorbed

(2 marks)

Test your understanding answers

Example 1

B

First of all - the profit under marginal costing:

Contribution per unit = $15 - (3.50 + 4.00 + 2.00) = $5.50

No of units sold = 2,400 - 180 = 2,220

	$
Contribution	
$5.50/unit x 2,220 units	12,210
Fixed cost	
$60,000 p.a. / 12 months	5,000
	7,210

As production is greater than sales, absorption costing will show the higher profit.

Difference in profit = change in stock x fixed production overhead per unit.

Difference in profit = 180 units x $2/unit = $360.

Therefore, profit reported under absorption costing = $7,210 + 360 = $7,570.

The FOAR was worked out as $\dfrac{\text{Budgeted Overheads}}{\text{Budgeted Level of Activity}} = \dfrac{\$60{,}000}{30{,}000 \text{ units}}$ = $2 per unit

Example 2

This is supposed to be a very simple little example, just emphasising the difference between the two systems.

(a)

(i)

		$	$
Sales	1,000 units x $50		50,000
Direct materials	1,000 units x $15	15,000	
Direct labour	1,000 units x $10	10,000	
Variable Overheads	1,000 units x $5	5,000	
Fixed Overheads		5,000	
			35,000
			15,000

(ii)

$$\text{Profit per unit} = \frac{\$15000}{1{,}000 \text{ units}} = 15/\text{unit}$$

(b)

(i) Contribution per unit = $50 – ($15 + $10 + $5) = $20

(ii) Total contribution = $20/unit x 1,000 units = $20,000

(iii)

	$
Contribution $20/unit x 1,000 units	20,000
Fixed cost	5,000
Profit	15,000

The 2 systems give the same profit provided there is no change in stock.

Example 3

Either marginal costing or absorption costing principles can be used. The 2 systems will give the same profit as there is no change in stock (production = sales). Marginal costing will be simpler and is illustrated first.

	$
Contribution	
$20/unit x 3,000 units	60,000
Fixed cost	5,000
Profit	55,000

This is a very simple, yet powerful format and would be used a lot in the answers for this topic.

or

		$	$
Sales	3,000 units x $50		150,000
Direct materials	3,000 units x $15	45,000	
Direct labour	3,000 units x $10	30,000	
Variable Overheads	3,000 units x $5	15,000	
Fixed Overheads		5,000	
			95,000
			55,000

Notice that we did not use the $15 per unit profit figure. Unlike contribution per unit, profit per unit is not constant.

Example 4

B

Test your understanding 1

As mentioned, it is relatively easy to complete the first two lines of the cost card. The difficult part is calculating the production overhead per unit, so let's start by considering this. We need to absorb the overheads into units of production. To do this, we will first need to calculate an overhead absorption rate (OAR):

$$OAR = \frac{\text{Production overhead}}{\text{Activity level}}$$

Production overhead (this is $80,000, as per the question)

Activity level (this must be chosen)

The activity level must be appropriate for the business. Saturn must choose between three activity levels:

- Units of production - This would not be appropriate since Saturn produces more than one type of product. It would not be fair to absorb the same amount of overhead into each product.
- Machine hours or labour hours – It is fair to absorb production overheads into the products based on the labour or machine hours taken to produce each unit. We must decide if the most appropriate activity level is machine or labour hours. To do this we can look at the nature of the process. Production appears to be more machine intensive than labour intensive because each unit takes more machine hours to produce than it does labour hours. Therefore, the most appropriate activity level is machine hours.

Working - OAR

$$OAR = \frac{\$80,000 \text{ production overhead}}{(0.01 \times 500k) + (0.04 \times 150k) + (0.02 \times 250k) \text{ hours}}$$

$$= \frac{\$80,000}{16,000 \text{ hours}}$$

$$= \$5 \text{ per machine hour}$$

We can now absorb these into the units of production:

	Sky Bar	Moon Egg	Sun Bar
Production overheads ($) = machine hours per unit x $5	0.05	0.20	0.10

This is the difficult part done. We can now quickly complete the cost card and answer the question:

	Sky Bar	**Moon Egg**	**Sun Bar**
	$	**$**	**$**
Direct labour cost per unit	0.07	0.14	0.12
Direct material cost per unit	0.17	0.19	0.16
Production overhead per unit	0.05	0.20	0.10
Full production cost per unit	**0.29**	**0.53**	**0.38**
Selling price per unit	0.50	0.45	0.43
Profit/ (loss) per unit	**0.21**	**(0.08)**	**0.05**

Outcome of absorption costing

Based on absorption costing, the Sky Bar and the Sun Bar are both profitable. However, the Moon Egg is loss making. Managers would need to consider the future of the Moon Egg. They may look at the possibility of increasing the selling price and/ or reducing costs. If this is not possible, they may make the decision to stop selling the product. However, this may prove to be the wrong decision because absorption costing does not always result in an accurate calculation of the full production cost per unit. ABC can be a more accurate method of calculating the full production cost per unit and as a result should lead to better decisions.

Test your understanding 2

D

The easiest way to answer this question is to make up a number for sales, say $1,000, then the relationships will be much easier to visualise.

If sales = $1,000, then:

Variable cost = 60% x $1,000 = $600

Current situation

	$
Sales	1,000
Variable cost	600
Contribution	400

New situation

	$
Sales (10% higher)	1,100
Variable cost	600
Contribution	500

Contribution increases by $100, which is an increase of 25% on its original value.

Fixed cost should be ignored as it does not affect contribution.

Test your understanding 3

B

Production is greater than sales, so absorption costing will have the higher profit.

Difference in profit = change in stock x fixed production overhead per unit.

Difference in profit = 2,500 units x $8/unit = $20,000.

Therefore, profit reported under marginal costing = $42,000 – 20,000 = $22,000.

Test your understanding 4 - KEATS PLC

(a)

(i)

	March		April	
	$	$	$	$
Sales		52,500		105,000
Cost of Sales				
Op. stock (W1)	0		10,000	
Production costs (@$20/unit)	40,000		64,000	
	40,000		74,000	
Less cl. stock (@$20/unit) (W2)	10,000		14,000	
		30,000		60,000
		22,500		45,000
(Under)/overabsorption (W3)		(5,000)		1,000
Gross profit		17,500		46,000
Selling etc costs				
Fixed (W4)	10,000		10,000	
Variable	7,875		15,750	
		17,875		25,750
Net Profit/Loss		(375)		20,250

(ii)

	March		April	
	$	$	$	$
Sales		52,500		105,000
Variable cost of Sales				
Op. stock (W1)	0		7,500	
Variable production costs (@$15/unit)	30,000		48,000	
	30,000		55,500	
Less cl. stock (@$15/unit) (W2)	7,500		10,500	
		22,500		45,000
		30,000		60,000
Variable selling etc costs		7,875		15,750
Contribution		22,125		44,250
Fixed costs				
Production	15,000		15,000	
Selling etc	10,000		10,000	
		25,000		25,000
Profit/Loss		(2,875)		19,250

Workings

(W1) The closing stock for March becomes the opening stock for April.

(W2)	March	April
	Units	Units
Op. stock	0	500
Production	2,000	3,200
	2,000	3,700
Less sales	1,500	3,000
Cl. stock	500	700

(W3) Under/overabsorption is the difference between overheads incurred and overheads absorbed.

"Overheads incurred" means actual overheads and we are told that the actual fixed overheads were as expected. Therefore the actual fixed overheads incurred are the same as the budgeted fixed overheads.

Budgeted fixed overhead = $5 per unit x 36,000 units = $180,000 per annum

÷ 12

= 15,000 per month

March

Overheads incurred	15,000
Overheads absorbed	
$5/unit x 2,000 units	10,000
Underabsorption	(5,000)

April

Overheads incurred	15,000
Overheads absorbed	
$5/unit x 3,200 units	16,000
Overabsorption	1,000

(W4) Selling, etc fixed overhead = $120,000/12 = $10,000 per month.

(b) If there is no change in stock, the 2 systems give the same profit. If production is greater than sales then absorption costing shows the higher profit.

Difference in profit = change in stock x fixed production overhead cost per unit

In both March and April, production is greater than sales and thus absorption costing will show the higher profit (the smaller loss in March).

	March	April
Marginal costing profit/loss	(2,875)	19,250
Difference in profit		
(2,000 - 1,500) x $5 per unit	2,500	
(3,200 - 3,000) x $5 per unit		1,000
Absorption costing profit/loss	(375)	20,250

This difference occurs because marginal costing writes off the entire fixed overhead in the period incurred, whereas absorption costing carries forward some fixed production overhead into the next period in the valuation of closing stock.

Test your understanding 5

(a) Contribution per unit = $(100 – 56) = $44

$$\text{C/S ratio} = \frac{\text{Contribution per unit}}{\text{Selling price per unit}} = \frac{\$44}{\$100} = 0.44$$

(b) Breakeven point in terms numbers of units sold

$$= \frac{\text{Fixed costs}}{\text{Contribution per unit}}$$

$$= \frac{\$220{,}000}{\$44} = 5{,}000 \text{ units}$$

(c) Breakeven point in terms of sales revenue

$$= \frac{\text{Fixed costs}}{\text{C/S ratio}}$$

$$= \frac{\$220{,}000}{0.44} = \$500{,}000 \text{ units}$$

(Proof: breakeven units × selling price per unit = 5,000 × $100 = $500,000)

(d) Margin of safety (as a % of Budgeted sales)

$$= \frac{\text{Budgeted sales} - \text{Break-even sales}}{\text{Budgeted sales}} \times 100\%$$

$$= \frac{7{,}500 - 5{,}000}{7{,}500} \times 100\%$$

= 33.33%

Test your understanding 6

B

Marginal costing values inventory at a lower amount because it does not include fixed overheads in the valuation. Therefore as inventory levels increase the value of closing inventory under marginal costing will be lower. This will give a higher cost of sales and a lower and profit.

Test your understanding 7

D

Under-absorption occurs when the amount absorbed is less than the actual overheads incurred.

Test your understanding 8

C

$$\text{Contribution margin} = \frac{160}{400} = 40\%$$

$$\text{Target revenue} = \frac{100 + 100}{40\%} = 500$$

$$\%\ \text{Increase in revenue} = \frac{500}{400} = 25\%$$

Test your understanding 9

D

Absorption rate	=	$\frac{\$450{,}000}{900{,}000}$	= $0.50/hour
Absorbed overheads		60,000 units × 18 hrs/unit × $0.50/hour	= $540,000
Actual overheads	=	$475,000	
Over-absorption	=	$65,000	

chapter

3

Production systems and environments

Chapter learning objectives

Lead	Component
A1. Discuss costing methods and their results.	(h) Explain the impact of just-in-time manufacturing methods on cost accounting and the use of 'back-flush accounting' when work-in-progress stock is minimal.
A2. Explain the role of MRP and ERP systems.	(a) Explain the role of MRP and ERP systems in supporting standard costing systems, calculating variances and facilitating the posting of ledger entries.

1 Session content diagram

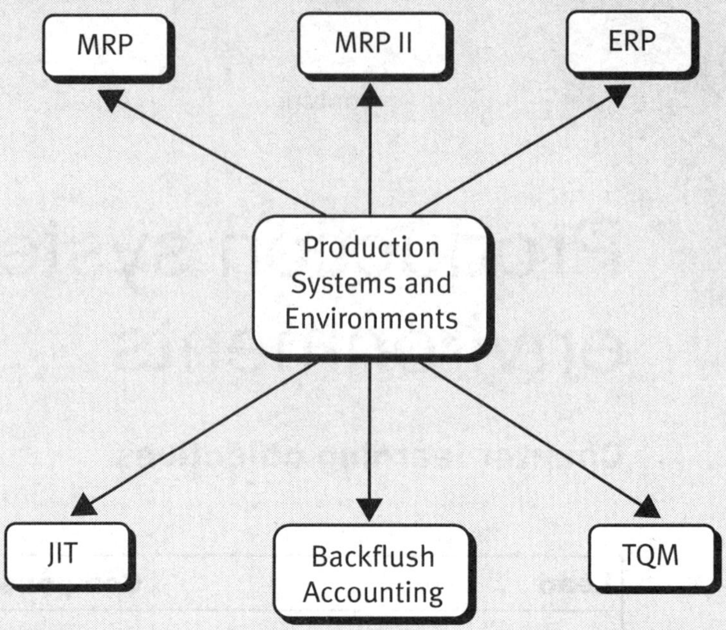

2 Modern business environment

'To compete successfully in today's highly competitive global environment companies are making customer satisfaction an overriding priority, adopting new management approaches, changing their manufacturing systems and investing in new technologies. These changes are having a significant influence on management accounting systems.

' Colin Drury in ' Management and Cost Accounting'.

The modern manufacturing environment is very different from the traditional production environment. It means that traditional costing methods covered in the previous chapter are becoming less relevant.

In this chapter we explore how the modern production system has changed. In the following two chapters we examine how costing has adapted to this and created new ways to calculate a product's production cost.

3 Characteristics of the modern business environment

The key changes in a modern production environment are as follows:

- greater use of Advanced Manufacturing Technolgy (**AMT**)
- a much more **global environment**
- a greater focus on **cost reduction**
- better **customer focus**

- a need for more **flexible** production systems
- more **employee participation**
- **shorter production cycles**
- a greater emphasis on **quality**

More details

Advanced manufacturing technology (AMT)

AMT is a collective term for a wide variety of modern practices and techniques based on computer systems. You do not need to know these in detail, just the effect they have on companies today - for instance the vast reduction in labour costs.

There are also systems such as MRP, ERP and JIT for controlling inventories and other resources and these systems are explored in more detail in this chapter.

Global environment

- Companies operate in a world economy
- Customers and competitors come from all over the world
- Products are made from components from around the world
- Firms have to be world class to compete.

Cost reduction

Clearly an important factor to the customer, a key part of World Class Manufacturing can be to be the lowest cost supplier. This means that during a price war the business has the opportunity to quote lower than its competitors, but also more importantly, in less severe circumstances similar pricing to competitors will lead to greater profitability.

Customer focus

In the past the linking of product to consumer was relatively hazy in many instances. A product would be produced within a large production run and then a customer would be 'sold' that unit. As competition increases, customers are demanding ever-improving levels of service in cost, quality, reliability, delivery and the choice of innovative new products. Companies need to be able to react quickly to changes in the environment to survive these days. They must be able to meet these customer requirements.

Flexibility

The move away from standardised units of production towards individual customised units means that mass production techniques are redundant, instead, it is of greatest importance to take an order from placement to completion in the shortest time possible. This means that production processes will be designed differently to accommodate flexibility of production rather than just throughput.

Employee participation

To ensure this flexibility, managers need to empower their employees to make decisions quickly, without reference to more senior managers. By empowering employees and giving them relevant information they will be able to respond faster to customers, increase process flexibility, reduce cycle times and improve morale.

The changes required in the way that the workforce is managed are frequently the most difficult aspects of World Class Manufacturing to implement. The changes often require a considerable amount of time and education so that trust, mutual respect and a common purpose can be established between the company's managers and production personnel. The employees are given a great deal more responsibility for production quality and scheduling. The operators are cross-trained so that they can perform a wide variety of tasks and therefore provide more production flexibility. A team approach is established which is designed to encourage all company employees to work co-operatively, eradicating the traditional job demarcation and incentive pay plans

Management Accounting Systems are moving from *providing information to managers* to monitor employees to *providing information to employees* to empower them to focus on continuous improvement.

Shorter product life cycles

Companies need to be continually developing new products in order to survive.

Quality

The World Class Manufacturing approach to quality is quite different from the traditional approach because the primary emphasis is placed on the resolution of the problems that cause poor quality, rather than merely detecting it. These systems are more proactive and try to prevent problems from occuring in the first place rather than waiting for them to occur and then fixing them.

The system might be developed formally under Total Quality Management.

Cost reduction

Cost reduction

Cost reduction in a loose sense is simply any action which results in a reduction in costs for an organisation. Used incorrectly, it is often just a reaction to a crisis, whereby for instance budgets for all activities of the company are cut by 5%, whether or not the activity is being run efficiently at present. More correctly: Cost reduction is a management technique concerned with reducing the unit cost of a product or a service on a permanent basis without affecting the perceived quality.

Value analysis

Value analysis is one example of a cost reduction technique. It is also known as value engineering. The CIMA definition of value analysis is 'A systematic inter-disciplinary examination of factors affecting the cost of a product or service, in order to devise means of achieving the specified purpose most economically at the required standard of quality and reliability'.

The purpose of value analysis is to identify any unnecessary cost elements within the components of goods and services. It is more comprehensive than simple cost reduction in that it examines the purposes or functions of the product and is concerned with establishing the means whereby these are achieved. Any cost data that does not add value to the product or service should be eliminated.

Value analysis will often lead to the reduction of components used in a product, the use of alternative, cheaper components and the standardisation of parts across several product lines.

Other AMT abbreviations

Your syllabus specifically mentions MRP and ERP systems, but there are other three-letter acronyms that you will need to be aware of, particularly if the examiner describes them briefly in objective test questions, include the following:

- Computer Aided Manufacturing **(CAM)** uses computer-based technology to program and control the production process.
- Computer Aided Design **(CAD)** is computer-based technology which allows products to be designed, modified and tested interactively on a computer screen.

- Flexible Manufacturing System **(FMS)** is a highly automated, integrated, computer controlled production system. An FMS is capable of producing a wide range of parts and can switch rapidly and economically from one production run to another, while maintaining the quality of output.
- Computer Integrated Manufacturing **(CIM)** is a feature of a Flexible Manufacturing System which enables an organisation to link all its functions, from the offices to the factory floor, to a system of total automation using computers. It brings together AMT, quality control activities and so on into a single coherent computerised system.
- Electronic Data Interchange **(EDI)** is a computer-to-computer system that facilitates the transmission of business data electronically, enabling an organisation to communicate directly and immediately with its customers and suppliers.
- Supply Chain Management **(SCM)** is the coordination and integration of the flow of information between all of the various organisations in a supply chain, from the supplier to the manufacturer and right through to the retailer and the final customer.
- Optimised Production Technology **(OPT)** is a technique that has developed from MRP systems and which requires similar operational and resource information. It seeks to identify and make optimum use of the bottleneck resources within a process, which prevent throughput from being higher. Non-bottleneck resources are scheduled around these and are utilised at an appropriate capacity to avoid the build up of excessive inventory.

4 Total quality management (TQM)

Total quality management (TQM) is a philosophy of quality management that has a number of important features.

- Total – means that everyone in the value chain is involved in the process, including employees, customers and suppliers.
- Quality – products and services must meet the customers' requirements.
- Management – quality is actively managed rather than controlled so that problems are prevented from occuring.

There are three basic principles of TQM:

(1) **'Get it right, first time'**

TQM considers that the costs of prevention are less than the costs of correction. One of the main aims of TQM is to achieve *zero* rejects and 100% quality.

(2) **Continuous improvement**

The second basic principle of TQM is dissatisfaction with the status-quo. Realistically a zero-defect goal may not be obtainable. It does however provide a target to ensure that a company should never be satisfied with its present level of rejects. The management and staff should believe that it is always possible to improve and to be able to get it more right next time!

(2) ***Customer focus***

Qulaity is examined from a customer perspective and the system is aimed at meeting customer needs and expectations.

TQM will often involve the use of Just-In-Time stock control in order to eliminate any waste in stock.

Quality related costs

Quality related costs

Failing to satisfy customers' needs and expectations, or failing to do so right first time, costs the average company between 15 and 30 per cent of sales revenue.

A quality-related cost is the 'cost of ensuring and assuring quality, as well as loss incurred when quality is not achieved. Quality costs are classified as prevention costs, appraisal cost, internal failure cost and external failure cost (BS6143).

(1) **Prevention cost**

Prevention costs represent the cost of any action taken to prevent or reduce defects and failures. It includes the design and development of quality control equipment and the maintenance of the equipment.

(2) **Appraisal costs**

Appraisal costs are the costs incurred, such as inspection and testing, in initially ascertaining the conformance of the product to quality requirements. They include the costs of goods inwards inspection, and the monitoring of the production output.

(3) **Internal failure cost**

Internal failure costs are the costs arising from inadequate quality where the problem is discovered before the transfer of ownership from supplier to purchaser. They include the cost of reworking or rectifying the product, the net cost of scrap, downtime of machinery due to quality problems, etc.

(4) **External failure cost**

The cost arising from inadequate quality discovered after the transfer of ownership from supplier to purchaser such as complaints, warranty claims, recall cost, costs of repairing or replacing returned faulty goods, etc.

Conformance costs and non-conformance costs

Appraisal costs and prevention costs may also be referred to as conformance costs, whilst internal failure costs and external failure costs may be referred to as non-conformance costs.

Example - COMPUTER UPGRADERS

E plc provides a computer upgrading, servicing and repair facility to a variety of business and personal computer users.

An issue which concerns the management of E plc is the quality of the service provided for clients. The Operations Manager has suggested that the company should introduce Total Quality Management (TQM) but the management team is unsure how to do this and of the likely costs and benefits of its introduction.

Required:

(a) Briefly explain Total Quality Management in the context of E plc.

(3 marks)

(b) Describe the likely costs and benefits that would arise if E plc introduced a TQM policy.

(12 marks)

(Total: 15 marks)

5 Just In Time

Just-in-time (JIT) is an approach to operations management based on the idea that goods and services should be **produced only when they are needed**.

At the same time, products (or services) must be **delivered to the customer at the time the customer wants them** ('just in time'). To be able to do this with no inventory, the production cycle must be short, and there can be no hold-ups in production due to defective items, bottlenecks or inefficiency.

JIT sees inventory as a cost burden and in its extreme form, a JIT system seeks to have **zero inventories**. When there are no inventories of raw materials, part-finished work-in-progress or finished goods, a break-down or disruption in one stage of the production chain will have an immediate impact on all the other stages of the chain. In practice, it might be impossible to have no inventory at all, but management should be trying continually to reduce and minimise inventory levels.

This means that another aspect of the JIT philosophy is **high quality**, and JIT is consistent with Total Quality Management or **TQM**.

Push and pull systems

- JIT can be described as a 'pull through' system. This is a system that responds to customer demand: components are drawn through the system as required, so that items are manufactured only when ordered by a customer. Similarly, raw materials are obtained from suppliers only when they are needed for production.
- This contrasts with a 'push' system, in which items are produced, and if there is no immediate demand, inventories build up.

The JIT philosophy is based on:

- continuous improvement ('kaizen') – doing things well and gradually doing them better, and
- the elimination of waste.

Examples of waste

Waste is defined as any activity that does not add value. Examples of waste are:

- **Overproduction**. Producing more than is needed immediately creates unnecessary inventory.
- **Waiting time**. Waiting time is evidence of a hold-up in the flow of production through the system. Set-up time is also non-productive time. ('Set-up' is the work needed at the end of one job or batch of work to get the production process ready for the next job or batch.) The aim is to achieve quick set-up times and low-cost set-up.
- **Unnecessary movement** of materials or people. Moving items around a production area does not add value.
- **Waste in the process**, caused by design defects in the product, or poor maintenance work. Work flow is an important element in JIT. Work needs to flow without interruption in order to avoid a build-up of inventory or unnecessary waiting times. The movement of materials and part-finished work is wasteful, and this waste can be reduced by laying out the work floor and designing the work flow so as to minimise movements. JIT production is associated with the use of work cells: a work cell is a small area on the factory floor that is given responsibility for the production of an entire product or part. The employees in the work cell do all the work on the product from the beginning to the end of the process, and so the work cell manager or supervisor is entirely responsible for the work flow and the product quality.
- **Inventory** is wasteful. The target should be to eliminate all inventory by removing the reasons why it builds up.
- **Complexity in work processes**. Simplification of work gets rid of waste in the system (the 'waste of motion') by eliminating unnecessary actions.
- **Defective goods** are a significant cause of waste in many operations.
- **Inspection time** is wasteful because it adds nothing to value. Inspection time can be eliminated by making the process free from errors and defects.

Pre-requisites for JIT

The operational requirements for the successful implementation of JIT production are as follows:

- **High quality.** Without high quality there will be disruptions in production, reducing throughput. Production must be reliable and not subject to hold-ups.
- **Speed.** Throughput in the operation must be fast, so that customer orders can be met by production. Without fast throughput, it will be necessary to hold some inventory to meet customer orders.
- **Flexibility.** The production system must be able to respond immediately to customer orders. Production must therefore be flexible, and in small batch sizes. The ideal batch size is 1.
- **Lower costs.** Fewer errors, less waste, greater reliability and flexibility and faster throughput should all help to reduce costs.

The most suitable conditions for applying JIT management are where:

- there are short set-up times and low set-up costs
- there are short lead times and low ordering costs for buying raw materials from suppliers
- work flow is fairly constant over time, and customer demand is not uneven and unpredictable
- production throughput time is very short
- there are no downtimes due to poor quality or stock-outs.

Benefits and problems of JIT

Benefits

- less cash tied up in inventory
- less storage space needed
- better quality
- more flexible production
- fewer bottlenecks
- better co-ordination
- more reliable and supportive suppliers

Problems

- relies on predictable demand, flexible supplier and a flexible workforce
- there will be initial set-up costs (e.g. in FMS)
- it is very difficult for businesses with a wide geographical spread
- there is no fallback position if disruptions occur in the supply chain
- it may be harder to switch suppliers

More details

Benefits from JIT

Successful adopters of JIT production have enjoyed tremendous savings. The most obvious saving arises from the much lower investment required to hold inventory. When inventory levels are reduced from three months to one month of sales (increasing the stock turnover from 4 to 12) financing costs are reduced by two-thirds. In fact, stock turnover can be increased to 30 or 60 once production problems, made visible by inventory reductions are solved

Beyond these obvious financing savings, companies also discovered large space savings. They found that up to 50% of factory space had previously been used to store in-process inventory. Having eliminated WIP, companies found another factory inside their old factory. Such savings permitted planned expansions to be curtailed, and previously dispersed operations could be consolidated inside a single location.

But even the carrying cost and floor space savings were smaller than the savings from improved JIT operations as companies attempted to reduce inventories, many problems emerged in the factory that had formerly been hidden by inventory buffers: quality problems, bottlenecks, co-ordination problems, inadequate documentation, and supplier unreliability, among others. Without the discipline to achieve JIT operations, these problems would remain unsolved. The rationalisation of production processes, the elimination of waste, and the more visible display of production problems that were achieved under successful JIT operations led to great reductions in material losses and great improvement in overall factory productivity.

6 Production management strategies - MRP and MRP II

Material requirements planning (MRP)

MRP can be defined as a computerised planning system that first determines the quantity and timing of the finished goods demanded, and then uses this to determine the requirements for raw materials, components and subassemblies at each of the prior stages of production.

Output from an MRP system

The output from an MRP system is an overall production schedule, and in addition it produces purchase orders and works orders that will initiate the purchasing of raw materials and the manufacture of parts and sub-assemblies

Benefits of the MRP system

A significant benefit of MRP systems is that if any change is necessary to the manufacturing schedule, for example due to an unexpected change in customer demand patterns, a new production schedule can be prepared in a very short time, together with new purchase orders and works orders.

A benefit claimed for MRP I is that it should reduce inventory levels. Through reliable scheduling of production requirements, it should be possible to avoid producing items that are not required in the foreseeable future, and so are held as inventory.

More details

Material requirements planning (MRP)

Traditionally material requirements were planned by continuously reviewing stock levels, and a predetermined quantity was ordered each time stocks fell below a predetermined level. This stock control approach was based on the assumption that replenishment of stocks could be planned *independently* of each other. However, the demand for materials is *dependent* on the demand for the assemblies of which they are part.

MRP originated in the early 1960s as a computerised approach for co-ordinating the planning of materials acquisition and production. MRP is a flow control system in the sense that it orders only what components are required to maintain the manufacturing flow. The orders can be for purchased parts or manufactured parts, and MRP thus provides the basis for production scheduling and materials purchasing. MRP can be defined as a computerised planning system that first determines the quantity and timing of the finished goods demanded, and then uses this to determine the requirements for raw materials, components and subassemblies at each of the prior stages of production.

Core data requirements

The core data requirements for operating an MRP system are:

(1) The **Master Production Schedule** (MPS). This specifies the quantity of each finished unit to be produced, and the time at which the unit will be required.

(2) The **Bill of Materials** file (BOM). This file sets out a detailed specification for each finished product in terms of subassemblies, components and materials. It distinguishes between those items which are purchased from outside the company and those which are internally manufactured.

(3) The **Inventory File.** This maintains details of current stock levels for each subassembly, component and part. It distinguishes between stock items that are already allocated to orders but which have not yet been released from stock, and those items which have not yet been allocated. It also records scheduled receipts of items.

Master production schedule

A master production schedule is a plan summarising the volume and timing of end-products required. The schedule is constructed from known customer orders (not yet fulfilled) and forecasts of future orders. It sets out how many units of each product will be required from production, and by when.

Having established the quantities and completion times for end products, the system works back to earlier stages of the production process, and prepares a schedule of the quantities of sub-assemblies, components and raw materials required, and the time by which these need to be available.

'The master production schedule (MPS) is the most important planning and control schedule in a business, and forms the main input to materials requirements planning.... In manufacturing, the MPS contains a statement of the volume and timing of the end products to be made; this schedule drives the whole operation in terms of what is assembled, what is manufactured and what is bought. It is the basis of planning the utilisation of labour and equipment and it determines the provisioning of materials and cash' (Operations Management, Slack, Chambers and Johnston).

Bills of materials

For every product manufactured by the business, there is a bill of materials. A bill of materials lists in detail the parts that make up the product and their production lead time. It also shows the relationship between the parts in the end-product.

Using the bills of materials for each product, the master production schedule is 'exploded' to work out:

- the number of sub-assemblies that are needed, and the quantities of raw materials and parts
- the time by which they are needed, and therefore
- the time by which their manufacture must begin or the purchase orders must be placed.

The scheduling is based on an assumption that lead times for purchasing and manufacture are constant and predictable, which might not be realistic in practice.

Inventory records

The MRP I system must have access to inventory records, so that current availability of inventories can be checked. The inventory records should relate to all raw material items, components and sub-assemblies as well as finished goods items.

The manufacturing schedule is prepared with allowances made for current inventory levels.

The data in the system are then analysed to produce a **materials requirements plan** for purchasing and manufacturing. This is a time phased schedule (usually in 'buckets' of one week) detailing when the orders are to be placed for subassemblies and components.

Manufacturing resources planning (MRP II)

When MRP is extended beyond the planning of raw materials, components and subassemblies to encompass other input resources, such as machine capacity and labour, so that the system provides a fully integrated planning approach to the management of all the company's resources it is known as Manufacturing Resources Planning. To produce MRP II schedules the database is extended to include labour resource data and machine availability data.

MRP and accounting

MRP I and accounting

An MRP I system is not integrated with other related systems within the organisation. From an accounting perspective, an MRP I system cannot produce a production cost budget or a materials purchases budget.

However, the system does provide information that can be used by accountants.

- The master production schedule provides the basis for drawing up a production cost budget.
- The schedule of materials purchase requirements can be used to prepare a materials purchases budget, by applying expected purchase prices to the quantities of purchases required.
- A bill of materials for each product can be used to construct a standard cost or budgeted cost for products, by applying a cost to each of the component parts of the end-product.

MRP II and accounting

MRP II systems offer integration between the production planning, inventory control and purchasing systems and the accounting system. The accounting function has access to bills of materials and production schedules through the common database. The system also holds data on prices for materials and labour.

It is therefore possible for the system to produce:

- a production cost budget from the master production schedule
- a materials purchases budget
- elements of a cash budget
- a standard cost for each unit produced.

In addition, when changes are made to production specifications, the bill of materials is amended, and this should work through to the accounting function, where a new, updated standard cost can be calculated for the product.

7 ERP: Enterprise resource planning

An enterprise resource system is a powerful computer system that integrates information from all parts of the organisation. It is an extension of the MRP philosophy, but provides more integration between different parts of the organisation.

An ERP system is expensive to acquire and install, given the size and complexity of many global businesses. However, the elements of an ERP system should include modules for:

- **manufacturing**: production planning and control, materials purchasing, plant maintenance, quality management
- **sales and distribution**: sales order management, customer management, distribution, transportation and shipping
- **accounting**: accounts receivable, accounts payable, budgeting, standard costing
- **human resources**: recruitment and workforce scheduling, payroll, training and development.

The system should also offer some decision support facilities, by giving decision-makers access to up-to-date company information.

8 Backflush accounting

Review of a traditional system

- In traditional accounting systems inventory is a key item. Traditional manufacturing firms hold high levels of inventory and much of the work of the management accountant is to put a value on this inventory.
- The traditional approach is to track the cost of products through the sequential stages of production, building up costing records for the direct material consumed, the direct labour cost and the overhead expense for each product.
- A traditional costing system will include the following accounts:

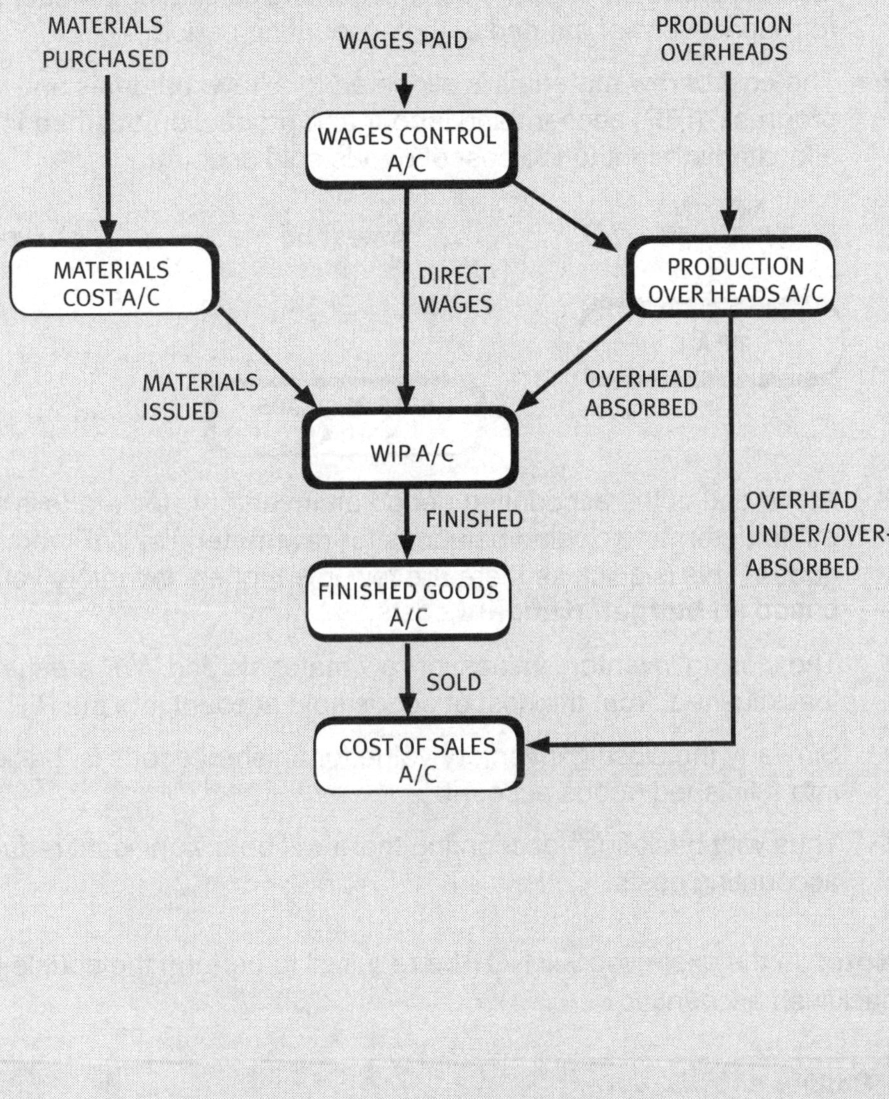

A backflush accounting system

- Backflush accounting offers a simplified apporach to costing by getting rid of unecessary costing records.
- It is suitable for use in a just-in-time (JIT) environment. A JIT company holds minimal amounts of stock; raw materials are only ordered when they are required, production is fast and efficient keeping work-in-progress to a minimum and once production is complete goods are delivered straight to the customer which minimises the amount of finished goods held.
- Instead of building up product costs sequentially from the start to the finish of production, back-flush accounting calculates product costs retrospectively, at the end of the accounting period.
- The cost of raw materials is allocated to a 'raw materials and in progress' (RIP) account and labour and production overheads are allocated straight to the cost of goods sold account.

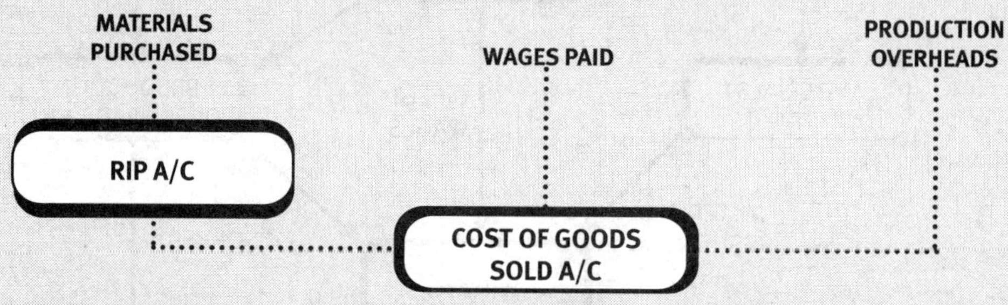

- At the end of the accounting period an inventory stock-take is carried out to determine closing balances for raw materials, WIP and finished goods. This is quick as there are few inventories. Inventory values are based on **budget/standard** costs.
- The closing inventory values for raw materials and WIP are then 'backflushed' from the cost of goods sold account into the RIP account.
- Similarly the closing inventory value for finished goods is 'backflushed' into a finished goods account.
- Thus with back-flush accounting there will be a significant reduction in accounting costs.

Note: In the exam you will NOT be required to perform the double entry for backflush accounting.

Double entries

Illustration

ABC Company manufactures calculators and uses a backflush cost accounting system. The standard material cost per unit is $2 and the standard conversion cost is $3 per unit. Ten units are manufactured during its first month of operation and six units are sold. During the month, $24 of Raw Material are purchased on credit.

Under a backflush accounting system, the point at which a sale occurs is taken also to be the point at which accounting entries are made. The following depicts this for the six units sold:

Cost of Goods Sold (6 units x $5)	30	
Conversion Costs (6 units x $3)		18
Creditors		12

Conversely, under a traditional cost accounting system, the following entries would be made:

1 Material Stock	24	
Creditors		24

To record purchase of raw material on credit

2 WIP (10 x $2)	20	
Material Stock		20

To record the issuing of raw material to WIP

3 WIP (10 x $3)	30	
Conversion Costs		30

To record the charging of conversion costs to WIP

4 Finished Goods	50	
WIP		50

To record transfer of finished goods to warehouse

5 Cost of Goods Sold (6 units x ($2 + $3))	30	
Finished Goods		30

To record the sale of 6 units

With the backflush accounting system, accounts for stock are not kept separately and the purchase of raw material is recognised at the point of sale.

Advantages and disadvantages of backflush accounting

Advantages	Disadvantages
• simple	• not appropriate if inventories are high
• less administration	• not appopriate for long production cycles
• gives the same results as traditional costing when inventories are low	• provides less detailed information

More details

Advantages of backflush accounting

The advantages of using backflush accounting are:

- It is a simple costing system.
- It avoids the need to record production costs sequentially as items move through step-by-step operations in the production process.
- When inventory levels are low or constant, it yields the same results as traditional costing methods would.

It is therefore appropriate in a mature JIT environment where there is a short production cycle and low inventories.

Disadvantages of backflush accounting

The main disadvantages of backflush accounting are:

- It is not appropriate for manufacturing environments where inventory levels are high, due to the problems of counting and valuing the inventory at the end of each period.
- It is probably inappropriate for production systems with a long production cycle. In such an environment, it is probably preferable to record the production costs as the work passes sequentially through each stage of the production system.
- It provides less detailed management information than traditional costing systems.

9 Chapter summary

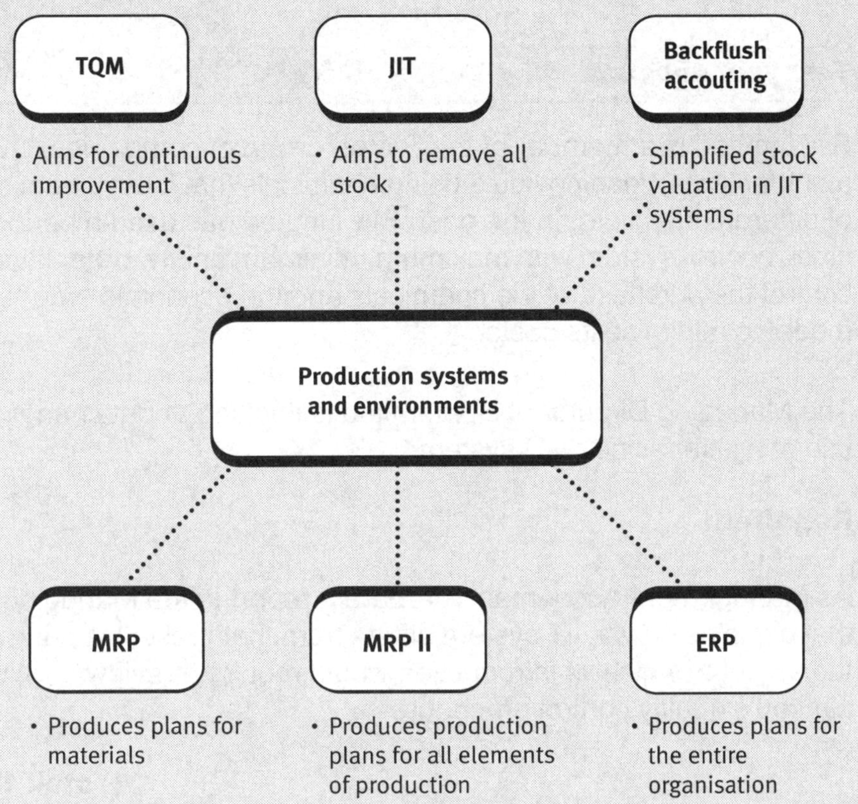

10 Practice questions

Test your understanding 1 - SW LIMITED

SW Limited is a member of the SWAL group of companies. SW Limited manufactures cleaning liquid using chemicals that it buys from a number of different suppliers. In the past, SW Limited has used a periodic review stock control system with maximum, minimum and re-order levels to control the purchase of the chemicals and the economic order quantity model to minimise its costs.

The Managing Director of SW Limited is thinking about changing to the use of a just-in-time (JIT) system.

Required:

As Management Accountant, prepare a report to the Managing Director that explains how a JIT system differs from that presently being used and the extent to which its introduction would require a review of SW Limited's quality control procedures.

(Total: 15 marks)

Test your understanding 2 - FOOD MANUFACTURER

SG plc is a long-established food manufacturer which produces semi-processed foods for fast food outlets. While for a number of years it has recognised the need to produce good quality products for its customers, it does not have a formalised quality management programme.

A director of the company has recently returned from a conference, where one of the speakers introduced the concept of Total Quality Management (TQM) and the need to recognise and classify quality costs.

Required:

(a) Explain what is meant by TQM and use examples to show how it may be introduced into different areas of SG plc's food production business.

(12 marks)

(b) Explain why the adoption of TQM is particularly important within a Just-in-Time (JIT) production environment.

(5 marks)

(c) Explain four quality cost classifications, using examples relevant to the business of SG plc.

(8 marks)

(Total: 25 marks)

Test your understanding 3

State whether back-flush accounting would be suitable for a major construction firm (which makes bridges, roads, buildings, etc.).

Test your understanding 4 - QUALITY COST

Explain how quality cost can be measured in a programme of Total Quality Management (TQM).

(5 marks)

Test your understanding 5

Identify which of the following statements are true:

(i) Enterprise Resource Planning (ERP) systems are accounting oriented information systems which aid in identifying and planning the enterprise wide resources needed to resource, make, account for and deliver customer orders.

(ii) Flexible Manufacturing Systems (FMS) are integrated, computer-controlled production systems, capable of producing any of a range of parts and of switching quickly and economically between them.

(iii) Just-In-Time (JIT) is a system whose objective is to produce, or to procure, products or components as they are required.

A (i) and (ii) only

B (i) and (iii) only

C (ii) and (iii) only

D (i), (ii) and (iii)

(2 marks)

Test your understanding answers

Example - COMPUTER UPGRADERS

(a) Total quality management (TQM) has two main concepts:

(1) **Get it right first time**
TQM considers that the costs of prevention are less than the costs of correction. One of the main aims of TQM is to achieve zero rejects and 100% quality.

(2) **Continuous improvement**
The second basic principle of TQM is dissatisfaction with the status quo. Realistically a zero-defect goal may not be obtainable. It does however provide a target to ensure that a company should never be satisfied with its present level of rejects. The management and staff should believe that it is always possible to improve and to be able to get it more right next time!

There must be a focus on the customer and what they require and there must be a constant review of costs and performance to ensure that the aims of the TQM programme are being met.

The aim is to build good quality in rather than inspect poor quality out. The aim in the end is to design such good products and processes and obtain such good materials that inspection is no longer necessary.

E plc should focus on the whole of its operation from start to finish if it wishes the TQM programme to be a success.

It must ensure that the input to its processes is defect-free. It must choose first-class suppliers who will guarantee the quality of their components. It must communicate with the suppliers to let them know what is expected of them. E plc is likely to have to pay a premium price to obtain these premium quality components.

It must also examine its own processes to ensure that there are as few quality problems as possible. Where there are known quality problems efforts should be directed at improving the processes by whatever means are appropriate, e.g. training, preventative maintenance, newer more reliable machines, etc.

The output process must also be controlled, i.e. the relationship with the customer. Efforts must be made to ensure that no defective products reach the customer, perhaps by means of final inspection before the goods leave the business and that where problems do occur, they are corrected as soon as possible. Communication with the customer is very important to ensure that the customer's needs are being met.

It is not enough to decide that a TQM system should be introduced. The programme should be carefully considered and communication to the staff should be clear. They should be educated as to the ideas behind TQM and given the necessary training to accomplish its aims. TQM should permeate the whole of the organisation and must be continually assessed to ensure that its goals are still being achieved.

(b) The likely costs that would arise include:

(1) **Extra prevention cost**
These are any costs incurred in order to prevent quality problems from occurring. Examples would include training, preventative maintenance, the purchase or hire of new, more reliable machines, the sourcing of better quality components, etc.

(2) **Extra appraisal costs**
Appraisal costs are the costs incurred in checking the raw materials and the product against the quality standard. These would include the wages and salaries of the quality control staff and any capital expenditure on testing equipment.

We would expect appraisal costs to increase at first when a TQM programme is introduced but then decline as quality is 'built in' rather than inspected out.

The likely benefits for E plc would be:

(1) A reduction in internal failure costs. Internal failure costs are the costs incurred as a result of quality problems where the problem is discovered before the product leaves the business, e.g. less mistakes when upgrading, servicing or repairing which then have to be corrected involving more labour and possibly more components.

(2) A reduction in external failure costs. External failure costs are the costs incurred as a result of quality problems where the problem is only discovered after the product leaves the business, e.g. loss of customer through delivering poor quality work, the material cost and labour cost of repairing poor quality which has been returned by the customer.

(3) An improvement in the company's reputation as a result of its good quality work.

Test your understanding 1 - SW LIMITED

REPORT

To: Managing Director
From: Management Accountant
Date: 21 November 2001
Subject: Just-in-time systems

Introduction

Further to our recent meeting, I have explained below how a just-in-time (JIT) system differs from the present stock control system and how the introduction of a JIT system would require a review of the quality control procedures.

Findings

The present system involves the use of three control levels: maximum, minimum and re-order levels. These will presumably have been determined on the basis of past data which could then lead to problems if the past data is not a reliable guide to the future. For instance the re-order level = Maximum lead time × Maximum usage and to illustrate we'll say that the maximum lead time in the past has been 2 weeks and that the maximum usage in any one week was 4,000 units of material, then the re-order level would be 2 × 4,000 = 8,000 units, and when stock falls to this level a new order must be placed.

Now at first this appears to be safe as it caters for the two worst possible outcomes, i.e. the longest delay before the new order arrives and the highest usage in that time, but this re-order level is only safe provided future usage and the future lead-times are not higher than the old figures. With the JIT system the suppliers will have to guarantee on-time delivery at very short notice. The uncertainty over lead time is completely removed as the supplier must deliver on demand and the supplier must be able to cope with fluctuations in demand. Because of the uncertainty associated with the present system there is a safety stock or buffer stock. With the JIT system there is no safety stock and there will be considerable savings in terms of holding costs such as the opportunity cost of the finance tied up in stock, insurance, storage costs and materials handling costs.

The present system uses an EOQ to minimise its costs. This may result in several weeks or months worth of stock being ordered at one time. This will then need storing and may require more storage space and more stores staff. With a JIT system the aim is to have very small batches being ordered on a much more frequent basis. Again this will result in a reduction in stock and in the associated cost.

Under the present system, SW buys its chemicals from a number of different suppliers. It is likely that the main emphasis will be on price and SW changes its suppliers frequently in accordance with the best deal that it can get. SW will accordingly not have a long-term relationship with its suppliers and sometimes the lowest cost supplier will only achieve its low cost at the expense of quality. With a JIT system the supplier must guarantee perfect quality material. The chemicals are ordered at very short notice and are not inspected when they arrive. SW will carry no safety stock and therefore cannot afford any defective chemicals. All the pressure seems to be on the supplier. It has to guarantee perfect quality materials and has to be able to deliver the required materials at very short notice. It therefore receives two benefits as a rule, firstly a premium price will be charged (this is reasonable as SW will be receiving a premium product) and, secondly, there will be a long-term agreement between SW and the supplier.

The implication in terms of quality goes beyond perfect quality materials from the supplier. The idea of zero defects must apply to all the company's operations. JIT is concerned with the elimination of waste, whether it be too much stock, unnecessary bureaucracy, machine breakdowns or production losses. If there were a 10% loss in a process, then SW would have to make more product than it really requires in order to cope with that loss. If a machine (say machine A) keeps breaking down under the present system, a common sense solution would be to have a buffer stock of completed items from that machine (machine A) at the next machine in line (say machine B), then if machine A does break down, machine B does not have to stop. It simply takes some items from its buffer stock until machine A comes on-line again. With JIT, instead of coping with the problem, we aim to eliminate the problem. Why does the machine keep breaking down? How can we fix it?

The emphasis should be in building good quality into everything we do, rather than inspecting bad quality out.

Conclusion

A just-in-time system can definitely bring advantages to a company's stock control systems, but must be implemented carefully, must be embraced by the workforce and must be carried through the whole of the supply chain to include the suppliers if it is work. If you require any further help or advice I will be only too happy to discuss matters further.

Signed: Management Accountant

Test your understanding 2 - FOOD MANUFACTURER

(a) Total Quality Management (TQM) has two main concepts:

(1) **Get it right first time**
TQM considers that the costs of prevention are less than the costs of correction. One of the main aims of TQM is to achieve zero rejects and 100% quality.

(2) **Continuous improvement**
The second basic principle of TQM is dissatisfaction with the status quo. Realistically a zero-defect goal may not be obtainable. It does, however, provide a target to ensure that a company should never be satisfied with its present level of rejects. The management and staff should believe that it is always possible to improve and to be able to get it more right next time!

There must be a focus on the customer and what they require and there must be a constant review of costs and performance to ensure that the aims of the TQM programme are being met.

The aim is to build good quality in rather than inspect poor quality out. The aim in the end is to design such good products and processes and obtain such good materials that inspection is no longer necessary.

SG plc should focus on the whole of its operation from start to finish if it wishes the TQM programme to be a success.

It must ensure that the input to its processes is defect-free. It must choose first-class suppliers who will guarantee the quality of their ingredients. It must communicate with the suppliers to let them know what is expected of them. SG plc is likely to have to pay a premium price to obtain these premium quality ingredients.

It must also examine its own processes to ensure that there are as few quality problems as possible. Where there are known quality problems, efforts should be directed at improving the processes by whatever means are appropriate, e.g. training, preventative maintenance, newer more reliable machines, etc.

The output process must also be controlled, i.e. the relationship with the customer. Efforts must be made to ensure that no defective products reach the customer, perhaps by means of final inspection before the goods leave the business and that where problems do occur, they are corrected as soon as possible. Communication with the customer is very important to ensure that the customer's needs are being met.

It is not enough to decide that a TQM system should be introduced. The programme should be carefully considered and communication to the staff should be clear. They should be educated as to the ideas behind TQM and given the necessary training to accomplish its aims. TQM should permeate the whole of the organisation and must be continually assessed to ensure that its goals are still being achieved.

(b) With a Just-In-Time (JIT) situation there are negligible stocks. There is no buffer stock. If there is a problem in production there is nothing to fall back on. The company does not keep a stock of raw materials or finished goods just-in-case. Thus, in a JIT system any problems can be catastrophic and therefore the idea is not to have any problems, i.e. perfect quality with zero defects. A TQM system is therefore necessary. In a JIT system quality is the responsibility of each employee.

(c) **Prevention costs**

These are the costs of preventing quality problems from occurring. They would include training, preventative maintenance, the purchase or hire of new more reliable machines, the sourcing of better quality ingredients, etc.

Appraisal costs

Appraisal costs are the costs incurred in checking the raw materials and products against the quality standard expected. They would include inspecting the ingredients and the semi-processed food destined for SG's customers, etc.

Internal failure costs

There are the costs incurred as a result of quality problems, where the problem is discovered before the product leaves the business, e.g. the cost of any out-of-date food which has to be disposed of, the material cost and labour cost of replacing a batch of defective product, etc.

External failure cost

These are the costs incurred as a result of quality problems, where the problem is discovered after the product leaves the business, e.g. loss of customer through delivering poor quality products, the material cost and labour cost of replacing a defective batch, the cost of being sued because of food poisoning, etc.

Test your understanding 3

The long manufacturing cycle and high levels of WIP make back-flush accounting unsuitable.

Test your understanding 4 - QUALITY COST

There are different philosophies about the cost of quality. Many businesses engineer quality into their processes while others set up systems to provide quality assurance.

The typical characteristics of quality cost are sometimes cited as follows:

Prevention cost

This would consist perhaps of the cost of the salaries of a quality control unit that carries out the sampling process to detect quality failures and prevents them from getting to the customer

Inspection/appraisal cost

This would include the cost of investigation into quality failures as well as the cost of consumable items used to carry out routine examinations.

Internal failure cost

This would cover the cost of scrapped items, reworking any defective output or undertaking any re-engineering process to improve quality.

External failure cost

This would cover the cost of warranties, free replacements, repairs and other efforts to repair the loss of customer goodwill.

Test your understanding 5

D

All of the statements are true.

chapter

4

Modern costing – throughput accounting

Chapter learning objectives

Lead	Component
A1. Discuss costing methods and their results.	(a) Compare and contrast marginal (or variable), throughput and absorption accounting methods in respect of profit reporting and stock valuation.

1 Session content diagram

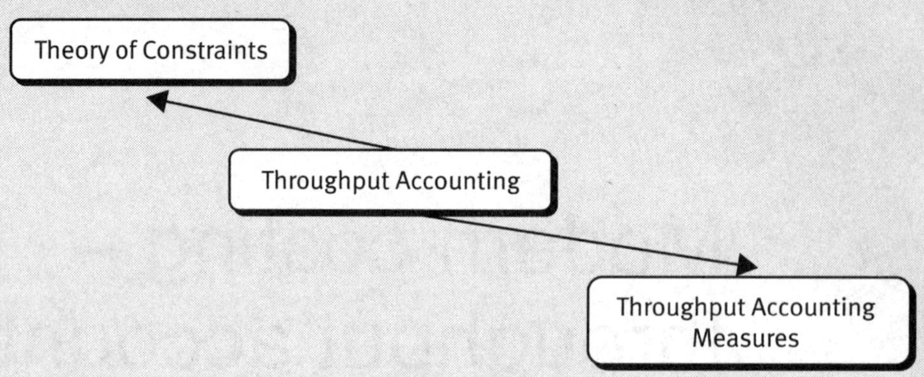

2 Introduction

Throughput accounting is very similar to marginal costing, but it can be used to make longer-term decisions about capacity/ production equipment.

Throughput accounting is based on three concepts: throughput, inventory (or investment) and operating expenses. **The aim of throughput accounting is to maximise the measure of throughput.** Goldratt and Cox advocate that managers should aim to increase throughput while simultaneously reducing inventory and operational expense.

Throughput

In throughput accounting, the only cost that is deemed to relate to volume of output is the direct material cost. All other costs (including all labour costs) are deemed to be fixed. These fixed costs may be called Total Factory Costs (TFC).

Throughput = Revenue – Totally variable costs

Throughput brings fresh money into the business from outside. Since totally variable costs are normally just raw materials and bought-in components, it is often convenient to define throughput as:

Throughput = Revenue – Raw material costs

Inventory

This is defined as all the money the business invests to buy the things that it intends to sell, or all the money tied up in assets so that the business can make the throughput. Inventory therefore includes unused raw materials, work-in-progress and unsold finished goods. It can also include non-current assets if these are used for buying raw materials.

Operating expenses

Operating expenses are defined as all the money a business spends to produce the throughput (i.e. to turn the inventory into throughput). It is not correct to think of operating expenses as fixed costs. They are costs that are not totally variable.

Origins and history

Throughput accounting emerged in the 1980s and 1990s as an alternative system of management accounting. It is associated with the work of Dr Eli Goldratt, who developed the Theory of Constraints (TOC) and the concept of throughput accounting comes from this theory.

Dr Goldratt described the approach of traditional accounting systems as 'Cost World', in which product cost is the main way to understand value. Costs are categorised as fixed and variable costs, and in absorption costing overheads are charged to labour time or to products using many arbitrary assumptions that have no commercial relevance. Even in marginal costing, it is assumed that direct labour costs vary with the activity level, and that fixed costs are the same for a given time period, regardless of the activity level.

Throughput accounting challenges these assumptions.

- Direct labour costs are not wholly variable. Skilled workers are paid fixed salaries, and so their cost does not vary directly with output volume.
- Fixed costs are 'less fixed' than they might have been in the past.
- The only totally variable cost is the purchase cost of raw materials and components that are bought from external suppliers.

3 Profit reporting

Since a business makes its money from throughput, management accounting systems should focus on the value of throughput created. Profit should therefore be reported as follows (illustrative figures are included):

		$
Revenue		750,000
Raw material cost	(totally variable cost)	200,000
Throughput		550,000
Operating expenses		400,000
Net profit		150,000

Super variable costing

Throughput accounting has been described as a form of 'super-variable costing' because the concept of throughput has similarities to the concept of contribution. It could therefore be seen as an alternative to marginal costing as a costing method. However, this is not an accurate description. This is because in throughput accounting, the concept of product cost is rejected. The throughput earned by individual products is calculated, but no attempt is made to charge operating expenses to products. This makes throughput accounting radically different from both traditional cost accounting systems such as absorption costing and marginal costing and also from activity based costing.

4 Inventory valuation

Inventory should be valued at the purchase cost of its raw materials and bought-in parts.

It should not include any other costs, not even labour costs. No value is added by the production process, not even by labour, until the item is sold.

It is impossible to create additional profit simply by producing more and adding to inventory. Profit is not created until there is throughput.

Example 1

A company makes 1,000 units of an item during a period and sells 800 units for $8,000. Costs of production were as follows:

	$
Materials	3,000
Direct labour	2,000
Fixed production overhead	1,000
Other overhead	1,000

Actual production volume and production overhead expenditure were both the same as budgeted.

Required:

Calculate the profit for the period using:

(a) absorption costing

(b) marginal costing

(c) throughput accounting.

5 Maximising throughput

Using throughput accounting, the aim should be to maximise throughput, on the assumption that operating expenses are a fixed amount in each period.

- If the business has more capacity than there is customer demand, it should produce to meet the demand in full, provided that each additional unit made and sold adds to total throughput.
- If the business has a constraint that prevents it from meeting customer demand in full, it should make the most profitable use that it can of the constraining resource. **This means giving priority to those products earning the highest throughput for each unit of the constraining resource that it requires**.

This goal is achieved by determining what factors prevent the throughput being higher. This constraint is called a *bottleneck*. A bottleneck may be a machine whose capacity limits the output of the whole production process. **The aim is to identify the bottlenecks and remove them, or, if this is not possible, ensure that they are fully utilised at all times**. Non-bottleneck resources should be scheduled and operated based on the constraints within the system, and should not be used to produce more than the bottlenecks can absorb.

Calculation - multi-product decision making

The usual objective in questions is to maximise profit. Given that fixed costs are unaffected by the production decision in the short run, the approach should be to maximise the throughput earned.

Step 1: identify the bottleneck constraint.

Step 2: calculate the throughput per unit for each product.

Step 3: calculate the throughput per unit of the bottleneck resource for each product.

Step 4: rank the products in order of the throughout per unit of the bottleneck resource.

Step 5: allocate resources using this ranking and answer the question.

Example 2

The following data relates to two products manufactured by DJ Ltd

	Product X	Product Y
Selling price per unit	\$15	\$20
Direct material cost per unit	\$10	\$11
Maximum demand (units)	25,000	30,000
Time required on the bottleneck (hours per unit)	2	6

The firm has 80,000 bottleneck hours available each period.

Total factory costs amount to \$128,000 in the period.

Requirement:

Calculate the optimum product mix and the maximum profit.

The theory of constraints

Goldratt and Cox (1992) describe the process of identifying and taking steps to remove the constraints that restrict output as the **theory of constraints** (TOC). The process involves 5 steps:

(1) Identify the system's bottlenecks.

(2) Decide how to exploit the bottlenecks.

(3) Subordinate everything else to the decision in Step 2.

(4) Elevate the system's bottlenecks.

(5) If, in the previous steps, a bottleneck has been broken, go back to Step 1.

The bottleneck is the focus of management's attention. Decisions regarding the optimum mix of products must be undertaken. Step 3 requires that the optimum production of the bottleneck activity determines the production schedule of the non-bottleneck activities. There is no point in a non-bottleneck activity supplying more than the bottleneck activity can consume. This would result in increased WIP inventories with no increased sales volume. The TOC is a process of continuous improvement to clear the throughput chain of all the constraints. Thus, step 4 involves taking action to remove, or elevate the constraint. This may involve replacing the bottleneck machine with a faster one, providing additional training for a slow worker or changing the design of the product to reduce the processing time required on the bottleneck activity. Once a bottleneck has been elevated it will generally be replaced by a new bottleneck elsewhere in the system. It then becomes necessary to return to step 1.

Constraints on throughput

The idea of constraints is central to the throughput approach. Examples of constraints may include:

- inadequately trained sales force
- poor reputation for meeting delivery dates
- poor physical distribution system
- unreliability of material supplies, delivery and/or quality
- inadequate production resources
- inappropriate management accounting system

6 Throughput accounting measures

Throughput Accounting Measures

Various performance measures have been devised to help measure throughput:

$$\text{Return per factory hour} = \frac{\text{Throughput}}{\text{Product' s time on the bottleneck resource}}$$

$$\text{Cost per factory hour} = \frac{\text{Total factory cost}}{\text{Total time on the bottleneck resource}}$$

$$\text{Throughput accounting ratio} = \frac{\text{Return per factory hour}}{\text{Cost per factory hour}}$$

The return per factory hour shows the value added by the organisation and managers are encouraged to maximise this (for example, by increasing throughput or reducing the time taken in the process).

The throughput accounting ratio measures the return from a product agains the cost of running the factory. Some people would argue that only products with a throughput accounting ratio greater than 1 are worthwhile.

But notice that the return per factory hours and the throughput accounting ratios are for each individual product, whereas the cost per factory hour is for the company as a whole. So it could be argued that a throughput accounting ratio of less than 1 does not reveal the full story.

Example 3

Calculate the Throughput Accounting ratio for each product in the previous example.

Criticism of throughput accounting

A criticism of throughput accounting is that it concentrates on the short term, when a business has a fixed supply of resources and operating expenses are largely fixed.

It is more difficult to apply throughput accounting concepts to the longer term, when all costs are variable, and vary with the volume of production and sales or another cost driver.

This criticism suggests that although throughput accounting could be a suitable method of measuring profit and performance in the short term, an alternative management accounting method, such as activity based costing, might be more appropriate for measuring and controlling performance from a longer-term perspective.

7 Chapter summary

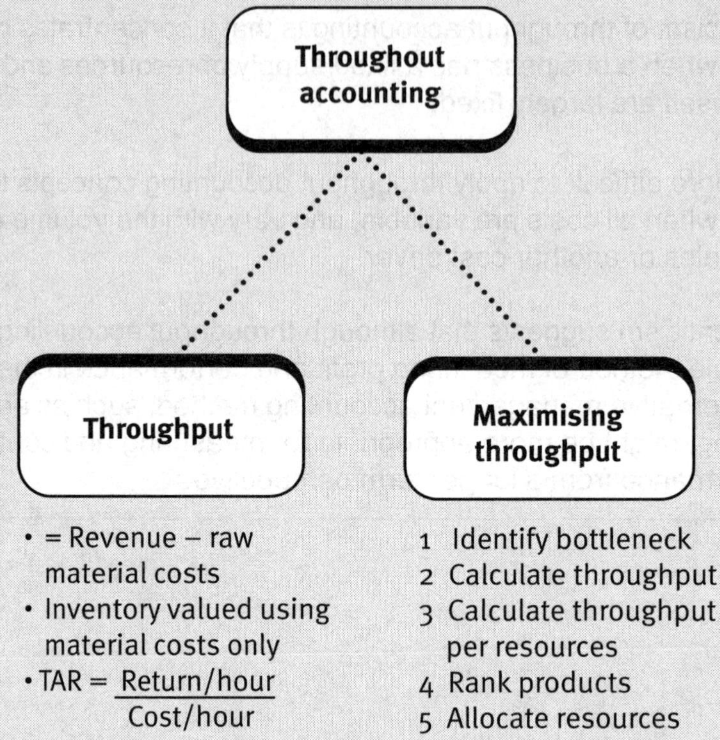

8 Practice questions

Test your understanding 1

A business makes four products, W, X, Y and Z. Information relating to these products is as follows:

	W	*X*	*Y*	*Z*
Sales price / unit	$20	$25	$18	$40
Materials required / unit	$10	$15	$11	$22
Labour hours / unit	4	5	2	6
Monthly sales demand (units)	500	800	1,000	400

There is a limit to the availability of labour, and only 8,000 hours are available each month.

Required:

Identify which products the business produce.

Test your understanding 2

A company manufactures a product that requires machine time of 1.5 hours per unit. Machine time is a bottleneck resource, due to the limited number of machines available. There are 10 machines available and each machine can be used for up to 40 hours each week.

The product is sold for $85 per unit and the material cost per unit is $42.50. Total operating expenses are $8,000 each week.

Required:

Calculate the throughput accounting ratio.

Test your understanding 3

X Limited manufactures a product that requires 1.5 hours of machining. Machine time is a bottleneck resource, due to the limited number of machines available. There are 10 machines available, and each machine can be used for up to 40 hours per week.

The product is sold for $85 per unit and the direct material cost per unit is $42.50. Total factory costs are $8,000 each week.

Calculate

(a) the return per factory hour

(b) the TPAR.

Test your understanding 4

Justin Thyme manufactures four products, A, B, C and D. Details of sales prices, costs and resource requirements for each of the products are as follows.

	Product A	Product B	Product C	Product D
	$	$	$	$
Sales price	1.40	0.80	1.20	2.80
Materials cost	0.60	0.30	0.60	1.00
Direct labour cost	0.40	0.20	0.40	1.00
	Minutes	Minutes	Minutes	Minutes
Machine time per unit	5	2	3	6
Labour time per unit	2	1	2	5
	Units	Units	Units	Units
Weekly sales demand	2,000	2,000	2,500	1,500

Machine time is a bottleneck resource and the maximum capacity is 400 machine hours each week. Operating costs, including direct labour costs, are $5,440 each week. Direct labour costs are $12 per hour, and direct labour workers are paid for a 38-hour week, with no overtime.

(a) Identify the quantities of each product that should be manufactured and sold each week to maximise profit and calculate the weekly profit.

(b) Calculate the throughput accounting ratio at this profit-maximising level of output and sales.

Test your understanding 5

The following data relate to the single product made by Squirrel Ltd:

Selling price per unit	£16
Direct material cost per unit	£10
Maximum demand (units) per period	40,000
Time required (hours) in Process X, per unit	1
Time required (hours) in Process Y, per unit	1.5

The capacities are 35,000 hours in Process X and 42,000 hours in Process Y.

The total factory costs are £105,000 in the period.

Required:

(a) Identify the process bottleneck.

(b) Calculate the throughput accounting ratio.

Test your understanding 6 - THROUGHPUT ACCOUNTING

Explain why throughput accounting has been described as a form of 'super variable costing' and how the concept of contribution in throughput accounting differs from that in marginal costing.

(5 marks)

Test your understanding 7

A company manufactures three products: W, X and Y. The products use a series of different machines, but there is a common machine that is a bottleneck. The standard selling price and standard cost per unit for each product for the next period are as follows:

	W	*X*	*Y*
	£	£	£
Selling price	180	150	150
Cost:			
Direct material	41	20	30
Direct labour	30	20	50
Variable production overheads	24	16	20
Fixed production overheads	36	24	30
	—	—	—
Profit	49	70	20
	—	—	—
Time (minutes) on bottleneck machine	7	10	7

The company is trying to plan the best use of its resources.

(a) **Using a traditional limiting factor approach, the rank order (best first) of the products would be:**

A W, X, Y

B W, Y, X

C X, W, Y

D Y, X, W

(2 marks)

(b) **Using a throughput accounting approach, the rank order (best first) of the products would be:**

A W, X, Y

B W, Y, X

C X, W, Y

D Y, X, W

(2 marks)

Test your understanding answers

Example 1

The valuation of closing inventory is:

- $1,200 ($6,000 × 200/1,000) in absorption costing
- $1,000 ($5,000 × 200/1,000) in marginal costing
- $600 ($3,000 × 200/1,000) in throughput accounting.

Example 2

	Product	
	X	Y
	$	$
Selling price	15	20
Direct material	10	11
	—	—
Throughput	5	9
No. of bottleneck hours per unit	2	6
Return per factory hour	2.50	1.50
	1st	2nd

	Units	Bottleneck hrs per unit	Bottleneck hrs	Throughput $
Product X	25,000	2	50,000	125,000
Product Y	5,000 Bal 2	6	30,000 Bal	45,000
			80,000	170,000
Total factory cost				128,000
				42,000

Example 3

				Product X	Product Y
Return per factory hour	=	Throughput per unit / Bottleneck hrs per unit	=	(15 – 10) / 2 hrs	(20 – 11) / 6 hrs
				= $2.50	= $1.50
Cost per factory hour	=	Total Factory Cost / Total Bottleneck Hrs	=	£128,000 / 80,000 hrs	
				= $1.60	
Throughput Accounting Ratio	=	Return per factory hour / Cost per factory hour	=	£2.50 / £1.60	£1.50 / £1.60
				= 1.56	= 0.94

Product X has the higher throughput accounting ratio and thus should be given priority over Product Y.

Test your understanding 1

The business should seek to maximise the total throughput.

	W	X	Y	Z
	$	$	$	$
Sales price / unit	20	25	18	40
Materials required / unit	10	15	11	22
Throughput / unit	10	10	7	18
Labour hours / unit	4	5	2	6
Throughput / labour hour	$2.50	$2.00	$3.50	$3.00
Priority	3rd	4th	1st	2nd

The production volumes that will maximise throughput and net profit are:

Product	**Units**	**Labour hours**	**Throughput**
			$
Y	1,000	2,000	7,000
Z	400	2,400	7,200
W	500	2,000	5,000
		6,400	
X (balance)	320	1,600	3,200
		8,000	22,400

Test your understanding 2

Throughput per bottleneck machine hour = ($85 – $42.50)/1.5 hours = $28.33

Operating expenses per bottleneck machine hour = $8,000/(10 × 40) = $20

Throughput accounting ratio = $28.33/$20 = 1.42

Test your understanding 3

Return per factory hour = ($85 – $42.50)/1.5 hours = $28.33

Cost per factory hour = $8,000/(10 × 40 hours) = $20

TPAR = $28.33/$20 = 1.4165

Test your understanding 4

(a)

Step 1: Determine the bottleneck constraint

The bottleneck resource is machine time. 400 machine hours available each week = 24,000 machine minutes.

Step 2: Calculate the throughput per unit for each product

	A	**B**	**C**	**D**
	$	$	$	$
Sales price	1.40	0.80	1.20	2.80
Materials cost	0.60	0.30	0.60	1.00
Throughput/ unit	0.80	0.50	0.60	1.80

Step 3: Calculate the throughput per machine minute

Machine time per unit	5 minutes	2 minutes	3 minutes	6 minutes
Throughput per minute	$0.16	$0.25	$0.20	$0.30

Step 4: Rank

Rank	4th	2nd	3rd	1st

Step 5: Allocate resources using this ranking and answer the question.

The profit-maximising weekly output and sales volumes are as follows.

Product	**Units**	**Machine minutes**	**Throughput per unit**	**Total throughout**
			$	$
D	1,500	9,000	1.80	2,700
B	2,000	4,000	0.50	1,000
C	2,500	7,500	0.60	1,500
		20,500		
A (balance)	700	3,500	0.80	560
		24,000		5,760
Operating expenses				5,440
Profit				320

(b) Throughput per machine hour: \$5,760/400 hours = \$14.40

Cost (operating expenses) per machine hour: \$5,440/400 hours = \$13.60.

TPAR: \$14.40/\$13.60 = 1.059.

Test your understanding 5

(a) Capacity in process X = $\frac{35,000}{1}$ = 35,000 units per period

Capacity in process Y = $\frac{42,000}{1.5}$ = 28,000 unit per period

∴ Process Y is the bottleneck

(b) Throughput per unit = £16 – £10 = £6

Return per factory hour = $\frac{£6}{1.5}$ = £4

Cost per factory hour = $\frac{£105,000}{42,000 \text{ hours}}$ = £2.50

Throughput accounting ratio = $\frac{£4}{£2.5}$ =1.6

As this is above 1, this is satisfactory.

Test your understanding 6 - THROUGHPUT ACCOUNTING

THROUGHPUT ACCOUNTING

Throughput accounting has been described as a form of 'super variable costing' because the concept of throughput has similarities to the concept of contribution. However there is a major difference in the definition of contribution in the two systems or, more specifically, in what is described as a variable cost.

The traditional marginal costing approach assumes that direct labour is a variable cost. Although this may have been true in the past when labour was typically paid a piece rate, this is no longer the case. In the short term, throughput accounting treats labour as a fixed cost.

Marginal costing also tends to emphasise cost behaviour, especially overheads, and usually attempts to separate these into fixed and variable components. As with labour costs, throughput accounting treats all production overhead as fixed in the short term and aggregates these with labour into what is referred to as 'total factory cost'. Consequently, in throughput accounting the only cost that is treated as variable is the direct material cost.

Furthermore, throughput accounting uses the total of direct materials purchased in the period in the calculation of throughput, rather than the cost of material actually used, as is the case with marginal costing.

Test your understanding 7

(a)

A

	W	X	Y
	£	£	£
Contribution	85	94	50
Time at bottle neck	7	10	7
Contribution per minute	12	9	7
Rank	1	2	3

(b)

B

	W	X	Y
	£	£	£
Throughput*	139	130	120
Time at bottle neck	7	10	7
Throughput per minute	20	13	17
Rank	1	3	2

* throughput = sales less material costs

chapter

5

Modern costing – activity-based costing

Chapter learning objectives

Lead	Component
A1. Discuss costing methods and their results.	(c) Discuss activity-based costing as compared with traditional marginal and absorption costing methods, including its relative advantages and disadvantages as a system of cost accounting.
A3. Apply principles of environmental costing.	(a) Apply principles of environmental costing in identifying relevant internalised costs and externalised environmental impacts of the organisation's activities.

1 Session content diagram

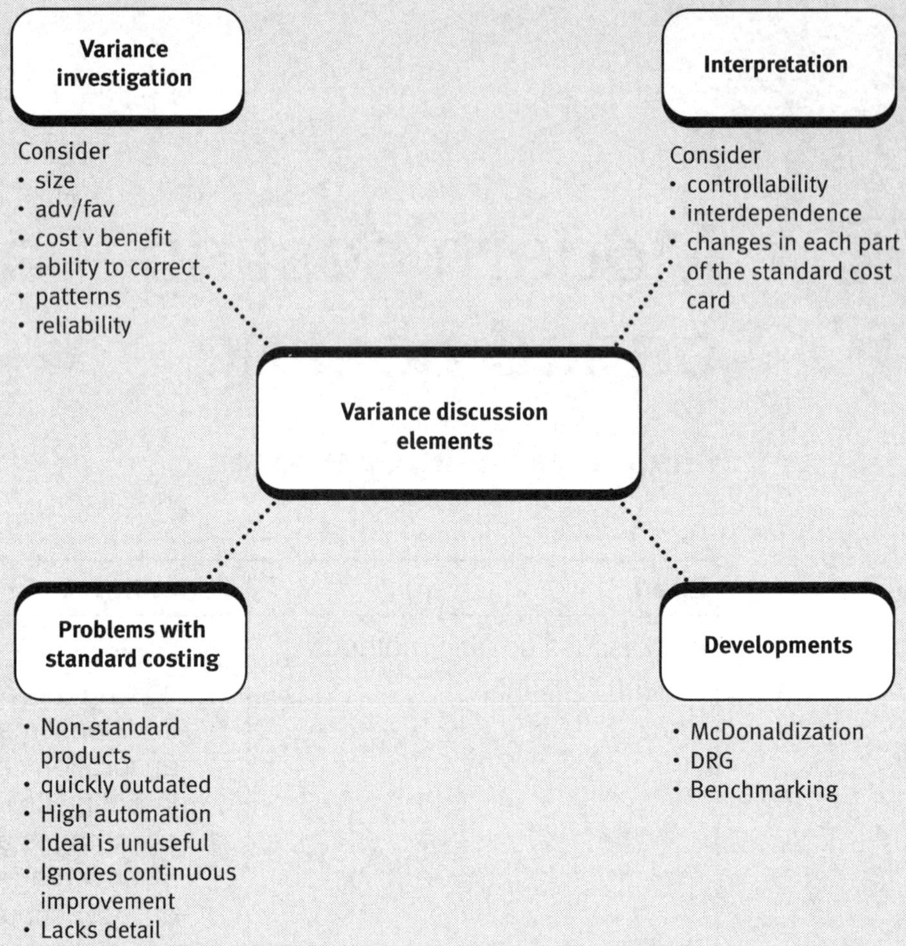

2 Modern production environments

Modern producers have changed the way that they produce so that they have:

- much more machinery and computers
- smaller batch sizes
- less use of 'direct' labour

This has had the following **impact on production costs:**

- more indirect overheads (for example, insurance and depreciation of the machines and computers)
- less direct labour costs

This means that the **traditional** methods of costing (marginal and absorption) produce **standard cost cards that are less useful**:

- the largest cost of production is indirect overheads but these are categorised together in one figure that lacks detail and is not useful to management
- because management does not now what the components are of the largest production cost (indirect overheads) they cannot implement proper cost control
- the costs are often allocated between products on the basis of direct labour hours - despite the fact that direct labour is becoming small and insigniicant in product costs and does not fairly reflect the relationship between the products and the indirect overheads
- because costs are badly shared between products it means that the total production cost can be wrong which can lead to poor pricing and production decisions

Activity based costing **(ABC) has been developed to solve the problems** that the traditional costing methods create in these modern environments.

Traditional costing problems

Problems with absorption costing

Traditional absorption costing charges overhead costs to products (or services) in an arbitrary way. In product costing, overheads are absorbed on the basis of the volume of production in each production department or centre. The basis for setting an absorption rate is volume-related, such as an overhead absorption rate per unit produced, a rate per direct labour hour or a rate per machine hour.

The assumption underlying this method of costing is that overhead expenditure is connected to the volume of production activity.

- This assumption was probably valid many years ago, when production systems were based on labour-intensive or machine-intensive mass production of fairly standard items. Overhead costs were also fairly small relative to direct materials and direct labour costs; therefore any inaccuracy in the charging of overheads to products costs was not significant.
- The assumption is not valid in a complex manufacturing environment, where production is based on smaller customised batches of products, indirect costs are high in relation to direct costs, and a high proportion of overhead activities – such as production scheduling, order handling and quality control – are not related to production volume.
- For similar reasons, traditional absorption costing is not well-suited to the costing of many services.

The criticism of absorption costing is that it cannot calculate a 'true' product cost that has any valid meaning. Overheads are charged to departments and products in an arbitrary way, and the assumption that overhead expenditure is related to direct labour hours or machine hours in the production departments is no longer realistic.

Problems with marginal costing

There are also major problems with marginal costing, but for different reasons. In marginal costing, products or services are valued at their marginal cost, and profitability is assessed by calculating the contribution earned from each product or service. Fixed costs are assumed to be time-related and are charged against profits as a cost for the period. This can be a useful costing method when variable costs are a large proportion of total costs.

The main criticisms of marginal costing as a method of measuring product costs and profitability are that:

- variable costs might be small in relation to fixed costs
- 'fixed' costs might be fixed in relation to production volume, but they might vary with other activities that are not production-related.

In many manufacturing and service environments, it is therefore inappropriate to treat overhead costs as fixed period costs, and indirect costs should be charged to products or services in a more meaningful way

3 Activity-based costing

Activity-based costing (ABC) is an alternative approach to product costing. It is a form of absorption costing, but , rather than absorbing overheads on a production volume basis it firstly allocates them to **cost pools** before absorbing them into units using **cost drivers**.

- A **cost pool** is an activity that consumes resources and for which overhead costs are identified and allocated. For each cost pool, there should be a cost driver.
- A **cost driver** is a unit of activity that consumes resources. An alternative definition of a cost driver is a factor influencing the level of cost.

e.g

Illustration 1

Imagine the machining department in a traditional absorption costing system. The OAR would be based on machine hours because many of the overheads in the machine department would relate to the machines, e.g. power, maintenance, machine depreciation, etc., so using a machine hour basis would seem fair, however, not only does the machine department have machine related costs, but also in an absorption costing system, it would also have picked up a share of rent and rates, heating, lighting, building depreciation, canteen costs, personnel cost, etc. These costs would also be absorbed on a machine hour basis, because everything in the machine department is absorbed on machine hours and whilst this is fair for power, maintenance and machine depreciation, it is inappropriate for the other costs.

ABC overcomes this problem by not using departments as gathering points for costs, but instead using activities, and there would for example be a machine-related activity to which power would be charged, machine depreciation would be charged, and machine maintenance would be charged. It would not pick up a share of personnel costs or rent or rates or indeed anything not machine related. ABC's flexibility thus reduces the incidence of arbitrary apportionments.

ABC vs absorption costing

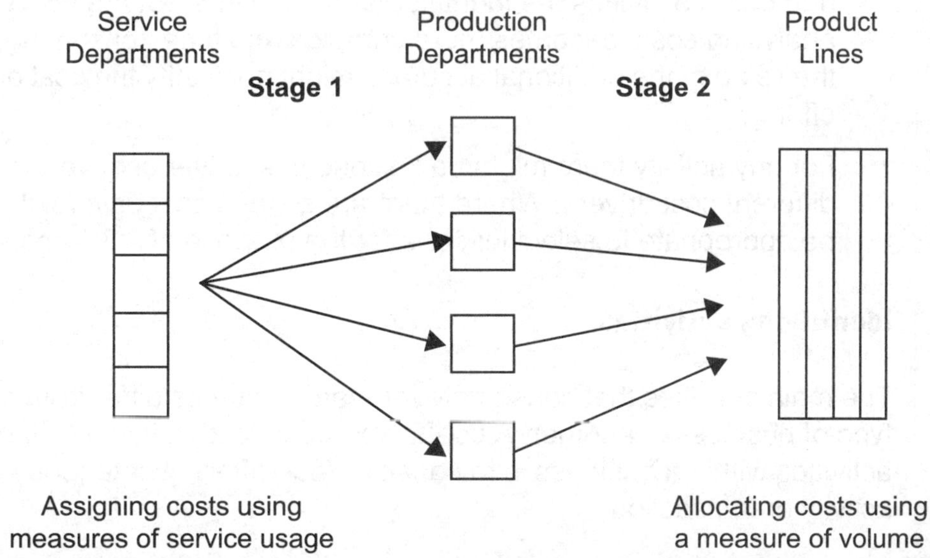

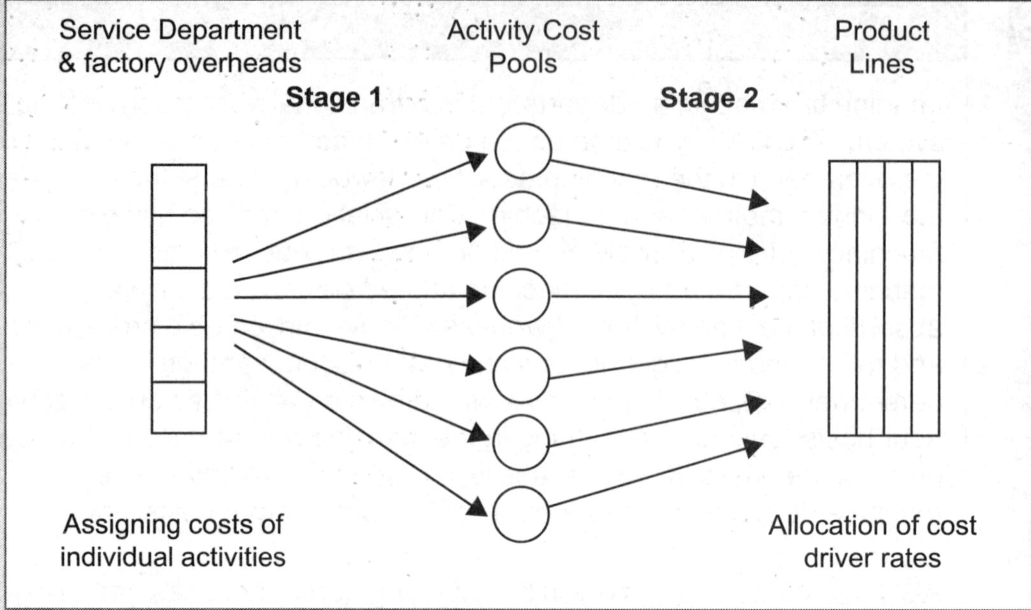

Identifying activities and drivers

If a business decides to adopt activity-based costing to measure the costs and profitability of its products or services, it must identify the key activities that consume resources and the cost driver for each of those activities.

- There might be a large number of different activities, but in an accounting system it is usually necessary to simplify the overhead cost analysis and select a fairly small number of activities. If a large number of activities are identified and used in ABC, the task of analysing costs becomes more complex and time-consuming, and the value of the additional accuracy might not justify the cost and effort.
- For any activity there might be just one cost driver or several different cost drivers. Where there are several cost drivers, it might be appropriate to select just one for the purpose of ABC analysis.

Identifying activities

The main activities that consume overhead resources differ from one type of business to another. A useful approach to identifying suitable activities within a business is to consider four different categories of activity or transaction:

- **Logistical transactions.** These are activities or transactions concerned with moving materials or people, and with tracking the progress of materials or work through the system.

- **Balancing transactions.** These are concerned with ensuring that the resources required for an operation are available. For example, the buying department has to make sure that raw materials are available to meet production requirements.
- **Quality transactions.** These are concerned with ensuring that output or service levels meet quality requirements and customer expectations. Inspections and handling customer complaints are both examples of quality transactions.
- **Change transactions.** These are activities required to respond to changes in customer demand, a change in design specifications, a scheduling change, a change in production or delivery methods, and so on.

For any business, there could be important resource-consuming activities in each of these categories.

Identifying cost drivers

For each selected activity, there should be a cost driver. The chosen cost driver must be:

- **Relevant.** In other words, there should be a connection between the cost driver and the consumption of resources for the activity.
- **Easy to measure.** Measuring the units of cost driver and identifying the products or services to which they relate needs to be a fairly easy and straightforward process.

Often, the cost driver is the number of transactions relating to the activity. For example:

- the cost of setting up machinery for a production run might be driven by the number of set-ups (jobs or batches produced)
- the cost of order processing might be related to the number of orders received
- the cost of despatch might be related to the number of orders despatched or to the weight of items despatched
- the costs of purchasing might be related to the number of purchase orders made
- the costs of quality control might be related to the number of inspections carried out, or to the incidence of rejected items.

Calculating the full production cost per unit using ABC

There are five basic steps to calculating an activity based cost:

Step 1: Group production overheads into activities, according to how they are driven.

A cost pool is an activity which consumes resources and for which overhead costs are identified and allocated. For each cost pool, there should be a cost driver. The terms 'activity' and 'cost pool' are often used interchangeably.

Step 2: Identify cost drivers for each activity, i.e. what causes these activity costs to be incurred.

A cost driver is a factor that influences (or drives) the level of cost.

Step 3: Calculate an OAR for each activity.

The OAR is calcuated in the same way as the absorption costing OAR. However, a separate OAR will be calcuated for each activity, by taking the activity cost and dividing by the cost driver information.

Step 4: Absorb the activity costs into the product.

The activity costs should be absorbed back into the individual products.

Step 5: Calculate the full production cost and/ or the profit or loss.

Some questions ask for the production cost per unit and/ or the profit or loss per unit.

Other questions ask for the total production cost and/ or the total profit or loss.

Example 1

A manufacturing business makes a product in two models, model M1 and model M2. details of the two products are as follows.

	Model M1	Model M2
Annual sales	8,000 units	8,000 units
Number of sales orders	60	250
Sales price per unit	$54	$73
Direct material cost per unit	$11	$21
Direct labour hours per unit	2.0 hours	2.5 hours
Direct labour rate per hour	$8	$8
Special parts per unit	2	8
Production batch size	2,000 units	100 units
Setups per batch	1	3
Production batch size	1	1

	$	Cost driver
Issues of material for each batch	97,600	Number of setups
Overhead analysis	42,000	Number of batches
Setup costs	50,000	Number of special parts
Material handling costs	31,000	Number of sales orders
Special part handling costs	108,000	Direct labour hours
Customer invoicing costs	328,600	

A customer has indicated an interest in placing a large order for either model M1 or M2, and the sales manager wished to try to sell the higher-priced model M2.

Required:

(a) Calculate the profit per unit for each model, using ABC.

(b) Using the information above identify which prodocut the sales manager should try to sell on the basis of the information provided by your ABC analysis

4 When is ABC relevant?

ABC is a more expensive system to operate than traditional costing, so it should only be introduced when it is appropriate to do so. Activity-based costing could provide much more meaningful information about product costs and profits when:

- indirect costs are high relative to direct costs
- products or services are complex
- products or services are tailored to customer specifications
- some products or services are sold in large numbers but others are sold in small numbers.

In these situations, ABC will often result in significantly different product or service overhead costs, compared with traditional absorption costing.

Advantages and disadvantages of ABC

ABC has a number of advantages:

- It provides a more accurate cost per unit. As a result, pricing, sales strategy, performance management and decision making should be improved (see next section for detail).
- It provides much better insight into what drives overhead costs.
- ABC recognises that overhead costs are not all related to production and sales volume.
- In many businesses, overhead costs are a significant proportion of total costs, and management needs to understand the drivers of overhead costs in order to manage the business properly. Overhead costs can be controlled by managing cost drivers.
- It can be applied to derive realistic costs in a complex business environment.
- ABC can be applied to all overhead costs, not just production overheads.
- ABC can be used just as easily in service costing as in product costing.

Disadvantages of ABC:

- ABC will be of limited benefit if the overhead costs are primarily volume related or if the overhead is a small proportion of the overall cost.
- It is impossible to allocate all overhead costs to specific activities.
- The choice of both activities and cost drivers might be inappropriate.

- ABC can be more complex to explain to the stakeholders of the costing exercise.
- The benefits obtained from ABC might not justify the costs.

The implications of switching to ABC

The use of ABC has potentially significant commercial implications:

- Pricing can be based on more realistic cost data.
  - Pricing decisions will be improved because the price will be based on more accurate cost data
- Sales strategy can be more soundly based.
  - More realistic product costs as a result of the use of ABC may enable sales staff to:
    - target customers that appeared unprofitable using absorption costing but may be profitable under ABC
    - stop targeting customers or market segments that are now shown to offer low or negative sales margins.
- Decision making can be improved.
  - Research, production and sales effort can be directed towards those products and services which ABC has identified as offering the highest sales margins.
- Performance management can be improved.
  - Performance management should be enhanced due to the focus on selling the most profitable products and through the control of cost drivers.
  - ABC can be used as the basis of budgeting and longer term forward planning of overhead costs. The more realistic budgeted overhead cost should improve the system of performance management.

5 Environmental management accounting

The importance of environmental management

Organisations are beginning to recognise that environmental awareness and management are not optional, but are important for long-term survival and profitability. All organisations:

- are faced with increasing legal and regulatory requirements relating to environmental management
- need to meet customers' needs and concerns relating to the environment

- need to demonstrate effective environmental management to maintain a good public image
- need to manage the risk and potential impact of environmental disasters
- can make cost savings by improved use of resources such as water and fuel
- are recognising the importance of sustainable development, which is the meeting of current needs without compromising the ability of future generations to meet their needs.

British Petroleum - an illustration

Environmental management at BP (British Petroleum)

BP plc's Annual Review 2006 describes a number of activities aimed at reducing the environmental impact of the company's operations:

- improving the integrity of its equipment and pipelines to reduce the spillage of oil
- reducing the emissions of greenhouse gases, which is measured and reported within the Annual Review
- introducing environmental requirements for new projects
- supporting the use of market mechanisms to bring about emission reductions across industry
- launching a new business providing energy from alternative sources
- investing in research into biofuels
- developing and marketing fuel which produces lower emissions compared with standard fuels.

The contribution of environmental management accounting (EMA)

EMA is concerned with the accounting information needs of managers in relation to corporate activities that affect the environment as well as environment-related impacts on the corporation. This includes:

- identifying and estimating the costs of environment-related activities
- identifying and separately monitoring the usage and cost of resources such as water, electricity and fuel and to enable costs to be reduced
- ensuring environmental considerations form a part of capital investment decisions
- assessing the likelihood and impact of environmental risks

- including environment-related indicators as part of routine performance monitoring
- benchmarking activities against environmental best practice.

EM and effect on financial performance

There are a number of ways in which environmental issues can have an impact on the financial performance of organisations.

Improving revenue

Producing new products or services which meet the environmental needs or concerns of customers can lead to increased sales. It may also be possible to sell such products for a premium price. Improved sales may also be a consequence of improving the reputation of the business.

It is possible that in the future, rather than good environmental management resulting in improved sales, poor management will lead to losses. All businesses will be expected to meet a minimum standard related to environmental issues.

Cost reductions

Paying close attention to the use of resources can lead to reductions in cost. Often simple improvements in processes can lead to significant costs savings.

Increases in costs

There may be increases in some costs, for example the cost of complying with legal and regulatory requirements, and additional costs to improve the environmental image of the organisation. However some of these costs may be offset by government grants and this expenditure may save money in the long-term as measures taken may prevent future losses.

Costs of failure

Poor environmental management can result in significant costs, for example the cost of clean-up and fines following an environmental disaster.

e.g

Illustration 2

Rolls-Royce Aerospace says up to a quarter of emissions can be cut by changes in airframe design. It adds that changes in its Environmentally Friendly Engine (EFE) programme will deliver up to another fifth and the remainder of the 50 per cent target can be met by changing the way the aircraft are operated.

Rolls are also developing fuel cell technology and alternatives to kerosene. A biofuel blended with kerosene will be used in one of the four Rolls-Royce RB211-524s powering an Air New Zealand Boeing 747-400 in the second half of 2008.

Another example of energy saving is McCain Foods, which buys an eighth of the UK's potatoes to make chips. It has cut its Peterborough plant's CO2 footprint by two-thirds, says corporate affairs director Bill Bartlett. It invested £10m in three 3MW turbines to meet 60 per cent of its annual electricity demand. McCain spent another £4.5m on a lagoon to catch the methane from fermenting waste water and particulates, which generates another 10 per cent of the site's electricity usage. It also wants to refine its used cooking oil, either for its own vehicles fleet or for selling on. McCain want to become more competitive and more efficient.

The Hull factory of Smith & Nephew Wound Management makes single-use sterile wound dressings for injuries and operations. It saved £250,000 a year by replacing a large absorption chiller with a vapour compression chiller. It also replaced four 500kW chillers with a 'ring main' run from one 1MW chiller for the whole factory; in winter this runs at 250kW. Hull saved £50,000 by shutting down four of its eight compres¬sors. These and other efforts have cut its energy use by 38 per cent to 48m kWh a year, saving £2m since 2003, says S&N energy and utilities manager Marc Beaumont, who adds: "And there's still more to go at." He says the main driver has been cost: "Energy prices are set to go only one way. If we can drive down costs we can increase our profits."

St Gobain are leaders in the design; production and distribution of materials for the construction; industrial and consumer markets. They used to pay contractors £75 a tonne for someone to take its cardboard away. Now it uses a baler that costs £238.33 a month to rent, maintain, operate and power. The baler crushes the cardboard into 500kg bales that it sells to a paper mill for £30 a tonne.

McLenaghan has a long list of sellable wastes, from mobile phones to scrap metal to cutting-wheels, thermocouples, cutting tools and vending machine cups. They believe waste can be reused, reallocated or put into a revenue stream.

Xerox has announced 'green software' that allows its machines to spot pages with just a URL, banner, logo or legal jargon and refuse to print them.

Canon advertising says its copiers' on-demand fixing technology saved seven million tonnes of CO_2 between 1999 and 2006. And in September 2007 Dell announced its aim to be carbon neutral.

EMA and TQM

Organisations should be striving to achieve an integrated environmental strategy underpinned by the same type of culture that is required for the successful operation of a programme of total quality management (TQM).

It is arguable that the two are inextricably linked insofar as good environmental management is increasingly recognised as an essential component of TQM. The focus is upon 'continuous improvement' and the pursuit of excellence. Such organisations pursue objectives that may include zero complaints, zero spills, zero pollution, zero waste and zero accidents. Information systems need to be able to support such environmental objectives via the provision of feedback – on the success or otherwise – of the organisational efforts in achieving such objectives. In this respect, the organisation becomes self-regulating and the undertaking of environmental audits on a regular basis provides the platform for organisations to adopt a self-critical and analytical posture as part of their routine organisational management processes.

This approach to environmental quality management requires the development of environmental performance measures and indicators that will enable a comprehensive review of environmental performance to be undertaken. Many – if not all – total quality management accounting techniques can be modified.

6 Identifying and accounting for environmental costs

Internal and external environmental costs

Management are often unaware of the extent of environmental costs and cannot identify opportunities for cost savings. Environmental costs can be split into two categories:

Internal costs

These are costs that directly impcat on the income statement of a company. There are many different types, for example:

- improved systems and checks in order to avoid penalties/fines
- waste disposal costs

- product take back costs (i.e. in the EU, for example, companies must provide facilities for customers to return items such as batteries, printer cartridges etc. for recycling. The seller of such items must bear the cost of these "take backs)
- regulatory costs such as taxes (e.g. companies with poor environmental management policies often have to bear a higher tax burden)
- upfront costs such as obtaining permits (e.g. for achieving certain levels of emmissions)
- back-end costs such as decommissioning costs on project completion

External costs

These are costs that are imposed on society at large but nor borne by the company that generates the cost in the irst instance. For example,

- carbon emissions
- usage of energy and water
- forest degradation
- health care costs
- social welfare costs

However, governments are becoming increasingly aware of these external costs and are using taxes and regulations to convert them to internal costs. For example, companies might have to have a tree replacement programme if they cause forest degradation, or they receive lower tax allowances on vehicles that cause a high degree of harm to the environment. On top of this, some companies are voluntarily converting external costs to internal costs.

Further examples of environmental costs

Regulatory	Upfront	Voluntary (beyond compliance)
Notification Reporting Monitoring / testing Studies / modelling Remediation Record keeping Plans Training Inspections Manifesting Labelling Preparedness Protective equipment Medical surveillance Environmental insurance Financial assurance Pollution control Spill response Storm water management Waste management Taxes / fees	Site studies Site preparation Permitting R&D Engineering and procurement Installation Conventional costs Capital equipment Materials Labour Supplies Utilities Structures Salvage value **Back-End** Closure / decommissioning Disposal of inventory Post-closure care Site survey	Community relations /outreach Monitoring / testing Training Audits Qualifying suppliers Reports (e.g. annual environmental reports) Insurance Planning Feasibility studies Remediation Recycling Environmental studies R&D Habitat and wetland protection Landscaping Other environmental projects Financial support to environmental groups and / or researchers

Accounting for environmental costs

Conventional management accounting practices do not provide adequate information for managing the environment in a world where environmental concerns, as well as environment-related costs, revenues, and benefits, are on the rise. Environmental costs are not traced to particular processes or activities and are instead "lumped in" with general business overheads or other activity costs.

Environmental activity-based accounting

In ABC, environmental costs are removed from general overheads and traced to products and services. This means that cost drivers are determined for these costs and products are charged for the use fo these environmental costs based on the amount of cost drivers that they contribute to the activity. This should give a good attribution of environmental costs to individual products.

Advantages of environmental costing	Disadvantages
• better/fairer product costs	• time consuming
• improved pricing - so that proucts that have the biggest environmental impact reflect this by having higher selling prices	• expensive to implement
• better environmental cost control	• determining accurate costs and appropriate costs drivers is difficult
• facilitates the quantification of cost savings from "environmentally-friendly" measures	• external costs not experienced by the company (e.g. carbon footprint) may still be ignored/unmeasured
• should integrate environmental costing into the strategic management process	• some internal environmental costs are intangible (e.g. impact on employee health) and these are still ignored
• reduces the potential for cross-subsidisation of environmentally damaging products	• a company that incorporates external costs voluntarily may be at a competitive disadvantage to rivals who do not do this

Input/output analysis

An alternative technique which can be used to identify and allocate environmental costs is Input/output analysis.

This technique records material flows with the idea that 'what comes in must go out – or be stored' (Jasch, 2003).

The purchased input is regarded as 100% and is balanced against the outputs – which are the produced, sold and stored goods and the residual (regarded as waste). Materials are measured in physical units and include energy and water. At the end of the process, the material flows can be expressed in monetary units. Process flow charts can help to trace inputs and outputs, in particular waste. They demonstrate the details of the processes so that the relevant information can be allocated to main activities.

The United Nations Centre for Sustainable Development (UNDSD) provides the following example:

Input	**Output**	
	Product	60%
	Scrap for recycling	20%
	Disposed of as waste	15%
	Not accounted for	5%
100%		100%

Flow management involves not only material flows, but also the organisational structure. Classic material flows are recorded as well as material losses incurred at various stages of production.

EMA can benefit from flow cost accounting because it aims to reduce the quantities of materials, which leads to increased ecological efficiency.

7 Chapter summary

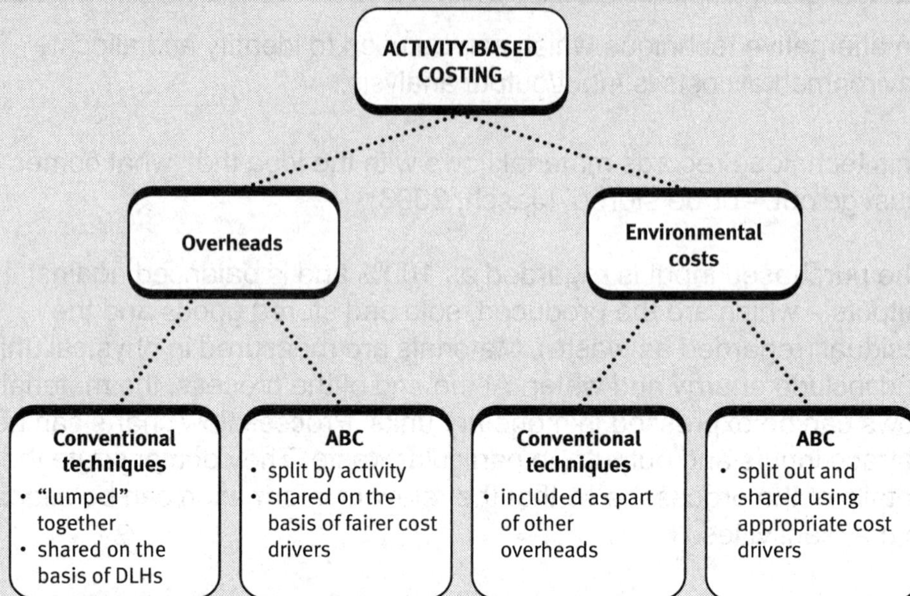

8 Practice questions

Test your understanding 1 - HENSAU LTD

Hensau Ltd has a single production process for which the following costs have been estimated for the period ending 31 December 20X1:

	$
Material receipt and inspection cost	15,600
Power cost	19,500
Material handling cost	13,650

Three products - X, Y and Z are produced by workers who perform a number of operations on material blanks using hand held electrically powered drills. The workers have a wage rate of $9 per hour.

The following budgeted information has been obtained for the period ending 31 December 20X1:

	Product X	**Product Y**	**Product Z**
Production quantity (units)	2,000	1,500	800
Batches of material	10	5	16
Data per product unit			
Direct material (sq. metres)	4	6	3
Direct material ($)	5	3	6
Direct labour (minutes)	24	40	60
Number of power drill operations	6	3	2

Overhead costs for material receipt and inspection, process power and material handling are presently each absorbed by product units using rates per direct labour hour.

An activity based costing investigation has revealed that the cost drivers for the overhead costs are as follows:

Material receipt and inspection: number of batches of material.

Process power: number of power drill operations.

Material handling: quantity of material (sq. metres) handled.

You are required:

(a) to prepare a summary which calculates the budgeted product cost per unit for each of the products X, Y and Z for the period ending 31 December 20X1 detailing the unit costs for each cost element:

(i) using the existing method for the absorption of overhead costs and

(ii) using an approach which recognises the cost drivers revealed in the activity based costing investigation

(22 marks)

(b) to explain the relevance of cost drivers in activity based costing. Make use of figures from the summary statement prepared in (a) to illustrate your answer.

(8 marks)

(Total: 30 marks)

Test your understanding 2 - SAPU PLC

Sapu plc make and sell a number of products. Products A and B are products for which market prices are available at which Sapu plc can obtain a share of the market as detailed below. Estimated data for the forthcoming period is as follows:

(i) Product data

	Product A	**Product B**	**Other products**
Production/sales (units)	5,000	10,000	40,000
	$000	$000	$000
Total direct material cost	80	300	2,020
Total direct labour cost	40	100	660

(ii) Variable overhead cost is $1,500,000 of which 40% is related to the acquisition, storage and use of direct materials and 60% is related to the control and use of direct labour.

(iii) It is current practice in Sapu plc to absorb variable overhead cost into product units using company wide percentages on direct material cost and direct labour cost as the absorption bases.

(iv) Market prices for Products A and B are $75 and $95 per unit respectively.

(v) Sapu plc require a minimum estimated contribution:sales ratio of 40% before proceeding with the production/sale of any product.

Required:

(a) Calculate estimated unit product costs for Product A and Product B where variable overhead is charged to product units as follows:

(i) Using the existing absorption basis as detailed above.

(6 marks)

(ii) Using an activity based costing approach where cost drivers have been estimated for material and labour related overhead costs as follows:

	Product A	**Product B**	**Other products**
Direct material related overheads - cost driver is material bulk. The bulk proportions per unit are:	4	1	1.5
Direct labour related overheads - cost driver is number of labour operations (not directly time related). Labour operations per product unit	6	1	2

(10 marks)

(b) Illustrate the decision strategy which Sapu plc may implement with regard to the production and sale of Products A and B. Use unit costs as calculated in (a) (i) and (a) (ii) together with other information given in the question in your analysis. Your answer should include relevant calculations and discussion and be prepared in a form suitable for presentation to management.

(10 marks)

(Total: 26 marks)

Test your understanding 3

Fixed overhead absorption rates are often calculated using a single measure of activity. It is suggested that fixed overhead costs should be attributed to cost units using multiple measures of activity (Activity Based Costing).

Explain Activity Based Costing and how it may provide useful information to managers.

(Your answer should refer to both the setting of cost driver rates and subsequent overhead cost control.)

(8 marks)

Test your understanding 4

Explain the benefits of using multiple activity bases for variable overhead absorption.

(5 marks)

Test your understanding 5

Cabal makes and sells two products, Plus and Doubleplus. The direct costs of production are $12 for one unit of Plus and $24 per unit of Doubleplus.

Information relating to annual production and sales is as follows:

	Plus	**Doubleplus**
Annual production and sales	24,000 units	24,000 units
Direct labour hours per unit	1.0	1.5
Number of orders	10	140
Number of batches	12	240
Number of setups per batch	1	3
Special parts per unit	1	4

Information relating to production overhead costs is as follows:

	Cost driver	Annual cost
		$
Setup costs	Number of setups	73,200
Special parts handling	Number of special parts	60,000
Other materials handling	Number of batches	63,000
Order handling	Number of orders	19,800
Other overheads	-	216,000
		432,000

Other overhead costs do not have an identifiable cost driver, and in an ABC system, these overheads would be recovered on a direct labour hours basis.

(a) Calculate the production cost per unit of Plus and of Doubleplus if the company uses traditional absorption costing and the overheads are recovered on a direct labour hours basis.

(b) Calculate the production cost per unit of Plus and of Doubleplus if the company uses ABC.

(c) Identify the reasons for the differences in the production cost per unit between the two methods.

(d) Explain the implications for management of using an ABC system instead of an absorption costing system?

Test your understanding 6

A supermarket chain is considering building a new shop. There are two possible locations. State the environmental factors that the management accountant should consider when providing information to support the decision making.

Test your understanding 7 - ABC COST DRIVERS

Explain the factors that should be considered when selecting cost drivers for an activity based costing system.

(5 marks)

Test your understanding answers

Example 1

Solution

(a)

Workings	**M1**	**M2**	**Total**
Number of batches	4	80	84
Number of setups	4	240	244
Special parts	16,000	64,000	80,000
Direct labour parts	16,000	20,000	36,000

Activity	**Cost**		**M1**	**M2**
	$		$	$
Setups	97,600	Cost per setup $400	1,600	96,000
Materials handling	42,000	Cost per batch $500	2,000	40,000
Special parts handling	50,000	Cost per part $0.625	10,000	40,000
Invoicing	31,000	Cost per order $100	6,000	25,000
Other overheads	108,000	Cost per hour $3	48,000	60,000
	328,600		67,600	261,000

	M1		**M2**	
	$	$	$	$
Sales		$432,000		584,000
Direct materials	88,000		168,000	
Direct labour	128,000		160,000	
Overheads	67,600		261,000	
Total costs		283,600		589,000
Profit/(loss)		148,400		(5,000)
Profit/loss per unit		18.55		(0.625)

(b) The figures suggest that model M2 is less profitable than M1. The sales manager should try to persuade the customer to buy model M1. Note that the apparent loss on M2 does not necessarily mean that production should be ceased. To assess this management should consider the incremental relevant cash flows involved - e.g. is the product making positive contribution, how many overheads are avoidable?

Test your understanding 1 - HENSAU LTD

(a)

(i) The existing overhead absorption rate is:

$$\frac{\$15{,}600 + \$19{,}500 + \$13{,}650}{(2{,}000 \times 24/60) + (1{,}500 \times 40/60) + (800 \times 60/60)} = \frac{\$48{,}750}{2{,}600 \text{ hours}}$$

= $18.75 per hour.

Unit cost

	Product X	*Product Y*	*Product Z*
Direct material	5.00	3.00	6.00
Direct labour	3.60	6.00	9.00
Production overhead	7.50	12.50	18.75
	$16.10	$21.50	$33.75

(ii) Cost driver rates

$$\text{Material receipt and inspection} = \frac{\$15{,}600}{10 + 5 + 16} = \$503.23 \text{ per batch}$$

$$\text{Process power} = \frac{\$19{,}500}{(2{,}000 \times 6) + (1{,}500 \times 3) + (8{,}000 \times 2)}$$

= $1.0773 per power drill operation

$$\text{Material handling} = \frac{\$13{,}650}{(2{,}000 \times 4) + (1{,}500 \times 6) + (8{,}000 \times 3)}$$

= $0.70361 per sq. metre handled

	Product		
	X	Y	Z
Direct material	5.00	3.00	6.00
Direct labour	3.60	6.00	9.00
Production overhead			
Material receipt/inspection (W1)	2.52	1.68	10.06
Process power (W2)	6.46	3.23	2.15
Material handling (W3)	2.81	4.22	2.11
Cost per unit	$20.39	$18.13	$29.32

Workings

(W1) Material receipt/inspection

Cost/unit

Product X 503.23/batch × 10 batches/2,000 units = $2.52/unit

Product Y 503.23/batch × 5 batches/1,500 units = $1.68/unit

Product Z 503.23/batch × 16 batches/800 units = $10.06/unit

(W2) Process power

Cost/unit

Product X $1.0773/operation × 6 operations = $6.46
Product Y $1.0773/operation × 3 operations = $3.23
Product Z $1.0773/operation × 2 operations = $2.15

(W3) Material handling

Cost/unit

Product X $0.70361/m^2 of material × 4m^2 = $2.81
Product Y $0.70361/m^2 of material × 6m^2 = $4.22
Product Z $0.70361/m^2 of material × 3m^2 = $2.11

(b) A cost driver is that factor which is most closely related to the way in which the costs of an activity are incurred. It could be said to cause the costs. Under ABC we do not restrict ourselves to just six possible OARs. We choose whatever basis we consider suitable to charge overheads to the product.

A good example of the superiority of ABC over absorption costing is that of process power in part (a) above. Under traditional absorption costing Product Z was the dearest for process power merely because it used the most labour hours per unit. - a fact completely and utterly unconnected with the way in which process power costs are incurred. Under ABC we investigate the business and actually take the time to find out what factor is most closely related to the cost and use that factor to charge overheads. Here we find that Product X should be the dearest because it uses the most power drill operations.

ABC supporters would argue that this cost/power drill operation is useful information. Costs are $1.0773 per power drill operation and thus product X costs $6.46. This cost is not insignificant and in fact is nearly as much as the direct material cost and direct labour cost combined. It would be inconceivable that the direct material costs and direct labour costs would not be very carefully controlled and yet under traditional absorption costing the process power costs would be included within the general overheads and would not be subject to such severe scrutiny.

Under ABC, once we realise that power drill operations cost $1.0773 each then when designing new products, we would have better cost information and thus would be able to make better informed decisions.

Test your understanding 2 - SAPU PLC

(a)

(i) **Workings**

Material related overhead cost	= 40% x $ 1,500,000 = $600,000
Overhead absorption rate	
($600,000/$2,400,000)	= 25% on direct material cost
Labour related overhead cost	= 60% x $1,500,000 = $900,000
Overhead absorption rate	
($900,000/$800,000)	= 112.5% on direct labour cost

Using the overhead absorption rates calculated above and average direct material and direct labour costs from the data in the question we have:

	Unit costs	
	Product A	**Product B**
	$	$
Direct material cost	16	30
Direct labour cost	8	10
	—	—
	24	40
Variable overhead		
Material related at 25%	4	7.5
Labour related at 112.5%	9	11.25
	—	—
Total variable cost	37	58.75
	—	—

(ii) **Workings**

Material related overhead has bulk as the cost driver.

Total bulk factor = (5,000 x 4) + (10,000 x 1) + (40,000 x 1.5) = 90,000

Material related overhead per unit of bulk = $600,000/90,000 = $6.67

Hence overhead cost per product unit:

Product A = $6.67 x 4 = $26.67

Product B = $6.67 x 1 = $6.67

Labour related overhead has the number of labour operations as the cost driver.

Total labour operations = (5,000 x 6) + (10,000 x 1) + (40,000 x 2) = 120,000

Labour related overhead per labour operation = $900,000/120,000 = $7.50

Hence overhead cost per product unit:

Product A = $7.50 x 6 = $45

Product B = $7.50 x 1 = $7.50

The amended unit product costs may now be shown as:

	Unit costs	
	Product A	**Product B**
	$	$
Direct material cost	16	30
Direct labour cost	8	10
	——	——
	24	40
Variable overhead		
Material related	26.67	6.67
Labour related	45.00	11.25
	——	——
Total variable cost	95.67	54.17
	——	——

(b)

From: Management accountant
To: Management team
Subject: Production strategy for Products A and B

The unit market prices for Products A and B are $75 and $95 respectively. At these prices we can obtain market share of 5,000 units of A and 10,000 units of B in the forthcoming period. The unit product cost and contribution information may be calculated using our existing basis for the absorption of variable overhead cost by product units or by using an ABC approach which recognises the cost drivers which cause costs to occur.

Unit product information is as follows:

	Product A		**Product B**	
	Existing approach	**ABC approach**	**Existing approach**	**ABC approach**
	$	$	$	$
Direct material cost	16	16	30	30
Direct labour cost	8	8	10	10
	—	—	—	—
	24	24	40	40
Variable overhead cost				
Material related	4	26.67	7.50	6.67
Labour related	9	45.00	11.25	7.50
	—	—	—	—
Total variable cost	37	95.67	58.75	54.17
Contribution	38	(20.67)	36.25	40.83
	—	—	—	—
Selling price	75	75.00	95.00	95.00
	—	—	—	—
Contribution: sales (%)	50.7%	negative	38.2%	43.0%

Based on the company policy of a minimum contribution: sales ratio of 40% before proceeding with the sale of any product, our current product costing procedure would confirm the production and sale of Product A with a CS ratio of 50.7%, but would reject Product B with a CS ratio of 38.2%.

The amended product costs using the ABC approach which recognises the cost drivers for overhead cost will reverse our decision. Product A would now be rejected with a negative CS ratio whereas Product B would be acceptable with a CS ratio of 43%. The ABC based calculations recognise the relatively high cost driver levels for Product A and 1 would recommend that we use the ABC calculations as the basis for our decision strategy and produce and sell Product B.

Test your understanding 3

Activity Based Costing (ABC) is a system of full costing which recognises that the more traditional method of absorption costing using cost centre absorption rates may not provide accurate product costs.

ABC identifies the activities of a production process and the extent to which individual products make use of those activities. Costs are then estimated for each of these activities which are referred to as cost pools. The number of times which the activity is expected to be carried out is also estimated and a cost driver rate calculated:

$$\frac{\text{Estimated cost of pool}}{\text{Estimated number of times activity is to be performed}}$$

An individual product will probably make use of a number of different activities, and a proportion of the cost of each activity will be attributed to the product using these predetermined cost driver rates.

The actual costs of each cost pool together with the number of times the activity is performed will be collected and a comparison made with the corresponding estimated values. This is similar to the comparison of actual and budgeted costs and volumes using the traditional absorption costing approach except that there are likely to be a greater number of cost driver rates using ABC than the one per cost centre absorption rate found in traditional absorption costing.

Test your understanding 4

Such an approach is beneficial because it identifies overhead costs with their cause, rather than assuming that they are all driven by a single cause.

This should enable management to control such costs more easily, the variances reported will be more meaningful and this will help management to control costs.

Test your understanding 5

(a) **Traditional absorption costing**

Budgeted direct labour hours (24,000 × 1.0) + (24,000 × 1.5)	60,000
Budgeted overhead costs	$432,000
Recovery rate per direct labour hour	$7.20

	Plus	**Double plus**
	$	$
Direct costs	12.00	24.00
Production overhead	7.20	10.80
Full production cost	19.20	34.80

(b) **ABC**

Workings

	Plus	Double plus	Total
Batches	12	240	252
Setups	12	720	732
Special parts	24,000	96,000	120,000
Orders	10	140	150
Direct labour hours	24,000	36,000	60,000

Cost driver rates

Setup costs	$73,200/732	$100 per setup
Special parts handling	$60,000/120,000	$0.50 per part
Order handling	$19,800/150	$132 per order
Materials handling	$63,000/252	$250 per batch
Other overheads	$216,000/60,000	$3.60 per hour

	Plus	Double plus	Total
	$	$	$
Setup costs	1,200	72,000	73,200
Special parts handling costs	12,000	48,000	60,000
Order handling costs	1,320	18,480	19,800
Materials handling costs	3,000	60,000	63,000
Other overheads	86,400	129,600	216,000
	103,920	328,080	432,000
Number of units	24,000	24,000	
	$	$	
Direct cost	12.00	24.00	
Overhead cost per unit	4.33	13.67	
Full cost	16.33	37.67	

Note: In the example above the full production costs were:

	Plus	Double plus
• Using traditional absoprtion costing	\$19.20	\$34.80
• Using ABC	\$16.33	\$37.67
• Assume the selling prices are	\$25.00	\$40.00
• Using absorption costing sales margins are	23.2%	13.0%
• ABC sales margins are	34.7%	5.8%

(c) The reasons for the difference in the production cost per unit between the two methods

- The allocation of overheads under absorption costing was unfair. This method assumed that all of the overheads were driven by labour hours and, as a result, the Double Plus received 1.5 times the production overhead of the Plus.
- However, this method of absorption is not appropriate. The overheads are in fact driven by a number of different factors. There are five acttivity costs, each one has its own cost driver. By taking this into account we end up with a much more accurate production overhead cost per unit.
- Using ABC, the cost per unit of a Double Plus is significantly higher. This is because the Double Plus is a much more complex product than the Plus. For example, there are 140 orders for the Double Plus but only 10 for the Plus and there are 4 special parts for the Double Plus compared to only one for the Plus. As a result of this complexity, the Double Plus has received more than three times the overhead of the Plus.
- This accurate allocation is important because the production overhead is a large proportion of the overall cost.

(d) **The implications of using ABC**

- Pricing - pricing decisions will be improved because the price will be based on more accurate cost data.
- Decision making - this should also be improved. For example, research, production and sales effort can be directed towards the most profitable products.
- Performance management - should be improved. ABC can be used as the basis of budgeting and forward planning. The more realsitic overhead should result in more accurate budgets and should improve the process of performance management. In addition, an improved understanding of what drives the overhead costs should result in steps being taken to reduce the overhead costs and hence an improvement in performance.

- Sales strategy - this should be more soundly based. For example, target customers with products that appeared unprofitable under absorption costing but are actually profitable, and vice versa.

Test your understanding 6

Suggestions for issues to consider

- The design of the shop and its usage of utilities such as water and electricity.
- The costs of ensuring that the building and the operation comply with any local environmental regulations and requirements such as those of planning authorities.
- The environmental impact on the local area and the cost of any measures needed to minimise it – for example the potential increase in traffic and the provision of a free bus service as an alternative for customers.
- The locations and their position relative to the chain's distribution network and the fuel costs of supplying goods.
- The views and influence of local environmental pressure groups and the likely cost of public relations activities and modifications to plans to address their concerns.
- The product range to be offered and the market locally for higher-priced environmentally-friendly products such as organic fruit and vegetables.

Test your understanding 7 - ABC COST DRIVERS

The cost driver for a particular activity is the factor that causes a change in the cost of the activity. For the cost driver to be useful there must be an identifiable relationship between the cost and the cost driver, i.e. changes in the number of cost drivers must cause corresponding changes in the total cost incurred on the activity.

Another major consideration is the ease of accurately recording the number of cost drivers incurred. If the process of recording the cost drivers is very complex and time-consuming then the cost of the recording system might outweigh the benefits derived from the information obtained.

It is possible to identify three types of cost driver:

Transaction drivers

Here, the cost of an activity is affected by the number of times a particular action is undertaken. Examples would include number of set-ups, number of power drill operations, number of batches of material received, number of purchase orders, etc.

Duration drivers

In this case, the cost of the activity is not so much affected by the number of times the action is undertaken as by the length of time that it takes to perform the action, e.g. set-up costs may not be related to the number of set-ups so much as to the set-up time, because some products involve more complicated and time consuming set-ups than others

Intensity drivers

In this case, efforts would be directed at determining what resources were used in the making of a product or service, e.g. rather than charging all purchase orders with the same cost per order, we might determine that overseas orders involve more work than home orders and apply a weighting to the overseas orders to reflect the extra work.

chapter

6

Variance analysis: calculations

Chapter learning objectives

Lead	Component
A1. discuss costing methods and their results.	(d) Apply standard costing methods, within costing systems, including the reconciliation of budgeted and actual profit margins.

Specific areas of indicative syllabus content of relevance here are the following:

- Manufacturing standards for material, labour, variable overhead and fixed overhead.
- Price/rate and usage/efficiency variances for materials, labour and variable overhead.
- Fixed overhead expenditure and volume variances. (Note: the subdivision of fixed overhead volume variance into capacity and efficiency elements will not be examined).
- Sales price and sales revenue/margin volume variances (calculation of the latter on a unit basis related to revenue, gross margin and contribution margin).

1 Session content diagram

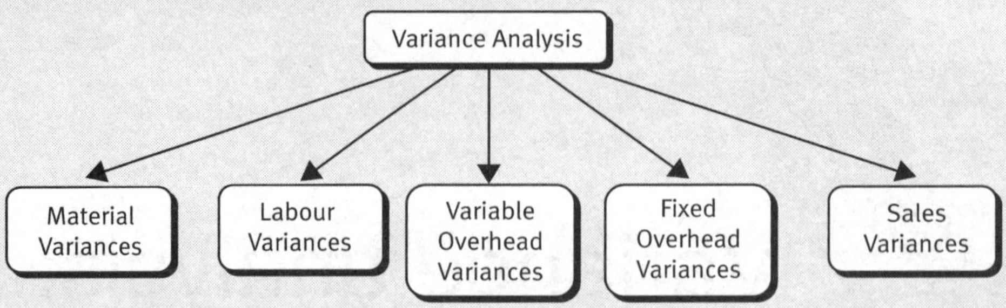

2 Standard costing

Whenever identical operations are performed or identical products are manufactured many times over, it should be possible to decide in advance not merely what they are *expected to cost*, but also what they *ought to cost.*

Similarly, when a standard service is provided many times over, it should be possible to establish in advance how the service should be provided, how long it should take and how much it should cost.

- **Standard costing** is a technique which establishes predetermined estimates of the costs of products and services and then compares these predetermined costs with actual costs as they are incurred. The predetermined costs are known as standard costs and the difference between the standard cost and actual cost is known as a variance.

  The process by which the total difference between actual cost and standard is broken down into its different elements is known as Variance Analysis.

- A **standard** is 'a benchmark measurement of resource usage, set in defined conditions' (CIMA *Official Terminology*).
- A **standard cost** for a product or service is a predetermined (planned) unit cost, based on a standard specification of the resources needed to supply it and the costs of those resources.

  A standard cost is based on technical specifications for the materials, labour time and other resources required and the prices and rates for the materials and labour.

  Standard costs can be prepared using either absorption costing or marginal costing.

- A **standard price** for a product or service is the expected price for selling the standard product or service. When there is a standard sales price and a standard cost per unit, there is also a **standard profit per unit** (absorption costing) or **standard contribution per unit** (marginal costing).

3 Standard costing variances

A variance is the difference between actual results and the budget or standard.

Variances can be calculated for both costs and sales. Cost variances analyse the difference between actual costs and standard costs. Sales variances analyse the difference between actual and budgeted sales prices and sales volumes.
Where standard costing is used, variance analysis can be an important aspect of performance measurement and control. It is defined in the CIMA Official Terminology as 'the evaluation of performance by means of variances, whose timely reporting should maximise the opportunity for managerial action'.

Taken together, cost and sales variances can be used to explain the difference between the budgeted profit for a period and the actual profit.

Variance reports comparing actual results with the standards or budget are produced regularly, perhaps monthly.

When actual results are *better than* expected results, a **favourable (F)** variance occurs.

When actual results are *worse than* expected results, an **adverse variance (A)** occurs.

Variance groups

Variances can be divided into three main groups:

- sales variances
- variable cost variances
  - material variances
  - labour variances
  - variable overhead variances
- fixed overhead variances

4 Sales variances

The difference between a budgeted profit and the actual profit achieved in a period is explained by both cost variances and sales variances. Cost variances explain the differences between actual costs and budgeted or standard costs. Sales variances explain the effect of differences between:

- actual and standard sales prices, and
- budgeted and actual sales volumes.

Sales price variance

A sales price variance shows the effect on profit of the difference between the standard sales prices for the items sold in a period and the actual sales revenue achieved. It is calculated as follows:

(a) Standard selling price multiplied by the actual number of units sold, and

(b) Actual selling price multiplied by the actual number of units sold.

Proforma

Sales price variance		$
Units sold should have sold for	(actual sales units × standard sales price per unit)	X
They did sell for	(actual sales revenue)	Y
Sales price variance		X–Y

This variance is favourable if actual sales revenue is higher than sales at the standard selling price, and adverse if actual sales revenue is lower than standard.

Sales volume profit variance

The sales volume margin variance is the difference between actual and budgeted sales volumes valued at either standard profit, in an absorption costing system, or standard contribution in a marginal costing system. Sales volumes can be measured:

- as the difference between actual and budgeted units of sale.

Proforma

A sales volume variance measured in units has to be calculated first. The variance is favourable if actual sales volume is higher than budgeted sales volume, and adverse if actual sales volume is lower than budget.

Sales volume variance	**Units of sale**
	Units
Actual sales volume	X
Budgeted sales volume	Y
Sales volume variance	X–Y

Example 1

Walter Dean Ltd has budgeted sales of 400 units at $25 each. The variable costs are expected to be $18 per unit, and there are no fixed costs.

The actual sales were 500 units at $20 each and costs were as expected.

Calculate the selling price variance and the sales volume profit variance.

The variance in units can then be valued in one of three ways:

- at the **standard gross profit per unit** - if using absorption costing
- at the **standard contribution per unit** - if using marginal costing
- at the **standard revenue per unit** - this is rarely used and we would only do so if it was specifically asked for in an exam question

Example 2

The following data is available for the most recent month of sales:

	Budget	**Actual**
Sales units	320	380
Selling price per unit	$45	$42
Full cost per unit	$23	$22
Variable cost per unit	$17	$15

Calculate the sales variances, calculating the sales volume variance using both absorption and marginal costing, as well as sales revenue.

5 Direct material cost variances

This section has three variances. The direct material total cost variance, which shows the impact of any overall change in the amount spent on materials, and this can also be split into two further components - the materials price and materials usage variances.

Direct material total variance

The difference between:

(a) the standard direct material cost of the actual production and

(b) the actual cost of direct material.

Proforma

Direct materials cost		$
Actual quantity of output	should cost (standard)	X
	did cost	Y
		——
Total cost variance		X-Y
		——

Example 3

James Marshall Ltd makes a single product with the following budgeted material costs per unit:

2 kg of material A at $10/kg

Actual details:

Output 1,000 units
Material purchased and used 2,200 kg
Material cost $20,900

Calculate appropriate variances for materials.

A total material variance actually conveys very little useful information. It needs to be analysed further. It can be analysed into two sub-variances:

(1) a Direct Material Price variance, i.e. paying more or less than expected for materials and

(2) a Direct Material Usage variance, i.e. using more or less material than expected.

Direct material price variance

The difference between:

(a) standard purchase price per kg and

(b) actual purchase price

multiplied by the actual quantity of material purchased or used.

Note that the material price variance can be calculated either at the time of purchase or at the time of usage. Generally, the former is preferable.

Proforma

Direct materials price variance		$
Actual quantity of materials	should cost (standard)	X
	did cost (actual)	Y
Direct materials price variance		X-Y

The impact of stock valuation

If stock is valued at standard cost, then the calculation should be performed using the quantity of materials *purchased*.

If stock is valued at actual cost, then the calculation should be performed using the quantity of materials *used*.

Direct material usage variance

The difference between:

(a) the standard quantity of material specified for the actual production and

(b) the actual quantity used

multiplied by the standard purchase price.

Proforma

Direct materials usage variance		$
Actual output produced	should use (standard quantity)	X
	did use (actual quantity)	Y
Direct materials usage variance	(in material quantity)	X-Y
x standard price	(per unit of material)	$P
Direct materials usage variance		$P x (X - Y)

Example 4

James Marshall Ltd makes a single product with the following budgeted material costs per unit:

2 kg of material A at $10/kg

Actual details:

Output 1,000 units
Material purchased and used 2,200 kg
Material cost $20,900

Calculate the price and usage variances for materials.

An alterntive method

Calculate the same variances for materials using the following format:

SQSP		
	Usage variance	
AQSP		Total variance
	Price variance	
AQAP		

Where SQ means Standard Quantity
SP means Standard Price
AQ means Actual Quantity
and AP means Actual Price

Standard Quantity means the standard quantity of the actual output.

Note: This assumes purchases = issues and/or the price variance is calculated at the time of issue.

					$	
SQSP	2 kg/unit x 1,000 units	x	$10/kg	=	20,000	Usage $2,000 A
AQSP	2,200 kg	x	$10/kg	=	22,000	
AQAP		x		=	20,900	$1,100 F Price

6 Direct labour variances

This section has four variances. The direct labour total cost variance, which shows the impact of any overall change in the amount spent on labour, and this can also be split into two further components - the labour rate and labour efficiency variances. In some scenarios we might also see a labour idle time variance.

Direct labour total cost variance

The difference between:

(a) the standard direct labour cost of the actual production and

(b) the actual cost of direct labour.

Proforma

Direct labour cost		$
Actual quantity of output	should cost (standard)	X
	did cost	Y
Total cost variance		X-Y

A total labour variance can also be analysed further. It can be analysed into two sub-variances:

(1) a Direct Labour Rate variance, i.e. paying more or less than expected per hour for labour and

(2) a Direct Labour Efficiency variance, i.e. using more or less labour per unit than expected.

Direct labour rate variance

The difference between:

(a) standard rate per hour and the

(b) actual rate per hour

multiplied by the actual hours that were paid for.

Proforma

Direct labour rate variance		$
Number of hours paid	should cost / hr (standard)	X
	did cost (actual)	Y
Direct labour rate variance		X-Y

Direct labour efficiency variance

The difference between:

(a) the standard hours specified for the actual production and

(b) the actual hours worked

multiplied by the standard hourly rate.

Example 5

Ivan Korshunov Ltd makes a single product and has the following budgeted/standard information:

Budgeted production	1,000 units
Labour hours per unit	3
Labour rate per hour	$8

Actual results:

Output	1,100 units
Hours paid for and worked	3,400 hours
Labour cost	$28,300

Calculate rate and efficiency variances for labour.

Another method

Using the same example, calculate appropriate variances for labour using the following format:

SHSR
} Efficiency variance
AHSR } Total variance
} Rate variance
AHAR

Where	SH	means Standard Hours
	SR	means Standard Rate
	AH	means Actual Hours
and	AR	means Actual Rate

Standard Hours means the standard hours of the actual output.

(this assumes that there is no idle time)

					$	
SHSR	3 hrs/unit x 1,100 units	x	$8/hr	=	26,400	Efficiency $800 A
AHSR	3,400 hrs	x	$8/hr	=	27,200	
AHAR				=	28,300	$1,100 A Rate

Idle time and idle time variances

The purpose of an efficiency variance should be to measure the efficiency of the work force in the time they are actively engaged in making products or delivering a service. During a period, there might be idle time, when the work force is not doing any work at all.

When idle time occurs, and if it is recorded, the efficiency variance should be separated into two parts:

- an idle time variance
- an efficiency variance during active working hours.

If there is no standard idle time set, then **the idle time variance is always adverse**, because it represents money 'wasted'. In some organisations a standard level of idle time may be set. If actual idle time is greater than standard then the variance is adverse; if it is less than standard then it would be favourable.

e.g

Illustration 1

A product has a standard direct labour cost of $15, consisting of 1.5 hours of work for each unit at a cost of $10 per hour. During April, 100 units were produced. The direct labour workers were paid $2,000 for 160 hours of attendance, but the idle time records show that 30 hours in the month were recorded as idle time.

(a) We can record an idle time variance of 30 hours (A). This is costed at the standard rate per hour, $10, to give an idle time variance of $300(A).

(b) The efficiency variance should then be calculated using the active hours worked, not the total hours paid for.

Direct labour efficiency variance		Hours	
Actual output produced	should take (standard hours)		
100 units	1.5 hrs per unit	150	
	did take (160hrs - 30hrs)	130	
Direct labour efficiency variance	(in hours)	20	F
x standard rate per hour		$10/ hr	
Direct labour efficiency variance		$200	F

Example 6

Melanie Mitchell Ltd makes a single product with the following information:

Budget/Standard

Output	1,000 units
Hours	6,000
Labour cost	$42,000

Actual

Output	900 units
Hours paid	5,500
Hours worked	5,200
Labour cost	$39,100

Calculate appropriate variances for labour

7 Variable overhead variances

Variable overhead variances are similar to direct materials and direct labour cost variances.

- In standard product costing, a variable production overhead total cost variance can be calculated, and this can be analysed into an expenditure or rate variance and an efficiency variance.
- With service costing, a variable overhead total cost variance can be calculated, but this might not be analysed any further.

Since variable production overheads are assumed to vary with labour hours worked, labour hours are used in calculations. This means, for example, that the variable production overhead efficiency variance uses exactly the same hours as the direct labour efficiency variance.

Details on the variances

Variable production overhead total cost variance

The difference between:

(a) the standard variable overhead cost of the actual production and

(b) the actual cost of variable production overheads.

Variable production overhead cost		$
Actual quantity of output	should cost (standard)	X
	did cost	Y
Total cost variance		X-Y

A total variable production overhead variance can also be analysed further. It can be analysed into two sub-variances:

(1) a variable overhead expenditure variance, i.e. paying more or less than expected per hour for variable overheads and

(2) a variable overhead efficiency variance, i.e. using more or less variable overheads per unit than expected.

Variable production overhead expenditure variance

Variable production overhead expenditure variance		$
Number of hours worked	should cost / hr (standard)	X
	did cost (actual)	Y
Variable production overhead expenditure variance		X-Y

Variable production overhead efficiency variance

Variable production overhead efficiency variance		Hours
Actual output produced	should take (standard hours)	X
	did take (actual hours)	Y
Efficiency variance	(in hours)	X-Y
x standard variable overhead rate per hour		$P
Variable production overhead efficiency variance		$P x (X - Y)

Example 7

The budgeted output for Kathryn Bennett Ltd for May was 1,000 units of product A. Each unit requires 2 direct labour hours. Variable overheads are budgeted at $3/labour hour.

Actual results:

Output	900 units
Labour hours worked	1,980 hours
Variable overheads	$5,544

Calculate appropriate variances for variable overheads.

Alternative method

Using the same example, calculate appropriate variances for variable overhead using the following format:

SHSR
                Efficiency variance }
AHSR   } Total variance
                Expenditure variance }
AHAR

Where	SH	means Standard Hours
	SR	means Standard Rate
	AH	means Actual Hours
and	AR	means Actual Rate

Standard Hours means the standard hours of the actual output.

					$	
SHSR	2 hrs/unit x 900 units	x	$3/hr	=	5,400	Efficiency $540 A
AHSR	1,980 hrs	x	$3/hr	=	5,940	
AHAR				=	5,544	$396 F Expenditure

Idle time variances and variable production overhead

The analysis of variable production overhead variances is affected by the existence of idle time. It is usually assumed that variable production overhead is incurred during active hours only.

The variable production overhead efficiency variance is calculated in the same way that the direct labour efficiency variance is calculated when there is idle time.

The variable production overhead expenditure variance, when there is idle time, is the difference between:

- the standard variable overhead cost of the active hours worked, and
- the actual variable overhead cost.

Example 8

Extracts from the standard cost of a product are as follows:

		$/unit
Direct labour	2 hours x $ 15/hour	30
Variable production overhead	2 hours x $ 4/hour	8

During May, 200 units were produced. The direct labour workers were paid $6,600 for 440 hours of work, but the idle time records show that 20 hours in the month were recorded as idle time. Actual variable production overhead expenditure incurred was $1,530.

Calculate the labour and variable overhead variances.

8 Fixed overhead cost variances

Fixed overhead total variance

In standard absorption costing, the total cost variance for fixed production overhead variances is the amount of over-absorbed or under-absorbed overhead. Over-absorbed overhead is a favourable variance, and under-absorbed overhead is an adverse variance.

The amount of overhead absorbed for each unit of output is the standard fixed overhead cost per unit. The total cost variance is therefore calculated as follows:

The difference between:

(a) the standard fixed overhead cost of the actual production and

(b) the actual fixed overheads incurred

Proforma

Fixed production overhead total cost variance	$
Overheads absorbed (Actual output x standard fixed cost per unit)	X
Actual fixed overhead incurred	Y
Fixed production overhead total cost variance	X-Y

Under/overabsorption

The fixed overhead total variance is equivalent to the amount of over/under absorption.

Under/over-absorption is the difference between the overheads incurred and the overheads absorbed.

The under/over-absorption occurs because the OAR is based upon two predictions - the budgeted fixed overhead and the budgeted level of activity. If either or both predictions are wrong there will be under/overabsorption and there will be a fixed overhead total variance.

- If the actual expenditure is different from the budgeted expenditure there is an expenditure variance and
- If the actual production is different from the budgeted production there is a volume variance

Fixed overhead expenditure variance

The difference between:

(a) Budgeted Fixed Cost and

(b) Actual Fixed Cost

Proforma

Fixed overhead expenditure variance	$
Budgeted fixed overhead	X
Actual fixed overhead incurred	Y
Fixed overhead expenditure variance	X-Y

An expenditure variance can be calculated for fixed production overhead. A similar variance can be calculated (if required) for other fixed overhead costs:

- a fixed administration overhead expenditure variance
- a fixed sales and distribution overhead expenditure variance.

A fixed production overhead volume variance represents the amount of fixed overhead that has been under- or over-absorbed due to the fact that actual production volume differed from the budgeted production volume.

The volume variance is calculated as the difference between:

(a) Budgeted output in units and

(b) Actual output in units

multiplied by the Standard Fixed Overhead Cost per unit

The fixed overhead volume variance does not occur in a marginal costing system.

Proforma

Fixed production overhead volume variance		Units
Actual output produced		X
Budgeted output		Y
Volume variance	(in units)	X-Y
x standard fixed overhead rate per hour		$F
Fixed production overhead volume variance		$F x (X - Y)

You may be aware that the fixed overhead volume variance can be sub-divided into a fixed overhead capacity and fixed overhead efficiency. These variances are most definitely **NOT** in the syllabus.

Example 9

The following data relates to the fixed production overhead costs of producing widgets in March:

Budgeted fixed production overhead	$4,375
Budgeted production volume (widgets)	1,750 units
Standard fixed production overhead cost:	
(0.25 hours @ $10 per hour)	$2.50
Number of widgets produced in March	1,800 units
Fixed production overhead expenditure	$4,800

Required:

Calculate the fixed production overhead expenditure and volume variances in March.

Marginal costing fixed overhed variances

In marginal costing, fixed overheads are not absorbed into the cost of production. For this reason, there is no fixed overhead volume variance.

The only fixed overhead variance reported in standard marginal costing is a fixed overhead expenditure variance. This is the difference between actual and budgeted fixed overhead expenditure, as described above for absorption costing

9 Operating statement

An operating statement is a top-level variance report, reconciling the budgeted and actual profit for the period.

An operating statement starts off with the expected figure, e.g. budgeted or standard profit or contribution or cost, etc. and ends up with the corresponding actual figure. In between we list all the appropriate variances in as much detail as possible.

The format will be similar to the following, the numbers have no significance. They are purely for illustration purposes.

Operating Statement for Period 12

		$	$	$
Budgeted gross profit				100,000
Sales volume profit variance				15,000F
Standard profit on actual sales				115,000
Selling price variance				28,750 F
				143,750
		Adverse	**Favourable**	
Cost variances				
Direct material A	Price	3,100		
	Usage		10,000	
Direct material B	Price		3,050	
	Usage		7,500	
Direct labour	Efficiency		7,000	
	Rate		12,000	
	Idle time		3,000	
Variable overhead	Efficiency	4,000		
	Expenditure		3,500	
Fixed Prod overhead	Expenditure		11,500	
	Volume	30,400		
		37,500	57,550	20,050 F
Actual gross profit				163,800

In some questions the usage variance will be sub-divided into mix and yield variances.

Variance reporting

Variances should be reported to management at the end of each control period, for example at the end of each month. There might be a hierarchy of control reports:

- a top level report reconciling budgeted and actual profit should be prepared for senior management

- variance reports might be prepared for individual managers with responsibility for a particular aspect of operations.

For example, regional sales managers might be sent variance reports showing sales price and sales volume variances for their region. Production managers might be sent variance reports relating to materials usage, labour efficiency and other items of expenditure under their control. Similarly, detailed reports on overhead expenditure variances might be sent to the managers responsible for departmental spending.

Variance reports should be provided as soon as possible after the end of each control period, since there is a risk that variance information might be considered 'out of date' if it is received several weeks after the control period has ended.

Example 10 - SAM MENDES LTD

Sam Mendes Ltd is a manufacturing company which produces a variety of products. The following information relates to one of its products - Product W:

Standard cost data

		$	$
Selling Price			100
Direct Material X	5 kg	15	
Direct Material Y	4 kg	20	
Direct Labour	@ $8/hr	24	
Variable Overheads		18	
Fixed Overheads		6	
		—	
			83
			—
Profit per unit			17
			═

The budgeted production is 24,000 units per annum evenly spread throughout the year, with each calendar month assumed to be equal. March is a bad month in terms of sales revenue and it is expected that sales will only be 1,700 units during the month. Fixed overheads were expected to be $144,000 per year and are absorbed on a labour hour basis.

Actual results for the month of March were that sales were 2,200 units at a price of $90. There was no change in stock of finished goods or raw materials.

The purchases during the month were 11,300 kg of material X at $2.80 per kg and 8,300 kg of material Y at $5.30 per kg.

4,800 labour hours were worked at a rate of $8.10 per hour and 1,600 hours at $8.30

The actual variable overheads for the period were $33,000 and the fixed overheads were $12,500

The company uses an absorption costing system and maintains its raw materials account at standard.

Required:

Calculate appropriate variances for the month of March in as much detail as possible and present an operating statement reconciling budgeted profit with actual profit.

You are not required to calculate mix or yield variances as Sam Mendes Ltd does not sub-analyse the material usage or labour efficiency variances.

10 Chapter summary

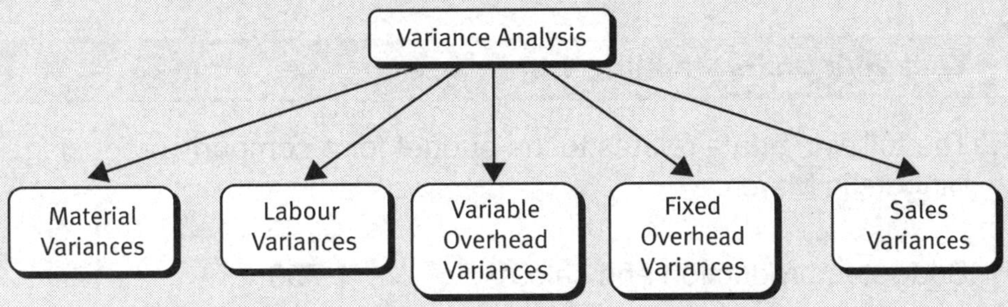

11 Practice questions

Test your understanding 1

The following data relates to the budget for a company producing widgets in March:

Budgeted production and sales (widgets)	1,750 units
Standard cost per unit:	$
Direct materials	6.00
Direct labour	3.00
Variable production overhead	0.75
Fixed production overhead	2.50
	12.25
Standard sales price	18.25
Standard profit per unit	6.00
Number of widgets produced in March	1,800 units
Actual sales revenue	$32,300

Required:

Calculate the sales price and sales volume profit variance. What would be the sales volume contribution variance if standard marginal costing were used?

Test your understanding 2

Major Caldwell Ltd makes and sells a single product. Each unit of the product requires 3 kg of material at $4 per kg.

The actual details for last period were that 1,200 units of finished goods were produced, 3,600 kg of material were purchased for $14,800 and 3,520 kg were used.

Major Caldwell Ltd maintains its raw materials account at standard.

Calculate appropriate variances for materials.

Test your understanding 3

The standard direct material and labour costs for a product are:

		$
Direct material A	2 kg x $ 4/kg	8
Direct material B	0.5 litres x $6 / ltr	3
Direct labour	0.75 hours x $12 per hour	9
		20

During November, the company made 3,200 units and sold 2,900. Actual production costs were:

		$
Direct material A	6,100 kgs	25,000
Direct material B	1,750 litres	11,600
Direct labour	2,200 hours paid (only 2,000 hours worked)	28.000

Required:

Calculate the following variances:

- direct materials price
- direct materials usage
- direct labour rate
- direct labour idle time
- direct labour efficiency

Test your understanding 4 - MAY LTD

May Ltd produces a single product for which the following data are given:

Standards per unit of product:

Direct material	4 kg at $3 per kg
Direct labour	2 hours at $6.40 per hour

Actual details for given financial period:

Output produced in units		38,000
Direct materials:		$
purchased	180,000 kg for	504,000
issued to production	154,000 kg	
Direct labour	78,000 hours worked for	546,000

There was no work in progress at the beginning or end of the period.

You are required to:

(a) Calculate the following variances:

(i) direct labour efficiency

(ii) direct labour rate

(iii) direct materials usage

(iv) direct materials price, based on issues to production.

(b) State whether in each of the following cases, the comment given and suggested as the possible reason for the variance, is consistent or inconsistent with the variance you have calculated in your answer to (a) above, supporting each of your conclusions with a brief explanatory comment.

Item in (a):

(i) Direct labour efficiency variance: the efficiency of labour was commendable

(ii) Direct labour rate variance: the union negotiated wage increase was $0.60 per hour lower than expected

(iii) Direct materials usage variance: material losses in production were less than had been allowed for in the standard.

(iv) Direct materials price variance: the procurement manager has ignored the economic order quantity and, by obtaining bulk quantities, has purchased material at less than the standard price

(Total: 10 marks)

Test your understanding 5

Jack Doherty Ltd makes a single product with the following standard cost details per unit.

				$
Direct materials	5 kg	@	$4/kg	20
Direct labour	4 hrs	@	$6/hr	24

Actual results were that 1,000 units were produced and sold. The actual hours paid for were 4,100 and the hours worked were 3,900. The actual labour cost was $27,060. The number of kg purchased in the month was 5,200 kg for $21,320 and the number of kg used was 4,900 kg. The company calculates the material price variance at the time of purchase.

Calculate appropriate variances for materials and labour.

Test your understanding 6

Col. Axelrod Ltd makes and sells a single product with the following information:

Std/Budget

Output	1,000 units
Material	3,000 kg @ $5/kg
Labour	5,000 hours @$6/hr

Actual

Output	1,100 units		
Material	Purchased	3,600 kg	for $18,720
	Used	3,400 kg	
Labour hrs	Paid for	5,200 hrs	for $32,760
	Worked	4,900 hrs	

Col. Axelrod Ltd maintains its raw material account at standard cost. Calculate the variances for materials and labour.

Test your understanding 7

Ivan Radek Ltd produces a single product which requires 3 standard hours. Fixed overheads are budgeted at $12,000 and are absorbed on a labour hour basis. Budgeted output is 1,000 units.

Actual results:

Output	1,100 units
Labour hours	3,080 hours
Overheads incurred	$13,000

Calculate appropriate variances for fixed overhead.

Test your understanding 8 - MALCOLM REYNOLDS LTD

Malcolm Reynolds Ltd makes and sells a single product, Product Q, with the following standard specification for materials:

	Quantity	**Price per kg**
	kg	$
Direct material X	12	40
Direct material Y	8	32

It takes 20 direct labour hours to produce one unit with a standard direct labour cost of $10 per hour.

The annual sales/production budget is 2,400 units evenly spread throughout the year. The standard selling price was $1,250 per unit.

The budgeted production overhead, all fixed, is $288,000 and expenditure is expected to occur evenly over the year, which the company divides into 12 calendar months. Absorption is based on direct labour hours.

For the month of October the following actual information is provided.

	$	$
Sales (220 units)		264,000
Cost of sales		
Direct materials used	159,000	
Direct wages	45,400	
Fixed production overhead	23,000	
		227,400
Gross profit		36,600
Administration costs	13,000	
Selling and distribution costs	8,000	
		21,000
Net profit		$15,600

Costs of opening stocks, for each material, were at the same price per kilogram as the purchases made during the month but there had been changes in the materials stock levels, viz.:

	1 October	**30 October**
	kg	kg
Material X	680	1,180
Material Y	450	350

Material X purchases were 3,000 kg at $42 each.

Material Y purchases were 1,700 kg at $30 each

The number of direct labour hours worked was 4,600 and the total wages incurred $45,400.

Work-in-progress stocks and finished goods stocks may be assumed to be the same at the beginning and end of October.

You are required:

(a) to prepare a standard product cost for one unit of product Q showing the standard selling price and standard gross profit per unit

(3 marks)

(b) to calculate appropriate variances for the materials, labour, fixed production overhead and sales, noting that it is company policy to calculate material price variances at time of issue to production and that RS Ltd does not calculate mix and yield variances

(12 marks)

(c) to prepare a statement for management reconciling the budgeted gross profit with the actual gross profit

(5 marks)

(Total: 20 marks)

Test your understanding 9 - GOOCH LTD

Gooch Ltd makes a single product and operates a standard costing system. The following variances, standard costs and actual results relate to period 6:

Variances	**Favourable**	**Adverse**
Direct material price variance		1,012
Direct material usage variance		1,380
Direct labour rate variance		920
Direct labour efficiency variance	3,680	
Variable overhead expenditure variance		1,288
Variable overhead efficiency variance	920	

Standard cost data

		$/unit
Direct materials	2 kg @ $3/kg	6
Direct labour	3 hrs @ $8/hr	24
Variable overheads	3 hrs @ $2/hr	6
Fixed overheads	3 hrs @ $4/hr	12
		—
		$48
		══

Fixed overheads were budgeted at $24,000 and the budgeted profit per unit was 20% of the selling price. Budgeted sales were 1,900 units.

Actual results

Material purchased and used	$16,192
Labour cost	$52,440
Variable overhead cost	$14,168
Fixed overhead cost	$23,500

Selling price per unit was $3 lower than budget and there was no change in stock levels.

You are required to calculate the:

(a) actual output

(b) actual material price per kg

(c) labour hours worked

(d) fixed overhead volume variance

(e) fixed overhead expenditure variance

(f) sales volume profit variance

(g) selling price variance

(h) budgeted profit

(i) actual profit.

(25 marks)

Test your understanding 10 - RBF TRANSPORT

RBF Transport, a haulage contractor, operates a standard costing system and has prepared the following report for April 20X0:

Operating statement

		$	$	$
Budgeted profit				8,000
Sales volume profit variance				880 (A)
				7,120
Selling price variance				3,560 (F)
				10,680
Cost variances		*A*	*F*	
Direct labour	- rate		1,086	
	- efficiency	240		
Fuel	- price	420		
	- usage	1,280		
Variable overhead	- expenditure		280	
	- efficiency	180		
Fixed overhead	- expenditure		400	
	- volume	1,760		
		3,880	1,766	2,114 (A)
Actual profit				8,566

The company uses delivery miles as its cost unit, and the following details have been taken from the budget working papers for April 20X0:

(1)	Expected activity	200,000 delivery miles
(2)	Charge to customers	$0.30 per delivery mile
(3)	Expected variable cost per delivery mile:	
	Direct labour (0.02 hours)	$0.08
	Fuel (0.1 litres)	$0.04
	Variable overhead (0.02 hours)	$0.06

The following additional information has been determined from the actual accounting records for April 20X0.

• Fixed overhead cost	$15,600
• Fuel price	$0.42 per litre
• Direct labour hours	3,620

Required:

(a) Calculate for April 20X0:

(i) the actual number of delivery miles;

(ii) the actual direct labour rate per hour;

(iii) the actual number of litres of fuel consumed;

(iv) the actual variable overhead expenditure.

(16 marks)

(b) State TWO possible causes of the fuel usage variance.

(4 marks)

(c) Prepare a report, addressed to the transport operations manager, explaining the different types of standard which may be set, and the importance of keeping standards meaningful and relevant.

(10 marks)

(Total: 30 marks)

Test your understanding 11

Flexed budgets for the cost of medical supplies in a hospital, based on a percentage of maximum bed occupancy, are shown below:

Bed occupancy	82%	94%
Medical supplies cost	$410,000	$429,200

During the period, the actual bed occupancy was 87% and the total cost of the medical supplies was $430,000.

Identify the medical supplies expenditure variance:

A $5,000 adverse

B $12,000 adverse

C $5,000 favourable

D $12,000 favourable

(2 marks)

Test your understanding answers

Example 1

Selling price variance

	$
Std selling price	25
Actual selling price	20
	5 A
x Actual no of units sold	x 500
	2,500 A

Sales volume profit variance

	Units
Budgeted sales	400
Actual sales	500
	100 F
x Std profit per unit	x 7
	$700 F

In this scenario there are no fixed costs, so the answer is the same whether we are uisng marginal or absorption costing.

Example 2

Sales price variance		$
Units sold should have sold for	(380 units × $45 per unit)	17,100
They did sell for	(actual sales revenue	15,960
Sales price variance		1,140 (A)

Absorption costing

Sales volume variance	Units	
Actual sales volume	380	
Budgeted sales volume	320	
Sales volume variance	60	
x standard profit per unit ($45 - $23)	x $22	
Sales volume profit variance	$1,320	(F)

Marginal costing

Sales volume variance	Units	
Actual sales volume	380	
Budgeted sales volume	320	
Sales volume variance	60	
x standard contribution per unit ($45 - $17)	x $28	
Sales volume contribution variance	$1,680	(F)

Sales revenue

Sales volume variance	Units	
Actual sales volume	380	
Budgeted sales volume	320	
Sales volume variance	60	
x standard sales price per unit	x $45	
Sales volume revenuevariance	$2,700	(F)

Example 3

Material total variance

	$
Std cost of actual output	
2kg x 1,000 units x $10/kg	20,000
Actual cost	20,900
	900 A

Material price variance

	$
Std price	10
Actual price $20,900/2,200 kg	9.50
	0.50 F
x Actual no of kg	x 2,000
	1,100 F

Material price variance – Alternative method

	$
Std cost of actual output	
$10/kg x 2,200 kg	22,000
Actual cost	20,900
	1,100 F
	2,200 A

Material usage variance

	kg
Std usage of actual output	
2kg x 1,000 units	2,000
Actual usage	2,200
	200 A
x Std price	x 10
	2,200 A

Example 4

Direct materials price variance:		$
Actual quantity of materials	should cost (standard)	
2,200kgs	$10 / kg	22,000
	did cost (actual)	20,900
Direct materials price variance		1,100 F

Direct materials usage variance:		$
Actual output produced	should use (standard quantity)	
1,000 units	2 ks / unit	2,000
	did cost (actual quantity)	2,200
Direct materials usage variance	(in material quantity)	200 A
× standard price	(per unit of material)	$10
Direct materials usage variance		2,000 A

Example 5

Direct labour rate variance:		$
Number of hours worked	should cost / hr (standard)	
3,400 hours	$8 / hr	27,200
	did cost (actual)	28,300
Direct labour rate variance		1,100 A

Direct labour efficiency variance:		Hours
Actual output produced	should take (standard hours)	
1,100 units	3 hrs per unit	3,300
	did take (actual hours)	3,400
Direct labour efficiency variance	(in hours)	100
x standard rate per hour		$8/ hr
Direct labour efficiency variance		$800 A

Example 6

					$	
SHSR	6 hrs/unit x 900 units	x	$7/hr	=	37,800	Efficiency $1,400 F
AHSR	5,200 hrs	x	$7/hr	=	36,400	

The efficiency variance looks at whether people **WORK** fast or slow and looks at hours **WORKED**.

					$	
AHSR	5,500 hrs	x	$7/hr	=	38,500	$600 A Rate
AHAR				=	39,100	

The rate variance looks at the rate of **PAY** so it looks at the hours **PAID**.

Idle time variance

(5,500 – 5,200) x $7 per hour $2,100 A

Or the idle time variance is simply the difference between the $38,500 and the $36,400 above = $2,100 A.

Example 7

Variable production overhead expenditure variance:		$	
Number of hours worked	should cost / hr (standard)		
1,980 hours	$3 / hour	5,940	
	did cost (actual)	5,544	
Variable production overhead expenditure variance		396	F

Variable production overhead efficiency variance:		Hours	
Actual output produced	should take (standard hours)		
900 units	2 hours / unit	1,800	
	did take (actual hours)	1,980	
Efficiency variance	(in hours)	180	A
x standard variable overhead rate per hour		$3	
Variable production overhead efficiency variance		$540	A

Example 8

(a) The idle time variance is 20 hours × $15 = $300 (A).

(b) The efficiency variances are then calculated based on the active hours worked, not on the total hours paid for.

Efficiency variances:		Hours
Actual output produced	should take	
200 units	(standard hours)	400
	2 hours / unit	
	did take (440 – 20)	420
Efficiency variance	(in hours)	20 A
× standard direct labour rate per hour		$15
Direct labour efficiency variance		$300 A
× standard variable overhead rate per hour		$4
Variable production overhead efficiency variance		$80 A

(c) The variable production overhead expenditure variance is based on active hours only, since variable production overhead cost is not incurred during idle time.

Variable production overhead expenditure variance:		$	
Number of hours worked	should cost / hr (standard)		
420 hours	$4 / hour	1,680	
	did cost (actual)	1,530	
Variable production overhead expenditure variance		150	F

Example 9

		$	
Fixed overhead expenditure variance:			
Budgeted fixed overhead		4,375	
Actual fixed overhead incurred		4,800	
Fixed overhead expenditure variance		425	(A)

		Units	
Fixed production overhead volume variance:			
Actual output produced		1,800	
Budgeted output		1,750	
Volume variance	(in units)	50	
x standard fixed overhead rate per hour		$2.50	
Fixed production overhead volume variance		$125	(F)

Example 10 - SAM MENDES LTD

Standard product cost

		$	$
Standard selling price			100
Material X	5 kg @ $3/kg	15	
Material Y	4 kg @ $5/kg	20	
Direct labour	3 hrs @ $8/hr	24	
Variable overheads	3 hrs @ $6/hr	18	
Fixed overheads (W1)	3 hrs @ $2/hr	6	
			83
Standard profit per unit			17

Material X variances

				$	
SQSP					
5 kg/unit x 2,200 units	x	$3/kg	=	33,000	Usage $900 A
AQSP					
11,300 kg	x	$3/kg	=	33,900	
AQAP					$2,260 F Price
11,300 kg	x	$2.8/kg	=	31,640	

Material Y variances

				$	
SQSP					
4 kg/unit x 2,200 units	x	$5/kg	=	44,000	Usage $2,500 F
AQSP					
8,300 kg	x	$5/kg	=	41,500	
AQAP					$2,490 A Price
8,300 kg	x	$5.30/kg	=	43,990	

Labour variances

				$	
SHSR					
3 hrs/unit x 2,200 units	x	$8/hr	=	52,800	Efficiency $1,600 F
AHSR					
6,400 hrs	x	$8/hr	=	51,200	
AHAR					$960 A Rate
(4,800 hrs x $8.10) + (1,600 hrs x $8.30)			=	52,160	

Variable overhead variances

				$	
SHSR					
3 hrs/unit x 2,200 units	x	$6/hr	=	39,600	Efficiency $1,200 F
AHSR					
6,400 hrs	x	$6/hr	=	38,400	
AHAR					$5,400 F Expenditure
			=	33,000	

Fixed overhead expenditure variance

	$
Budgeted Cost	12,000
Actual Cost	12,500
	500 A

Fixed overhead volume variance

	Units
Budgeted output	2,000
Actual output	2,200
	200 F
x Std Fixed Overhead Cost per unit	x 6
	$1,200 F

Sales volume profit variance

	Units
Budgeted sales	1,700
Actual sales	2,200
	500 F
x Std profit per unit	x 17
	$8,500 F

Sales price variance

	$
Std selling price	100
Actual selling price	90
	10 A
x Actual No of units sold	x 2,200
	$22,000 A

Operating statement

		$	$	$
Budgeted gross profit (W2)				28,900
Sales volume profit variance				8,500 F
Standard profit on actual sales				37,400
Selling price variance				22,000 A
				15,400
		Favourable	**Adverse**	
Cost variances				
Material X	Usage		900	
	Price	2,260		
Material Y	Usage	2,500		
	Price		2,490	
Direct labour	Efficiency	1,600		
	Rate		960	
Variable Overhead	Efficiency	1,200		
	Expenditure	5,400		
Fixed Prod Overhead	Expenditure		500	
	Volume	1,200		
		14,160	4,850	9,310 F
Actual profit (W3)				24,710

Workngs

(W1)

Budgeted fixed overheads are $144,000 per year and the budgeted output is 24,000 units for the year. Thus the budgeted/standard fixed cost per unit is $6.

The overheads are absorbed on direct labour hours and each unit takes 3 hours. Therefore the budgeted/standard fixed overhead is $2 per hour ($6 ÷ 3 hours).

(W2)

Budgeted profit = $17 per unit x Budgeted **sales** of 1,700 units = $28,900

(W3)

		$	$
Sales	2,200 units x $90		198,000
Material X	11,300 kg x $2.80/kg	31,640	
Material Y	8,300 kg x $5.30/kg	43,990	
Direct labour	(4,800 hrs x $8.10) + (1,600 hrs x $8.30)	52,160	
Variable overhead		33,000	
Fixed overhead		12,500	
			173,290
Actual Profit			24,710

Test your understanding 1

Sales price variance:		$	
Units sold should have sold for	(1.800 units x $18.25 per unit)	32,850	
They did sell for	(actual sales revenue)	32,300	
Sales price variance		550	(A)

Sales volume variance	Units	
Actual sales volume	1,800	
Budgeted sales volume	1,750	
Sales volume variance	50	
x standard profit per unit	x $6	
Sales volume profit variance	$300	(F)

Marginal costing

The contribution per unit is $ 8.50 ($18.25 - 6.00 - 3.00 - 0.75)

Sales volume variance	Units	
Actual sales volume	1,800	
Budgeted sales volume	1,750	
Sales volume variance	50	
x standard contribution per unit	x $8.50	
Sales volume contribution variance	$425	(F)

Test your understanding 2

					$		
SQSP	3 kg/unit x 1,200 units	x	$4/kg	=	14,400	}	Usage $320 F
AQSP	3,520 kg	x	$4/kg	=	14,080		

For a **USAGE** variance the quantity must be the quantity **USED**

					$		
AQSP	3,600 kg	x	$4/kg	=	14,400	}	$400 A Price
AQAP				=	14,800		

As the price variance is calculated at the time of **PURCHASE** then the quantity must be the quantity **PURCHASED** and we had to use the more complicated format.

Test your understanding 3

Direct material A price variance:		$
Actual quantity of materials 6,100 kgs	should cost (standard) $4 / kg	24,400
	did cost (actual)	25,000
Direct material A price variance		600 A

Direct material A usage variance:		$
Actual output produced 3,200 units	should use (standard quantity) 2 kgs / unit	6,400
	did cost (actual quantity)	6,100
Direct materials price variance	(in material quantity)	300 F
× standard price	(per unit of material)	$4
Direct material A usage variance		1,200 F

Direct material B price variance:

		$
Actual quantity of materials	should cost (standard)	
1,750 ltrs	$6 / ltr	10,500
	did cost (actual)	11,600
Direct material B price variance		1,100 A

Direct material B usage variance:

		$
Actual output produced	should use (standard quantity)	
3,200 units	0.5 ltrs / unit	1,600
	did cost (actual quantity)	1,750
Direct materials usage variance	(in material quantity)	150 A
× standard price	(per unit of material)	$6
Direct material B usage variance		900 A

Direct labour rate variance:

		$
Number of hours paid	should use / hr (standard)	
2,200 hours	$12 / hr	26,400
	did cost (actual)	28,000
Direct labour rate variance		1,600 A

Idle time variance:

There are 200 hours of idle time. At a standard cost of $12 per hour, this gives an idle time variance of

= 200 hours x $12 / hour

= $2,400 A

Direct labour efficiency variance:			$
Actual output produced	should use (standard hours)		
3,200 units	0.75 hrs per unit		2,400
	did take (actual hours)		2,000
Direct labour efficiency variance	(in hours)		400 F
× standard rate per hour			$12/hr
Direct labour efficiency variance			$4,800 F

Test your understanding 4 - MAY LTD

(a) **Direct labour variances**

						$	
SHSR	2 hrs/unit x 38,000 units	x	$6.40/hr	=	486,400		Efficiency $12,800 A
AHSR	78,000 hrs	x	$6.40/hr	=	499,200		$46,800 A
AHAR		x		=	546,000		Rate

(i) $12,800 A
(ii) $46,800 A

Direct material variances

						$	
SQSP	4 kg/unit x 38,000 units	x	$3/kg	=	456,000		Usage $6,000 A
AQSP	154,000 kg	x	$3/kg	=	462,000		$30,800 F
AQAP	154,000 kg	x	$2.80/kg	=	431,200		Price

The requirement in part (iv) asks for the price variance to be calculated at the time of issue, which is the same as at the time of usage, so the quantity must be the quantity issued/used.

The actual price of the material is $504,000/180,000 kg.

(iii) $6,000 A

(iv) $30,800 F

(b)

(i) Inconsistent. The workforce were inefficient.

(ii) Inconsistent. In fact the wage increase was $0.60 per hour higher than expected.

(iii) Inconsistent. If the losses had been less than expected then the usage variance would have been favourable.

(iv) Consistent. A bulk purchase discount should lead to cheaper materials and hence a favourable material price variance.

Test your understanding 5

Material variances

					$	
SQSP						
	5 kg/unit x 1,000 units	x	$4/kg	=	20,000	Usage $400 F
AQSP						
	4,900 kg	x	$4/kg	=	19,600	

For a **USAGE** variance the quantity must be the quantity **USED**

					$	
AQSP						
	5,200 kg	x	$4/kg	=	20,800	$520 A Price
AQAP						
				=	21,320	

As the price variance is calculated at the time of **PURCHASE** then the quantity must be the quantity **PURCHASED** and we had to use the more complicated format.

Labour variances

					$	
SHSR						
	4 hrs/unit x 1,000 units	x	$6/hr	=	24,000	Efficiency $600 F
AHSR						
	3,900 hrs	x	$6/hr	=	23,400	

The efficiency variance looks at whether people **WORK** fast or slow and looks at hours **WORKED**.

					$	
AHSR						
	4,100 units	x	$6/hr	=	24,600	$2,460 A Rate
AHAR						
				=	27,060	

The rate variance looks at the rate of **PAY** so it looks at the hours **PAID**.

Idle time variance

(4,100 – 3,900) x $6 per hour $1,200 A

Or the idle time variance is simply the difference between the $23,400 and the $24,600 above = $1,200 A.

Test your understanding 6

Material variances

					$	
SQSP						
	3 kg/unit x 1,100 units	x	$5/kg	=	16,500	Usage $500 A
AQSP						
	3,400 kg	x	$5/kg	=	17,000	

For a **USAGE** variance the quantity must be the quantity **USED.**

					$	
AQSP						
	3,600 kg	x	$5/kg	=	18,000	$720 A Price
AQAP						
				=	18,720	

As the price variance is calculated at the time of **PURCHASE** then the quantity must be the quantity **PURCHASED** and we had to use the more complicated format.

Labour variances

					$	
SHSR						
	5 hrs/unit x 1,100 units	x	$6/hr	=	33,000	Efficiency $3,600 F
AHSR						
	4,900 hrs	x	$6/hr	=	29,400	

The efficiency variance looks at whether people **WORK** fast or slow and looks at hours **WORKED**.

					$	
AHSR						
	5,200 hrs	x	$6/hr	=	31,200	$1,560 A Rate
AHAR						
				=	32,760	

The rate variance looks at the rate of **PAY** so it looks at the hours **PAID**.

Idle time variance

(5,200 – 4,900) x $6 per hour $1,800 A

Or the idle time variance is simply the difference between the $29,400 and the $31,200 above = $1,800 A.

Test your understanding 7

Fixed overhead total variance

	$
Std cost of actual output	
$12/unit x 1,100 units	13,200
Actual cost	13,000
	200 F

Fixed overhead expenditure variance

	$
Budgeted Cost	12,000
Actual Cost	13,000
	1,000 A

Fixed overhead volume variance

	Units
Budgeted output	1,000
Actual output	1,100
	100 F
x Std Fixed Overhead Cost per unit	x12
	$1,200 F

Under/overabsorption

	$
Overheads incurred	13,000
Overheads absorbed	
$4/direct labour hour x (3 hours x 1,100 units)	13,200
Overabsorption	200

The overhead absorption rate is based on direct labour hours and =

$$\frac{\text{Budgeted overheads}}{\text{Budgeted level of activity}}$$

$$\text{OAR} = \frac{\$12{,}000}{1{,}000 \text{ units} \times 3 \text{ hrs}} \quad \$4\text{/direct labour hour}$$

It would now be very natural to calculate the overheads absorbed by multiplying the OAR by the actual number of hours, i.e. 3,080, but in a standard costing system, the overheads are absorbed on the standard hours, not the actual hours.

The standard hours are the standard hours of actual output, 3 hours x 1,100 units = 3,300 hours.

Test your understanding 8 - MALCOLM REYNOLDS LTD

(a) **Standard product cost**

		$	$
Standard selling price			1,250
Material X	12 kg @ $40/kg	480	
Material Y	8 kg @ $32/kg	256	
Direct labour	20 hrs @ $10/hr	200	
Production overhead (W1)		120	
			1,056
Standard gross profit			194

(b) **Material X variances**

				$	
SQSP					
12 kg/unit x 220 units	x	$40/kg	=	105,600	
AQSP					Usage $5,600 F
2,500 kg (W2)	x	$40/kg	=	100,000	
AQAP					$5,000 A Price
2,500 kg	x	$42/kg	=	105,000	

Material Y variances

				$	
SQSP					
8 kg/unit x 220 units	x	$32/kg	=	56,320	
AQSP					Usage $1,280 A
1,800 kg (W2)	x	$32/kg	=	57,600	
AQAP					$3,600 F Price
1,800kg	x	$30/kg	=	54,000	

Direct labour variances

				$	
SHSR					
20 hrs/unit x 220 units	x	$10/hr	=	44,000	
AHSR					Efficiency $2,000 A
4,600 hrs	x	$10/hr	=	46,000	
AHAR					$600 F Rate
			=	45,400	

Fixed Overhead Expenditure variance

	$
Budgeted Cost (W3)	24,000
Actual Cost	23,000
	1,000 F

Fixed overhead volume variance

	Units
Budgeted output (2,400 units p.a. ÷ 12 months)	200
Actual output	220
	20 F
x Std Fixed Overhead Cost per unit	x120
	$2,400 F

Sales price variance

	$
Std selling price	1,250
Actual selling price ($264,000/220 units)	1,200
	50 A
x Actual no of units sold	x 220
	$11,000 A

Selling volume profit variance

	Units
Budgeted sales	200
Actual sales	220
	20 F
x Std profit per unit	x 194
	$3,880 F

(c) **Operating statement**

		$	$	$
Budgeted gross profit (W4)				38,800
Sales volume profit variance				3,880 F
				–––––
Standard profit on actual sales				42,680
Sales price variance				11,000 A
				–––––
				31,680
		Favourable	**Adverse**	
Cost variances				
Material X	Usage	5,600		
	Price		5,000	
Material Y	Usage		1,280	
	Price	3,600		
Direct labour	Efficiency		2,000	
	Rate	600		
Fixed Prod overhead	Expenditure	1,000		
	Volume	2,400		
		–––––	–––––	
		13,200	8,280	4,920 F
		–––––	–––––	–––––
Actual gross profit				36,600
				–––––

Workings

(W1) Fixed over head per unit = $288,000/2,400 units = $120 per unit

(W2)

	Material X	Material Y
	Kg	Kg
Op stock	680	450
+ Purchases	3,000	1,700
	3,680	2,150
- Cl stock	1,180	350
Materials issued/used	2,500	1800

(W3) Budgeted fixed overhead per month = $288,000/12 = $24,000

(W4) Budgeted profit = 200 units x $194 = $38,800

Test your understanding 9 - GOOCH LTD

(a) This is a 'backwards' question. Rather than calculating the variances ourselves, we have been given some of them. We have to find some other information which is missing. We will use the variances to work backwards to find that missing information.

The starting point is usually to find a variance which mentions the missing information, i.e. for part (a) we are asked for the actual output. We need to find a variance which mentions the actual output somewhere along the line.

One set of variances which would work are the material variances. The first line of the format is SQSP, where SQ is the standard quantity of the **actual output**.

We plug in the information that we know, and we can then work backwards to find the missing information.

Material variances

				$	
SQSP					
2 kg/unit x ? units	x	$3/kg	=	?	Usage $1,380 A
AQSP					
? kg	x	$3/kg	=	?	
AQAP					$1,012 A Price
? kg	x	$?/kg	=	16,192	

We know that AQAP is 16,192 and we know that the price variance is 1,012 A, so we can work backwards to find AQSP.

AQSP = 16,192 - 1,012 = 15,180

Material variances

				$	
SQSP					
2 kg/unit x ? units	x	$3/kg	=	?	Usage $1,380 A
AQSP					
? kg	x	$3/kg	=	15,180 Bal 1	
AQAP					$1,012 A Price
? kg	x	$?/kg	=	16,192	

Now, we know AQSP is 15,180 and the usage variance is 1,380 A, so we can work backwards to find SQSP.

SQSP = 15,180 - 1380 A = 13,800

Material variances

					$	
SQSP						
	2 kg/unit x ? units	x	$3/kg	=	13,800[Bal 2]	Usage
AQSP						$1,380 A
	? kg	x	$3/kg	=	15,180[Bal 1]	
AQAP						$1,012 A
	? kg	x	$?/kg	=	16,192	Price

Finally, for the first line, we know SQSP, i.e. we know 2 kg x something x $3/kg = 13,800. We can work backwards to find the actual output.

Actual output = 13,800 ÷ 2kg ÷ $3/kg = 2,300 units

Material variances

					$	
SQSP						
	2 kg/unit x 2,300[Bal 3] units	x	$3/kg	=	13,800[Bal 2]	Usage
AQSP						$1,380 A
	? kg	x	$3/kg	=	15,180[Bal 1]	
AQAP						$1,012 A
	? kg	x	$?/kg	=	16,192	Price

(b) We have already worked out a lot of the figures that we need for the material variances. We can carry on from where we left off in part (a).

Material variances

					$	
SQSP						
	2 kg/unit x 2,300 [Bal 3] units	x	$3/kg	=	13,800 [Bal 2]	Usage
AQSP						$1,380 A
	? kg	x	$3/kg	=	15,180[Bal 1]	
AQAP						$1,012 A
	? kg	x	$?/kg	=	16,192	Price

For the second line, we know AQSP = 15,180, i.e. we know that AQ x 3 = 15,180.

Actual quantity = 15,180 ÷ 3 = 5,060 kg

AQ appears on both the second line and the third line, so we can write 5,060 kg on both lines.

Material variances

					$	
SQSP						
	2 kg/unit x 2,300 [Bal 3] units	x	$3/kg	=	13,800 [Bal 2]	Usage
AQSP						$1,380 A
	5,060 [Bal 4] kg	x	$3/kg	=	15,180 [Bal 1]	
AQAP	⇩					$1,012 A
	5,060 [Bal 4] kg	x	$?/kg	=	16,192	Price

Finally for the third line, AQAP = 5,060 Kg x something = 16,192

Actual price = 16,192 ÷ 5,060 = $3.20 per kg.

Material variances

					$	
SQSP						
	2 kg/unit x 2,300 [Bal 3] units	x	$3/kg	=	13,800 [Bal 2]	Usage
AQSP						$1,380 A
	5,060 [Bal 4] kg	x	$3/kg	=	15,180 [Bal 1]	
AQAP	⇩					$1,012 A
	5,060 [Bal 4] kg	x	$3.20/kg [Bal 5]	=	16,192	Price

(c) Labour variances

				$	
SHSR					
3 hrs/unit x 2,300 units	x	$8/hr	=	55,200	Efficiency $3,680 F
AHSR					
? hrs	x	$8/hr	=	?	$920 A Rate
AHAR					
? hrs	x	$?/hr	=	52,440	

To find out the labour hours we can use the labour variances format. We can find AHSR by subtracting the efficiency variance of 3,680 F from SHSR to get 51,520 or by adding the adverse rate variance of 920 to AHAR.

Once we know that AHSR is $51,520, we know that something x $8/hr = $51,520.

Actual hours = 51,520 ÷ 8 = 6,440 hours

Labour variances

				$	
SHSR					
3 hrs/unit x 2,300 units	x	$8/hr	=	55,200	Efficiency $3,680 F
AHSR					
6,440 Bal 2 hrs	x	$8/hr	=	51,520 Bal 1	
AHAR					$920 A rate
? hrs	x	$?/hr	=	52,440	

(d) Fixed overhead volume variance

	Units
Budgeted output	2,000
Actual output	2,300
	300F
x Std Fixed Overhead Cost per unit	x 12
	$3,600F

(e) Fixed overhead expenditure variance

	$
Budgeted Cost	24,000
Actual Cost	23,500
	500 F

(f) **Selling volume profit variance**

	Units
Budgeted sales	1,900
Actual sales	2,300
	400 F
x Std profit per unit	x 12
=	$4,800 F

The profit margin is 20% of selling price. A profit margin of 20% is the same as a mark-up of 25%. Thus we know standard cost to be $48 per unit, standard profit must be 25% of that, must be $12 per unit.

(g) **Selling price variance**

	$
Std selling price	60
Actual selling price	57
	3 A
x Actual no of units sold	x 2,300
=	6,900 A

We know that standard cost is $48 per unit and we the standard profit (from part (f)) is $12. Therefore standard selling price = $48 + $12 = $60.

(h) Budgeted profit = 1,900 units x $12 per unit = $22,800.

(i)

		$	$
Sales	2,300 units x $57		131,100
Direct material		16,192	
Direct labour		52,440	
Variable overhead		14,168	
Fixed overhead		23,500	
			106,300
Actual profit			24,800

Test your understanding 10 - RBF TRANSPORT

Key answer tips

This is a very good test of the depth of your knowledge of variances. The basic technique is to set out your normal computations of the variances, putting in the figures you know and working back to those you don't. Often the results from one will be needed in another, so do all the related variances together.

(a)

(i) Budgeted fixed overhead cost/mile =

$$= \frac{(\$15,600 + \$400)}{200,000} = \$0.08/\text{mile}$$

Volume variance = $1,760 (A)

Volume difference = $1,760 ÷ $0.08

= 22,000 miles(A)

Actual miles = 200,000 - 22,000

178,000

(ii)

Standard rate/hr $= \frac{\$0.08}{0.02}$

= $4/hour

Rate variance = $1,086 (F)

$= \frac{\$1,086}{3,260} = \$0.30/\text{hr (F)}$

Actual rate $4.00 - $0.30 = $3.70/hr

(iii)

$$\text{Standard price/litre} = \frac{\$0.04}{0.1}$$

= $0.40/litre

Actual price/litre = $0.42/litre

Price variance/litre = $0.02 (A)

Total price variance = $420 (A)

$$\text{Actual number of litres} = \frac{\$420}{£0.02} = 21{,}00$$

(c) **Variable overhead variances**

				$		
SHSR						
0.02 hrs × 178,000 delivery miles	×	$3/hr	=	10,680	Efficiency $180 A	
AHSR						
	×	$3/hr	=	?		
AHAR					$280 F Expenditure	
			=	?		

We know all the above infor mation, but are trying to find the missing information represented by question marks. In particular we are trying to find the bottom question mark, the actual hours at the actual rate, i.e. the actual variable overhead expenditure. We can do this in one step or two. Taking it in two steps, we can find the middle question mark:

SHSR					
0.02 hrs × 178,000 delivery miles	×	$3/hr	= 10,680		Efficiency $180 A
AHSR				Bal 1	
	×	$3/hr	= 10,860		
AHAR					$280 F Expenditure
			= ?		

And then, the bottom question mark:

SHSR					
0.02 hrs × 178,000 delivery miles	×	$3/h	= 10,680		Efficiency $ 180 A
AHSR				Bal 1	
	×	$3/hr	= 10,860		
AHAR				Bal 2	$280 F Expenditure
			= 10,580		

The actual variable overhead expenditure is $10,580

(b) Two possible causes of an adverse fuel usage variance are:

(i) Spillage of fuel occurred on filling vehicle fuel tanks.

(ii) Vehicles are in need of servicing and as a result fuel usage is excessive.

(c) **To:** Transport Operations Manager

From: Management Accountant

Date: XX - XX - XX

Subject: Standard costs

Introduction

This report explains the type of standard cost which may be set and importance of keeping standards meaningful and relevant.

Types of standard

A standard cost is a prediction of the cost per unit expected in a future period. It is dependent on estimates of resource requirements per output unit and the price to be paid per resource unit.

There are three types of standard which may be set and these are often referred to as:

- current standard;
- attainable standard; and
- ideal standard.

The current standard uses existing efficiency and achievement levels as the standard for the future period. This does not encourage improvement and may also allow existing inefficiencies to continue unnoticed.

The attainable standard sets a target which requires improvements in performance if it is to be achieved, but these are small and are considered to be achievable (or attainable). This form of standard is believed to be the best motivator to a manager.

The ideal standard assumes a perfect working environment (which never exists for a prolonged period). This is impossible to achieve.

Keeping standards useful

Standards are useful as a basis for performance evaluation. If such comparisons are to be valid the standard must reflect the current method of working AND resource prices which are realistic. If standards are not kept up to date they are no longer meaningful and thus their usefulness is reduced.

Conclusion

I recommend that attainable standards should be used, and that they should be reviewed regularly. Please contact me if you wish to discuss this further.

Test your understanding 11

B

$$\text{Contribution margin} = \frac{429{,}200 - 410{,}000}{94\% - 82\%}$$

= £1600 for every 1% change

Budget for 87% occupancy = £429,200 – (7 × 1600)

= £418,000

Medical expenditure variance = 418,000 – 430,000

= 12,000 Adverse

chapter

7

Variance analysis: discussion elements

Chapter learning objectives

Lead	Component
A1. discuss costing methods and their results.	(e) Explain why and how standards are set in manufacturing and in service industries with particular reference to the maximisation of efficiency and minimisation of waste. (f) Interpret material, labour, variable overhead, fixed overhead and sales variances. (g) Prepare reports using a range of internal and external benchmarks and interpret the results.

Specific areas of indicative syllabus content of relevance here are the following:

- Criticisms of standard costing in general and in advanced manufacturing environments in particular.
- Standards and variances in service industries (including the phenomenon of 'McDonaldization'), public services (e.g. Health), (including the use of 'diagnostic related' or 'reference' groups), and the professions (e.g. labour mix variances in audit work).
- Application of these variances to all sectors, including professional services and retail analysis.

1 Session content diagram

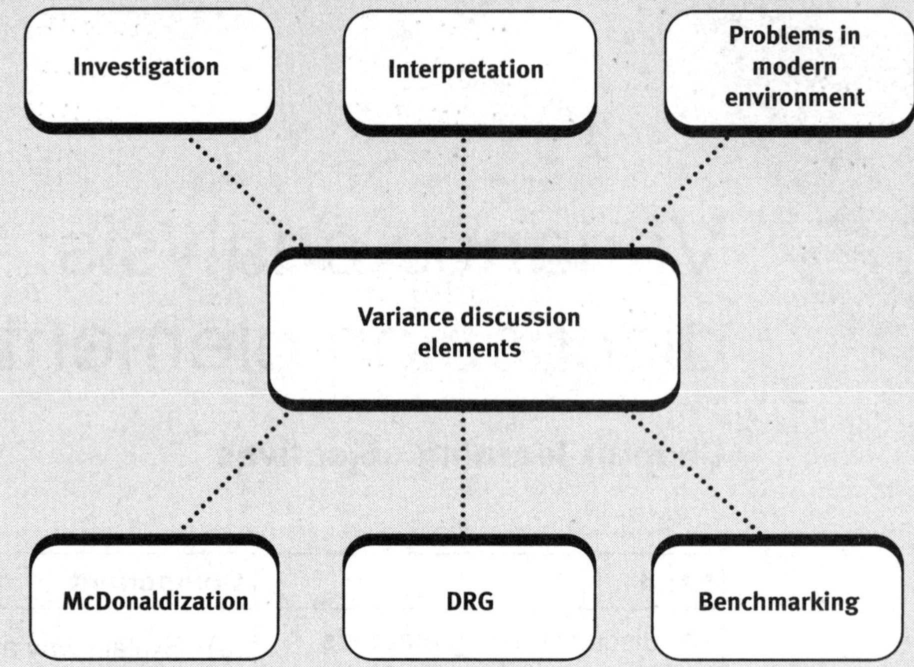

2 Variance investigation

Variances arise naturally in standard costing because a standard cost is a long term average cost. In any period actual costs may be higher or lower than standard but in the long run these should cancel out if the process is under control.

Variances may also arise because of:

- poor budgeting
- poor recording of cost
- operational reasons (the key emphasis in exam questions)
- random factors.

It is important to identify the reason for a variance so that appropriate action can be taken, but time and effort will be wasted if all variances are investigated as many will arise as a normal part of the process.

When should a variance be investigated?

Factors to consider include the following:

- the size of the variance
- whether favourable/adverse – firms often treat adverse variances as more important than favorable
- correction costs versus benefits

- ability to correct
- past pattern
- budget reliability
- reliability of measurement/recording systems.

Variance investigation techniques

Reporting by exception

Variance reports might identify significant variances. This is a form of reporting by exception, in which particular attention is given to the aspects of performance that appear to be exceptionally good or bad.

Alternatively, a rule might be applied generally that any adverse variance or favourable variance should be investigated if it exceeds more than a given percentage amount of the standard cost. For example, a rule might be applied that all adverse variances exceeding 5% of standard cost should be investigated and all favourable variances exceeding 10% of the standard should also be investigated.

Cummulative variances and control charts

An alternative method of identifying significant variances is to investigate the cause or causes of a variance only if the cumulative total for the variance over several control periods exceeds a certain limit.

The reason for this approach is that variances each month might fluctuate, with adverse variances in some months and favourable variances in the next. Provided that over time, actual results remain close to the standard, monthly variances might be acceptable.

For example, actual fixed overhead expenditure will not be exactly the same every month. Budgeted monthly expenditure, on the other hand, might be calculated by dividing the budgeted annual expenditure by 12. Consequently, there will inevitably be favourable or adverse expenditure variances from one month to the next, although over the course of the financial year, actual and budgeted expenditure should be the same.

This approach to identifying significant variances can be illustrated by the concept of a variance control chart. Variances should only be investigated when the cumulative total of variances exceeds predetermined control limits.

Setting the control limits

The control limits used as a basis for determining whether a variance should be investigated may be set statistically based on the normal distribution.

Using historical data a standard can be set as an expected average cost and a standard deviation can also be established. By assuming that a cost conforms to the normal distribution a variance will be investigated if it is statistically significant and has not arisen according to chance.

- If a company has a policy to investigate variances that fall outside the range that includes 95% of outcomes, then variances which exceed 1.96 standard deviations from the standard would be investigated.
- If a company has a policy to investigate variances that fall outside the range that includes 99% of outcomes, then variances which exceed 2.58 standard deviations from the standard would be investigated.

For control purposes, management might need to establish why a particular variance has occurred. Once the reason for the variance has been established, a decision can then be taken as to what control measures, if any, might be appropriate:

- to prevent the adverse variance continuing in the future, or
- to repeat a favourable variance in the future, or
- to bring actual results back on course to achieve the budgeted targets.

3 Interpretation of variances

Possible operational causes of variances are as follows:

Material price

(1) Using a different supplier, who is either cheaper or more expensive.

(2) Buying in larger-sized orders, and getting larger bulk purchase discounts. Buying in smaller-sized orders and losing planned bulk purchase discounts.

(3) An unexpected increase in the prices charged by a supplier.

(4) Unexpected buying costs, such as high delivery charges.

(5) Efficient or inefficient buying procedures.

(6) A change in material quality, resulting in either higher or lower purchase prices

Material usage

(1) A higher-than-expected or lower-than-expected rate of scrap or wastage.

(2) Using a different quality of material (higher or lower quality) could affect the wastage rate.

(3) Defective materials.

(4) Better quality control.

(5) More efficient work procedures, resulting in better material usage rates.

(6) Changing the materials mix to obtain a more expensive or less expensive mix than the standard.

Labour rate

(1) An unexpected increase in basic rates of pay.

(2) Payments of bonuses, where these are recorded as direct labour costs.

(3) Using labour that is more or less experienced (and so more or less expensive) than the 'standard'.

(4) A change in the composition of the work force, and so a change in average rates of pay.

Labour efficiency

(1) Taking more or less time than expected to complete work, due to efficient or inefficient working.

(2) Using labour that is more or less experienced (and so more or less efficient) than the 'standard'.

(3) A change in the composition or mix of the work force, and so a change in the level of efficiency.

(4) Improved working methods.

(5) Industrial action by the work force: 'working to rule'.

(6) Poor supervision.

(7) Improvements in efficiency due to a 'learning effect' amongst the work force.

(8) Unexpected lost time due to production bottlenecks and resource shortages.

Overhead variances

(1) Fixed overhead expenditure adverse variances are caused by spending in excess of the budget. A more detailed analysis of the expenditure variance would be needed to establish why actual expenditure has been higher or lower than budget.

(2) Variable production overhead efficiency variances: the causes are similar to those for a direct labour efficiency variance.

Sales price

(1) Higher-than-expected discounts offered to customers to persuade them to buy, or due to purchasing in bulk.

(2) Lower-than-expected discounts, perhaps due to strength of sales demand.

(3) The effect of low-price offers during a marketing campaign.

(4) Unexpected price increases.

(5) Unexpected price cuts.

Sales volume

(1) Successful or unsuccessful direct selling efforts.

(2) Successful or unsuccessful marketing efforts (for example, the effects of an advertising campaign).

(3) Unexpected changes in customer needs and buying habits.

(4) Failure to satisfy demand due to production difficulties.

(5) Higher demand due to a cut in selling prices, or lower demand due to an increase in sales prices.

4 Possible interdependence between variances

In many cases, the explanation for one variance might also explain one or more other variances in which case the variances are inter-related.

For control purposes, it might therefore be necessary to look at several variances together and not in isolation.

Some examples of interdependence between variances are listed below.

- Using cheaper materials will result in a favourable material price variance, but using the cheaper material in production might increase the wastage rate (adverse material usage) and cause a fall in labour productivity (adverse labour and variable overhead efficiency).

  A more expensive mix of materials (adverse mix variance) might result in higher output yields (favourable yield variance).
- Using more experienced labour to do the work will result in an adverse labour rate variance, but productivity might be higher as a result (favourable labour and variable overhead efficiency).
- Changing the composition of a team might result in a cheaper labour mix (favourable mix variance) but lower productivity (adverse yield variance).
- Workers trying to improve productivity (favourable efficiency variance) in order to win a bonus (adverse rate variance) might use materials wastefully in order to save time (adverse materials usage).

- Cutting sales prices (adverse sales price variance) might result in higher sales demand from customers (favourable sales volume variance).

5 The controllability principle

Controllability means the extent to which a specific manager can control costs or revenues or any other item (such as output quality). The controllability principle is that a manager should only be made accountable and responsible for costs and revenues that he or she can control directly.

In variance reporting, this means that variances should be reported to the managers who are in a position to control the costs or revenues to which the variances relate.

Composite variances

Sometimes a variance might be caused by a combination of two factors. The variance is a composite variance, because it is the result of the two factors combined. To apply the controllability principle, the variance should be reported to each of the managers who are in a position to control one of the factors.

6 Standard costing in the modern manufacturing environment

Standard product costs are associated with traditional manufacturing systems producing large quantities of standard items.

Standard costing may not be appropriate in the modern production environment because:

Non-standard products

Standard product costs apply to manufacturing environments in which quantities of an identical product are output from the production process. They are not suitable for manufacturing environments where products are non-standard or are customised to customer specifications.

Standard costs become outdated quickly

Shorter product life cycles in the modern business environment mean that standard costs will need to be reviewed and updated frequently. This will increase the cost of operating a standard cost system but, if the standards are not updated regularly, they will be of limited use for planning and control purposes. The extra work involved in maintaining up-to-date standards might limit the usefulness and relevance of a standard costing system.

Production is highly automated

It is doubtful whether standard costing is of much value for performance setting and control in automated manufacturing environments. There is an underlying assumption in standard costing that control can be exercised by concentrating on the efficiency of the workforce. Direct labour efficiency standards are seen as a key to management control. However, in practice, where manufacturing systems are highly automated, the rates of production output and materials consumption, are controlled by the machinery rather than the workforce.

Ideal standard used

Variances are the difference between actual performance and standard, measured in cost terms. The significance of variances for management control purposes depends on the type of standard cost used. JIT and TQM businesses often implement an ideal standard due to the emphasis on continuous improvement and high quality. Therefore, adverse variances with an ideal standard have a different meaning from adverse variances calculated with a current standard.

Emphasis on continuous improvement

Standard costing and adherence to a preset standard is inconsistent with the concept of continuous improvement, which is applied within TQM and JIT environments.

Detailed information is required

Variance analysis is often carried out on an aggregate basis (total material usage variance, total labour efficiency variance and so on) but in a complex and constantly changing business environment more detailed information is required for effective management control.

Monitoring performance is important

Variance analysis control reports tend to be made available to managers at the end of a reporting period. In the modern business environment managers need more 'real time' information about events as they occur.

7 McDonaldization

The concept of McDonaldization comes from the successes of the fast food company. Although the principles are perhaps best understood by applying them to the way McDonalds has operated, it is important to remember that they can be applied to many other services, such as hairdressing, dentistry, or opticians' services.

Ritzer identified four dimensions to McDonaldization which are critical to the success of the model.

(1) **Efficiency**. This means choosing the optimum means to achieve a given end. Consumers should be able to get what they need more quickly and with less effort. Workers should perform tasks more quickly and with less effort. In McDonalds, for example, drinks dispensers, automatic coffee brewers, microwave ovens, automatic potato peelers, dishwashers and pre-programmed cash registers have saved time, reduced the need for human input and reduced the scope for error.

(2) **Calculability**. This means the ability to produce and obtain large quantities of something very quickly. A problem with fast high-volume production is that quality might suffer consequently non-human technologies should be used as much as possible to perform tasks. 'Quantity has become equivalent to quality, a lot of something, or the quick delivery of it, means that it must be good.

(3) **Control**. There should be effective controls over both employees and customers. In McDonalds restaurants, for example, customers are expected to clear their own tables after eating.

(4) **Predictability**. Customers (and employees) should know exactly what they are going to get at any service point anywhere in the world. In the case of McDonalds, for example, the predictability of what customers get in any outlet has been a significant factor in expansion through franchising.

The relevance of standard costing to services of this nature should be apparent. Management should be able to set accurate standards for what is takes, in terms of materials and time, to provide standard items to customers. This in turn means that costs are both minimised and predictable, and with predictable costs, it becomes possible to set prices that customers see as fair (or even better) and still make a large profit.

More details

The term was defined by George Ritzer (1996) as 'the process by which the principles of the fast-food restaurant are coming to dominate more and more sectors of American society, as well as the rest of the world'.

Other principles on which McDonaldization is based are that:

- When goods and services are more uniform in quality, quality will be better.
- Standardisation of services is less expensive than customisation.
- Customers like familiarity, and feel that it is safer to do things within a controlled regime.
- People like to be treated in the same way as everyone else.

Features of the McDonalds service, which are probably familiar to you, are automation, speed, the use of disposable paper products and plastic wraps, pre-sliced cheese and packs of tomato ketchup, getting customers to do the work and having a limited menu of items with a short preparation time. Customers feel they are getting a good deal in terms of generous portions for a reasonable price and in a short time.

8 Diagnostic related groups

Diagnostic related groups are another application of standards in a service industry.

A diagnostic related group (DRG) is a category of disease or medical condition for which diagnosis and treatment are similar. For each DRG, a standard cost is calculated for diagnosis and treatment, according to the age of the patient, based on estimates of the standard consumption of hospital resources required and the expected length of stay in hospital. This uniform cost for each DRG is then used by medical insurers, such as Medicare in the US, as the basis for payments to the hospitals.

Since the system sets a maximum amount that will be paid for the care of Medicare patients, it provides an incentive to hospital management to meet the standards (or improve on them) and keep their costs down.

More details

DRGs have been defined as 'systems for classifying patient care by relating common characteristics such as diagnosis, treatment and age to an expected consumption of hospital resources and length of stay. Its aim is to provide a framework for specifying care mix and to reduce hospital costs' (www.online-medical-dictionary.org).

The concept was developed in US healthcare in the early 1980s as a means of controlling the costs of the Medicare health service. In broad terms, patients are placed into one of several standard categories of condition and treatment, and the amount that Medicare will pay the hospitals providing the treatment is based on a standard price for that category.

9 Benchmarking

In addition to monitoring performance through variance analysis, or as an alternative to variance reporting, organisations might use benchmarking to:

- monitor their performance, and
- set targets for improved performance.

The basic idea of benchmarking is that performance should be assessed through a comparison of the organisation's own products or services, performance and practices with 'best practice' elsewhere.

Definition of benchmarking

'Benchmarking is 'the establishment, through data gathering, of targets and comparators, through whose use relative levels of performance (and particularly areas of under-performance) can be identified. By adoption of identified best practices it is hoped that performance will improve' (CIMA *Official Terminology*).

Alternative definitions

'Benchmarking is simply about making comparisons with other organisations and then learning the lessons that those comparisons throw up' (The European Benchmarking Code of Conduct).

'Benchmarking is the continuous process of measuring products, services and practices against the toughest competitors … recognised as industry leaders (best in class)' (The Xerox Corporation).

Benchmarking was pioneered by Xerox Business Systems in the late 1970s as a tactical planning tool, in response to the challenge from rival Japanese producers of photocopier machines.

The reasons for benchmarking might be summarised as:

- to receive an alarm call about the need for change
- learning from others in order to improve performance
- gaining a competitive edge (in the private sector)
- improving services (in the public sector).

Different types of benchmarking

Benchmarking can be categorised according to what is being benchmarked and whose performance is being used for comparison (as 'best in class').

- Internal benchmarking
- Competitive benchmarking
- Functional benchmarking
- Strategic benchmarking

Further details

It is important to remember that in order to use benchmarking, it is necessary to gather information about best practice. This leads on to the problem of how much information is available and where it can be obtained.

Benchmarking can be categorised according to what is being benchmarked and whose performance is being used for comparison (as 'best in class').

Internal benchmarking. With internal benchmarking, other units or departments in the same organisation are used as the benchmark. This might be possible if the organisation is large and divided into a number of similar regional divisions. Internal benchmarking is also widely used within government. In the UK for example, there is a Public Sector Benchmarking Service that maintains a database of performance measures. Public sector organisations, such as fire stations and hospitals, can compare their own performance with the best in the country.

Competitive benchmarking. With competitive benchmarking, the most successful competitors are used as the benchmark. Competitors are unlikely to provide willingly any information for comparison, but it might be possible to observe competitor performance (for example, how quickly a competitor processes customer orders). A competitor's product might be dismantled in order to learn about its internal design and its performance: this technique of benchmarking is called **reverse engineering**.

Functional benchmarking. In functional benchmarking, comparisons are made with a similar function (for example selling, order handling, despatch) in other organisations that are not direct competitors. For example, a fast food restaurant operator might compare its buying function with buying in a supermarket chain.

Strategic benchmarking. Strategic benchmarking is a form of competitive benchmarking aimed at reaching decisions for strategic action and organisational change.

Companies in the same industry might agree to join a **collaborative benchmarking process**, managed by an independent third party such as a trade organisation. With this type of benchmarking, each company in the scheme submits data about their performance to the scheme organiser. The organiser calculates average performance figures for the industry as a whole from the data supplied. Each participant in the scheme is then supplied with the industry average data, which it can use to assess its own performance.

The benchmarking process

The benchmarking process can be summarised as follows:

- Identify gaps in performance through comparisons with other organisations.
- Seek a fresh approach to achieve an improvement in performance where significant gaps are found. This does not necessarily mean copying what the other organisation does.
- Implement the improvements.
- Monitor progress.
- Repeat the process.

Benchmarking should be a continual process, not a 'one-off' exercise.

Performance measures

Gaps in performance are identified by comparing an organisation's own performance with the performance of the organisation acting as the benchmark.

- Several measures of performance will be used. Each measure should be a key performance measure, critical to the success of the organisation.
- Performance measures can be financial or non-financial.
- Ideally performance should be quantifiable and measurable, although qualitative assessments and comparisons might be necessary.
- The information available for comparison will depend on whether it has been provided voluntarily by the benchmark. Co-operative benchmarking should provide more extensive information.

The performance measures used will vary. For your examination, you might be required to:

- Suggest suitable performance measures. Performance measures should allow for direct comparisons. For example, a profit/sales ratio might provide a useful comparison, but earnings per share would not. Remember that both financial and non-financial data might be significant.
- Comment on a benchmarking report, by comparing the performance of an organisation with a benchmark such as a leading competitor or another region in the same organisation.

10 Chapter summary

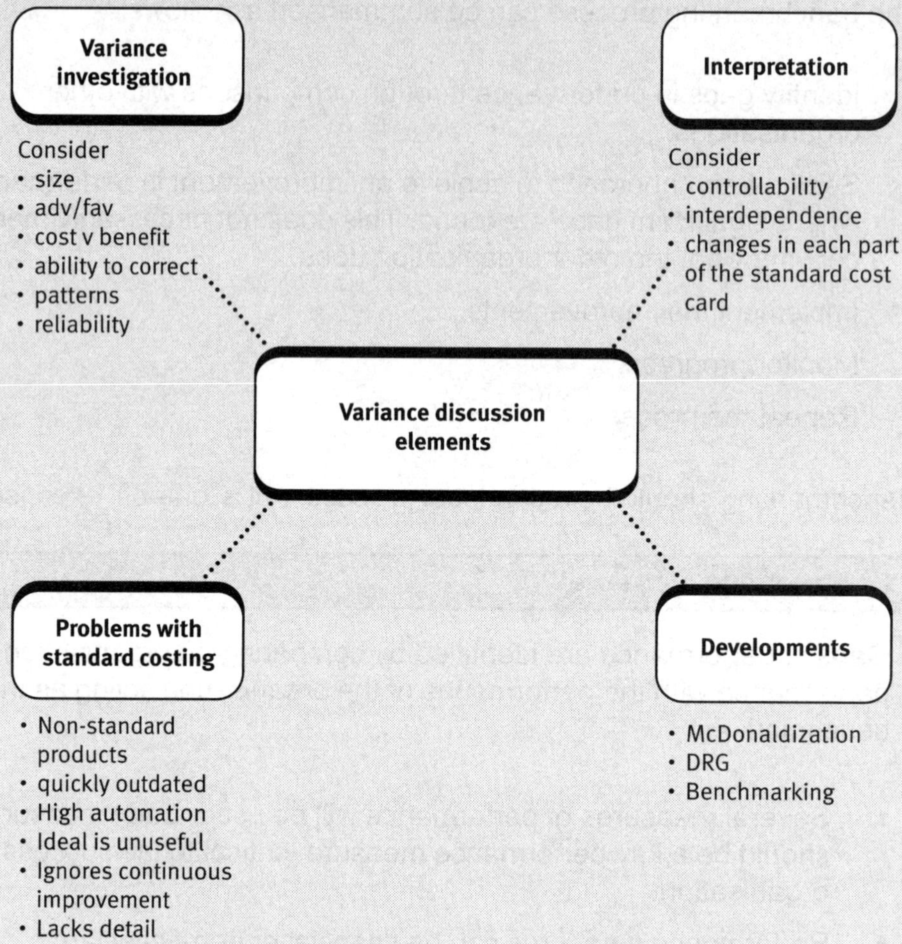

11 Practice questions

Test your understanding 1

Describe whether standard costing applies in both manufacturing and service businesses and how it may be affected by modern initiatives of continuous performance improvement and cost reduction.

Test your understanding 2 - BUSINESS EQUIPMENT SOLUTIONS

CM Limited was formed 10 years ago to provide business equipment solutions to local businesses. It has separate divisions for research, marketing, product design, technology and communication services, and now manufactures and supplies a wide range of business equipment (copiers, scanners, printers, fax machines and similar items).

To date it has evaluated its performance using monthly financial reports that analyse profitability by type of equipment.

While on a course, the Managing Director of CM Limited overheard someone mention how the performance of their company had improved after they introduced 'Benchmarking'.

Required:

Explain 'Benchmarking' and how it could be used to improve the performance of CM Limited.

(12 marks)

Test your understanding answers

Test your understanding 1

Standard costing is most suited to organisations whose activities consist of a series of common or repetitive operations. Typically, mass production manufacturing operations are indicative of its area of application. It is also possible to envisage operations within the service sector to which standard costing may apply, though this may not be with the same degree of accuracy of standards which apply in manufacturing. For example, hotels and restaurants often use standard recipes for preparing food, so dealing with conference attendance can be like a mass production environment. Similarly, banks will have common processes for dealing with customer transactions, processing cheques, etc. It is possible therefore that the principles of standard costing may be extended to service industries.

In modern manufacturing and service businesses, continuous improvement and cost reduction are topical. In order to remain competitive it is essential that businesses address the cost levels of their various operations. To do this they have to deal with the costing of operations. But the drive to 'cost down' may mean in some cases that standards do not apply for long before a redesign or improvement renders them out of date. In such a setting an alternative to the use of standard costs is to compare actual costs with those of the previous operating period. We have seen above that a standard costing system has a variety of purposes. It is for management to judge their various reasons for employing standard costing and, consequently, whether their aims of continuous improvement and cost reduction render the system redundant.

Test your understanding 2 - BUSINESS EQUIPMENT SOLUTIONS

Benchmarking is the continuous process of comparing products, services and activities against best practice. The best practice information could be taken from internal sources, e.g. other divisions or from external organisations which may be competitors or may even be companies in completely different industries, but with some similar processes.

By comparing the performance against best practice elsewhere, where company performance falls short of the target, questions can be asked as to why this is so and efforts directed at improving.

CM Ltd should determine what performance measures are important, which ones are critical to the company's success. It should be the divisional managers who choose the measures which are important for their divisions. Then, the source of the benchmark should be established. Some of the benchmarks will be internal, e.g. other divisions within the group and there will not be any problem obtaining the information, but some of the benchmarks will be external and this could cause more problems. Where the external benchmark is based upon performance by a non-competing company then there are no commercial confidence considerations to take into account, but even competing companies do sometimes agree to share information with the aim that both companies improve their performance. Sometimes various companies in the same industry agree to pool information to a trade association or other body which will collect information in confidence and then publish various statistics which the individual companies can then use for benchmarking. It is also possible to benchmark against an unwilling competitor but this relies on the information being publicly available.

For the manufacturing arm of CM Ltd, information about competing companies could be obtained by 'reverse engineering', i.e. literally taking a competitor's product apart to see what components and materials are used and what processes must have been involved.

CM Ltd could agree to benchmark with similar companies in the same industry, but operating in a different geographical area, hence not competing.

chapter

8

Advanced variances

Chapter learning objectives

Lead	**Component**
A1. Discuss costing methods and their results.	(f) Interpret material, labour, variable overhead, fixed overhead and sales variances, distinguishing between planning and operational variances.

Specific areas of indicative syllabus content of relevance here are the following:

- A1: Further subdivision of total usage/efficiency variances into mix and yield components.

(**Note:** The calculation of mix variances on both individual and average valuation bases is required).

1 Session content diagram

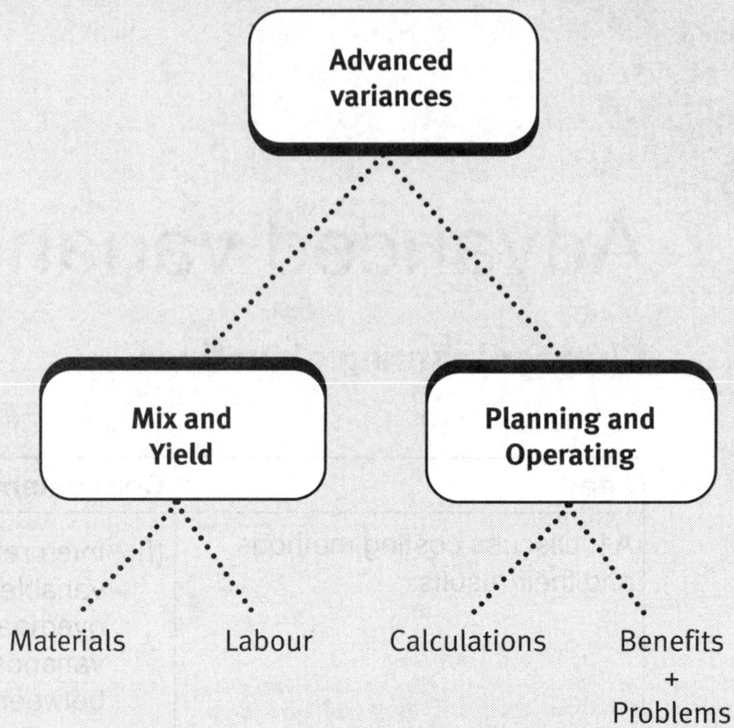

2 Advanced material variances - mix and yield

In many industries, particularly process industries, input consists of more than one type of material and it is possible to vary the mix. In many cases this would then affect the quantity of output produced. To analyse this the usage variance can be broken down into mix and yield variances.

Material mix variance

The material mix variance arises when the mix of materials used differs from the predetermined mix included in the calculation of the standard cost of an operation. If the mixture is varied so that a larger than expected proportion of a more *expensive* material is used there will be an *adverse* variance. When a larger than expected proportion of a *cheaper* material is included in the mix, then a *favourable* variance occurs.

Material yield variance

The material yield variance arises when there is a difference between the standard output for a given level of input and the actual output attained. A materials yield variance is similar to a materials usage variance. However, instead of calculating a usage variance for each material separately, a single yield variance is calculated for all the materials as a whole. The yield variance is calculated first of all in terms of units of material, and is converted into a money value at the weighted average standard price per unit of material.

Further details

The meaning of the mix variance

For materials and labour variances, a mix variance measures whether the actual mix that occurred was more or less expensive than the standard mix. For example, suppose that a product consists of two materials, X and Y, thestandard mix of the two items is 50:50, and material X is much more expensive than material Y.

- If the actual mix used to make the product contains more than 50% of X and less than 50% of Y, the actual mix will be more expensive than the standard mix, because it includes a bigger-than-standard proportion of the expensive material. The mix variance will be adverse.
- Similarly, if the actual mix used to make the product contains less than 50% of X and more than 50% of Y, the actual mix will be less expensive than the standard mix, and the mix variance will be favourable.

The meaning of the yield variance

When a mix variance is calculated, it is assumed that the mix of materials or labour can be controlled.

- The material usage should therefore be assessed for all the materials combined, not for each item of material separately.
- Similarly, the labour efficiency variance should be assessed for the labour team as a whole, not for each grade of labour separately.

A yield variance is therefore an overall usage variance or efficiency variance for all the items in the mix.

3 Calculating mix and yield variances

There are two different methods of calculating mix and yield variances mentioned in the syllabus - the individual units method and the weighted average method.

The individual units method is easier to calculate and understand (so you should use this in the exam if you have a choice), but the weighted average is technically superior.

Both methods produce exactly the same total figure for the mix variance.

Both methods compare the actual mix of materials with the standard mix.

- The actual mix = the actual quantities of materials used (for each material individually and in total).
- The standard mix = the actual total quantity of materials used, with the total divided between the individual materials in the standard proportions.
- The mix variance in units of material is the difference between the actual mix and the standard mix. A mix variance is calculated for each individual material in the mix.

Individual units method

Mix variance

(1) Write down the actual input. (This is the **actual mix**.)

(2) Take the actual input in total and push it down one line and then work it back in the standard proportions. (This is the **standard mix**.)

(3) Calculate the difference between the standard mix (line 2) and the actual mix (line 1). This is the mix variance in terms of physical quantities and must add up to zero in total. (If you use a higher than expected proportion of one material, you must use a lower than expected proportion of something else!)

(4) Multiply by the standard price per kg

(5) This gives the mix variance in financial terms.

	Material A	**Material B**		**Total**
	Kg	Kg		Kg
1 Actual input	X	X		XX
				⇓
2 Actual input in std proportions	X	X	⇐	XX
	—	—		—
3 Difference in quantity	X	X		
4 x Std Price	x X	x X		
5 Mix variance	X	X		X
	—	—		—

Yield variance

The yield variance only happens in total. CIMA and the examiner do not consider individual yield variances to be meaningful.

(1) Calculate the **standard yield**. This is the expected output from the actual input

(2) Compare this to **actual yield**.

(3) The difference is the yield variance in physical terms.

(4) To express the variance in financial terms we multiply by the standard cost. One thing to be careful of however is that the yield variance considers outputs and so the standard cost is the standard cost per kg **of output.**

(5) This gives the yield variance in financial terms.

		Kg
1	Standard yield of actual input	X
2	Actual yield	X
		—
3		X
4	x std cost per kg of output	x X
		—
		X
		—

Example 1

Leopard Airlines has estimated that on any flight, the free drinks consumed by passengers will be *(for every 10 passengers)*:

	Number of drinks	Cost per drink	Total cost $
Low cost	5	$0.25	1.25
Medium cost	8	$0.50	4.00
High cost	12	$1.00	12.00
	—		——
	25		17.25
	—		——

On a flight to Bermuda with 300 passengers on board, the actual number of free drinks consumed was as follows:

	Number of drinks
Low cost	215
Medium cost	280
High cost	355
	——
	850
	——

If the company calculates materials mix and yield variances for the cost of its free in-flight drinks, calculate the materials mix and yield variances for this flight.

Weighted average method

The individual units method is easier to understand, but is slightly flawed. The weighted average method is theoretically superior, is recommended by CIMA and is much more likely to be asked for by the examiner. The superiority of the weighted average method will be seen in the next question - Hordru.

The format is similar to that used for the individual units method, except that once the difference in quantity has been calculated, instead of multiplying by the individual material price, we multiply by the difference between the individual price and the weighted average price

Calculate the weighted average std cost of the materials. (This is needed for step 4). *You have to be very careful here. This weighted average is the weighted average cost per kg of input as we are just about to compare* ***inputs****.*

Yield variance

The yield variance is calculated in the same way under both methods. Again it only happens in total.

Using mix and yield variances

Mix variances might be calculated when there is a mix of two or more items, and the mix is regarded as **controllable** by management.

- Two or more materials might be used in making a product or providing a service. If standard costing is used and the mix of the materials is seen as controllable, a materials mix variance and a materials yield variance can be calculated. These provide a further analysis of the materials usage variance.
- Two or more different types of labour might be used to make a product or provide a service. If standard costing is used and the labour mix in the team is seen as controllable, a labour mix variance and a labour yield variance can be calculated. These provide a further analysis of the labour efficiency variance.

It is also possible to calculate a sales mix variance, when a business sells more than one product or service, but these variances are not included in the syllabus, and are not described here.

If the mix cannot be controlled, it is inappropriate to calculate a mix and yield variance. Instead, a usage variance should be calculated for each individual material or an efficiency variance should be calculated for each individual type or grade of labour. *In other words, if the mix cannot be controlled, the usage or efficiency variance should not be analysed into a mix and yield variance.*

4 Advanced labour variances - mix and yield

Labour mix variance

The labour mix variance arises when the mix of labour used differs from the predetermined mix included in the calculation of the standard cost of an operation. If the mixture is varied so that a larger than expected proportion of a higher grade of labour is used there will be an *adverse* variance. When a larger than expected proportion of a *lower grade of labour* is included in the mix, then a *favourable* variance occurs.

Labour yield variance

The labour yield variance arises when there is a difference between the standard output for a given level of input (measured in terms of hours) and the actual output attained.

Calculations

These are **calculated in exactly the same way as the material mix and yield variances** except that the situation will involve different grades of labour instead of different types of material.

Calculations

Individual units method

Mix variance

A labour mix variance is sometimes called a team composition variance. It measures whether the actual composition of the labour team was more or less expensive than the standard mix.

(1) Write down the actual hours. (This is the **actual mix**.)

(2) Take the actual hours in total and push it down one line and then work it back in the standard proportions. (This is the **standard mix**.)

(3) Calculate the difference between the standard mix (line 2) and the actual mix (line 1). This is the mix variance in terms of hours and must add up to zero in total. (If you use a higher proportion of one type of labour, you must use a lower proportion of another type!)

(4) Multiply by the standard rate per hour

(5) This gives the mix variance in financial terms.

	Skilled Labour	Unskilled Labour	Total
	Hrs	Hrs	Hrs
1 Actual hours	X	X	XX ⇓
2 Actual hours in std proportions	X	X	⇐ XX
	—	—	—
3 Difference in quantity	X	X	
4 x Std Rate	x X	x X	
5 Mix variance	X	X	X
	—	—	—

Yield variance

The yield variance only happens in total. CIMA and the examiner do not consider individual yield variances to be meaningful.

(1) Calculate the **standard yield**. This is the expected output from the actual input

(2) Compare this to **actual yield**.

(3) The difference is the yield variance in physical terms.

(4) To express the variance in financial terms we multiply by the standard cost. One thing to be careful of however is that the yield variance considers outputs and so the standard cost is the standard cost per kg **of output.**

(5) This gives the yield variance in financial terms.

		Kg
1	Standard yield of actual hours	X
2	Actual yield	X
		—
3		X
4	x std cost per kg of output	x X
		—
		X
		—

Weighted average method

The format is similar to that used for the individual units method, except that once the difference in quantity has been calculated, instead of multiplying by the individual labour rate, we multiply by the difference between the individual standard rate and the weighted average standard rate.

Calculate the weighted average standard cost of the labour. (This is needed for step 4). *You have to be very careful here. This weighted average is the weighted average cost per hour as we are just about to compare* ***inputs****.*

(1) Write down the actual hours. (This is the **actual mix**.)

(2) Take the actual hours in total and push it down one line and then work it back in the standard proportions. (This is the **standard mix**.)

(3) Calculate the difference between the standard mix (line 2) and the actual mix (line 1). This is the mix variance in terms of hours and must add up to zero in total. (If you use a higher proportion of one type of labour, you must use a lower proportion of another type!)

Remember what a mix variance means - using a higher proportion of an expensive grade of labour is adverse, but using a higher proportion of a cheap grade would actually be regarded as a good thing.

We have just found out for each grade of labour whether we have used a higher or lower proportion of that grade. In order to decide whether the variance is favourable or adverse we need to know whether that grade of labour is cheap or expensive. We determine this by comparing the individual labour rate with the weighted average rate.

(4) Determine for each grade of labour whether it is cheap or expensive compared to a weighted average price.

(5) Multiply the results from line 3 and line 4.

(6) This gives the mix variance in financial terms.

	Skilled Labour	Unskilled Labour	Total
	Hrs	*Hrs*	*Hrs*
1 Actual hours	X	X	XX ⇓
2 Actual hours in std proportions	X	X	⇐ XX
	—	—	—
3 Difference in quantity	X	X	
4 x Difference in rate (weighted average std rate - individual labour std rate)			
x (X - X)	x X		
x (X - X)		x X	
	—	—	—
5 Mix variance	X	X	X
	—	—	—

Yield variance

A labour yield variance is sometimes called a team productivity variance. It measures the efficiency of the team as a whole, rather than the efficiency of each grade of labour separately.

The yield variance is calculated in the same way under both methods. Again it only happens in total.

(1) Calculate the **standard yield**. This is the expected output from the actual input.

(2) Compare this to **actual yield**.

(3) The difference is the yield variance in physical terms.

(4) To express the variance in financial terms we multiply by the standard cost. One thing to be careful of however is that the yield variance considers outputs and so the standard cost is the standard cost per kg **of output.**

(5) This gives the yield variance in financial terms.

		Kg
1	Standard yield of actual hours	X
2	Actual yield	X
		—
3		X
4	x std cost per kg of output	x X
		—
		X
		—

Limitations of mix variances

Mix and yield variances can provide useful control information, but only where the mix of materials or labour is controllable, and where the information about total yield is more useful than usage/efficiency variances for the individual materials or labour grades separately.

Using mix variances also has some other limitations.

- It is often found that the mix and yield variances are interdependent, and one variance cannot be assessed without also considering the other. For example, the inefficiency of a team (adverse labour yield variance) could be explained by the fact that the team has a larger-than-expected proportion of inexperienced, cheaper employees (favourable labour mix variance).
- If management is able to achieve a cheaper mix of materials or labour, without affecting yield, the standard becomes obsolete. The cheaper mix should become the new standard mix.
- Control measures to improve the mix by making it cheaper are likely to affect the quality of the output or the work done. Analysing mix and yield variances for control purposes does not take quality issues into consideration.
- Mix and yield variances are based on standard prices for material and standard rates for labour. Actual prices/rates may differ from standard and this will be measured using the material price/labour rate variances. For an overall assessment of performance these will also have to be taken into consideration.

5 Planning and operational variances

Forecasts by their nature are unreliable, and yet most standards are set on a forecast basis, i.e. ***ex ante*** or before the event. A planning variance arises from an inability to make exact predictions of future costs and revenues at the budgeting stage.

If it were possible to set standards with the benefit of hindsight, i.e. ***ex post*** or after the event managers would be able to see more clearly what amount of variances was genuinely attributable to operating performance (***operational variances***) and what amount to difficulties or errors in setting the original standard (***planning variances***). Such information should improve operational control and may also provide guidance for the improvement of planning procedures.

The calculations

Planning variance	= Original standard	– Revised standard	**PRO**
Operational variance	= Revised standard	– Actual	**OAR**

The planning variance is usually regarded as uncontrollable and has arisen because the original standard was not reflective of the attainable standard. The operational variance is controllable.

Further explanation

Operational variances

Operational variances are variances that are assumed to have occurred due to operational factors. These are materials price and usage variances, labour rate and efficiency variances, variable overhead expenditure and efficiency variances, overhead expenditure variances, and sales variances.

Operational variances are calculated with the 'realistic' ex post standard. They are calculated in exactly the same way as described in earlier chapters, the only difference being that the ex post standard is used, not the original standard.

Planning variances

A planning variance measures the difference between the budgeted and actual profit that has been caused by errors in the original standard cost. It is the difference between the ex ante and the ex post standards.

- A planning variance is **favourable** when the ex post standard cost is lower than the original ex ante standard cost.
- A planning variance is **adverse** when the ex post standard cost is higher than the original ex ante standard cost.

Example 2

The following data concerns Material X

Original standard price $2 per kg	Revised standard price $3.50 per kg
Standard usage 1,000 kg	
Actual price $3 per kg	Actual usage 1,200 kg

Required:

Calculate material price and usage variances using a planning and operational approach.

6 Causes of planning variances

There must be a good reason for deciding that the original standard cost is unrealistic. Deciding in retrospect that expected costs should be different from the standard should not be an arbitrary decision, aimed perhaps at shifting the blame for poor results from poor operational management to poor cost estimation.

A good reason for a change in the standard might be:

- a change in one of the main materials used to make a product or provide a service
- an unexpected increase in the price of materials due to a rapid increase in world market prices (for example, the price of oil or other commodities)
- a change in working methods and procedures that alters the expected direct labour time for a product or service
- an unexpected change in the rate of pay to the work force.

7 More than one planning error

A situation might occur where the difference between the standards is in two (or more) items.

In these circumstances, the rules for calculating planning and operational variances are as follows:

- Operational variances are calculated using the ex post standard.
- The planning variance is the difference between the ex ante and the ex post standard cost per unit, multiplied by the number of units.
- It might be possible to analyse the planning variance into the amount of planning variance caused by each of the differences between the ex post and ex ante standard.

8 Benefits and problems

Benefits of Planning and Operational Variances

(1) In volatile and changing environments, standard costing and variance analysis are more useful using this approach.

(2) Operational variances provide up to date information about current levels of efficiency.

(3) Operational variances are likely to make the standard costing system more acceptable and to have a positive effect on motivation.

(4) It emphasises the importance of the planning function in the preparation of standards and helps to identify planning deficiencies.

Problems of Planning and Operational Variances

(1) There is an element of subjectivity in determining the ex-post standards as to what is 'realistic'.

(2) There is a large amount of labour time involved in continually establishing up to date standards and calculating additional variances.

(3) There is a great temptation to put as much as possible of the total variances down to outside, uncontrollable factors, i.e. planning variances.

(4) There can then be a conflict between operating and planning staff. Each laying the blame at each other's door.

9 Chapter summary

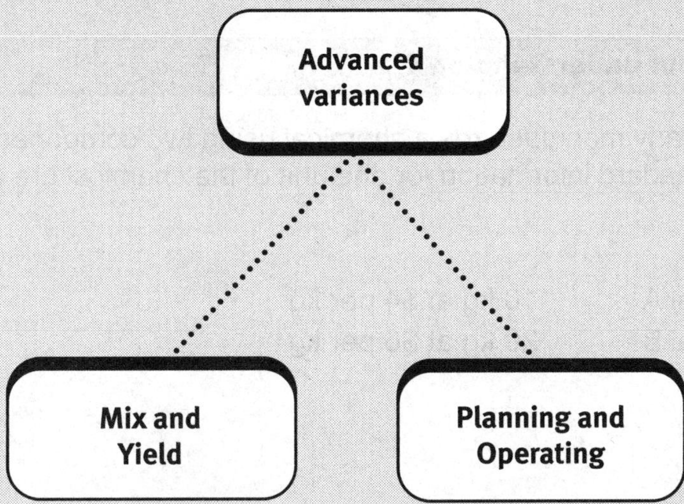

Mix and Yield

- Mix is adverse if we use more of the expensive material/ labour
- Yield is adverse if we use more materials/ labour overall

Planning and Operating

- Planning variance = original standard – revised standard
- Operational variance = revised standard – actual results

10 Practice questions

Test your understanding 1

A company manufactures a chemical using two components, A and B. The standard information for one unit of the chemical are as follows:

		$
Material A	10 kg at $4 per kg	40
Material B	20 kg at $6 per kg	120
		160

In a particular period, 160 units of the chemical were produced, using 1,000 kgs of material A and 1,460 kgs of material B.

Required:

Calculate the material usage, mix and yield variances for each material.

Test your understanding 2 - HORDRU LTD

Hordru Ltd operates a standard costing system.

The standard direct material mix to produce 1,000 kilos of output is as follows:

Material grade	Input quantity (kilos)	Standard price per kilo input $
A	600	1.10
B	240	2.40
C	360	1.50

During April the actual output of the product was 21,000 kilos.

The actual materials issued to production were:

Material grade	Quantity (kilos)
	(kilos)
A	14,000
B	5,500
C	5,500

Required:

(a) Calculate material mix variances for each material grade and in total, and the material yield variance in total where individual material prices per kilo are used as the variance valuation base.

(6 marks)

(b) Calcualte the same range of variances as in (a) above but using the budgeted weighted average material price per kilo as the valuation base.

(7 marks)

(Total: 13 marks)

Test your understanding 3 - BUZZ LIGHTYEAR LTD

Buzz Lightyear Ltd makes a single product, of which the standard labour input per unit is:

Skilled labour	6 hrs @ $12/hr
Unskilled labour	4 hrs @ $7/hr

During Period 1:
1,000 units were produced

5,250 hours of skilled labour were used and

5,250 hours of unskilled labour were used

Calculate the labour mix variances for each grade of labour and the labour yield variance in total.

Use both the weighted average method and the individual units method.

Test your understanding 4

Pan-Ocean Chemicals has one product, which requires inputs from three types of material to produce batches of Synthon. Standard cost details for a single batch are shown below:

Material type	Standard quantity (kgs)	Standard price per kg ($)
S1	8	0.30
S2	5	0.50
S3	3	0.40

A standard loss of 10% of input is expected. Actual output was 15,408 kgs for the previous week. Details of the material used were:

Material type	Quantity (kgs)
S1	8,284
S2	7,535
S3	3,334

Required:

Calculate the individual material mix and yield and the total usage variance.

Test your understanding 5

The following data relates to Skilled Labour Grade ST1

Standard labour hours per unit	5 hours
Standard labour rate	$10 per hour
Actual production	250 units
Actual labour hours	1,450 hours
Actual labour cost	$13,050

During the month there was an unforeseen shortage of the Skilled Labour Grade ST1. Semi skilled workers (Grade ST2) were hired. As a consequence of this, the standard time was revised to 6 hours per unit.

Required:

Calculate labour rate and efficiency variances using a planning and operational approach.

Test your understanding 6

Holmes Ltd uses one raw material for one of their products. The standard cost per unit at the beginning of the year was $28, made up as follows:

Standard material cost per unit = 7 kg per unit at $4 per kg = $28.

In the middle of the year the supplier had changed the specification of the material slightly due to problems experienced in the country of origin, so that the standard had to be revised as follows:

Standard material cost per unit = 8 kg per unit at $3.80 per kg = $30.40.

The actual output for November was 1,400 units. 11,000 kg of material was purchased and used at a cost of $41,500.

Calculate

(a) material price and usage variances using the traditional method

(b) all planning and operational material variances.

Test your understanding 7 - ATS LTD

The expected contribution per unit of the product manufactured by ATS Ltd is $26, ascertained as below:

		$	$
Selling price			110
Material	8 kg x $3/kg	24	
Labour	6 hours x $10/hour	60	
		—	
			84
			—
Contribution/unit			26
			═

The expected contribution was $31,200. The actual contribution was $38,800 as shown below:

		$	$
Actual sales revenue	1,000 units @ $135		135,000
Actual material cost	7,800 kg x $4/kg	31,200	
Actual labour cost	6,250 hours x $10.40/hour	65,000	
			96,200
Actual contribution			38,800

The Sales Director made the policy decision to sell at $5 above the prevailing market price of $125, suggesting that if they did suffer a decrease in volume, ATS Ltd would still be better off. It was also accepted that an efficient purchasing officer could have purchased at around $4.50 per kg.

There was no stock movement of either materials or finished goods in the period.

Required:

Prepare a variance statement which would be most helpful to the management of ATS Ltd, which clearly takes planning and operational variances into consideration.

Test your understanding 8

POV Ltd uses a standard costing system to control and report upon the production of its single product.

An abstract from the original standard cost card of the product is as follows:

	$	$
Selling price per unit		200
Less: 4 kgs materials @ $20 per kg	80	
6 hours labour @ $7 per hour	42	
		122
Contribution per unit		78

For period 3, 2,500 units were budgeted to be produced and sold but the actual production and sales were 2,850 units.

The following information was also available:

(1) At the commencement of period 3 the normal material became unobtainable and it was necessary to use an alternative. Unfortunately, 0.5 kg per unit extra was required and it was thought that the material would be more difficult to work with. The price of the alternative was expected to be $16.50 per kg In the event, actual usage was 12,450 kg at $18 per kg

(2) Weather conditions unexpectedly improved for the period with the result that a 50c per hour bad weather bonus, which had been allowed for in the original standard, did not have to be paid. Because of the difficulties expected with the alternative material, management agreed to pay the workers $8 per hour for period 3 only. During the period 18,800 hours were paid for.

After using conventional variances for some time, POV Ltd is contemplating extending its system to include planning and operational variances.

(a) Prepare a statement reconciling budgeted contribution for the period with actual contribution, using conventional material and labour variances.

(b) Prepare a similar reconciliation statement using planning and operational variances.

(c) Explain the meaning of the variances shown in statement (b).

Test your understanding 9

A company budgeted to make and sell 2,000 units of its only product, for which the standard marginal cost is:

		$
Direct materials	4 kilos at $2 per kilo	8
Direct labour	3 hours at $6 pr hour	18
		26

The standard sales price is $50 per unit and the standard contribution $24 per unit. Budgeted fixed costs were $30,000, giving a budgeted profit of $18,000.

Due to severe material shortages, the company had to switch to a less efficient and more expensive material, and it was decided in retrospect that the realistic (ex post) standard direct material cost should have been 5 kilos at $3 per kilo = $15 per unit.

Actual results were as follows:

Actual production and sales: 2,400 units

		$	$
Sales revenue			115,000
Direct materials	12,300 kilos at $3 per kilo	36,900	
Direct labour	7,500 hours at $6.10 per hour	45,750	
Total variable costs			82,650
Actual contribution			32.350
Actual fixed costs			32,000
Actual profit			350

Required:

Prepare an operating statement with planning and operational variances that reconciles the budgeted and actual profit figures.

Test your understanding 10

It might be argued that only operational variances have significance for performance measurement. Planning variances cannot be controlled and so have little or no value for performance reporting.

Required:

State briefly, with your reason(s), whether you agree with this point of view.

Test your understanding 11 - FB

FB makes and sells a single product. The standard cost and revenue per unit are as follows:

		$
Selling price		400
Direct material A	5 kg at $25 per kg	125
Direct material B	3 kg at $22 per kg	66
Direct labour	3 hours at $10 per hour	30
Variable overheads	3 hours at $7 per hour	21
Standard contribution		158

The budgeted production and sales for the period in question were 10,000 units.

The mix of materials can be varied and therefore the material usage variance can be sub-divided into mix and yield variances.

For the period under review, the actual results were as follows:

Production and sales		9,000 units
		$
Sales revenue		4,455,000
Material cost	A - 35,000 kg	910,000
	B - 50,000 kg	1,050,000
Labour cost	30,000 hours	385,000
Variable overhead		230,000

The general market prices at the time of purchase for material A and material B were $21 per kg and $19 per kg respectively.

There were no opening or closing inventories during the period.

Required:

(a) Prepare a statement detailing the variances (including planning and operational, and mix and yield variances) which reconciles the budgeted contribution and the actual contribution.

(22 marks)

(b) Explain the results and usefulness to FB of the planning and operational, and mix and yield variances that you have calculated in your answer to part (a).

(8 marks)

(Total: 30 marks)

Test your understanding 12

Product XYZ is made by mixing three materials (X, Y and Z). There is an expected loss of 20% of the total input.

The budgeted and actual results for Period 1 are shown below. There were no opening or closing inventories of any materials or of the finished product.

	Budget		Actual	
Output of XYZ	**800 kg**		**960 kg**	
Material				
X		500 kg @ $5.00 per kg		600 kg @ $4.70 per kg
Y		300 kg @ $6.00 per kg		380 kg @ $6.50 per kg
Z		200 kg @ $7.00 per kg		300 kg @ $7.10 per kg
Total input	**1,000 kg**		**1,280 kg**	

Calculate for Period 1:

(i) the total materials mix variance;

(2 marks)

(ii) the total materials yield variance

(2 marks)

Test your understanding answers

Example 1

Average number of drinks per passenger = 25 / 10 = 2.5

Weighted standard average cost per drink = £17.25 / 25 = $0.69

	Drinks	
300 passengers should consume (x 2.5 drinks)	750	
They did consume	850	
Yield variance in number of drinks	100	(A)
x weighted standard average cost per drink	$0.69	
Yield variance	$69	(A)

	Actual usage		Standard mix	Mix variance	Standard cost per drink	Mix variance	
	Drinks		Drinks	Drinks		$	
Low cost	215	(5)	170	45 (A)	$0.25	11.25	(A)
Medium cost	280	(8)	272	8 (A)	$0.50	4.00	(A)
High cost	355	(12)	408	53 (F)	$1.00	53.00	(F)
	850		850			**37.75**	**(F)**

Example 2

Traditional approach

			$	
SQSP				
1,000 kg x	$2/kg	=	2,000	Usage $400 A
AQSP				
1,200 kg x	$2/kg	=	2,400	
AQAP				$1,200 A Price
1,200 kg x	$3/kg	=	3,600	

Planning and operational approach

Planning variance

Price	($2 - $3.50) x 1000 kg	$1,500 A

Operational variances

SQSP				
1,000 kg x	$3.50/kg	=	3,500	Usage $700 A
AQSP				
1,200 kg x	$3.50/kg	=	4,200	
AQAP				$600 F Price
1,200 kg x	$3/kg	=	3,600	

Test your understanding 1

Material A usage variance

AQ SP = 1,000 × $4 = $4,000

Variance = $2,400 F

SQ SP = (160 units × 10kg/unit) × $4 = $6,400

Material B usage variance

AQ SP = 1,460 × $6 = $8,760

Variance = $10,440 F

SQ SP = (160 units × 20kg/unit) × $6 = $19,200

Total usage variance = $2,400 + $10,440 = $12,840

Material mix variance

Material	Std mix	Actual material usage (kgs)	Actual usage @ std mix (kgs)	Mix variance (kgs)	Std cost per kg ($)	Mix variance ($)
A	10/30	1,000	820	180 A	4	720 A
B	20/30	1,460	1,640	180 F	6	1,080 F
		2,460	2,460	0	-	360 F

Material yield variance

Material	Std usage for actual output (kgs)	Actual usage @ std mix (kgs)	Yield variance (kgs)	Std cost per kg ($)	Yield variance ($)
A	160 × 10kg = 1,600	820	780 F	4	3,120 F
B	160 × 20kg = 3,200	1,640	1,560 F	6	9,360 F
	4,800	2,460	2,340 F	-	12,480 F

Alternatively, the material yield variance can be calculated in total using the following method:

(1) Total input = 1,000 kgs + 1,460 kgs = 2,460 kgs.	
This should produce (÷ 30 kgs)	82 units of output
(2) 2,460 kgs did produce	160 units of output
(3) Difference = yield variance in units	78 units F
(4) Value at the standard cost of	$160 per unit
(5) Yield variance	$12,480 F

Total mix and yield variance = $12,480 F + $360 F = $12,840 F (as per the usage variance)

Test your understanding 2 - HORDRU LTD

(a) **Mix variance**

		Material A	Material B	Material C	Total
		Kg	Kg	Kg	Kg
1	Actual input	14,000	5,500	5,500	25,000
2	Actual input in std proportions				⇓
	50%:20%:30%	12,500	5,000	7,500	⇐ 5,000
3	Difference in quantity	1,500 A	500 A	2,000 F	
4	x Std Price	x 1.10	x 2.40	x 1.50	
5	Mix variance	$1,650 A	$1,200 A	$3,000F	$150 F

Yield variance

$$\text{Std cost per kg of output} = \frac{600 \times 1.10 + 240 + 2.40 + 360 + 1.50}{1{,}000 \text{ kg}} = \$1.776/\text{kg}$$

		Kg
1	Std yield	
	$25{,}000 \times \frac{1{,}000}{1{,}200}$	20,833.33
2	Actual yield	21,000
3		166.67 F
4	x Std price/cost per kg of output	x 1.776
	Yield variance	296 F

(b)

$$\text{Weighted average std cost} = \frac{600 \times 1.10 + 240 + 2.40 + 360 + 1.50}{1{,}200\text{ kg}} = \$1.48/\text{kg}$$

Mix variance

		Material A	Material B	Material C	Total
		Kg	Kg	Kg	Kg
1	Actual input	14,000	5,500	5,500	25,000
2	Actual input in std proportions				⇓
	50%:20%:30%	12,500	5,000	7,500	⇐25,000
3	Difference in quantity	1,500	500	– 2,000	
4	x Difference in price (weighted av. std price - Ind. material std price)				
	x (1.48 – 1.10)	x 0.38			
	x (1.48 – 2.40)		x – 0.92		
	x (1.48 – 1.50)			– 0.02	
5	Mix variance	$570 F	$460 A	$40 F	$150 F

Yield variance

This is calculated in exactly the same way under both methods.

$$\text{Std cost per kg of output} = \frac{600 \times 1.10 + 240 + 2.40 + 360 + 1.50}{1{,}000\text{ kg}} = \$1.776/\text{kg}$$

		Kg
1	Std yield	
	25,000 x $\frac{1,000}{1,200}$	20,833.33
2	Actual yield	21,000
3		166.67 F
4	x Std price/cost per kg of output	x 1.776
	Yield variance	296 F

Test your understanding 3 - BUZZ LIGHTYEAR LTD

Individual units method

Mix variance

		Skilled Labour	**Unskilled Labour**	**Total**
		Hrs	*Hrs*	*Hrs*
1	Actual input	5,250	5,250	10,500
2	Actual input in std proportions			⇓
	6:4	6,300	4,200 ←	10,500
3	Difference in quantity	1,050 F	1,050 A	
4	x Std Price	x 12	x 7	
5	Mix variance	$12,600 F	$7,350 A	$5,250F

Yield variance

$$\text{Std cost per unit of output} = \frac{6 \times \$12 + 4 \times \$7}{1 \text{ unit}} = \$100 \text{ per unit}$$

		Hrs
1	Std yield	
	10,500 hours $\frac{1 \text{ unit}}{10 \text{ hours}}$	1,050
2	Actual yield	1,000
3		50 A
4	x Std price/cost per kg of output	x 100
	Yield variance	$5,000 A

Weighted average method

$$\text{Weighted average std rate} = \frac{6 \times \$12 + 4 \times \$7}{6 \text{ hours} + 4 \text{ hours}} = \$10 \text{ per hour}$$

Mix variance

		Skilled Labour	Unskilled Labour	Total
		Hrs	*Hrs*	*Hrs*
1	Actual input	5,250	5,250	10,500
2	Actual input in std proportions			⇓
	6:4	6,300	4,200	⇐10,500
3	Difference in hours	-1,050	1,050	
4	x Difference in rate (weighted average std rate - individual labour std rate)			
	x (10 - 12)	x -2		
	x (10 - 7)		x 3	
5	Mix variance	$570 F	$3,150 F	$5,250 F

Yield variance

$$\text{Std cost per unit of output} = \frac{6 \times \$12 + 4 \times \$7}{1 \text{ unit}} = \$100 \text{ per unit}$$

		Hrs
1	Std yield	
	$10{,}500 \text{ hours} \times \dfrac{1 \text{ unit}}{10 \text{ hours}}$	1,050
2	Actual yield	1,000
3		50 A
4	x Std price/cost per kg of output	x 100
	Yield variance	$5,000 A

Test your understanding 4

Material mix variance

The material mix variance is not affected by the material wastage and should be calculated in the normal way:

Material	Std mix	Actual material usage (kgs)	Actual usage @ std mix (kgs)	Mix variance (kgs)	Std cost per kg ($)	Mix variance ($)
S1	8/16	8,284	9,576.5	1,292.5 F	0.30	387.75 F
S2	5/16	7,535	5,985.3	1,549.7 A	0.50	774.85 A
S3	3/16	3,334	3,591.2	257.2 F	0.40	102.88 F
		19,153	19,153	0	-	284.22 A

Material yield variance

The yield variance will take account of the material wastage of 10%:

Material	Std usage for actual output (kgs)	Actual usage @ std mix (kgs)	Yield variance (kgs)	Std cost per kg ($)	Yield variance ($)
S1	8/16 = 8,560	9,576.5	1,016.5 A	0.30	304.95 A
S2	5/16 = 5,350	5,985.3	635.3 A	0.50	317.65 A
S3	3/16 = 3,210	3,591.2	381.2 A	0.40	152.48 A
	15,408 × 100/90 = 17,120	19,153	2,033 A	-	775. 08 A

Material usage variance

Total = $775.08 A + $284.22 A = $1,059.3 A

Test your understanding 5

Conventional approach

				$	
SHSR 5 hrs/unit x 250 units	x	$10/hr	=	12,500	Efficiency $2,000 A
AHSR 1,450 hrs	x	$10/hr	=	14,500	
AHAR			=	13,050	$1,450 F Rate

Planning and operational approach

Planning variance

Efficiency (5 hrs/unit – 6 hrs/unit) x 250 units x $10/hr $2,500 A

Operational variances

				$	
SHSR 6 hrs/unit x 250 units	x	$10/hr	=	15,000	Efficiency $500 F
AHSR 1,450 hrs	x	$10/hr	=	14,500	
AHAR			=	13,050	$1,450 F Rate

Test your understanding 6

(a) **Traditional variances**

AQAP =		$41,500	
		Price variance	$2,500 F
AQSP =	11,000 × $4 =	$44,000	
		Usage variance	$4,800 A
SQSP =	1400 × 7 × $4 =	$39,200	

(b) **Planning variances**

RSQ × RSP =	1,400 × 8 × $3.80=	$42,560	
		Price variance	$2,240 F
RSQ × SP =	1,400 × 8 × $4 =	$44,800	
		Usage variance	$5,600 A
SQ × SP =	1,400 × 7 × $4 =	$39,200	

(c) **Operational variances**

AQ × AP =		$41,500	$300 F
		Price variance	
AQ × RSP =	11,000 × $3.80 =	$41,800	
		Usage variance	$760 F
RSQ × RSP =	1,400 × 8 × $3.80=	$42,560	

Test your understanding 7 - ATS LTD

Revised standards

		$	$
Selling price			130
Direct Material	8 kg x $4.50 per kg	36	
Direct Labour	6 hours x $10 per hr	60	
			96
Contribution per unit			34

Operating Statement for ATS Ltd

		$	$
Original budgeted contribution	1,200 x $26		31,200
Planning variances			
Sales price	($110 – $130) x 1,200	24,000 F	
Material price	($3 – $4.50) x 8 x 1,200	14,400 A	
			9,600 F
Revised contribution	($34 x 1,200)		40,800

Operational variances

Sales volume	(1,200 – 1,000) x $34	6,800 A	
Sales price	($130 – $135) x 1,000	5,000 F	
Material price	($4.50 – $4) x 7,800	3,900 F	
Material usage	(8,000 – 7,800) x $4.50	900 F	
Labour rate	($10 – $10.40) x 6,250	2,500 A	
Labour efficiency	(6,000 – 6,250) x $10	2,500 A	
			2,000 A
Actual contribution			38,800

Test your understanding 8

(a) Reconciliation of budgeted and actual contribution using conventional variances

				$
Budgeted contribution:		2,500 × $78		195,000
Variances:		**Favourable**	**Adverse**	
		$	$	
Sales volume		27,300		
Direct material	– Price	24,900		
	– Usage		21,000	
Direct labour	– Rate		18,800	
	– Efficiency		11,900	
		52,200	51,700	
				500
Actual contribution				195,500

Assumption: No sales price variance.

Workings

Conventional variances

(i) **Materials**

Price = (Actual material purchased × standard price) — (Actual cost of material purchased)

= (12,450 × $20) – (12,450 × $18)

= $249,000 – $224,100

= $24,900 F

Usage = (Standard quantity for actual production × standard price)— (Actual material used at standard price)

= (2,850 × 4 0215 $20) – (12,450 × $20)

= $228,000 – $249,000

= $21,000 A

(ii) **Labour**

Rate = (Actual hours worked × standard direct labour rate) – (Actual hours worked × actual hourly rate)

= (18,800 × $7) – (18,800 × $8)

= $131,600 – $150,400

= $18,800 A

Efficiency = (Standard hours of actual production × standard rate) – (Actual hours worked × standard rate)

= (2,850 × 6 × $7) – (18,800 × $7)

= $119,700 – $131,600

= $11,900 A

Sales volume

Contribution = (Budgeted sales units × standard contribution per unit) – (Actual sales units × standard contribution per unit)

= (2,500 × $78) – (2,850 × $78)

= $195,000 – $222,300

= $27,300 F

(b) Reconciliation statement using planning and operational variances

			$
Budgeted contribution			
for actual sales:	2,850 × $78	222,300.00	
Planning variances:	**Favourable**	**Adverse**	
	$	$	
Material – Price	44,887.50		
– Usage		28,500	
Labour – Rate: weather	8,550.00		
– Rate: material		25,650	
	53,437.50	54,150	
			(712.50)
Revised budgeted contribution ($77.75 × 2,850)			221,587.50
Operational variances:	**Favourable**	**Adverse**	
	$	$	
Material – Price		18,675.00	
– Usage	6,187.50		
Labour – Rate	0		
– Efficiency		13,600.00	
	6,187.50	32,275.00	
			26,087.50
Actual contribution			195,500.00

Workings

Planning variances

(i) **Material**

= (Standard material cost) – (Revised standard material cost)

Price = (2,850 × (4 + 0.5) × \$20) – (2,850 × (4 + 0.5) × \$16.50)

= \$256,500 – \$211,612.50

= \$44,887.50 F

Usage = (2,850 × 4 × \$20) – (2,850 × 4.5 × \$20)

= \$228,000 – \$256,500

= \$28,500 A

(ii) **Labour rate**

(1) Weather bonus

= (2,850 × 6 × \$7) – (2,850 × 6 × \$6.50)

= \$119,700 – \$111,150

= \$8,550 (F)

(2) Alternative material difficulties

= (2,850 × 6 × \$6.50) – (2,850 × 6 × \$8)

= \$111,150 – \$136,800

= \$25,650 A

Therfore, revised unit contribution is as follows.

		$	$
Selling price			200.00
Direct material:	4.5 × $16.50	74.25	
Direct labour:	6 × $8	48.00	
			(122.25)
Contribution			77.75

Operational variances

(i) **Material**

Price = (12,450 × $16.50) – (12,450 × $18)

= $205,425 – $224,100

= $18,675 A

Usage = (2,850 × 4.50 × $16.50) – (12,450 × $16.50)

= $211,612.5 – $205,425

= $6,187.5 F

(ii) **Labour**

Rate = 0

Efficiency = (2,850 × 6 × $8) – (18,800 × $8)

= $136,800 – $150,400

= $13,600 A

(c) The analysis of variances in part (b) makes it possible to separate those variances which are non-controllable (the planning variances) from the variances which are controllable by the individual managers (the operational variances).

In this case the change in type of material used was unavoidable. Similarly, the change in weather conditions could not have been anticipated. The cost implications of these changes are reflected in the planning variances. Management's attention should be focused primarily on the operational variances.

In particular, why did the firm pay $18 per kg for material when this was expected to cost $16.50?

The operational material usage variance indicates that less material was used than expected – this could be due to the workers spending longer working with the material (as evidenced by the adverse efficiency variance.

Test your understanding 9

Operational variances

	$	
12,300 kilos should cost (× $3)	36,900	
They did cost	36,900	
Direct materials price variance	0	
	Kilos	
2,400 units of product should use (× 5 kilos)	12,000	
They did use	12,300	
Direct materials usage variance (in kilos)	300	(A)
Standard price per kilo (ex post)	$3	
Direct materials usage variance	$900	
	$	
7,500 hours should cost (× $6)	45,000	
They did cost	45,750	
Direct labour rate variance	750	(A)
	Hours	
2,400 units of product should take (× 3 hours)	7,200	
They did take	7,500	
Direct labour efficiency variance (in hours)	300	(A)
Standard rate per hour	$6	
Direct labour efficiency variance	$1,800	(A)
	$	
2,400 units should sell for (× $50)	120,000	
They did sell for	115,000	
Sales price variance	5,000	(A)
	$	
Budgeted fixed costs	30,000	
Actual fixed costs	32,000	
Fixed cost expenditure variance	2,000	(A)

	Units	
Budgeted sales	2,000	
Actual sales	2,400	
Sales volume variance (in units)	400	(F)
Ex post standard contribution per unit	$17	
Sales volume contribution variance	$6,800	

Planning variances

Material costs	*$ / unit*	
Ex ante standard per unit (4 kilos × $2)	8.0	
Ex post standard per unit (5 kilos × $3)	15.0	
Planning variance per unit	7.0	(A)
Units produced	x 2,000	
Total planning variance	$14,000	(A)

The planning variance is due to changes in the standard for both the material usage per unit of product and the material price per kilo. This could be analysed as follows:

Planning variance due to:	$	
Change in material usage:		
1 kilo per unit × $2 per kilo × 2,000 units	4,000	(A)
Change in material price:		
$1 per kilo × 4 kilos per unit × 2,000 units	8,000	(A)
Composite variance:		
$1 per kilo × 1 kilo per unit × 2,000 units	2,000	(A)
Total planning variance	$14,000	(A)

In this example, since the change in both the material usage and material price are inter-related, the total planning variance only is reported in the operating statement below.

	$
Budgeted profit	18,000
Budgeted fixed costs	30,000
Budgeted contribution	48,000
Sales volume contribution variance	6,800 (F)
	54,800
Planning variance	14,000 (A)
	40,800
Operational variances	
Sales price	5,000 (A)
Materials usage	900 (A)
Direct labour rate	750 (A)
Direct labour efficiency	1,800 (A)
Actual contribution	32,350
Budgeted fixed costs	30,000
Fixed cost expenditure variance	2,000 (A)
Actual profit	350

Test your understanding 10

A performance reporting and management control system depends on both reliable planning as well as control over operating activities.

Some planning variances might be caused by factors that could not have been foreseen in advance. However, some planning variances might be caused by weaknesses in the planning process. If so, they can be significant and indicate the need for better planning procedures in the future.

Test your understanding 11 - FB

Key answer tips

The planning variances may be based upon budget or actual level of activity, depending upon at what point the sales volume variance was calculated. If the first calculation is sales volume variance, then ALL variances AFTER this should be based upon the actual output of 9,000 units. However, if the first calculations are the planning variances, these would be based upon the budget volume of 10,000 units. Full marks should be obtained using either approach.

The mix variance may be calculated using either the individual units method or the weighted average price method. The total result, which is the important figure in this question, will be the same.

(a)

	$000	$000
Original budgeted contribution (10,000 × $158)		1,580
Planning variances		
Material A price ($25 - $21) × 5 kg × 10,000	200 F	
Material B price ($22 - $19) × 3 kg × 10,000	90 F	
	—	
		290 F
		—
Revised budgeted contribution (10,000 × $187) (W1)		1,870

Operational variances

Sales volume (contribution) (10,000 - 9,000) × $187	187 A	
Selling price ($400 - $495) × 9,000	855 F	
Material A price (35,000 × $21) - $910,000	175 A	
Material B price (50,000 × $19) - $1,050,000	100 A	
Mix variance (W2)	36.25 F	
Yield variance (W3)	263.25 A	
Direct labour rate (30,000 hr × $10) - $385,000	85 A	
Direct labour efficiency (9,000 × 3 - 30,000) × $10	30 A	
Variable overhead expenditure (30,000 hr × $7) - $230,000	20 A	
Variable overhead efficiency (9,000 × 3 - 30,000) × $7	21 A	
	—	
Total operational variances		10 A
		1,880

The above variances can also be calculated as follows:

Material A variance

					$	
AQSP						
	35,000 kg	×	$21 / kg	=	735,000	$175,000 A Price
AQAP				=	910,000	

Material B variance

					$	
AQSP						
	50,000kg	×	$19 / kg	=	950,000	$100,000 A Price
AQAP				=	1,050,000	

Labour variances

					$	
SHSR						
	3 hrs / unit × 9,000 units	×	$10 / hr	=	270,000	Efficiency $30,000 A
AHSR						
	30,000 hrs	×	$10 / hr	=	300,000	
AHAR						$85,000 A Rate
				=	385,000	

Variable overhead variances

					$	
SHSR						
	3 hrs / unit × 9,000 units	×	$7 / hr	=	189,000	Efficiency $21,000 A
AHSR						
	30,000 hrs	×	$7 / hr	=	210,000	
AHAR						$20,000 A Rate
				=	230,000	

Sales price variance

	$
Std selling price	400
Actual selling price $4,455,000/9,000 units	495
	95 F
× Actual no of units sold	× 9,000
	$855,000 F

Sales volume contribution variance

	Units
Budgeted sales	10,000
Actual sales	9,000
	1,000A
× Std contribution per unit	× 187
	$187,000 A

Workings

(W1) Revised contribution per unit

	$
Selling price	400
Material A 5 kg × $21	(105)
Material B 3 kg × $19	(57)
Direct labour 3 hr × $10	(30)
Variable overhead 3 hr × $7	(21)
Contribution	187

(W2) Mix variance

Note: A method is not specified. Use individual units method if given a choice as it is quicker and easier than the weighted average price method.

Material	**Standard mix**	**Actual mix**	**Difference**	**@ Standard price**	**Variance**
	000s	000s	000s		$000
A	53.125	35	18.125 F	$21	380.625 F
	31.875	50	18.125 A	$19	344.375 A
B	85	85	Nil		36.25 F

Standard mix of A : B is 5 kg : 3 kg

Hence, standard mix of actual input is:

$$A = 85 \times \frac{5}{8} = 53.125$$

$$A = 85 \times \frac{3}{8} = 31.875$$

(W3) Yield variance

Standard yield from actual input 85,000 kg ÷ 8 kg pu	10,625	units
Actual yield (output)	9,000	units
	1,625	units
@ Average price per unit of **output** (5 kg × $21) + (3 kg × $19)	$162	
Variance	$263,250	A

(W4)

	$000
Sales revenue	4,455
Less: Material A	(910)
Material B	(1,050)
Labour cost	(385)
Variable overhead	(230)
	1,880

(b) **Planning and operational variances**

The actual contribution is $300,000 higher than budget, despite sales volume falling from 10,000 units to 9,000 units. At first this appears to be an extraordinarily strong result. However, by calculating planning variances a new perspective emerges.

Both materials A and B were originally budgeted at prices that were quite substantially higher than the general market prices that emerged during the period. Material A could be bought at $4 less per kg than originally planned. This reduction in general market price immediately leads to a saving of $200,000 on the original budgeted cost. This is a significant saving. Similarly, material B's reduction in market price lead to a saving in the budget of $90,000. Planning variances indicate this large uncontrollable saving experienced by FB.

Once the budget is amended to reflect the new standard costs of the materials, actual results can be compared to the new budget. This exercise involves calculating operational variances. The operational variances for FB are quite revealing. There was a selling price variance of $855,000 favourable. However, virtually all the other variances were adverse. This would seem to indicate that FB did not perform particularly well in the latest period.

Planning and operational variances are useful for several reasons:

(1) They permit actual results to be compared to realistic up-to-date standards.

(2) The system is likely to provide more useful information for management.

(3) Operational staff may be more motivated by the feedback information, as their performance is judged against realistic standards.

(4) The importance of the planning function is emphasised – poor forecasting may be highlighted.

Mix and yield variances

The mix variance was $36,250 favourable. This was due to a far smaller proportion of the more expensive material A being used than was standard. The standard stated that 62.5% of material input should be material A. During the period, however, only 41% of input was material A. This is a significant difference. In each case the balance of material was material B (cheaper than A).

It is possible for FB to vary the input mix of raw materials. As this is the case, it would seem to be a useful exercise to examine how a deviation of the actual material mix from the expected mix has had an impact on costs.

Perhaps because of this mix variance there has been a massive drop in expected output. 85,000 kg of input should have produced 10,625 units of output. During the period only 9,000 units of output were produced. This is 15% below expectations. This has given rise to an adverse variance of $263,250 adverse. FB should investigate this significant variance and discover whether this variance was partly caused by the unusual mix in the period. It is probably important that FB correct the problems behind the yield variance and avoid it recurring in the future.

Test your understanding 12

Mix and yield variances

Actual output was 960; therefore the standard input material quantity (with an expected loss of 20%) is 960/0.8 = 1,200 kg (to be mixed 50% X, 30% Y and 20% Z).

The standard cost per litre of input was

Material	***Input***	**Standard price**	**Total cost**
	kg	$	$
X	500	5.00	2,500
Y	300	6.00	1,800
Z	200	7.00	1,400
	1,000		5,700

Standard price per kg = $5.70

(i) *Yield variance*

Standard input	1,200	
Actual input	1,280	
Variance	80kg	Adverse
Standard price per kg of input	$5.70	
Yield variance	$456.00	Adverse

(ii) *Mix variance*

Material	Standard mix	Actual mix	Mix variance	Standard price	Mix Variance
	kg			$	$
X	640	600	40 F	5.00	200 F
Y	384	380	4 F	6.00	24 F
Z	256	300	44 A	7.00	308 A
	1,280 kg	1,280 kg			84 A

chapter

9

The budgeting framework

Chapter learning objectives

Lead	Component
B1. Explain the purposes of forecasts, plans and budgets.	(a) Explain why organisations prepare forecasts and plans. (b) Explain the purposes of budgets, including planning, communication, co-ordination, motivation, authorisation, control and evaluation, and how these may conflict.
B2. Prepare forecasts of financial results.	(b) Calculate projected revenues and costs based on product/service volumes, pricing strategies and cost structures.
B3. Prepare budgets based on forecasts.	(a) Prepare a budget for any account in the master budget, based on projections/forecasts and managerial targets.

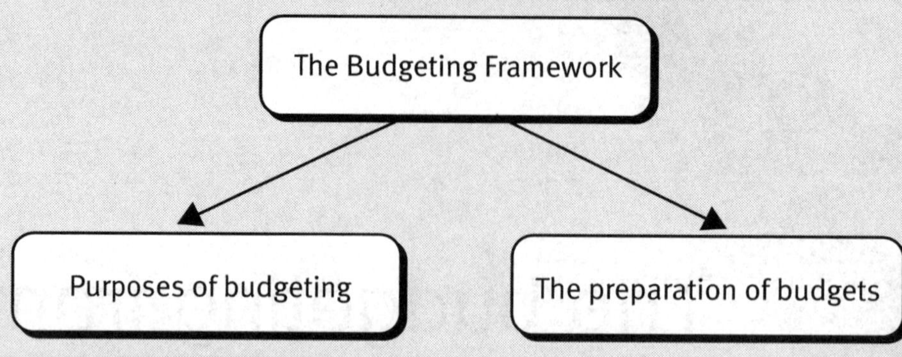

1 Budget

A quantitative or financial plan relating to the future. It can be for the company as a whole or for departments or functions or products or for resources such as cash, materials, labour, etc. It is usually for one year or less.

2 Purposes of budgeting

Budgets have several different purposes:

(1) **Planning**

Budgets **compel** planning. The budgeting process forces management to look ahead, set targets, anticipate problems and give the organisation purpose and direction. Without the annual budgeting process the pressures of day-to-day operational problems may tempt managers not to plan for future operations. The budgeting process encourages managers to anticipate problems before they arise, and hasty decisions that are made on the spur of the moment, based on expediency rather than reasoned judgements, will be minimised. Corporate planners would regard budgeting as an important technique whereby long-term strategies are converted into shorter-term action plans.

(2) **Control**

The budget provides the plan against which actual results can be compared. Those results which are out-of-line with the budget can be further investigated and corrected.

(3) **Co-ordination**

The budget serves as a vehicle through which the actions of the different parts of an organisation can be brought together and reconciled into a common plan. Without any guidance managers may each make their own decisions believing that they are working in the best interests of the organisation. A sound budgeting system helps to co-ordinate the different activities of the business and to ensure that they are in harmony with each other.

(4) **Communication**

Budgets communicate targets to managers. Through the budget, top management communicates its expectations to lower-level management so that all members of the organisation may understand these expectations and can co-ordinate their activities to attain them.

(5) **Motivation**

The budget can be a useful device for influencing managerial behaviour and motivating managers to perform in line with the organisational objectives.

(6) **Evaluation**

The performance of a manager is often evaluated by measuring his success in achieving his budgets. The budget might quite possibly be the only quantitative reference point available.

(7) **Authorisation**

A budget may act as formal authorisation to a manager for expenditure, the hiring of staff and the pursuit of the plans contained in the budget.

3 Functional budgets and the master budget

A master budget for the entire organisation brings together the departmental or activity budgets for all the departments or responsibility centres within the organisation.

The structure of a budget depends on the nature of the organisation and its operations. In a manufacturing organisation, the budgeting process will probably consist of preparing several functional budgets, beginning with a sales budget.

- **Sales budget**. Budget for future sales, expressed in revenue terms and possibly also in units of sale. The budget for the organisation as a whole might combine the sales budgets of several sales regions.

- **Production budget**. A production budget follows on from the sales budget, since production quantities are determined by sales volume. The production volume will differ from sales volume by the amount of any planned increase or decrease in inventories of finished goods (and work-in-progress).

In order to express the production budget in financial terms (production cost), subsidiary budgets must be prepared for materials, labour and production overheads. Several departmental managers could be involved in preparing these subsidiary budgets.

- **Direct materials usage budget**. This is a budget for the quantities and cost of the materials required for the planned production quantities.
- **Materials purchasing budget**. This is a budget for the cost of the materials to be purchased in the period. The purchase cost of direct materials will differ from the material usage budget if there is a planned increase or decrease in direct materials inventory. The purchases budget should also include the purchase costs of indirect materials.
- **Direct labour budget**. This is a budget of the direct labour costs of production. If direct labour is a variable cost, it is calculated by multiplying the production quantities (in units) by the budgeted direct labour cost per unit produced. If direct labour is a fixed cost, it can be calculated by estimating the payroll cost.
- **Production overheads**. Budgets can be produced for production overhead costs. Where a system of absorption costing is used, overheads are allocated and apportioned, and budgeted absorption rates are determined.
- **Administration and sales and distribution overheads**. Other overhead costs should be budgeted.
- **Budgeted income statement, cash budget and balancesheet**. Having prepared budgets for sales and costs, the master budget can be summarised as an income statement for the period, a cash budget (or cash flow forecast) and a balance sheet as at the end of the budget period.

If the budgeted profit, cash position or balance sheet are unsatisfactory, the budgets should be revised until a satisfactory planned outcome is achieved.

These stages in budgeting are illustrated in the following diagram.

Budget preparation

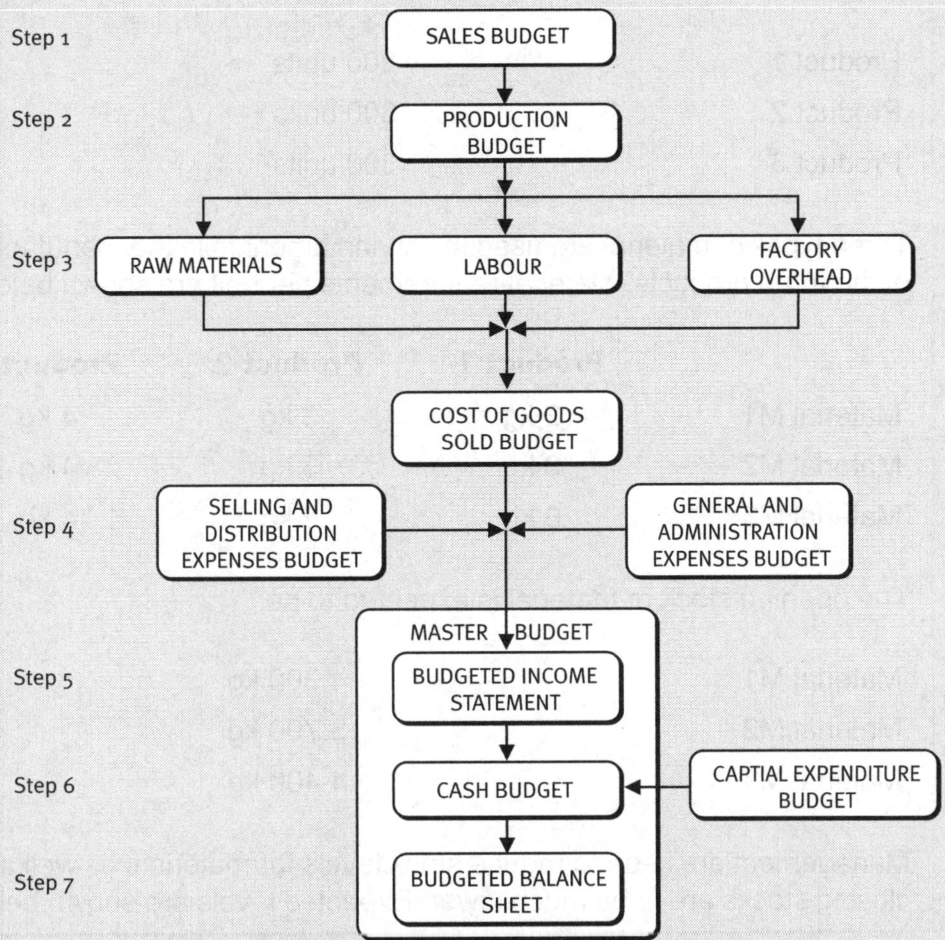

Example 1 - NEWTON LTD

Newton Ltd manufactures three products; the expected sales for each product are shown below.

	Product 1	**Product 2**	**Product 3**
Sales in units	3,000	4,500	3,000

Opening stock is expected to be:

Product 1	500 units
Product 2	700 units
Product 3	500 units

Management have stated their desire to reduce stock levels and closing stocks are budgeted as:

Product 1	200 units
Product 2	300 units
Product 3	300 units

Three types of material are used in varying amounts in the manufacture of the three products. Material requirements per unit are shown below:

	Product 1	**Product 2**	**Product 3**
Material M1	2 kg	3 kg	4 kg
Material M2	3 kg	3 kg	4 kg
Material M3	6 kg	2 kg	4 kg

The opening stock of material is expected to be:

Material M1	4,300 kg
Material M2	3,700 kg
Material M3	4,400 kg

Management are keen to reduce stock levels for materials as well and closing stocks are to be much lower. Expected levels are shown below:

Material M1	2,200 kg
Material M2	1,300 kg
Material M3	2,000 kg

Material prices are expected to be 10% higher than this year and current prices are $1.10/kg for material M1, $3.00/kg for material M2 and $2.50/kg for material M3.

Two types of labour are used in producing the three products. Standard times per unit (in hours) are shown below:

	Product 1	**Product 2**	**Product 3**
Skilled labour	3	1	3
Semi-skilled labour	4	4	2

Skilled labour are to be paid at the rate of $6/hour and semi-skilled labour at the rate of $4/hour.

Required:

Prepare budgets for:

(a) production (in quantity);

(b) materials usage (in quantity);

(c) materials purchases (in quantity and value);

(d) labour (in hours and value).

(25 marks)

4 Principal budget factor

It is usually assumed in budgeting that sales demand will be the key factor setting a limit to what the organisation can expect to achieve in the budget period. Occasionally, however, there might be a shortage of a key resource, such as cash, raw material supplies, skilled labour or equipment. If a resource is in restricted supply, and the shortage cannot be overcome, the budget for the period should be determined by how to make the best use of this key budget resource, rather than be sales demand.

When a key resource is in short supply and affects the planning decisions, it is known as the **principal budget factor** or **limiting budget factor**.

5 Chapter summary

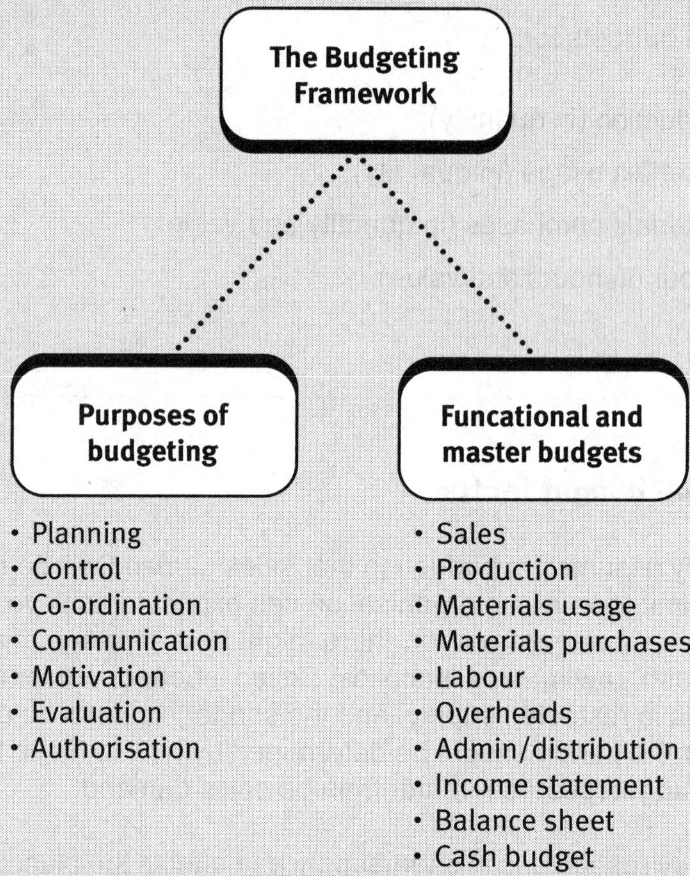

6 Practice questions

Test your understanding 1

Hash makes two products – P1 and P2. Sales for next year are budgeted at 5,000 units of P1 and 1,000 units of P2. Planned selling prices are £230 and £300 respectively.

Hash expects to have the following opening inventory and required closing inventory levels of finished products:

	P1 Units	P2 Units
Opening inventory	100	50
Required closing inventory	1,100	50

Each product goes through two production processes, whittling and fettling. Budgeted production data for the products are as follows:

Finished products:	P1	P2
Raw materials X: Kilos per unit	12	12
Raw materials Y: Kilos per unit	6	8
Direct labour hours per unit	8	12
Machine hours per unit: whittling	5	8
Machine hours per unit: fettling	3	4

Raw material inventories	Raw material X	Y
Opening inventory (kilos)	5,000	5,000
Planned closing inventory (kilos)	6,000	1,000

Standard rates and prices:

Direct labour rate per hour	$7
Material X purchase price per kilo	$2
Material Y purchase price per kilo	$5

You should assume that the following production overhead absorption rates have already been established:

Production overhead absorption rates

Variable	$1 per direct labour hour
Fixed	$8 per direct labour hour

Budgeted administration and marketing overheads are $225,000.

The opening balance sheet is expected to be as follows:

	$	$
Non current assets		950,000
Inventory	66,000	
Trade receivables	260,000	
Cash	25,000	
	351,000	
Trade payables	86,000	
Other short-term liabilities	24,000	
	110,000	
Net current assets		241,000
Net assets		1,191,000

Non-current assets in the balance sheet are expected to increase by $40,000, but no change is expected in trade receivables, trade payables and other short-term liabilities.

There are no plans at this stage to raise extra capital by issuing new shares or obtaining new loans. The company currently has an overdraft facility of $300,000 with its bank.

Required:

For the budget period, prepare:

(a) a sales budget

(b) a production budget in units

(c) materials usage and purchases budgets

(d) a direct labour cost budget

(e) a machine utilisation budget

(f) a production cost budget

(g) a budgeted income statement

(h) a budgeted balance sheet as at the end of the period.

Test your understanding 2 - FLEMING PLC

Fleming plc has established a new subsidiary company on 1 November specifically for the manufacture and selling of a new product. The holding company will inject, for working capital purposes, $30,000 cash on 1 December. Fixed capital assets are being transferred from another company in the group.

Using the data given you are required to prepare a cash budget for each of the months of December, January, February and March. Calculations are to be made to the nearest $1.

Data

The variable production cost per unit is expected to be:

	$
Direct materials	4.0
Direct wages	3.0
Variable production overhead	1.5
Variable production cost	8.5

Fixed overhead estimated at $48,000 per annum is expected to be incurred in equal amounts each month from 1 December.

Production will commence in December and sales on 1 January. The estimated sales for the first four months are:

20X7	**Units**	**Sales Value**
		$
January	6,200	65,100
February	6,800	70,720
March	5,400	59,400
April	6,000	63,000

The following information is to be taken into consideration:

(1) Stocks, finished goods: 75% of each month's invoiced sales units to be produced in the month of sale and 25% of each month's invoiced sales units to be produced in the previous month.

(2) Stocks, direct materials: 50% of direct materials required for each month's production to be purchased in the previous month. Direct materials to be paid for in the month following purchase.

(3) Direct wages to be paid 75% in the month used and 25% in the following month.

(4) Variable production overhead: 40% to be paid in the month of use and the balance in the following month.

(5) Fixed overhead: 30% to be paid in the month in which it is incurred and 40% in the following month, the balance represents depreciation of fixed assets.

(6) Payments to be received from customers as follows:

January	$12,369
February	$45,987
March	$59,666

Prepare a cash budget

(30 marks)

Test your understanding answers

Example 1 - NEWTON LTD

(a) **Production budget**

	Product 1	Product 2	Product 3
	units	units	units
Sales	3,000	4,500	3,000
+ Cl. inventory	200	300	300
	3,200	4,800	3,300
- Op. inventory	500	700	500
Production Qty	2,700	4,100	2,800

(b) **Material usage budget**

	Material M1	Material M2	Material M3
	Kg	Kg	Kg
Production Requirement			
2,700 Product 1	5,400	8,100	16,200
4,100 Product 2	12,300	12,300	8,200
2,800 Product 3	11,200	11,200	11,200
Usage Qty	28,900	31,600	35,600

(c) **Material purchases budget**

	Material M1	Material M2	Material M3
	Kg	Kg	Kg
Usage Qty	28,900	31,600	35,600
+ Cl. inventory	2,200	1,300	2,000
	31,100	32,900	37,600
- Op. inventory	4,300	3,700	4,400
Purchase Qty	26,800	29,200	33,200
	x $1.21	x $3.30	x $2.75
	$32,428	$96,360	$91,300

(d) **Labour budget**

	Skilled	Semi-skilled
	hrs	hrs
Production Requirement		
2,700 Product 1	8,100	8,100
4,100 Product 2	4,100	12,300
2,800 Product 3	8,400	11,200
Usage Qty	20,600	31,600
	x $6/hr	x $4/hr
	$123,600	$126,400

Test your understanding 1

(a) **The sales budget**

The sales budget is the plan for the volume of sales, in quantities and sales revenue. Unless there is a production limiting factor, the sales budget is the starting point for preparing the master budget.

Here, the sales budget is:

	Product P1		Product P2		Total
	Units	$	Units	$	$
Sales	5,000	1,150,000	1,000	300,000	1,450,000

In practice, organisations prepare their sales budget in more detail, with planned sales analysed by region and area as well as by product.

Comparative figures for the previous year will also usually be shown, to indicate whether planned sales are higher or lower than in the previous period, and by how much.

(b) **The production budget**

The production budget can be calculated by taking the sales budget in units and adjusting the figures for planned changes in inventories of finished goods (and work in progress). If there is a planned increase in inventory levels, production volume will exceed the planned sales volume. If inventory levels are planned to fall, production will be lower than sales.

	Product P1	**Product P2**
	Units	Units
Sales budget	5,000	1,000
planned closing inventory (finished goods)	1,100	50
	6,100	1,050
Trade payables	(100)	(50)
	6,000	1,000

Having established the production budget in quantity terms, the various elements of production cost can be budgeted.

(c) **The raw materials usage and purchases budget**

The raw materials usage budget is calculated from production quantities, in both units of raw material and direct material production cost.

The raw materials purchases budget is the usage budget adjusted for any planned increase or decrease in raw materials inventories.

In this example, raw materials are assumed to be direct materials only. In practice, a purchases budget is also required for indirect materials, where these are significant in volume and cost.

	Material X		Material Y		Total
To produce	*Kilos*	*$*	*Kilos*	*$*	*$*
6,000 units of P1	72,000	144,000	36,000	180,000	324,000
1,000 units of P2	12,000	24,000	8,000	40,000	64,000
Materials usage budget	84,000	168,000	44,000	220,000	388,000
Planned closing inventory	6,000	12,000	1,000	5,000	17,000
	90,000	180,000	45,000	225,000	405,000
Opening inventory	(5,000)	(10,000)	(5,000)	(25,000)	(35,000)
Materials purchases budget	85,000	170,000	40,000	200,000	370,000

(d) **The direct labour cost and production overhead budgets**

The cost budget for direct labour is also derived from the budgeted production volumes.

Since production overhead costs are being absorbed on a direct labour hour basis, the production overhead costs for each product can also be calculated.

	Product P1 6,000 units		Product P2 1,000 units		Total
	Hours	*$*	*Hours*	*$*	*$*
Direct labour cost	48,000	336,000	12,000	84,000	420,000
Variable production o/h	48,000	48,000	12,000	12,000	60,000
Fixed production o/h	48,000	384,000	12,000	96,000	480,000

(e) **The machine utilisation budget**

This is a budget for the number of machine hours required for production. A separate budget is required for each different group of machines. Once again, the starting point for preparing the budget is the production volume for each product. Since machine hours are not specifically costed, the budget is in hours only.

	Whittling	**Fettling**
To produce:	Machine hours	Machine hours
6,000 units of P1	30,000	18,000
1,000 inits of P2	8,000	4,000
Machine utilisation budget	38,000	22,000

(f) **Production cost budget**

The production budget has already been prepared in units. A production cost budget can now be prepared, for each product and in total.

	Product P1	**Product P2**	**Total**
	6,000	1,000	
	$	$	$
Direct materials:			
Material X	144,000	24,000	168,000
Material Y	180,000	40,000	220,000
	324,000	64,000	388,000
Direct labour	336,000	84,000	420,000
Variable production overhead	48,000	12,000	60,000
Fixed production overhead	384,000	96,000	480,000
Total production cost	1,092,000	256,000	1,348,000
Production cost per unit	$182	$256	

(g) **Budgeted income statement**

A budgeted income statement can now be prepared. The production cost of sales is calculated by adjusting the production cost budget to allow for changes in inventories of finished goods. Here, it is assumed that opening units of inventory have the same production cost per unit as units produced in the budget period.

	Product P1		**Product P2**	
Cost per unit	$182		$256	
	Units	*$*	*Units*	*$*
Opening inventory	100	18,200	50	12,800
Closing inventory	1,100	200,200	50	12,800

Administration and marketing overheads are deducted as a period charge from the gross profit.

	Product P1	**Product P2**	**Total**
	$	$	$
Sales	1,150,000	300,000	1,450,000
Opening inventory	18,200	12,800	31.000
Cost of production	1,092,000	256,000	1,348,000
	1,110,200	268,800	1,379,000
Closing inventory	(200,200)	(12,800)	(213,000)
Production cost of sales	910,000	256,000	1,166,000
Gross profit	240,000	44,000	284,000
Administration/marketing costs			(225,000)
Net profit			59,000

(h) **Budgeted closing balance sheet**

A closing balance sheet can be constructed from the information provided.

The net assets of the business will increase by the amount of the net profit, minus any drawings or dividends paid to the owners. If we assume that drawings/dividends will be nil, the net assets at the year end will be:

	$
Opening net assets	1,191,000
Budgeted net profit	59,000
Closing net assets	1,250,000

The non-current assets will increase by $40,000, closing inventory has been calculated in the budget, and budgeted assumptions are available for receivables and payables. We can calculate the total closing inventory as follows:

	$
Finished goods	213,000
Raw materials	17,000
	230,000

The last figure that we need for the balance sheet is the cash balance. We could deduce this as a balancing figure but it can be proved as follows:

	$
Opening cash balance	25,000
Profit	59,000
Purchase of non-current assets	(40,000)
Cash effect of inventory increase	(164,000)
(Closing inventory - opening inventory)	
Closing cash balance (overdraft)	(120,000)

The closing balance sheet is as follows (assuming no dividend payments):

	$	$
Non current assets		990,000
Inventory	230,000	
Trade receivables	260,000	
	490,000	
Bank overdraft	120,000	
Trade payables	86,000	
Other short-term liabilities	24,000	
	230,000	
Net current assets		260,000
Net assets		1,250,000

This budget is for the entire year. For control purposes, the budget should be analysed in much greater detail. A sales and production budget will be prepared for each control period (typically each month or each quarter).

Test your understanding 2 - FLEMING PLC

Cash budget

	December	January	February	March
	$	$	$	$
Receipts -		12,369	45,987	59,666
Payments				
Materials	3,100	15,800	25,600	24,000
Wages	3,488	15,450	19,275	17,325
Variable overheads	930	5,205	9,585	9,135
Fixed overheads	1,200	2,800	2,800	2,800
	8,718	39,255	57,260	53,260
Net cash flow for month	(8,718)	(26,886)	(11,273)	6,406
Balance b/d	30,000	21,282	(5,604)	(16,877)
Balance c/d	21,282	(5,604)	(16,877)	(10,471)

Workings

	Nov	Dec	Jan	Feb	March	April
1 Production budget						
Sales			6,200	6,800	5,400	6,000
75% current			4,650	5,100	4,050	4,500
25% previous		1,550	1,700	1,350	1,500	?
		1,550	6,350	6,450	5,550	

	Nov	Dec	Jan	Feb	March	April
2 Materials budget						
Production (units)		1,550	6,350	6,450	5,550	
×$/unit		× 4	× 4	× 4	× 4	
Production required ($)		6,200	25,400	25,800	22,200	
50% previous	3,100	12,700	12,900	11,100	?	
50% current		3,100	12,700	12,900	11,100	
	3,100	15,800	25,600	24,000		
Payment 1 month delay		3,100	15,800	25,600	24,000	
3 Wages budget						
Production (units)		1,550	6,350	6,450	5,550	
× $/unit		× 3	× 3	× 3	× 3	
Production required ($)		4,650	19,050	19,350	16,650	
75% current		3,488	14,288	14,513	12,488	
25% following			1,162	4,762	4,837	
		3,488	15,450	19,275	17,325	
4 Variable overhead budget						
Production (units)		1,550	6,350	6,450	5,550	
× $/unit		× 1.50	× 1.50	× 1.50	1.50	
Production required ($)		2,325	9,525	9,675	8,325	
40% current		930	3,810	3,870	3,330	
60% following		–	1,395	5,715	5,805	
		930	5,205	9,585	9,135	

	Nov	Dec	Jan	Feb	March	April
5 Fixed overhead budget						
Cost per month ($)		4,000	4,000	4,000	4,000	4,000
30% current		1,200	1,200	1,200	1,200	1,200
40% following		–	1,600	1,600	1,600	1,600
		1,200	2,800	2,800	2,800	2,800

chapter

10

Alternative approaches to budgeting

Chapter learning objectives

Lead	Component
B3. Prepare budgets based on forecasts.	(b) Apply alternative approaches to budgeting.

1 Session content diagram

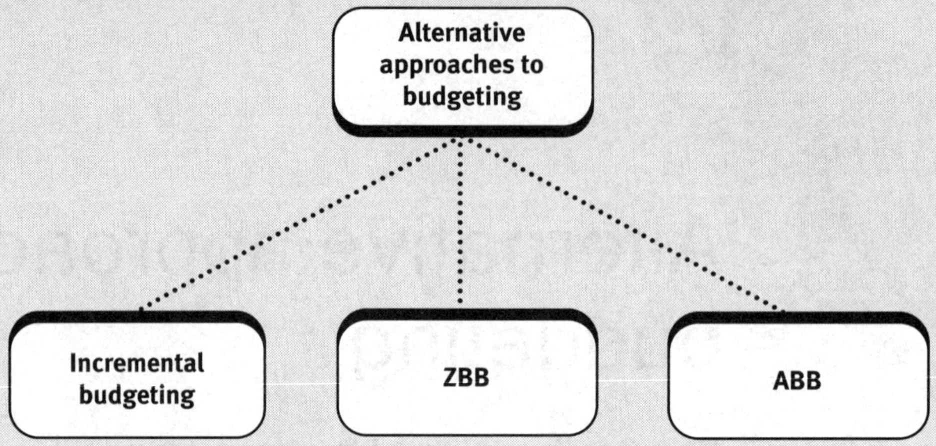

2 Incremental budgeting

The traditional approach to budgeting is to take the previous year's budget and to add on a percentage to allow for inflation and other cost increases. In addition there may be other adjustments for specific items such as an extra worker or extra machine.

Further explanation

- Fairly small changes are made to the current year's budget. For example, adjustments might be made to allow for a planned increase or decline in sales volume, and for inflationary increases in sales prices and costs.
- A check is then made to ensure that the budget produced in this way meets the performance targets of the organisation. For example, the company might have a target of keeping the operating costs to sales ratio at less than, say, 60%.

In a static business environment, incremental budgets are little more than 'last year's budget plus a percentage amount for inflation'.

Advantages and disadvantages

Advantages	Disadvantages
• simple	• backward looking
• cheap	• builds on previous inefficiencies
• suitable in stable environments	• doesn't remove waste / inefficiencies
• most practical	• unsuited to changing environments
	• targets are too easy
	• activities are not justified
	• envourages over-spending

ZBB is one method which may be used to overcome these problems.

Further explanation

The advantage of incremental budgeting is that it is an easy, quick and cheap method of preparing budgets for what may be many cost centres in a large organisation. However, the traditional approach has severe disadvantages.

Advanatges

(1) It is a simple, low-cost budgeting system.

(2) If the business is fairly stable, the budgets produced by this method might be sufficient for management needs.

(3) There are some items of cost where an incremental budgeting approach is probably the most practical. For example, the easiest way of budgeting telephone expenses for the next year might be to base the planned cost on the previous year's budget (or possibly actual costs in the current year).

Disadvantages

(1) The main disadvantage is that it assumes that all current activities should be continued at the current level of operations and with the same allocation of resources.

(2) It is backward-looking in nature, since next year's budget is based on what has been expected in the past. In a dynamic and rapidly-changing business environment, this approach to planning is inappropriate.

(3) It is often seen as a desk-bound planning process, driven by the accounts department.

(4) The performance targets in the budget are often unchallenging, based on past performance. Incremental budgeting does not encourage managers to look for ways of improving the business.

(5) When there are excessive costs in the budget for the current year, these will be continued in the future. Incremental budgeting is not a planning system for cutting out waste and overspending.

(6) Consideration will not be given to the justification for each activity. They will be undertaken merely because they were undertaken the previous year.

(7) Different ways of achieving the objective will not be examined.

(8) Past inefficiencies will be continued.

(9) Managers know that if they fail to spend their budget, it is likely to be reduced next period. They therefore try to spend the whole budget, regardless of whether or not the expenditure is justified.

3 Zero-based budgeting

ZBB may be defined as:

'A method of budgeting whereby all activities are re-evaluated each time a budget is formulated. Each functional budget starts with the assumptions that the function does not exist, and is at zero cost. Increments of costs are compared with increments of benefits, culminating in the planned maximum benefit for a given budgeted cost.'

Zero-based budgeting (ZBB) is a radical alternative to incremental budgeting. In ZBB, all activities and costs are budgeted from scratch (a zero base). For every activity, managers look at its costs and its purpose, and consider whether there are alternative ways of doing it. Inessential activities and costs are identified and eliminated, by removing them from next year's budget.

Implementation of ZBB

The technique was first introduced by **Peter Pyhrr** at **Texas Instruments** in 1969. It is especially useful for:

(1) service departments such as stores, maintenance, marketing, finance, etc.

(2) discretionary costs such as research and development

(3) public sector organisations such as local authorities.

Implementation

It is important that managers involved in ZBB examine their current practices very carefully. Questions they should ask themselves include:

(1) Is the activity essential? What would happen if it ceased?

(2) Is the provision of the activity at the correct level?

(3) Are there other alternatives for achieving the same effect?

There are four distinct stages in the implementation of ZBB:

(1) Managers should specify, for their responsibility centres, those activities that can be individually evaluated.

(2) Each of the individual activities is then described in a **decision package.** The decision package should state the costs and revenues expected from the given activity. It should be drawn up in such a way that the package can be evaluated and ranked against other packages.

Pyhrr identifies two types of package:

(i) mutually exclusive packages. These contain different methods of obtaining the same objective

(ii) incremental packages. These divide the activity into a number of different levels of activity. The base package describes the minimum effort and cost that is needed to carry out the activity. The other packages describe the incremental costs and benefits when added to the base.

(3) Each decision package is evaluated and ranked usually using cost/benefit analysis.

(4) The resources are then allocated to the various packages.

e.g

Illustration 1

A company is conducting a ZBB exercise, and a decision package is being prepared for its materials handling operations.

- The manager responsible has identified a base package for the minimum resources needed to perform the materials handling function. This is to have a team of five workers and a supervisor, operating without any labour-saving machinery. The estimated annual cost of wages and salaries, with overtime, would be $375,000.

- In addition to the base package, the manager has identified an incremental package. The company could lease two fork lift trucks at a cost of $20,000 each year. This would provide a better system because materials could be stacked higher and moved more quickly. Health and safety risks for the workers would be reduced, and there would be savings of $5,000 each year in overtime payments.
- Another incremental package has been prepared, in which the company introduces new computer software to plan materials handling schedules. The cost of buying and implementing the system would be $60,000, but the benefits are expected to be improvements in efficiency that reduce production downtime and result in savings of $10,000 each year in overtime payments.

The base package would be considered essential, and so given a high priority. The two incremental packages should be evaluated and ranked. Here, the fork lift trucks option might be ranked more highly than the computer software.

In the budget that is eventually decided by senior management, the fork lift truck package might be approved, but the computer software package rejected on the grounds that there are other demands for resources with a higher priority.

Advantages and disadvantages

Advantages	Disadvantages
• creates an environment that accepts change	• time-consuming
• better focus on goals	• expensive
• forward looking	• encourages short-termism
• improves resource utilisation	• less useful in controlled environments
• better performance measures	• managers require new budgeting skills
• focuses managers to examine activities	• can result in arbitrary decisions

Further details

Advantages

- It helps to create an organisational environment where change is accepted.
- It helps management to focus on company objectives and goals. It moves budgeting away from number-crunching, towards analysis and decision-making.
- It focuses on the future rather than on the past.
- It helps to identify inefficient operations and wasteful spending, which can be eliminated.
- Establishing priorities for activities provides a framework for the optimum utilisation of resources. This assists decision-makers when some expenditures are discretionary.
- It establishes a measure of performance for each decision package. This measure can be used to monitor actual performance and compare actual with budget.
- It involves managers in the budgeting process. Unlike incremental budgeting, it is not a desk-bound exercise driven by the accounting department.

Disadvantages

- It is a time-consuming exercise. It is unlikely that an organisation will have the time to carry out a ZBB exercise every year.
- There is a temptation to concentrate on short-term cost savings at the expense of longer-term benefits.
- It might not be useful for budgeting for production activities or service provision, where costs and efficiency levels should be well-controlled, so that budgets can be prepared from forecasts of activity volume and unit costs.
- It might require skills from management that the management team does not possess.
- The ranking process can be difficult, since widely-differing activities cannot be compared on quantitative measures alone. For example, it might be difficult to rank proposals for spending on better service quality, improvements in safety in the work place or more spending on new product development.

4 Activity-based budgeting

Introduction

In a manufacturing business, budgeting for direct costs is relatively straightforward. The costs of direct materials and direct labour are assumed to vary with production, and once production levels have been estimated, budgeting the direct costs of production is a matter of simple arithmetic.

Budgeting for overhead costs is not so simple. Traditionally, there has been a tendency to take an incremental approach in budgeting for overhead costs, and prepare next year's budget by simply adding a percentage to the current year budget, to allow for inflation. Zero-based budgeting is one method of bringing greater discipline to the process of budgeting for overhead activities and costs. Another method is activity-based budgeting.

As its name should suggest, activity-based budgeting (ABB) takes a similar approach to activity-based costing. ABB is defined as: 'a method of budgeting based on an activity framework and utilising cost driver data in the budget-setting and variance feedback processes' (CIMA *Official Terminology*).

Whereas ZBB is based on budgets (decision packages) prepared by responsibility centre managers, ABB is based on budgeting for activities.

The basic approach of ABB is to budget the costs for each cost pool or activity.

(There will also be some general overhead costs that are not activity-related, such as factory rental costs and the salary cost of the factory manager. General overhead costs are budgeted separately.)

(1) The cost driver for each activity is identified. A forecast is made of the number of units of the cost driver that will occur in the budget period.

(2) Given the estimate of the activity level for the cost driver, the activity cost is estimated. Where appropriate, a **cost per unit of activity** is calculated.

Advantages and disadvantages

Advantages	Disadvantages
• useful when overheads are significant	• expensive to implement
• better cost control	• only suited to ABC users
• better information for management	
• useful for TQM environments	

Further details

The advantages of ABB are similar to those provided by activity-based costing.

- It draws attention to the costs of 'overhead activities'. This can be important where overhead costs are a large proportion of total operating costs.
- It provides information for the control of activity costs, by assuming that they are variable, at least in the longer term.
- It provides a useful basis for monitoring and controlling overhead costs, by drawing management attention to the actual costs of activities and comparing actual costs with what the activities were expected to cost.
- It also provides useful control information by emphasising that activity costs might be controllable if the activity volume can be controlled.
- ABB can provide useful information for a total quality management (TQM) programme, by relating the cost of an activity to the level of service provided (for example, stores requisitions processed) – Do the user departments feel they are getting a cost-effective service?

5 Chapter summary

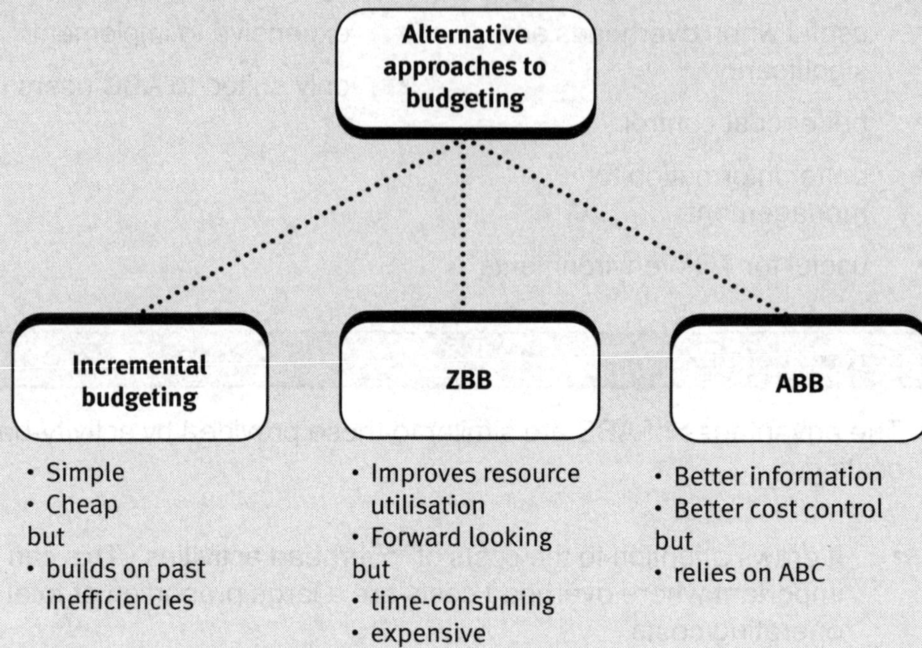

6 Practice questions

Test your understanding 1 - RESEARCH DIVISION

For a number of years, the research division of Z plc has produced its annual budget (for new and continuing projects) using incremental budgeting techniques. The company is now under new management and the annual budget for 2004 is to be prepared using zero based budgeting techniques.

Required:

(a) Explain the differences between incremental and zero based budgeting techniques.

(5 marks)

(b) Explain how Z plc could operate a zero based budgeting system for its research projects.

(8 marks)

The operating divisions of Z plc have in the past always used a traditional approach to analysing costs into their fixed and variable components. A single measure of activity was used which, for simplicity, was the number of units produced. The new management does not accept that such a simplistic approach is appropriate for budgeting in the modern environment and has requested that the managers adopt an activity-based approach to their budgets for 2004.

Required:

(c)

(i) Briefly explain activity-based budgeting (ABB)

(3 marks)

(ii) Explain how activity-based budgeting would be implemented by the operating divisions of Z plc.

(9 marks)

(Total: 25 marks)

Test your understanding 2

AW Inc produces two products, A and C. In the last year (20X4) it produced 640 units of A and 350 units of C incurring costs of $672,000. Analysis of the costs has shown that 75% of the total costs are variable. 60% of these variable costs vary in line with the number of A produced and the remainder with the number of C.

The budget for the year 20X5 is now being prepared using an incremental budgeting approach. The following additional information is available for 20X5:

- All costs will be 4% higher than the average paid in 20X4.
- Efficiency levels will remain unchanged.
- Expected output of A is 750 units and of C is 340 units.

Calculate the budgeted total variable cost of products A and C for the full year 20X5?

Test your understanding 3

For a number of years, the research division of Z Inc has produced its annual budget (for new and continuing projects) using incremental budgeting techniques. The company is now under new management and the annual budget for 20X4 is to be prepared using ZBB techniques.

Explain how Z Inc could operate a ZBB system for its research projects.

Test your understanding 4

Identify which of the following statements is correct regarding the benefits to be gained from using ABB?

A If there is much inefficiency within the operations of a business then ABB will identify and remove these areas of inefficiency.

B In a highly direct labour intensive manufacturing process, an ABB approach will assist management in budgeting for the majority of the production costs.

C In an organisation currently operating efficiently, where the next period will be relatively unchanged from the current one, then ABB will make the budgeting process simpler and quicker.

D If an organisation produces many different types of output using different combinations of activities then ABB can provide more meaningful information for budgetary control.

Test your understanding answers

Test your understanding 1 - RESEARCH DIVISION

(a) An incremental budget starts off with last year's budget or last year's actual results and adds on a certain percentage to take account of expected inflation and/or any expected changes in the level of activity. It is a very simple, quick and cheap budget to produce, but it does not promote a questioning attitude. Activities are undertaken without thought. They are simply incorporated into the next budget because they were in the last budget and nobody has given any thought as to whether the activity is still really worthwhile.

With ZBB, each manager sets out what he or she wishes to accomplish over the forthcoming period. For each activity they want to undertake, they look at different ways of achieving the objective and they look at providing the service at different levels. They estimate the costs and benefits and the activity only takes place if the benefits exceed the costs. Also once all the activities have been evaluated, they can be ranked against each other and the company's resources directed to the best activities.

(b) The managers/researchers responsible for each project should decide which projects they wish to undertake in the forthcoming period. These projects will be a mixture of continued projects and new projects. For the projects which have already been started and which the managers want to continue in the next period, we should ignore any cash flows already incurred (they are sunk costs), and we should only look at future costs and benefits. Similarly, for the new projects we should only look at the future costs and benefits. Different ways of achieving the same research goals should also be investigated and the projects should only go ahead if the benefit exceeds the cost. Once all the potential projects have been evaluated if there are insufficient funds to undertake all the worthwhile projects, then the funds should be allocated to the best projects on the basis of a cost-benefit analysis.

ZBB is usually of a highly subjective nature. (The costs are often reasonably certain, but usually a lot of uncertainty is attached to the estimated benefits.) This will be even truer of a research division where the researchers may have their own pet projects which they are unable to view in an objective light.

(c)

(i) Activity based budgeting is where the budget is based upon a number of different levels of activity, i.e. on a number of different cost drivers, rather than being based on just one level of activity such as machine hours or output in units.

The activity based budget will be based upon the number of units of the cost driver multiplied by the cost per unit of cost driver. The cost driver is that factor which actually causes the cost and therefore should lead to a more accurate budget as the budgeted cost will be based on the thing that should influence that cost. The alternative is to use absorption costing and assume that all overheads vary with output or machine hours or labour hours or that they are fixed.

(ii) Z plc may employ an outside specialist such as a management consultant who will investigate the business and determine what activities the business undertakes during the course of its operations.

The consultant will discuss matters with the staff and the process will normally be time consuming. For each activity, efforts will be made to determine the factor which is most closely related to the costs of that activity, i.e. the cost driver. The investigation may bring to light non-value-added activities which can then be eliminated. It should improve the understanding of all those involved as to the true relationship between cost and level of activity.

Managers would then estimate the expected incidence of their cost drivers and multiply by the budgeted cost driver rate to get the budget for the forthcoming period. ABB would be more complicated than a traditional budget and the overheads would be broken down into many activities such as set-up costs, materials, handling costs, etc rather than expenses such as rent, heating, depreciation, etc.

With ABB the majority of the overhead costs would be perceived as variable rather than fixed. Of course it is not necessary to employ an outside consultant. The company may feel that they have their own managers with sufficient skills and time to undertake the exercise.

Test your understanding 2

	Total variable cost	Variable cost per unit
20X4:		
Product A	\$672,000 × 75% × 60% = \$302,000	\$302,000 ÷ 640 units = \$472.50
Product C	\$672,000 × 75% × 40% = \$201,600	\$201,600 ÷ 350 units = \$576
20X5:		
Product A	\$472.50 × 1.04 × 750 units = \$368,550	n/a
Product C	\$576 × 1.04 × 340 units = \$203,674	n/a

Test your understanding 3

Stage 1: Managers should specify the activities that can be evaluated

The managers/researchers responsible for each project should decide which projects they wish to undertake in the forthcoming period. These projects will be a mixture of continued projects and new projects.

Stage 2: Each activity is described in a decision package

For the projects which have already been started and which the managers want to continue in the next period, we should ignore any cash flows already incurred (they are sunk costs), and we should only look at future costs and benefits. Similarly, for the new projects we should only look at the future costs and benefits.

Stage 3: Each decision package is evaluated and ranked

Different ways of achieving the same research goals should also be investigated and the projects should only go ahead if the benefit exceeds the cost.

Stage 4: Resources are allocated to the various packages

Once all the potential projects have been evaluated if there are insufficient funds to undertake all the worthwhile projects, then the funds should be allocated to the best projects on the basis of a cost-benefit analysis.

ZBB is usually of a highly subjective nature. (The costs are often reasonably certain, but usually a lot of uncertainty is attached to the estimated benefits.) This can be shown by the example of a research division where the researchers may have their own pet projects, which they are unable to view in an objective light.

Test your understanding 4

D is the correct answer.

Situation A would be best suited by implementing Zero Base Budgeting. Situation B does not require ABB since it has relatively low overheads. Situation C would be suitable for incremental budgeting. ABB will certainly not be quicker.

chapter

11

Forecasting techniques

Chapter learning objectives

Lead	Component
B2. Prepare forecasts of financial results.	(a) Calculate projected product/service volumes employing appropriate forecasting techniques. (b) Calculate projected revenues and costs based on product/service volumes, pricing strategies and cost structures.

1 Session content diagram

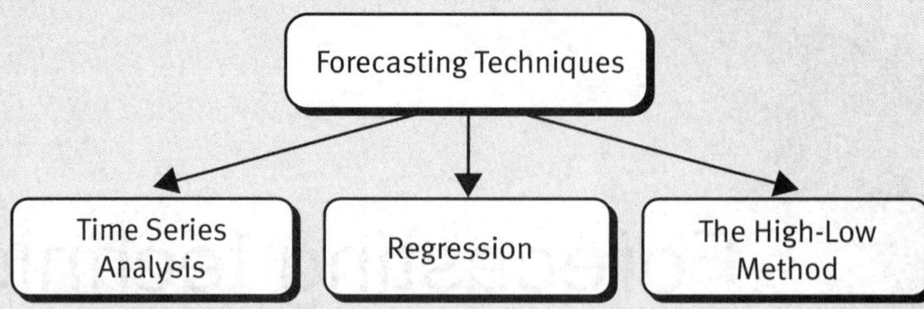

Forecasts in budgeting

Budgets are based on forecasts. Forecasts might be prepared for:

- the volume of output and sales
- sales revenue (sales volume and sales prices)
- costs.

The purpose of forecasting in the budgeting process is to establish realistic assumptions for planning. Forecasts might also be prepared on a regular basis for the purpose of feed-forward control reporting.

A forecast might be based on simple assumptions, such as a prediction of a 5% growth in sales volume or sales revenue. Similarly, budgeted expenditure might be forecast using a simple incremental budgeting approach, and adding a percentage amount for inflation on top of the previous year's budget.

On the other hand, forecasts might be prepared using a number of forecasting models, methods or techniques. The reason for using these models and techniques is that they might provide more reliable forecasts.

This chapter describes:

- the high-low method
- the uses of linear regression analysis
- techniques of time series analysis.

More complex models might be used in practice, but these are outside the scope of the syllabus.

2 The high-low method

This is a method of breaking semi-variable costs into their two components. A semi-variable cost being a cost which is partly fixed and partly variable.

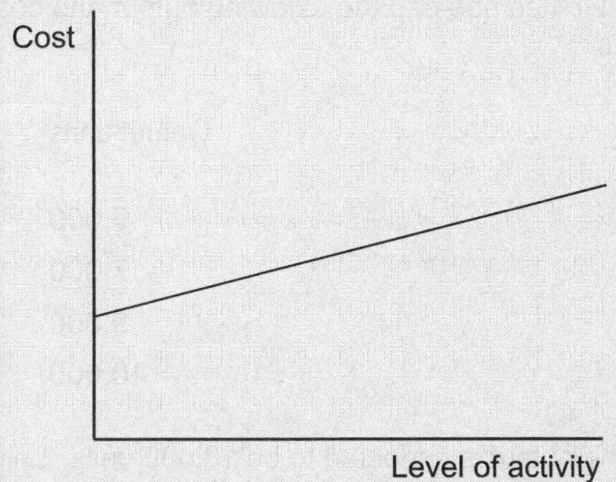

In the exam in computational questions, semi-variable costs must be broken down into their 2 components using the *high-low method.*

The following example will be used to illustrate the method:

Step 1 Find the variable cost per unit

$$\text{Variable cost per unit} = \frac{\text{Increase in cost}}{\text{Increase in activity}}$$

Step 2 Find the fixed cost

A semi-variable cost consists of 2 components. We have found the variable part. The bit that is left must be fixed.

Step 3 Calculate the expected cost

Example 1

Great Auk Limited has had the following output and cost results for the last 4 years:

	Output units	Cost $
Year 1	5,000	26,000
Year 2	7,000	34,000
Year 3	9,000	42,000
Year 4	10,000	46,000

In year 5 the output is expected to be 13,000 units. Calculate the expected costs?

Inflation may be ignored.

3 Regression analysis

Regression analysis is concerned with establishing the relationship between a number of variables. We are only concerned here with linear relationships between 2 variables.

There are a variety of methods available for identifying the relationship:

(1) Least Squares Regression Analysis

(2) The high-low method.

(3) Draw a *scatter diagram* and a line of best fit

The scatter diagram

The data is plotted on a graph. The y-axis represents the *dependent* variable, i.e. that variable that depends on the other. The *x*-axis shows the *independent* variable, i.e. that variable which is not affected by the other variable:

From the scatter diagram, the line of best fit can be estimated. The aim is to use our judgement to draw a line through the middle of data with the same slope as the data.

Least squares regression analysis

Regression analysis finds the line of best fit computationally rather than by estimating the line on a scatter diagram. It seeks to minimise the distance between each point and the regression line.

The equation of a straight line is:

$$y = a + bx$$

where y = dependent variable
a = intercept (on y-axis)
b = gradient
x = independent variable

and
$$b = \frac{n\Sigma xy - \Sigma x\Sigma y}{n\Sigma x^2 - (\Sigma x)^2}$$

where n = number of pairs of data

and
$$a = \bar{y} - b\bar{x}$$

Example 2

Marcus Aurelius Ltd is a small supermarket chain, that has 6 shops. Each shop advertises in their local newspapers and the marketing director is interested in the relationship between the amount that they spend on advertising and the sales revenue that they achieve. She has collated the following information for the 6 shops for the previous year:

Shop	Advertising expenditure	Sales revenue
	$000	$000
1	80	730
2	60	610
3	120	880
4	90	750
5	70	650
6	30	430

She has further performed some calculations for a linear regression calculation as follows:

- the sum of the advertising expenditure (x) column is 450
- the sum of the sales revenue (y) column is 4,050
- when the two columns are multiplied together and summed (xy) the total is 326,500

- when the advertising expenditure is squared (x^2) and summed, the total is 38,300, and
- when the sales revenue is squared (y^2) and summed, the total is 2,849,300

Calculate the line of best fit using regression analysis.

Detailed proof of totals in example 2

Advertising Expenditure $000	**Sales** $000			
x	y	xy	x^2	y^2
80	730	58,400	6,400	532,900
60	610	36,600	3,600	372,100
120	880	105,600	14,400	774,400
90	750	67,500	8,100	562,500
70	650	45,500	4,900	422,500
30	430	12,900	900	184,900
450	4,050	326,500	38,300	2,849,300

Interpretation of the line

Mathematical interpretation (No good! No marks!)

If x = 0, then y = 300 and then each time x increases by 1 y increases by 5

Business interpretation (This is what the examiner wants.)

If no money is spent on advertising then sales would still be $300,000. Then for every additional $1 increase in advertising sales revenue would increase by $5.

Linear regression in budgeting

Linear regression analysis can be used to make forecasts or estimates whenever a linear relationship is assumed between two variables, and historical data is available for analysis.

Two such relationships are:

- **A time series and trend line.** Linear regression analysis is an alternative to calculating moving averages to establish a trend line from a time series. (Time series is explained later in this chapter)
  - The independent variable (x) in a time series is time.
  - The dependent variable (y) is sales, production volume or cost etc.
- **Total costs, where costs consist of a combination of fixed costs and variable costs** (for example, total overheads, or a semi-variable cost item). Linear regression analysis is an alternative to using the high-low method of cost behaviour analysis. It should be more accurate than the high-low method, because it is based on more items of historical data, not just a 'high' and a 'low' value.
  - The independent variable (x) in total cost analysis is the volume of activity.
  - The dependent variable (y) is total cost.
  - The value of a is the amount of fixed costs.
  - The value of b is the variable cost per unit of activity.

When a linear relationship is identified and quantified using linear regression analysis, values for a and b are obtained, and these can be used to make a forecast for the budget. For example:

- a sales budget or forecast can be prepared, or
- total costs (or total overhead costs) can be estimated, for the budgeted level of activity.

Forecasting

The regression equation can be used for predicting values of y from a given *x* value.

(1) If the value of *x* is within the range of our original data, the prediction is known as *Interpolation*.

(2) If the value of *x* is outside the range of our original data, the prediction is known as *Extrapolation*.

In general, interpolation is much safer than extrapolation.

Example 2 - CONTINUED

Marcus Aurelius Ltd has just taken on 2 new stores in the same area and the predicted advertising expenditure is expected to be $150,000 for one store and $50,000 for the other.

(a) Calculate the predicted sales revenues?

(b) Explain the reliability of the forecasts.

Limitations of simple linear regression

(1) Assumes a linear relationship between the variables.

(2) Only measures the relationship between two variables. In reality the dependent variable is affected by many independent variables.

(3) Only interpolated forecasts tend to be reliable. The equation should not be used for extrapolation.

(4) Regression assumes that the historical behaviour of the data continues into the foreseeable future.

(5) Interpolated predictions are only reliable if there is a significant correlation between the data.

4 Correlation

Regression analysis attempts to find the relationship between a number of variables. Correlation is concerned with establishing how strong the relationship is.

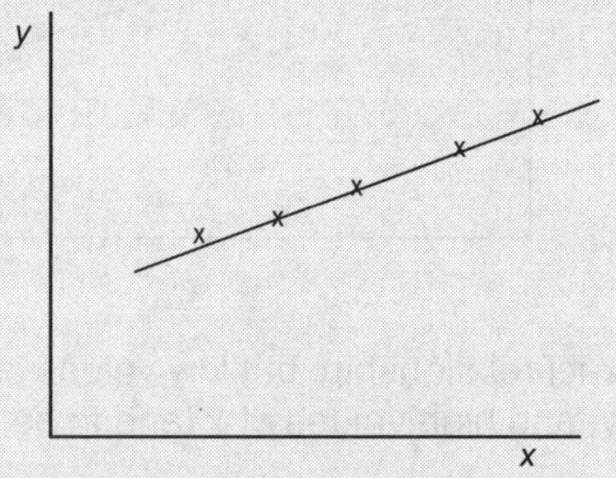

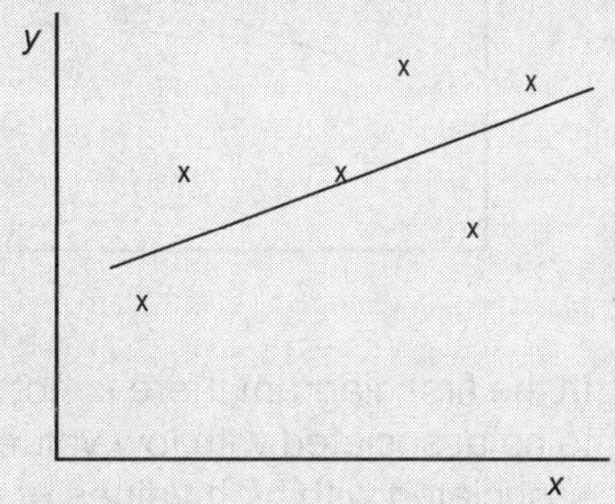

Clearly in the first diagram, the regression line would be a much more useful predictor than the regression line in the second diagram.

Degrees of correlation

Two variables might be:

(a) perfectly correlated
(b) partly correlated
(c) uncorrelated

Perfect correlation

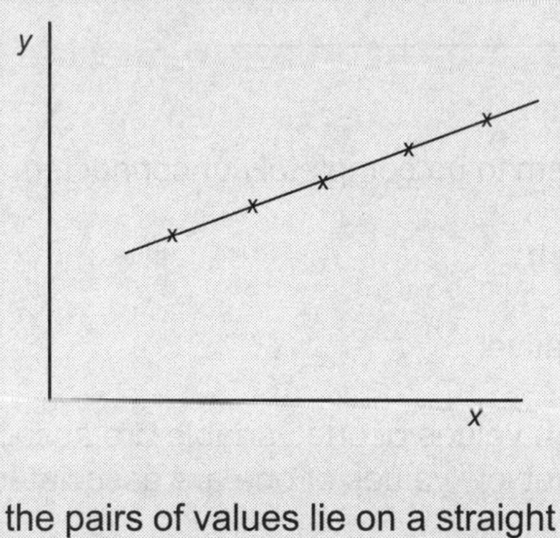

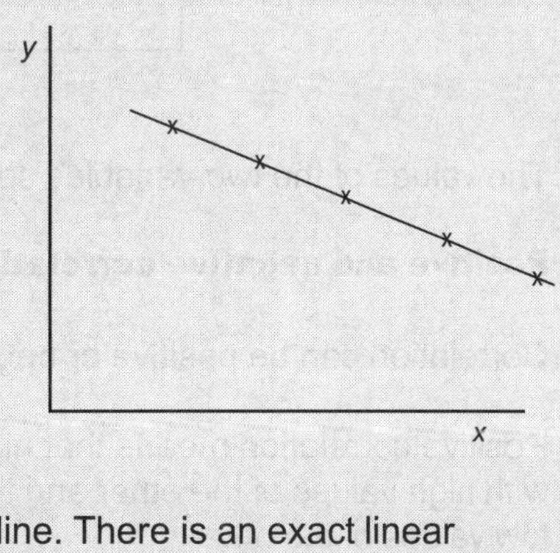

All the pairs of values lie on a straight line. There is an exact linear relationship between the two variables.

Partial correlation

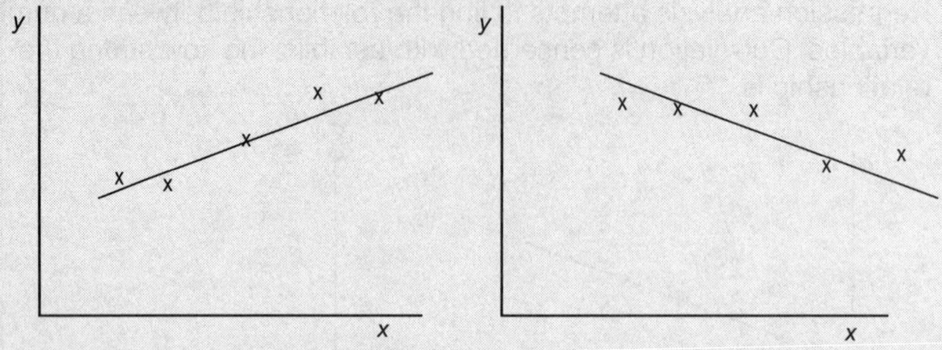

In the first diagram there is not an exact relationship, but low values of *x* tend to be associated with low values of y, and high values of *x* tend to be associated with high values of y.

In the second diagram again there is not an exact relationship, but low values of *x* tend to be associated with high values of y and vice versa.

No correlation

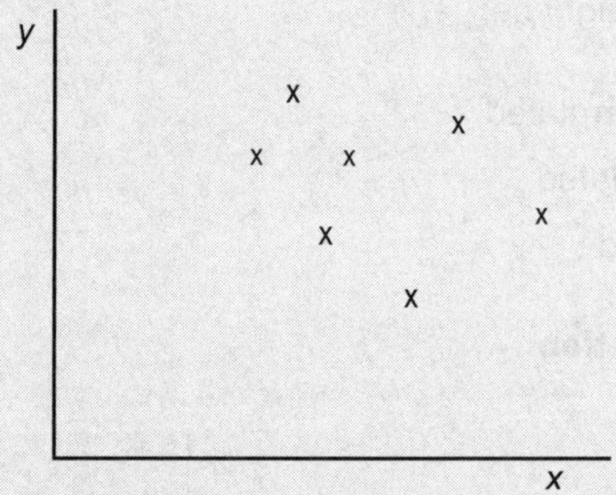

The values of the two variables seem to be completely unconnected.

Positive and negative correlation

Correlation can be positive or negative.

Positive correlation means that high values of one variable are associated with high values of the other and that low values of one are associated with low values of the other.

Negative correlation means that low values of one variable are associated with high values of the other and vice versa.

The correlation coefficient

The degree of correlation can be measured by the Pearsonian correlation coefficient, r (also known as the product moment correlation coefficient).

r must always be between -1 and +1.

If r = 1, there is perfect positive correlation

If r = 0, there is no correlation

If r = -1, there is perfect negative correlation

For other values of r, the meaning is not so clear. It is generally taken that if r > 0.8, then there is strong positive correlation and if r < -0.8, there is strong negative correlation, however more meaningful information can be gathered from calculating the coefficient of determination, r^2.

$$r = \frac{n\sum xy - \sum x \sum y}{\sqrt{\left(n\sum x^2 - \left(\sum x\right)^2\right)\left(n\sum y^2 - \left(\sum y\right)^2\right)}}$$

Example 2 - AGAIN

Required:

Calculate the coefficient of correlation for the previous scenario.

The coefficient of determination, r^2

The coefficient of determination, r^2 measures the proportion of changes in y that can be explained by changes in *x*. Calculate the coefficient of determination for Example 2 and comment.

5 Adjusting forecasts for inflation

The accuracy of forecasting is affected by the need to adjust historical data and future forecasts to allow for price or cost inflation.

- When historical data is used to calculate a trend line or line of best fit, it should ideally be adjusted to the same index level for prices or costs. If the actual cost or revenue data is used, without adjustments for inflation, the resulting line of best fit will include the inflationary differences.
- When a forecast is made from a line of best fit, an adjustment to the forecast should be made for anticipated inflation in the forecast period.

Example 3

Production overhead costs at company BW are assumed to vary with the number of machine hours worked. A line of best fit will be calculated from the following historical data, with costs adjusted to allow for cost inflation over time.

Year	Total production overheads	Number of machine hours	Cost index
	$		
20X5	143,040	3,000	192
20X6	156,000	3,200	200
20X7	152,320	2,700	224
20X8	172,000	3,000	235

Required:

(a) Reconcile the cost data to a common price level, to remove differences caused by inflation.

(b) If the line of best fit, based on current (20X4) prices, is calculated as:

$y = 33{,}000 + 47x$

where y = total overhead costs in $ and x = machine hours:

calculate the expected total overhead costs in 20X5 if expected production activity is 3,100 machine hours and the expected cost index is 250.

6 Time series analysis

A time series is a series of figures recorded over time, e.g. unemployment over the last 5 years, output over the last 12 months, etc.

A graph of a time series is called a *historigram*.

Examples of a time series

Examples of time series might include the following:

- quarterly sales revenue totals over a number of years
- annual overhead costs over a number of years
- daily production output over a month.

Where the item being measured is subject to 'seasonal' variations, time series measurements are usually taken for each season. For example, if sales volume varies in each quarter of the year, a time series should be for quarterly sales. Similarly, if the sales in a retail store vary according to the day of the week, a time series might measure daily sales

A time series has 4 components:

(1) The trend
(2) Seasonal variations
(3) Cyclical variations
(4) Residual variations

We are only interested in the first two - the trend and the seasonal variation.

Time series analysis is a term used to describe techniques for analysing a time series, in order to:

- identify whether there is any **underlying historical trend** and if there is, measure it
- use this analysis of the historical trend to forecast the trend into the future
- identify whether there are any **seasonal variations** around the trend, and if there is measure them
- apply estimated seasonal variations to a trend line forecast in order to prepare a forecast season by season.

In other words, a trend over time, established from historical data, and adjusted for seasonal variations, can then be used to make predictions for the future.

The trend

Most series follow some sort of long term movement - upwards, downwards or sideways. In time series analysis the trend is measured.

Seasonal variations

Seasonal variations are short-term fluctuations in value due to different circumstances which occur at different times of the year, on different days of the week, different times of day, etc e.g.:

- Ice cream sales are highest in summer
- Sales of groceries are highest on Saturdays
- Traffic is greatest in the morning and evening rush hours.

e.g

Illustration 1

A business might have a flat trend in sales, of $1 million each six months, but with sales $150,000 below trend in the first six months of the year and $150,000 above trend in the second six months. In this example, the sales would be $850,000 in the first six months of the year and $1,150,000 in the second six months.

- If there is a straight-line trend in the time series, seasonal variations must cancel each other out. The total of the seasonal variations over each cycle should be zero.
- Seasonal variations can be measured:
  - in units or in money values, or
  - as a percentage value or index value in relation to the underlying trend.

Cyclical and residual factors

Cyclical variations

Cyclical variations are medium-term to long term influences usually associated with the economy. These cycles are rarely of consistent length. A further problem is that we would need 6 or 7 full cycles of data to be sure that the cycle was there. Cyclical variations are often associated with the economy.

Residual or random factors

The residual is the difference between the actual value and the figure predicted using the trend, the cyclical variation and the seasonal variation, i.e. it is caused by irregular items, which could not be predicted.

Calculation of the trend

There are three main methods of finding the underlying trend of the data:

(1) *Inspection*. The trend line can be drawn by eye with the aim of plotting the line so that it lies in the middle of the data.

(2) *Least squares regression analysis*. The x axis represents time and the periods of time are numbers, e.g. January is 1, February is 2, March is 3, etc.

(3) *Moving averages*. This method attempts to remove seasonal or cyclical variations by a process of averaging.

Calculating a moving average

A moving average is in fact a series of averages, calculated from time series historical data.

- The first moving average value in the series is the average of the values for time period 1 to time period n. (So, if n = 4, the first moving average in the series would be the average of the historical values for time period 1 to time period 4.)
- The second moving average value in the series is the average of the values for time period 2 to time period (n + 1). (So, if n = 4, the second moving average in the series would be the average of the historical values for time period 2 to time period 5.)
- The third moving average value in the series is the average of the values for time period 3 to time period (n + 2). (So, if n = 4, the third moving average in the series would be the average of the historical values for time period 3 to time period 6.)

The moving average value is associated with the mid-point of the time periods used to calculate the average.

The moving average time period

When moving averages are used to estimate a trend line, an important issue is the choice of the number of time periods to use to calculate the moving average. How many time periods should a moving average be based on?

There is no definite or correct answer to this question. However, where there is a regular cycle of time periods, it would make sense to calculate the moving averages over a full cycle.

- When you are calculating a moving average of daily figures, it is probably appropriate to calculate a seven-day moving average.
- When you are calculating a moving average of quarterly figures, it is probably appropriate to calculate a four-quarter moving average.
- When you are calculating a moving average of monthly figures, it might be appropriate to calculate a 12-month moving average, although a shorter-period moving average might be preferred.

The seasonal variation

Once the trend has been found, the seasonal variation can be determined. A seasonal variation means that some periods are better than average (the trend) and some worse. Then the model can be used to predict future values. There are two main models:

(1) *The additive model*. Here the seasonal variation is expressed as an absolute amount to be added on to the trend to find the actual result, e.g. ice-cream sales in summer are good and in general we would expect sales to be $200,000 above the trend.

Actual/Prediction = T + S + C + R

In exam questions we would not be required to calculate the cyclical variation, and the random variations are by nature random and cannot be predicted and also ignored. The equation simplifies to:

Prediction = T + S

(2) *The multiplicative model.* Here the seasonal variation is expressed as a ratio/proportion/ percentage to be multiplied by the trend to arrive at the actual figure, e.g. ice-cream sales in summer are good and in general we would expect sales to be 50% more than the trend

Actual/Prediction = T x S x C x R

Again this simplifies to:

Prediction = T x S

Measuring seasonal variations

The technique for measuring seasonal variations differs between an additive model and a multiplicative model. The additive model method is described here.

- Seasonal variations can be estimated by comparing an actual time series with the trend line values calculated from the time series.
- For each 'season' (quarter, month, day etcetera), the seasonal variation is the difference between the trend line value and the actual historical value for the same period.
- A seasonal variation can be calculated for each period in the trend line. When the actual value is higher than the trend line value, the seasonal variation is positive. When the actual value is lower than the trend line value, the seasonal variation is negative.
- An average variation for each season is calculated.
- The sum of the seasonal variations has to be zero in the additive model. If they do not add up to zero, the seasonal variations should be adjusted so that they do add up to zero.
- The seasonal variations calculated in this way can be used in forecasting, by adding the seasonal variation to the trend line forecast if the seasonal variation is positive, or subtracting it from the trend line if it is negative.

When a multiplicative model is used to estimate seasonal variations, the seasonal variation for each period is calculated by expressing the actual sales for the period as a percentage value of the moving average figure for the same period.

Example of the calculation

A small business operating holiday homes in Scotland wishes to forecast next year's sales for the budget, using moving averages to establish a straight-line trend and seasonal variations. Next year is 20X7. The accountant has assumed that sales are seasonal, with a summer season and a winter season each year.

Seasonal sales for the past seven years have been as follows:

	Sales	
	Summer	*Winter*
	$000	*$000*
20X4	124	70
20X5	230	180
20X6	310	270
20X7	440	360
20X8	520	470
20X9	650	

Required:

(a) Calculate a trend line based on a two-season moving average.

(b) Calculate the average increase in sales each season.

(c) Calculate seasonal variations in sales.

(d) Use this data to prepare a sales forecast for each season in 20Y0.

Solution

(a)

Season and year	**Actual sales**	**Two-season moving total**	**Seasonal moving average**	**Centre the moving average**	**Seasonal variation**
	(A)			(B)	= (A) - (B)
	$000	*$000*	*$000*	*$000*	*$000*
Summer 20X4	124				
		194	97		
Winter 20X4	70			123.5	- 53.5
		300	150		
Summer 20X5	230			177.5	+ 52.5
		410	205		

Winter 20X5	180			225.0	- 45.0
		490	245		
Summer 20X6	310			267.5	+ 42.5
		580	290		
Winter 20X6	270			322.5	- 52.5
		710	355		
Summer 20X7	440			377.5	+ 62.5
		800	400		
Winter 20X7	360			420.0	- 60.0
		880	440		
Summer 20X8	520			467.5	+ 52.5
		990	495		
Winter 20X8	470			527.5	- 57.5
		1,120	560		
Summer 20X9	650				

The trend line is shown by the moving averages.

(b) The average increase in sales each season in the trend line is:

($527,500 - $123,500) / 8 seasons = $50, 500 each season

(c) Seasonal variations need to add up to zero in the additive model. The seasonal variations calculated so far are:

Year	Summer	Winter
	$000	$000
20X4		- 53.5
20X5	+ 52.5	- 45.0
20X6	+ 42.5	- 52.5
20X7	+ 62.5	- 60.0
20X8	+ 52.5	- 57.5
Total variations	+ 210.0	- 268.5

	Summer	Winter	Total
Number of measurements	4	5	
Average seasonal variation	+ 52.5	- 53.7	- 1.2
Reduce to 0 (share equally)	+ 0.6	+ 0.6	+ 1.2
Adjusted seasonal variation	+ 53.1	- 53.1	0.0

The seasonal variations could be rounded to + $53,000 in summer and - $53,000 in winter.

Example 4

W plc is preparing its budgets for next year.

The following regression equation has been found to be a reliable estimate of W plc's deseasonalised sales in units:

$y = 10x + 420$

Where *y* is the total sales units and *x* refers to the accountancy period. Quarterly seasonal variations have been found to be:

Q1	Q2	Q3	Q4
+10%	+25%	-5%	-30%

In accounting period 33 (which is quarter 4) identify the seasonally adjusted sales units:

A 525

B 589

C 750

D 975

(3 marks)

Advantages and disadvantages

The advantages of forecasting using time series analysis are that:

- forecasts are based on clearly-understood assumptions
- trend lines can be reviewed after each successive time period, when the most recent historical data is added to the analysis; consequently, the reliability of the forecasts can be assessed
- forecasting accuracy can possibly be improved with experience.

The disadvantages of forecasting with time series analysis are that:

- there is an assumption that what has happened in the past is a reliable guide to the future
- there is an assumption that a straight-line trend exists
- there is an assumption that seasonal variations are constant, either in actual values using the additive model (such as dollars of sales) or as a proportion of the trend line value using the multiplicative model.

None of these assumptions might be valid.

However, the reliability of a forecasting method can be established over time. If forecasts turn out to be inaccurate, management might decide that they are not worth producing, and that different methods of forecasting should be tried. On the other hand, if forecasts prove to be reasonably accurate, management are likely to continue with the same forecasting method.

7 Learning curves

It has been observed in some industries that there is a tendency for labour time per unit to reduce as more of the units are produced and thus workers become more familiar with the task.

From the experience of aircraft production during World War II, aircraft manufacturers found the rate of improvement was so regular that it could be reduced to a formula and the labour hours required could be predicted with a high degree of accuracy from a learning curve.

The first time a new operation is performed, both the workers and the operating procedures are untried. As the operation is repeated, the workers become more familiar with the work, labour efficiency increases and the labour cost per unit declines.

The learning process starts from the point when the first unit comes off the production line. From then on, each time **cumulative** production is doubled, the **cumulative average time per unit** is a fixed percentage of its previous level. An 80% learning curve means that each time cumulative output doubles the cumulative average time per unit falls to 80% of its previous value.

Example 5

A new product will take 100 hours for the first unit. An 80% learning curve applies.

Required:

Complete the table.

Cumulative			**Incremental**		
Units	**Average time per unit**	**Total time**	**Units**	**Total time**	**Average time per unit**

Learning curve formula

$y = a.x^b$ **GIVEN**

where y = average labour hours per unit

a = number of labour hours for first unit

x = cumulative number of units

b = the learning coefficient

$$b = \frac{\log \text{learning curve rate}}{\log 2}$$

For example an 80% learning curve:

$$b = \frac{\log 0.8}{\log 2} =$$

Note: the value of 'b' may be given in exam questions.

Example 5 - CONTINUED

The first unit of a new product is expected to take 100 hours. An 80% learning curve is known to apply.

Calculate:

(a) the average time per unit for the first 16 units;

(b) the average time per unit for the first 25 units;

(c) the time it takes to make the 20th unit.

General conditions for a learning curve to apply

(1) The activity should be labour intensive.

(2) The process should be repetitive for each unit.

(3) Labour turnover should be low.

(4) No prolonged breaks between production.

Applications of the learning curve effect

(1) Pricing decisions – an ability to accurately predict costs of a new product is often a very important factor when pricing a new product.

(2) Work scheduling – understanding the learning curve allows correct scheduling of labour and enables deliveries to take place on time.

(3) Standard setting – it is difficult to set labour standards where a learning curve applies. Standards should not be set until the 'steady state' has been achieved.

(4) Budgeting – cash budgets should take into account the effect of the reduction in variable costs.

Experience curves

Experience curves are very similar to learning curves but they cover all costs, not just labour costs. Material costs may decrease slightly with quantity discounts, etc. but will not decrease by a large amount. Variable overheads often follow the pattern of direct labour and so may decrease in a similar way. Fixed overheads will decrease per unit as more units are made.

Knowledge of the experience curve for a new product can be very useful. The initial cost estimates for a new product may be very high, but if they fall through the experience curve, it may allow the company to sell at a lower and hence more competitive price.

For example, it is estimated that the cost of the first unit of a new product is £650, but an 80% experience curve is expected to apply. It is estimated that the company will make and sell 2,000 units during the first year. The average cost per unit for the first 2,000 units can be calculated as follows:

$b = -0.322$ (80% learning/experience)

$y = £650 \times 2000^{-0.322} = £56.23$ per unit

This means that the selling price can be set at far below the cost of the first unit.

8 Chapter summary

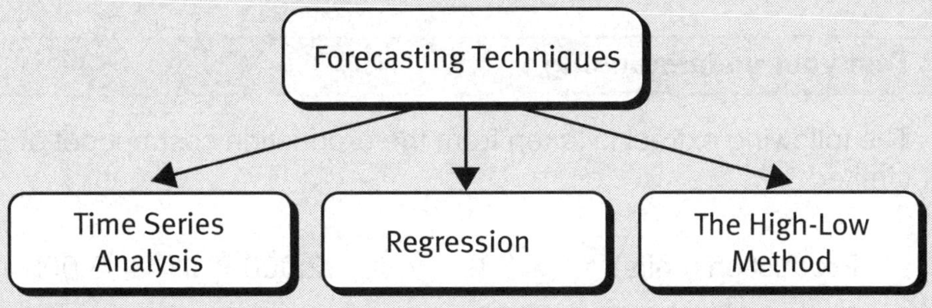

9 Practice questions

Test your understanding 1

The following extract is taken from the production cost budget of S Limited:

Production (units)	2,000	3,000
Production cost ($)	11,100	12,900

Identify the budget cost allowance for an activity level of 4,000 units:

A $7,200.

B $14,700.

C $17,200.

D $22,200.

Test your understanding 2

The following data have been extracted from the budget working papers of BL Limited

Production volume	*1,000*	*2,000*
	$/unit	*$/unit*
Direct materials	4.00	4.00
Direct labour	3.50	3.50
Production overhead - department 1	6.00	4.20
Production overhead - department 2	4.00	2.00

Identify the total fixed cost and variable cost per unit

	Total fixed cost	**Variable cost per unit**
A	3,600	7.50
B	3,600	9.90
C	7,600	7.50
D	7,600	9.90

Test your understanding 3 - DOMESTIC ELECTRICAL

A domestic electrical appliance was introduced on to the market in 2003. At the point of sale customers are offered the chance to purchase an insurance policy to cover repairs and parts for the first five years of operation these policies cannot be purchased later on, only when the appliance is first bought. The table below shows the total industry sales of this appliance for the years 2003 to 2009 together with the number of insurance policies sold and a general price index for electrical goods.

Year	Sales of Appliance ($000)	Policy sales (number)	Price index for Electrical Goods (2001 = 100)
2003	3,600	400	120
2004	6,250	300	125
2005	9,170	600	131
2006	14,000	1,200	140
2007	21,600	1,700	144
2008	27,000	2,200	150
2009	41,600	2,000	160

Required:

(a) Explain why it is important to adjust the original appliance sales figures for inflation when identifying the relationship between the sales of the appliance and the number of insurance policies sold. Deflate the appliance sales figures to 2001 prices.

(5 marks)

(b) Calculate the coefficient of determination between the deflated appliance sales figures and the insurance policy sales, and interpret your value.

(6 marks)

(c) Calculate the least squares regression equation to predict insurance policy sales from deflated appliance sales.

(3 marks)

(d) The total sales of the electrical appliance in 2010 are estimated at $51 million at 2010 prices and the price index for electrical goods in the year 2010 based on 2001 is predicted to be 170.

Use the least squares regression equation to obtain a forecast of insurance policy sales for 2010.

(3 marks)

(e) Explain the pitfalls of using this type of approach for predicting insurance policy sales in 2010.

(3 marks)

(Total: 20 marks)

Test your understanding 4

A company will forecast its quarterly sales units for a new product by using a formula to predict the base sales units and then adjusting the figure by a seasonal index.

The formula is BU = 4,000 + 80Q

Where BU = Base sales units and Q is the quarterly period number.

The seasonal index values are:

Quarter 1	105%
Quarter 2	80%
Quarter 3	95%
Quarter 4	120%

Identify the forecast increase in sales units from Quarter 3 to Quarter 4:

A 25%

B 80 units

C 100 units

D 1,156 units

(2 marks)

Test your understanding 5

A firm produces 100 units and the average time per unit is 5.32 hours. A 90% learning curve applies.

Required:

(a) Find the average time per unit if 500 units are produced.

(b) Find the average time per unit for the next 250 units.

Test your understanding 6

The first unit produced in a manufacturing process took 50 hours. However, once 250 units had been produced the average time per unit had fallen to 15 hours.

Required:

Find the learning curve rate.

Test your understanding 7

Department F assembles, by hand, widgets. A new product line was commenced last week. The first widget produced took five hours. The labour hours were fully utilised making 2,000 widgets in the first week of production. No additional labour hours are available in the short term.

Note: the department bases its learning curve calculations on the model:

$y = a.x^{-0.23}$

Production in the second week was:

A 4,920 units

B 3,482 units

C 1,741 units

D 2,920 units

(3 marks)

Test your understanding 8

Captain Bligh has designed a new type of sailing boat, for which the cost and sales price of the first boat to be produced have been estimated as follows:

	£
Direct materials	5,000
Direct labour (800 hours × £5 per hour)	4,000
Overhead (150% of labour cost)	6,000
	15,000
Profit mark-up (20%)	3,000
Sales price	18,000

It is planned to sell the yachts at full cost plus 20%. An 80% learning curve is expected to apply to the production work. Only one customer has expressed interest in buying the yacht so far, but he thinks £18,000 is too high a price to pay. He might want to buy two or even four of the yachts during the next six months.

He has asked the following questions:

(a) If he paid £18,000 for the first yacht, what price would he have to pay later for the second yacht?

(b) Could Captain Bligh quote the same unit price for the two yachts, if the customer ordered two yachts initially?

(c) If the customer bought two yachts now at one price, what price would be quoted per unit for the third and fourth yacht, if he ordered them both together later on?

Assuming that there are no other prospective customers for the yachts, how would the questions be answered?

(8 marks)

Test your understanding answers

Example 1

Step 1 Calculate the variable cost per unit

$$\text{Variable cost per unit} = \frac{\text{Increase in cost}}{\text{Increase in level of activity}}$$

$$= \frac{\$46{,}000 - \$26{,}000}{10{,}000 \text{ units} - 5{,}000 \text{ units}}$$

$$= \$4 \text{ per unit}$$

Step 2 Find the fixed cost

A semi-variable cost has only got 2 components - a fixed bit and a variable bit. We now know the variable part. The bit that's left must be the fixed cost. It can be determined either at the high level or the low level.

	High Level	Low Level
	$	$
Semi-variable cost	46,000	26,000
Variable part		
$4/unit x 10,000 units	40,000	
$4/unit x 5,000 units		20,000
Fixed cost	6,000	6,000

Step 3 Calculate the expected cost

Therefore cost for 13,000 units = 13,000 units x $4 per unit + $6,000 = $58,000

Example 2

$$b = \frac{n\Sigma xy - \Sigma x \Sigma y}{n\Sigma x^2 - (\Sigma x)^2}$$

$$= \frac{6 \times 326{,}500 - 450 \times 4{,}050}{6 \times 38{,}300 - 450^2}$$

$$= \frac{136{,}500}{27{,}300} = 5$$

$$a = \overline{y} - b\overline{x}$$

$$a = \frac{4{,}050}{6} - 5 \times \frac{450}{6} = 300$$

The regression equation is $y = 300 + 5x$

Example 2 - CONTINUED

(a)

				$000
Sales	=	300 + 5 x 150	=	1,050
Sales	=	300 + 5 x 50	=	550

(b) The second prediction is the more reliable as it involves interpolation. The first prediction goes beyond the original data upon which the regression line was based and thus assumes that the relationship will continue on in the same way, which may not be true.

Example 2 - AGAIN

$$r = \frac{n\Sigma xy - \Sigma x\Sigma y}{\sqrt{(n\Sigma x^2 - (\Sigma x)^2)(n\Sigma y^2 - (\Sigma y)^2)}}$$

$$r = \frac{6 \times 326{,}500 - 450 \times 4{,}050}{\sqrt{(6 \times 38{,}300 - 450^2)(6 \times 2{,}849{,}300 - 4{,}050^2)}}$$

$$r = \frac{136{,}500}{\sqrt{27{,}300 \times 693{,}300}}$$

$$r = 0.992$$

The coefficient of determination

$r^2 = 0.992^2 = 0.984$

This means that 98.4% of the changes in sales can be explained by changes in advertising. The other 1.6% of changes are caused by other factors.

Example 3

(a) As the line of best fit is based on 20X4 prices, use this as the common price level. Costs should therefore be adjusted by a factor:

$$\frac{\text{Index level to which costs will be adjusted}}{\text{Actual index level of costs}}$$

Year	Actual overheads	Cost index	Adjustment factor	Costs at 20X8 price level
	$			$
20X5	143,040	192	x 235/192	175,075
20X6	156,000	200	x 235/200	183,300
20X7	152,320	224	x 235/224	159,800
20X8	172,000	235	x 235/235	172,000

(b) If the forecast number of machine hours is 3,100 and the cost index is 250:

Forecast overhead costs = [$33,000 + ($47 × 3,100 hours)] × (250/235)

= $178,700 × (250/235)

= $190,106

Example 4

A

y = 10x + 420

We are told that x refers to the accountancy period, which is 33, therefore:

y = 420 + 33 x 10 = 750

This is the trend, however and we need to consider the seasonal variation too. Accounting period 33 is quarter 4. Quarter 4 is a bad quarter and the seasonal variation is -30%, therefore the expected results for period 33 are 30% less than the trend.

Expected sales = 750 x 70% = 525 units

Example 5

Cumulative			**Incremental**		
Units	**Average time p.u.**	**Total time**	**Units**	**Total time**	**Average time p.u.**
1	100	100	1	100	100
2	80	160	1	60	60
4	64	256	2	96	48
8	51.2	409.6	4	153.6	38.4
16	40.96	655.36	8	245.76	30.72

Example 5 - CONTINUED

(a)	a	= 100	b = –0.3219 x = 16
	y	= $100.16^{-0.3219}$	
		= 40.96 hours	
(b)	x	= 25	
	y	= $100.25^{-0.3219}$	
		= 35.48 hours	
(c)	x	= 20	
	y	= $100.20^{-0.3219}$	
		= 38.12 hours	
	Total time for 20 units = 38.12 × 20	= 762.42	
	x	= 19	
	y	= $100.19^{-0.3219}$	
		= 38.76 hours	
	Total time for 19 units = 38.76 × 19	= 736.35	
		= 762.42 – 736.35	
		= **26.07 hours**	

Test your understanding 1

B

The high-low method

Step 1 Calculate the variable cost per unit

$$\text{Variable cost per unit} = \frac{\text{Increase in cost}}{\text{Increase in level of activity}}$$

$$= \frac{\$12{,}900 - \$11{,}100}{3{,}000 \text{ units} - 2{,}000 \text{ units}}$$

$$= \$1.80 \text{ per unit}$$

Step 2 Find the fixed cost

A semi-variable cost has only got 2 components - a fixed bit and a variable bit. We now know the variable part. The bit that's left must be the fixed cost. It can be determined either at the high level or the low level.

	High Level	Low Level
	$	$
Semi-variable cost	12,900	11,100
Variable part		
$1.80/unit x 3,000 units	5,400	
$1.80/unit x 2,000 units		3,600
Fixed cost	7,500	7,500

Therefore cost for 4,000 units = 4,000 units x $1.80 per unit + $7,500 = $14,700.

Test your understanding 2

D

We know the cost per unit. We need to multiply by the number of units so that we can find the total cost for 1,000 units and 2,000 units. Then we can apply the high-low method.

Production volume	**1,000**	**2,000**
	$/unit	*$/unit*
Direct materials	4.00	4.00
Direct labour	3.50	3.50
Production overhead - department 1	6.00	4.20
Production overhead - department 2	4.00	2.00
	17.50	13.70
x No of units	x 1,000	x 2,000
Total cost	17,500	27,400

Now we can do the high-low method.

The high-low method

Step 1 Calculate the variable cost per unit

$$\text{Variable cost per unit} = \frac{\text{Increase in cost}}{\text{Increase in level of activity}}$$

$$= \frac{\$27{,}400 - \$17{,}500}{2{,}000 \text{ units} - 1{,}000 \text{ units}}$$

$$= \$9.90 \text{ per unit}$$

Step 2 Find the fixed cost

A semi-variable cost has only got 2 components - a fixed bit and a variable bit. We now know the variable part. The bit that's left must be the fixed cost. It can be determined either at the high level or the low level.

	High Level	Low Level
	$	$
Semi-variable cost	27,400	17,500
Variable part		
$9.90/unit x 2,000 units	19,800	
$9.90/unit x 1,000 units		9,900
Fixed cost	7,600	7,600

Test your understanding 3 - DOMESTIC ELECTRICAL

(a) The factor affecting the number of policies sold is the number of appliances sold. We do not know the number of appliances sold, however, just the value, which is distorted by inflation. If we deflate the appliance sales we can remove the distorting effect and see the underlying change in the level of activity.

Year	**Sales of Appliances** $000		**Deflated Sales** $000
2003	3,600	x 100/120	3,000
2004	6,250	x 100/125	5,000
2005	9,170	x 100/131	7,000
2006	14,000	x 100/140	10,000
2007	21,600	x 100/144	15,000
2008	27,000	x 100/150	18,000
2009	41,600	x 100/160	26,000

(b)

Deflated Appliance Sales $m	*Policy Sales 000s*			
x	y	xy	x2	y2
3	0.4	1.2	9	0.16
5	0.3	1.5	25	0.09
7	0.6	4.2	49	0.36
10	1.2	12.0	100	1.44
15	1.7	25.5	225	2.89
18	2.2	39.6	324	4.84
26	2.0	52.0	676	4.00
84	8.4	136.0	1408	13.78

$$r = \frac{n\Sigma xy - \Sigma x\Sigma y}{\sqrt{(n\Sigma x^2 - (\Sigma x)^2)(n\Sigma y^2 - (\Sigma y)^2)}}$$

$$r = \frac{7 \times 136 - 84 \times 8.4}{\sqrt{(7 \times 1{,}408 - 84^2)(7 \times 13.78 - 8.4^2)}}$$

$$r = \frac{246.4}{\sqrt{2{,}800 \times 25.9}}$$

$$r = 0.915$$

$$r^2 = 0.915^2 = 0.837$$

This means that 83.7% of the changes in policy sales can be explained by changes in the level of the deflated appliance sales. The other 16.3% of changes are caused by other factors.

(c)

$$b = \frac{n\Sigma xy - \Sigma x\Sigma y}{n\Sigma x^2 - (\Sigma x)^2}$$

$$= \frac{7 \times 136 - 84 \times 8.4}{7 \times 1{,}408 - 84^2}$$

$$= \frac{246.4}{2{,}800} = 0.088$$

$$a = \bar{y} - b\bar{x}$$

$$a = \frac{8.4}{7} - 0.088 \times \frac{84}{7} = 0.144$$

The Regression equation is $y = 0.144 + 0.088x$

Where x is deflated appliance sales ($m)

And y is policy sales (000s)

(d) Deflated appliance sales = 51m x 100/170 = $30m

Policy sales = 0.144 + 0.088 x 30

= 2.784 (000s)

= 2,784 policies

(e) (1) We are extrapolating. We have determined a regression equation showing the relationship between deflated appliance sales and policy sales for activity levels between $3m and $26m in terms of deflated sales. We are making a prediction for activity levels outside this range and assuming that the relationship would continue in the same way. This might not be so.

(2) Even if we had not been extrapolating we would be assuming that the historic pattern that we had established in the past would continue into the future. Again this might not be so.

Test your understanding 4

D

Sales in quarter 3 (Q=3)			
Base = 4000 + (80 ×3)	=	4,240	
Seasonal adjustment		95%	
Actual sales	=	4,028	
Sales in quarter 4 (Q=4)			
Base = 4000 + (80 ×4)	=	4,320	
Seasonal adjustment		120%	
Actual sales	=	5,184	
Overall increase in sales	=	5,184 – 4,028	= 1,156 units

Test your understanding 5

(a) x = 100 units y = 5.32 hours $b = \frac{\log 0.9}{\log 2} = -0.1520$

$y = a.x^b$

$5.32 = a.100^{-0.1520}$

$\therefore$ a = 10.71 hours

when x = 500 units

$y = 10.71 \times 500^{-0.1520}$

y = 4.16 hours per unit

Average time per unit is 4.16 hours

(b) Cumulative output = 750 units

Therefore

When x = 750,

$y = 10.71 \times 750^{-0.1520}$

= 3.915 hours per unit

Total hours for 750 units	= 3.915 × 750	= 2,936.52 hours
Total hours for 500 units	= 4.16 × 500	= 2,080 hours
Total hours for last 250 units	= 2,936.52 – 2,080	= 856.52
Therefore, time per unit	= 856.52 ÷ 250	= **3.43 hours per unit**

Test your understanding 6

$y = a.x^b$

$15 = 50 \times 250^b$

$0.30 = 250^b$

$\log 0.30 = \log 250^b$

$\log 0.30 = b \times \log 250$

$$\frac{\log 0.30}{\log 250} = b$$

$-0.2180533 = b$

$$\frac{\log \text{rate}}{\log 2} = -0.2180533$$

$\log \text{rate} = -0.2180533 \times \log 2$

$\log \text{rate} = -0.0656405$

$\therefore$ rate = 0.8597, i.e. **86%**

Test your understanding 7

a	=	5
x	=	2,000
b	=	–0.23
y	=	$5.2000^{-0.23}$
	=	0.8704 hours per unit
Total labour hours available each week	= 2,000 × 0.8704	= 1,740.857 hours
Cumulative hours after two weeks	= 1,740.857 × 2	= 3,481.71 hours

Let 'x' be total production in two weeks

$$y = a \,.\, x^{b}$$

$$\frac{3{,}481.71}{x} = 5 \,.\, x^{-0.23}$$

$$\frac{3{,}481.71}{5} = x^{1} \,.\, x^{-0.23}$$

When multiplying the two x terms together, it is necessary to add the powers, i.e. 1 + – 0.23 = + 0.77

$$696.34 = x^{0.77}$$

$$\sqrt[0.77]{696.34} = x$$

$$4{,}920.12 = x$$

Total production after two years = 4,920 units

Therefore production in the second year = 4,920 – 2,000 = 2,920 units

Answer D

Test your understanding 8

Number of yachts	Cumulative average time per unit (hours)	Total hours	Incremental hours
1	800	800	800
2	640	1,280	480
4	512	2,048	768

(a) Price for the second yacht:

	£
Direct materials	5,000
Direct labour (480 hours x £5 per hour)	2,400
Overhead (150% of labour cost)	3,600
	11,000
Profit mark-up (20%)	2,200
Sales price	13,200

(b) Average price per yacht for the first two yachts =

$$\frac{£18,000 + £13,200}{2} = £15,600$$

(c) Average hours per yacht = 768 ÷ 2 = 384 hours

A single price for yachts 3 and 4:

	£
Direct materials	5,000
Direct labour (384 hours × £5 per hour)	1,920
Overhead (150% of labour cost)	2,880
	9,800
Profit mark-up (20%)	1,960
Sales price	11,760

chapter

12

The treatment of uncertainty and risk in decision making

Chapter learning objectives

Lead	Component
D1. Analyse information to assess the impact on decisions of variables with uncertain values.	(a) Analyse the impact of uncertainty and risk on decision models that may be based on relevant cash flows, learning curves, discounting techniques etc. (b) Apply sensitivity analysis to both short and long-run decision models to identify variables that might have significant impacts on project outcomes. (c) Analyse risk and uncertainty by calculating expected values and standard deviations together with probability tables and histograms. (d) Prepare expected value tables. (e) Calculate the value of information. (f) Apply decision trees.

1 Session content diagram

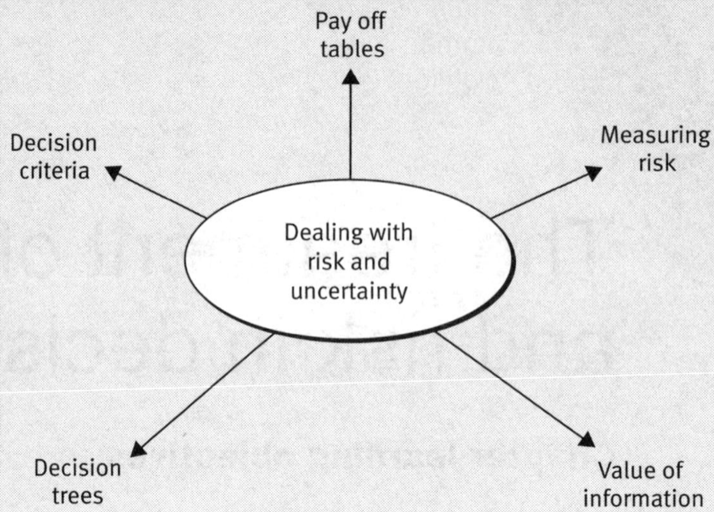

2 Introduction

Over the next few chapters we explore some decision making problems such as whether to launch new products, whether to buy machines, choosing between products etc.

All of these decisions will involve an element of risk and uncertainty. This chapter looks at how risk and uncertainty can be built into the decision making process. This is often achieve by building in probabilities for expected outcomes and using expected values and decision trees to assess the problem.

Topic overview

Forecasting and decision making often inlcude an element of risk or uncertainty. Because they look to the future they often involve estimates of future costs and benefits. In this chapter we look at how these risks and uncertainty can be built into the decision making process.

Decision making involves making decisions now about what will happen in the future. Events in the future can be predicted, but managers can rarely be 100% confident that these predicted future events will actually arise. As actual results emerge managers are likely to discover that they have achieved better or worse results than those predicted originally.

There are several ways of dealing with this variability of outcomes. In this session we will consider several different possible outcomes that may arise. It is common in practice to consider three possible outcomes; the most likely outcome, the pessimistic (worst possible) outcome and the optimistic (best possible) outcome. Analysts may consider more than these three possibilities, but more information will become more complicated and cumbersome to analyse and understand.

Examination questions will generally provide all the different possible outcomes that may arise, together with the associated chance (probability) of the outcome occurring. It is our task to analyse the information given, recommend an appropriate strategy for management to follow and finally to highlight the potential risk involved in the various choices.

3 Risk and uncertainty

The difference between risk and uncertainty

Investment appraisal faces the following problems:

- all decisions are based on forecasts
- all forecasts are subject to uncertainty
- this uncertainty needs to be reflected in the financial evaluation.

The decision maker must distinguish between:

- **risk** – quantifiable – possible outcomes have associated probabilities, thus allowing the use of mathematical techniques
- **uncertainty** – unquantifiable – outcomes cannot be mathematically modelled.

Illustration 1

Risk: there are a number of possible outcomes and the probability of each outcome is known.

For example, based on past experience of digging for oil in a particular area, an oil company may estimate that they have a 60% chance of finding oil and a 40% chance of not finding oil.

Uncertainty: there are a number of possible outcomes but the probability of each outcome is not known.

For example, the same oil company may dig for oil in a previously unexplored area. The company knows that it is possible for them to either find or not find oil but it does not know the probabilities of each of these outcomes.

Risk attitudes

The selection criterion applied by the manager will often depend upon the manager's attitude towards risk. It is common to recognise three different attitudes:

Risk neutral	This person considers all possible outcomes and will select the strategy that maximises the expected value of benefit.
Risk seeker	The decision maker is likely to select the strategy with the best possible outcomes, regardless of the likelihood that they will occur. This person will apply the maximax criterion.
Risk averse	This person will consider the worst outcome each time. They will apply the maximin criterion or the minimax regret approach.

4 Probabilities and expected values

An expected value summarises all the different possible outcomes by calculating a single weighted average. It is the long run average (mean).

The expected value is not the most likely result. It may not even be a possible result., but instead it finds the average outcome if the same event was to take place thousands of times.

Expected value formula

EV = Σpx **LEARN**

where x represents the future outcome

and p represents the probability of the outcome occurring

Example 1 – Calculating an expected value

A company expects the following monthly profits:

Monthly profit	Probability
£10,000	0.70
£20,000	0.30

Calculate the expected value of monthly profit.

Advantages and disadvatages of EVs

Advantages:

- Takes risk into account by considering the probability of each possible outcome and using this information to calculate an expected value.
- The information is reduced to a single number resulting in easier decisions.
- Calculations are relatively simple.

Disadvantages:

- The probabilities used are usually very subjective.
- The EV is merely a weighted average and therefore has little meaning for a one-off project.
- The EV gives no indication of the dispersion of possible outcomes about the EV, i.e. the risk.
- The EV may not correspond to any of the actual possible outcomes.

5 Pay off tables and decision criteria

When evaluating alternative courses of action, management's decision will often depend upon their attitude towards the risk. To consider the risk borne by each alternative it is necessary to consider ALL the different possible profits/losses that may arise. A pay off table is simply a table that illustrates all possible profits/losses.

Example 2 - Profit tables

- Hofgarten Newsagents stocks a weekly magazine which advertises local second-hand goods. Marie, the owner, can:
  - buy the magazines for 15c each
  - sell them at the retail price of 25c
- At the end of each week unsold magazines are obsolete and have no value.

- Marie estimates a probability distribution for weekly demand which looks like this:

Weekly demand in units	Probability
10	0.20
15	0.55
20	0.25
	1.00

Required:

(i) Calculate the expected value of demand?

(ii) If Marie is to order a fixed quantity of magazines per week, calculate how many should that be. Assume no seasonal variations in demand.

Decision making criteria

When managers are faced with mutually exclusive options and there are several possible outcomes that may arise for each given decision, there are four basic decision criteria that may be applied to enable the manager to make their decision. Namely:

The expected value criterion	This considers all possible outcomes. A weighted average profit (benefit) is calculated for each decision strategy. The option with the highest expected value is then chosen.
The maximax criterion	Find the best pay off for each supply option. Then select the strategy with the highest of these various maximums. Choose the best of the best.
The maximin criterion	Find the worst pay off for each supply option. Select the supply level with the highest of these worst pay offs. The best of the worst is chosen.
The minimax regret criterion	In order to apply this criterion it is necessary to construct a regret (or opportunity loss) table first. This table illustrates the opportunity that is lost if a decision has been undertaken that was not the optimum decision for that particular demand. Then establish the maximum regret for each possible supply strategy. Select the strategy with the minimum of these maximum regrets. The aim is to avoid opportunity losses.

Perfect and imperfect information

In many questions the decision makers receive a forecast of a future outcome (for example a market research group may predict the forthcoming demand for a product). This forecast may turn out to be correct or incorrect. The question often requires the candidate to calculate the value of the forecast.

Perfect information The forecast of the future outcome is always a correct prediction. If a firm can obtain a 100% accurate prediction they will always be able to undertake the most beneficial course of action for that prediction.

Imperfect information The forecast is usually correct, but can be incorrect. Imperfect information is not as valuable as perfect information. Imperfect information may be examined in conjunction with Decision Trees (see later in this chapter).

The value of information (either perfect or imperfect) may be calculated as follows:

Expected profit (outcome) WITH the information

minus

Expected profit (outcome) WITHOUT the information

Example 3 – Pay off tables and decision criteria

Geoffrey Ramsbottom runs a kitchen that provides food for various canteens throughout a large organisation. A particular salad is sold to the canteen for £10 and it costs £8 to prepare.

Based upon past demands, it is expected that during the 250-day working year the canteens will require the following quantities;

On 25 days	40 salads
On 50 days	50 salads
On 100 days	60 salads
On 75 days	70 salads

The kitchen must prepare the salad in batches of 10 meals and it has to decide how many it will supply for each day of the forthcoming year.

Required:

(a) Tabulate a pay off table.

(6 marks)

(b) Calculate how many salads should be made by the kitchen each day if the following decision criteria are applied:

(i) expected value criterion;

(ii) maximax rule;

(iii) maximin rule;

(iv) minimax regret rule.

(10 marks)

(c) A new ordering system is being considered, whereby customers must order their salad online the day before. With this new system Mr Ramsbottom will know for certain the daily demand 24 hours in advance. He can adjust production levels on a daily basis. Calcualte how much this new system is worth to Mr Ramsbottom.

(4 marks)

6 Decision trees and multi-stage decision problems

A decision tree is a diagrammatic representation of a decision problem, where all possible courses of action are represented, and every possible outcome of each course of action is shown. Decision trees should be used where a problem involves a series of decisions being made and several outcomes arise during the decision-making process. Decision trees force the decision maker to consider the logical sequence of events. A complex problem is broken down into smaller, easier-to-handle sections. The financial outcomes and probabilities are shown separately, and the decision tree is 'rolled back' by calculating expected values and making decisions. In the examination ensure that only relevant costs and revenues are considered, and that all cash is expressed in present value terms.

Three-step method

Step 1: Draw the tree from left to right showing appropriate decisions and events/outcomes.

Symbols to use:

□ A square is used to represent a decision point. At a decision point the decision maker has a choice of which course of action he wishes to undertake.

○ A circle is used at a chance outcome point. The branches from here are always subject to probabilities.

Label the tree and relevant cash inflows/outflows (discounted to present values) and probabilities associated with outcomes.

Step2: Evaluate the tree from right to left carrying out these two actions:

Calculate an EV at each outcome point.

Choose the best option at each decision point.

Step 3: Recommend a course of action to management.

Example 4 - Decision trees

An oil company has recently acquired rights in a certain area to conduct surveys and geological test drillings that may lead to lifting oil where it is found in commercially exploitable quantities.

The area is already considered to have good potential for finding oil in commercial quantities. At the outset the company has the choice to conduct further geological tests or to carry out a drilling programme immediately. On the known conditions, the company estimates that there is a 70% chance of further tests indicating that a significant amount of oil is present.

Whether the tests show the possibility of oil or not, or even if no tests are undertaken at all, the company could still pursue its drilling programme or alternatively consider selling its rights to drill in the area.

Thereafter, however, if it carries out the drilling programme, the likelihood of final success or failure in the search for oil is considered dependent on the foregoing stages. Thus:

(i) If the tests indicated that oil was present, the expectation of success in drilling is given as 80%.

(ii) If the tests indicated that there was insufficient oil present, then the expectation of success in drilling is given as 20%.

(iii) If no tests have been carried out at all, the expectation of finding commercially viable quantities of oil is given as 55%.

Costs and revenues have been estimated for all possible outcomes and the net present value of each is given below:

Outcome	**Net present value**
	£ millions
Geological testing	(10)
Drilling cost	(50)
Success in finding oil	150
Sale of exploitation rights:	
Tests indicate oil is present	65
Tests indicate 'no oil'	15
Without geological tests	40

Required:

(a) Prepare a decision tree diagram to represent the above information.

(8 marks)

(b) For the management of the company, calculate its best course of action.

(7 marks)

(c) Explain the value of decision trees in providing management with guidance for decision making. Illustrate examples of any situations where you consider their use would be of benefit.

(5 marks)

(Total: 20 marks)

7 Sensitivity analysis

Sensitivity analaysis takes each uncertain factor in turn, and calculates the change that would be necessary in that factor before the original decision is reversed.

By using this technique it is possible to establish which estimates (variables) are more critical than others in affecting a decision.

The process is as follows:

- Best estimates for variables are made and a decision arrived at. For example, a NPV calculation may indicate accepting a project.
- Each of the variables is analysed in turn to see how much the original estimate can change before the original decision is reversed. For example, it may be that the estimated selling price can fall by 5% before the NPV becomes negative and the project would be rejected.
- Estimates for each variable can then be reconsidered to assess the likelihood of the decision being wrong. For example, what is the chance of the selling price falling by more than 5%?

Example 5 - Sensitivity analysis

A manager is considering a make v buy decision based on the following estimates:

	If made in-house	**If buy in and re-badge**
	$	$
Variable production costs	10	2
External purchase costs	-	6
Ultimate selling price	15	14

Identify the sensitivity of the decision to the external purchase price.

Strengths and weaknesses

Strengths of sensitivity analysis

- There is no complicated theory to understand.
- Information will be presented to management in a form which facilitates subjective judgement to decide the likelihood of the various possible outcomes considered.
- It identifies areas which are crucial to the success of the project. If the project is chosen, those areas can be carefully monitored.

Weaknesses of sensitivity analysis

- It assumes that changes to variables can be made independently, e.g. material prices will change independently of other variables. Simulation allows us to change more than one variable at a time.
- It only identifies how far a variable needs to change; it does not look at the probability of such a change.
- It provides information on the basis of which decisions can be made but it does not point to the correct decision directly.

8 Chapter summary

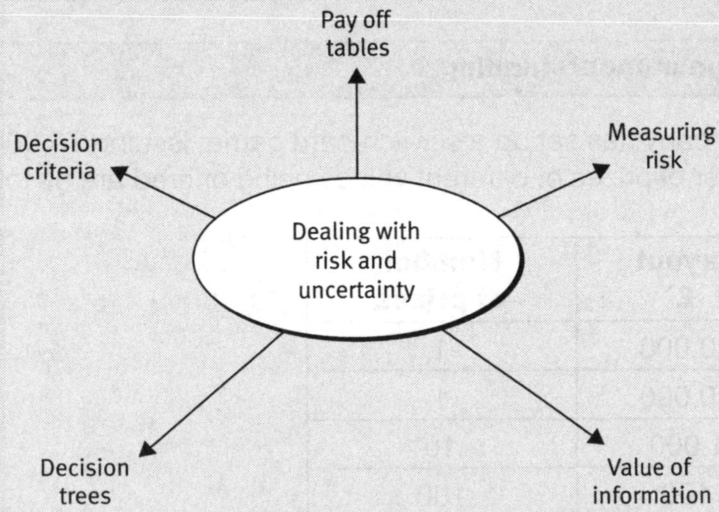

9 Practice questions

Test your understanding 1

A company has set up a scratch-card game, issuing 75,000 cards. The number of prizes of different values being offered are as follows:

Payout £	Number of prizes
20,000	1
10,000	1
1,000	10
100	100
5	2,000

Assuming they sell all 75,000 tickets for £1 each, identify the expected gain per card to the company:

A 15p

B 20p

C 41p

D 59p

(2 marks)

Test your understanding 2

Identify the correct description of imperfect information:

A costs more to collect than its value to the business;

B is available only after preliminary decisions on a business venture have been taken;

C does not take into account all factors affecting a business;

D may contain inaccurate predictions.

(2 marks)

Test your understanding 3

A company is considering investing in one of the following projects.

Project	Expected value £000	Standard deviation £000
A	850	500
B	1,200	480
C	150	200
D	660	640

It wishes to select the project with the lowest risk factor (coefficient of variation). Identify which project should it select:

A Project A

B Project B

C Project C

D Project D

(2 marks)

Test your understanding 4 – SITERAZE LTD

Siteraze Ltd is a company which engages in site clearance and site preparation work. Information concerning its operations is as follows:

(a) It is company policy to hire all plant and machinery required for the implementation of all orders obtained, rather than to purchase its own plant and machinery.

(b) Siteraze Ltd will enter into an advance hire agreement contract for the coming year at one of three levels – high, medium or low, which correspond to the requirements of a high, medium or low level of orders obtained.

(c) The level of orders obtained will not be known when the advance hire agreement contract is entered into. A set of probabilities have been estimated by management as to the likelihood of the orders being at high, medium or low level.

(d) Where the advance hire agreement entered into is lower than that required for the level of orders actually obtained, a premium rate must be paid to obtain additional plant and machinery required.

(e) No refund is obtainable where the advance hire agreement for plant and machinery is at a level in excess of that required to satisfy the site clearance and preparation orders actually obtained.

A summary of the information relating to the above points is as follows:

			Plant and machinery hire costs	
Level of orders	**Revenue** £000	**Probability**	**Advance hire** £000	**Conversion remium** £000
High	15,000	0.25	2,300	
Medium	8,500	0.45	1,500	
Low	4,000	0.30	1,000	
Low to medium				850
Medium to high				1,300
Low to high				2,150

Variable cost (as a percentage of turnover) 70%

Required:

(a) Prepare a summary which shows the forecast net margin earned by Siteraze Ltd for the coming year for each possible outcome.

(8 marks)

(b) On the basis of maximising expected value, calculate for Siteraze whether the advance contract for the hire of plant and machinery should be at the low, medium or high level.

(6 marks)

(c) Explain how the risk preferences of the management members responsible for the choice of advance plant and machinery hire contract may alter the decision reached in (b) above.

(6 marks)

(d) Siteraze Ltd are considering employing a market research consultant who will be able to say with certainty in advance of the placing of the plant and machinery hire contract, which level of site clearance and preparation orders will be obtained. On the basis of expected value, calculate the maximum sum which Siteraze Ltd should be willing to pay the consultant for this information.

(5 marks)

(Total: 25 marks)

Test your understanding 5 - CHARITY ORGANISATION

For the past 20 years a charity organisation has held an annual dinner and dance with the primary intention of raising funds.

This year there is concern that an economic recession may adversely affect both the number of persons attending the function and the advertising space that will be sold in the programme published for the occasion.

Based on past experience and current prices and quotations, it is expected that the following costs and revenues will apply for the function:

			£
Cost:	Dinner and dance:	Hire of premises	700
		Band and entertainers	2,800
		Raffle prizes	800
		Photographer	200
		Food at £12 per person (with a guarantee of 400 persons minimum)	
	Programme:	A fixed cost of £2,000 plus £5 per page	
Revenues:	Dinner and dance:	Price of tickets	£20 per person
		Average revenue from:	
		Raffle	£5 per person
		Photographs	£1 per person
	Programme:	Average revenue from advertising	£70 per page

A sub-committee, formed to examine more closely the likely outcome of the function, discovered the following from previous records and accounts:

Number of tickets sold	Number of past occasions
250 to 349	4
350 to 449	6
450 to 549	8
550 to 649	2

Number of programme pages sold	Number of past occasions
24	4
32	8
40	6
48	2

Required:

Calculate the expected value of the profit to be earned from the dinner and dance this year.

Test your understanding 6 - APPLYING MAXIMAX

A company is choosing which of three new products to make (A, B or C) and has calculated likely pay-offs under three possible scenarios (I, II or III), giving the following pay-off table.

Profit (loss)	Product chosen		
Scenario	A	B	C
I	20	80	10
II	40	70	100
III	50	(10)	40

Required:

Using maximax, calculate which product would be chosen.

(5 marks)

Apply the maximin rule to decide which product should be made.

(5 marks)

Apply the minimax regret rule to decide which product should be made.

(8 marks)

Test your understanding 7 - RS GROUP

The RS Group owns a large store in Ludborough. The store is old-fashioned and profits are declining. Management is considering what to do – there appear to be three possibilities:

(1) Shut down and sell the site for £15m.

(2) Continue as before with profits declining.

(3) Upgrade the store.

The Group has had problems in the past and experience suggests that when stores are upgraded, 60% achieve good results and 40% poor results.

Because of the doubts, management is considering whether to contact a leading market research company to carry out consumer research in Ludborough for £1m. It has been fortunate in obtaining details of the track record of the research company, as follows:

		Actual outcome	
		Good	Poor
Attitude predicted by research	Positive	0.85 *	0.10
	Negative	0.15	0.90

* This means that when the actual results were good the research had predicted this 85% of the time.

If the research indicates a positive attitude, management will consider deluxe upgrading which will generate more profit but will cost £12m, as compared with standard upgrading costing £6m.

If the research indicates a negative attitude, then management will consider standard upgrading compared with shutting down and selling the site.

The time scale for the analysis is 10 years and the following estimates of returns have been made:

With Deluxe upgrading:	Good results	£40m total present value
	Poor results	£20m total present value
With Standard upgrading:	Good results	£25m total present value
	Poor results	£10m total present value

If operations continue as before, returns over the next 10 years will be £13.03m in present value terms.

You are required:

(a) prepare a decision tree to represent the above information;

(19 marks)

Note: No discounting is necessary for this question as the values are already expressed in present value terms.

(b) calculate what decisions should be taken;

(3 marks)

(c) explain the basis of your analysis.

(3 marks)

(Total: 25 marks)

Test your understanding 8

A company can make either of two new products, X and Y, but not both. The profitability of each product depends on the state of the market, as follows:

Market state	Profit from product		Probability of market state
	X £	Y £	
Good	20,000	17,000	0.2
Fair	15,000	16,000	0.5
Poor	6,000	7,000	0.3

Calculate the expected value of perfect information as to the state of the market

A £0

B £600

C £800

D £1,000

(2 marks)

Test your understanding 9 - SENSITIVITY ANALYSIS

A manager has identified the following two possible outcomes for a process.

Outcome	Probability	Financial implications ($000s)
Poor	0.4	Loss of 20
Good	0.6	Profit of 40

The expected value has been calculated as EV = (0.4 × -20) + (0.6 × 40) = +16. This would suggest that the opportunity should be accepted.

Required:

(a) Suppose the likely loss if results are poor has been underestimated. Calculate the level of loss would change the decision? (In effect we want a break-even estimate.)

(b) Suppose the probability of a loss has been underestimated. Calculate the break-even probability?

Test your understanding 10

The Venus Department Store operates a customer loan facility. If one of its new customers requests a loan then Venus either refuses it, gives a high loan limit, or gives a low loan limit. From a number of years past experience the probability that a new customer makes a full repayment of a loan is known to be 0.95, whilst the probability of non-repayment is 0.05 (these probabilities being independent of the size of loan limit). The average profit in £, per customer made by Venus is given by the following table.

	Loan Limit	
	High	**Low**
Full-repayment	50	20
Non-repayment	–200	–30

Required:

(a) In the past the company has used a selection criterion that is totally arbitrary (i.e. it is not influenced by the customer's ability to repay).

Prepare a decision tree to represent the information. Calculate the expected value and explain what the management of Venus should do if a new customer requests a loan?

(6 marks)

(b) Venus can apply to an agency to evaluate the credit-rating of a customer. This agency would provide a rating for the customer as either a good risk or as a bad risk, this credit-rating being independent of the size of the loan being considered. Analysis of the last 1,000 customer ratings by this agency revealed the following information.

Agency	Type of customer		
Credit Rating	**Full-repayment**	**Non-repayment**	**Total**
Good risk	790	10	800
Bad risk	160	40	200
Total	950	50	1,000

Determine the value of this credit rating to Venus

(9 marks)

(c) The Venus management believe that this first agency is not very good at selecting full-payers and non-payers. It considers contacting a second agency which guarantees perfect information concerning the credit rating of the customers.

Explain the meaning of the term 'perfect information' in the context of this question.

Calculate the value of this perfect information.

(5 marks)

(Total: 20 marks)

Test your understanding answers

Example 1 – Calculating an expected value

Expected value formula

$$EV = \Sigma px$$

Monthly profit	Probability	px
£10,000	0.70	7,000
£20,000	0.30	6,000
		13,000

Expected profit is £13,000 per month.

Example 2 - Profit tables

(i) EV of demand = (10 × 0.20) + (15 × 0.55) + (20 × 0.25) = 15.25 units per week.

(ii) The first step is to set up a decision matrix of possible strategies (numbers bought) and possible demand, as follows:

Outcome (number demanded)	**Strategy (number bought)** 10	15	20
10			
15			
20			

The 'pay-off' from each combination of action and outcome is then computed:

No sale: cost of 15c per magazine.

Sale: profit of 25c — 15c = 10c per magazine

Pay-offs are shown for each combination of strategy and outcome.

Probability	**Outcome (number demanded)**	**Decision (number bought)** 10	15	20
0.20	10	100	25	(50)
0.55	15	100	150	75
0.25	20	100	150	200
1.00	EV	100c	125c	81.25c

Conclusion: The strategy which gives the highest expected pay-off is to stock 15 magazines each week.

Workings

(i) If 10 magazines are bought, then 10 are sold no matter how many are demanded and the payoff is always 10 × 10c = 100c.

(ii) If 15 magazines are bought and 10 are demanded, then 10 are sold at a profit of 10 × 10c = 100c, and 5 are scrapped at a loss of 5 × 15c = 75c, making a net profit of 25c

(iii) The other contributions are similarly calculated.

Example 3 – Pay off tables and decision criteria

(a)

			Daily Supply			
		Probability	40	50	60	70
Daily Demand	40	0.10	£80	£0	(£80)	(£160)
	50	0.20	£80	£100	£20	(£60)
	60	0.40	£80	£100	£120	£40
	70	0.30	£80	£100	£120	£140

Profit if an item is sold = £10 − £8 = £2

$$P(\text{demand of }40) = \frac{25}{250} = 0.10$$

$$P(\text{demand of }50) = \frac{50}{250} = 0.20 \quad \text{etc}$$

(b) (i)

Supply	Expected value	Working
40	£80	
50	£90	(0 × 0.1) + (£100 × 0.9)
60	£80	(–£80 × 0.1) 20 × 0.2) + (£120 × 0.7)
70	£30	(–£160 × 0.1) + (–£60 × 0.2) + (£40 × 0.4) + (140 × 0.3)

To maximise expected profits, the company should supply 50 salads per day.

(ii) Maximax criterion

Supply	Maximum pay off
40	£80
50	£100
60	£120
70	£140 Highest

Supply 70 salads each day

(iii) Maximin criterion

Supply	Minimum pay off
40	£80 Highest
50	£0
60	(£80)
70	(160)

Supply 40 salads each day

(iv) Regret table

			Daily Supply			
		Probability	40	50	60	70
Daily Demand	40	0.10	£0	£80	£160	£240
	50	0.20	£20	£0	£80	£160
	60	0.40	£40	£20	£0	£80
	70	0.30	£60	£40	£20	£0

To calculate the regrets find the biggest payoff for each demand row, then subtract all other numbers in this row from the largest number.

Minimax regret criterion

Supply	Maximum regret
40	£60 Lowest
50	£80
60	£160
70	£240

Supply 50 salads each day

(c)

Supply = demand	X Pay off	P Probability	px
40	80	0.1	8
50	£100	0.2	20
60	£120	0.4	48
70	£140	0.3	42
			118
E.V. with perfect information =			£118
E.V. without perfect information =			£90
			——
Value of perfect information			£28 per day
			——

Example 4 - Decision trees

(a) and (b)

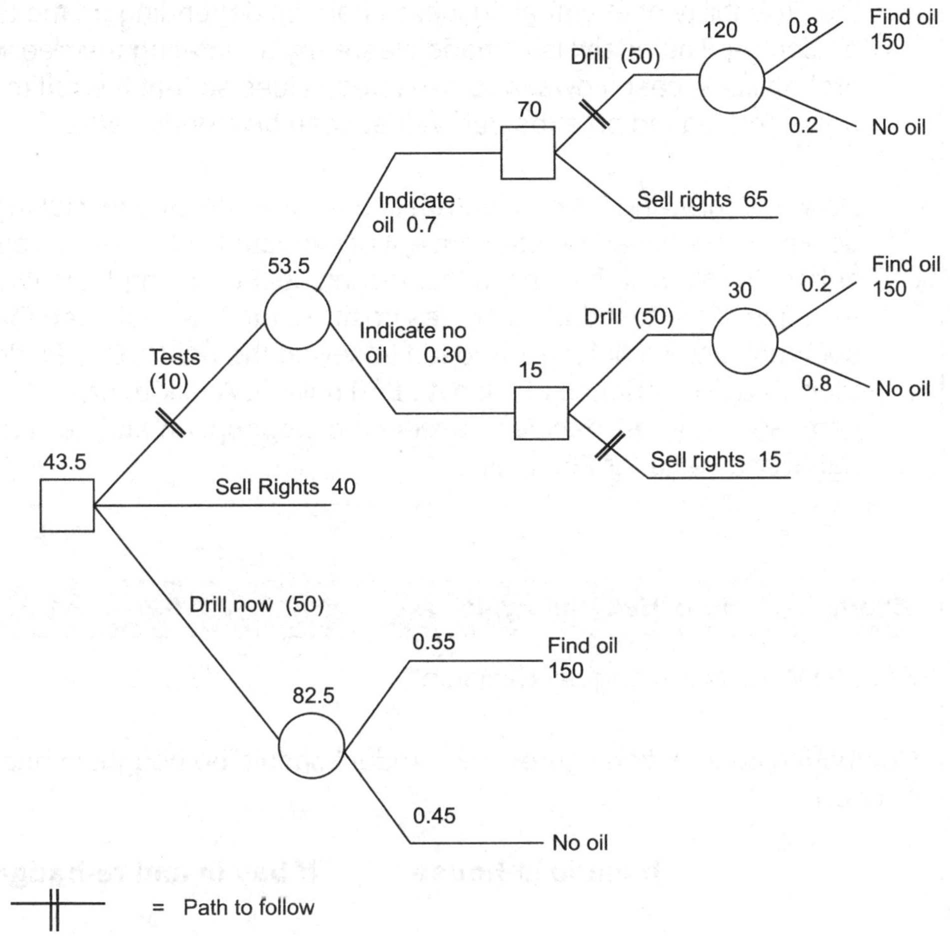

Advice:

The company should undertake geological tests. If the tests indicate that oil is present then a drilling programme should be carried out. However, if the tests indicate that there is no oil then the company should sell the drilling rights.

This strategy will maximise expected returns at £43.5m.

(c) The main value of a decision tree is that it maps out clearly all the decisions and uncertain events and exactly how they are interrelated. They are especially beneficial where the outcome of one decision affects another decision. For example in the above, the probability of eventual success changes depending on the test outcomes. The analysis is made clearer by annotating the tree with probabilities, cash flows, and expected values so that the optimum decisions (based on expected values) can be clearly seen.

However, drawing a tree diagram is only one way of undertaking a decision. It is based on the concept of expected value and as such suffers from the limitations of this technique. For example, in this example, if the test drilling proves positive, the tree indicated the company should drill, as opposed to selling the rights. But if it does there is a 20% chance of it losing £50 million. A risk-averse company may well decide to accept the safer option and sell the rights and settle for £65 million.

Example 5 - Sensitivity analysis

Step 1: What is the original decision?

Comparing contribution figures, the product should be bought in and re-badged:

	If made in-house	If buy in and re-badge
	$	$
Contribution	5	6

Step 2: Calculate the sensitivity (to the external purchase price)

For indifference, the contribution from outsourcing needs to fall to $5 per unit. Thus the external purchase price only needs to increase by $1 per unit (or $1/ $6 = 17%).

If the external purchase price rose by more than 17% the original decision would be reversed.

Test your understanding 1

Payout £	Number of prizes	Total payout £
20,000	1	20,000
10,000	1	10,000
1,000	10	10,000
100	100	10,000
5	2,000	10,000
Total		**60,000**

Revenue £1 × 75,000	=	£75,000
Cost		£60,000
Gain to the company		£15,000

$$\text{Expected gain per card} = \frac{15,000}{75,000} = 0.20$$

Test your understanding 2

D

Perfect information is certain to be right about the future. Imperfect information may predict wrongly.

Test your understanding 3

B

Project	Expected value £000	Standard deviation £000	Coefficient of variation
A	850	500	0.59
B	1,200	480	0.40
C	150	200	1.33
D	660	640	0.97

Test your understanding 4 – SITERAZE LTD

(a) Calculate the contribution for each turnover figure.

There is a 30% C/S ratio

Turnover £000	Contribution £000
15,000	4,500
8,500	2,550
4,000	1,200

Calculate the net margin for each of the different possible outcomes.

Advance hire level	Demand level	Contribution £000	Advance hire costs £000	Extra hire costs £000	Net margin £000
High	High	4,500	2,300	–	2,200
	Medium	2,550	2,300	–	250
	Low	1,200	2,300	–	(1,100)
Medium	High	4,500	1,500	1,300	1,700
	Medium	2,550	1,500	–	1,050
	Low	1,200	1,500	–	(300)
Low	High	4,500	1,000	2,150	1,350
	Medium	2,550	1,000	850	700
	Low	1,200	1,000	–	200

(b) High hire level

EV = (2,200 × 0.25) + (250 × 0.45) + (–1,100 × 0.30) = £332,500

Medium hire level

EV = (1,700 × 0.25) + (1,050 × 0.45) + (–300 × 0.30) = £807,500

Low hire level

EV = (1,350 × 0.25) + (700 × 0.45) + (200 × 0.30) = £712,500

The expected net gain is maximised at the medium hire level.

(c) Managers could either seek risk or avoid it. While the calculations of expected values seem to indicate that the medium-usage advance hire contract was the best option, this is only the result when using the weighted average and probabilities. A risk-averse manager will examine the options to see which of the demand levels is providing the worst net gains. He/she will then select the best from these worst outcomes. In the case of Siteraze this would mean selecting the low hire level. With a low hire level a net gain of £200,000 or higher is guaranteed. However, if the manager was a risk seeker, he would select the high hire level in the hope that demand would subsequently be high. This combination would yield a net gain of £2,200,000.

(d)

Demand level	**Hire decision**	**Net gain** £000	**Probability**	**px**
High	High	2,200	0.25	550.00
Medium	Medium	1,050	0.45	472.50
Low	Low	200	0.30	60.00
				1,082.50

EV with perfect information	£1,082,500
EV without perfect information	£807,500
Value of the information	£275,000

Siteraze should not pay more than £275,000 to the consultant.

Test your understanding 5 - CHARITY ORGANISATION

Revenue per person = £20 + £5 + £1

Number of tickets	Probability	Revenue	Food cost	Net benefit	Prob. × benefit
		£	£	£	£
300	0.2	7,800	(4,800)	3,000	600
400	0.3	10,400	(4,800)	5,600	1,680
500	0.4	13,000	(6,000)	7,000	2,800
600	0.1	15,600	(7,200)	8,400	840
	1.0			**Expected value = 5,920**	

Number of pages	Probability	Contribution £65 per page	Prob. × contribution
		£	£
24	0.2	1,560	312
32	0.4	2,080	832
40	0.3	2,600	780
48	0.1	3,120	312
	1.0		**Expected value = 2,236**

Total contribution	£5,920 + £2,236	=	£8,156
Less fixed costs		=	(£6,500)
Expected profit			£1,656

Test your understanding 6 - APPLYING MAXIMAX

Using maximax, an optimist would consider the best possible outcome for each product and pick the product with the greatest potential.

Here C would be chosen with a maximum possible gain of 100.

- Using maximin, a pessimist would consider the poorest possible outcome for each product and would ensure that the maximum pay-off is achieved if the worst result were to happen.
- Therefore, product A would be chosen resulting in a minimum pay-off of 20 compared to a minimum pay-off of 10 for products B and C.

In the pay-off matrix above, if the market state had been scenario I:

The correct decision would have been:	B (net income $80)
If A had been chosen instead:	The company would have been out of pocket by $60 (i.e. 80 – 20)
If C had been chosen:	It would have been out of pocket by $70 (i.e. 80 – 10)

- The opportunity loss associated with each product is: A = $60, B =$0, C = $70.

Scenario II and III can be considered in the same way and the results can be summarised in a regret table.

The completed opportunity loss ('regret') table is thus as follows.

	Decision		
State	**A**	**B**	**C**
I	60	0	70
II	60	30	0
III	0	60	10
Maximum regret	60	60	70

The maximum regret value for:

A = $60

B = $60

C = $70

The minimum value of these is $60, hence the minimax regret strategy would be either A or B.

B would probably be adopted because its second-highest regret outcome ($30) is lower than the second-highest for A ($60).

Test your understanding 7 - RS GROUP

(a)

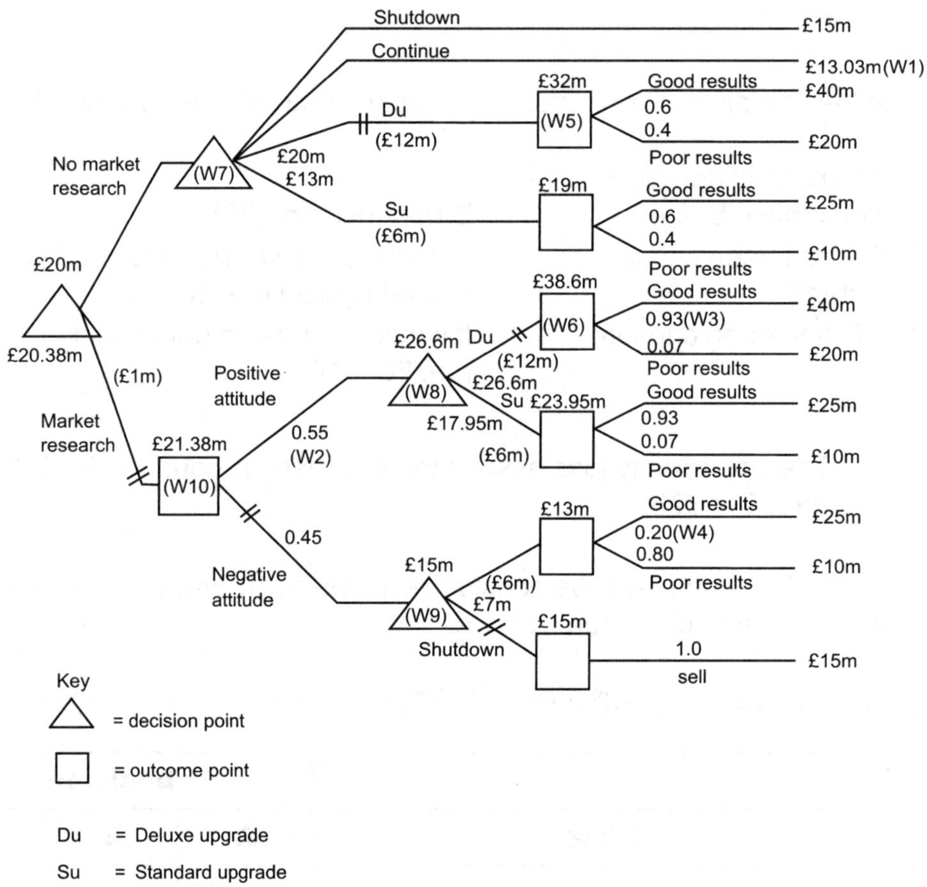

Workings 2, 3 and 4

A probability tree is the best way of understanding the dependent probabilities given in the question.

The probability of the prediction depends upon whether the results are good or poor.

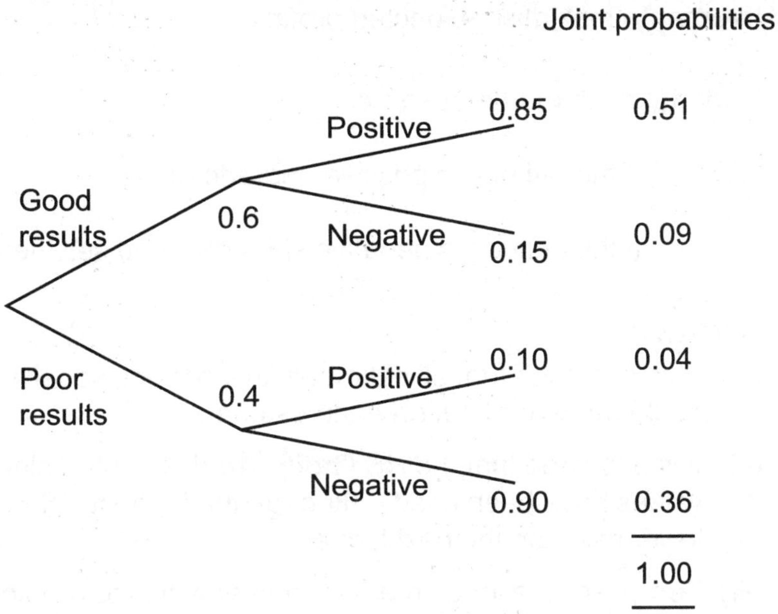

(W2) p(positive attitude) = 0.51 + .04 = 0.55

(W3) p(good results/positive attitude) =

$$\frac{\text{p (good results and positive attitude)}}{\text{p (positive attitude)}}$$

$$= \frac{0.51}{0.55} = 0.93$$

(W4) p(good results/negative attitude) = $\frac{\text{p (good results and negative attitude)}}{\text{p (negative attitude)}}$

$$= \frac{0.09}{0.45} = 0.20$$

(W5) Expected profit = £40m × 0.6 + £20m × 0.4 = £32m

(W6) Expected profit = £40m × 0.93 + £20m × 0.07 = £38.6m

(W7) The deluxe upgrade provides an expected profit of (£32m – £12m) £20m

(W8) Deluxe upgrade profit = £38.6m – £12m = £26.6m

Standard upgrade profit = £23.95 – £6m = £17.95m

∴ Deluxe upgrade is recommended.

(W9) Standard upgrade profit = £7m

Shutdown and sell site = £15m

∴ Shutdown and sell is recommended

(W10) Expected profit = £26.6m × 0.55 + £15m × 0.45 = £21.38m

(b) In order to maximise expected profit:

Undertake the market research.

If the attitude is positive upgrade deluxe.

If the attitude is negative shutdown and sell the site.

(c) Comment

(i) This assumes that all estimates are correct; sensitivity analysis could be carried out on each estimate.

(ii) It is assumed that the RS Group are risk neutral since expected values have been used - although the highest ENPV has a lower risk than the next highest.

(iii) Ten years is a long time period over which to predict profits - a reasonable period for the life of the store but this makes estimation difficult.

(iv) Comments on the courses of action open to the RS Group have been made in (a).

Test your understanding 8

B

Without information, the expected profits are:

Product X: £20,000 × 0.2 + £15,000 × 0.5 + £6,000 × 0.3	= £13,300
Product Y: £17,000 × 0.2 + £16,000 × 0.5 + £7,000 × 0.3	= £13,500

So without information, product Y would be selected.

With perfect information, product X would be selected if the market was good, and product Y in the other two cases. The expected value would then be:

£20,000 × 0.2 + £16,000 × 0.5 + £7,000 × 0.3 = £14,100

The expected value of perfect information is therefore £14,100 – £13,500 = £600

Test your understanding 9 - SENSITIVITY ANALYSIS

(a) The EV would have to decrease by \$16,000 before the original decision is reversed, i.e. this is the break-even point.

– Let the loss be L

Currently, EV = (0.4 × L of 20) + (0.6 × 40)

If EV falls to zero:

EV of 0 = (0.4 × L) + (0.4 × 40)

0 = 0.4L + 24

– 24 = 0.4L

– 24/ 0.4 = L

L = – 60

– The loss would have to increase from \$20,000 to \$60,000 before the decision is reveresed. This is a 200% increase in the loss.

(b) The EV would have to decrease by \$16,000 before the original decision is reversed, i.e. this is the break-even point.

– Let the probability of a loss be P and the probability of a profit be 1 – P.

Currently, EV = (P × –20) + (1–p × 40)

If EV falls to zero:

EV of 0 = (P × –20) + (1–p × 40)

0 = –20P + 40 –40P

60P = 40

P = 40/60

P = 0.67

– The probability of a loss would have to increase to 0.67 from 0.4 before the decision is reversed.

Test your understanding 10

(a)

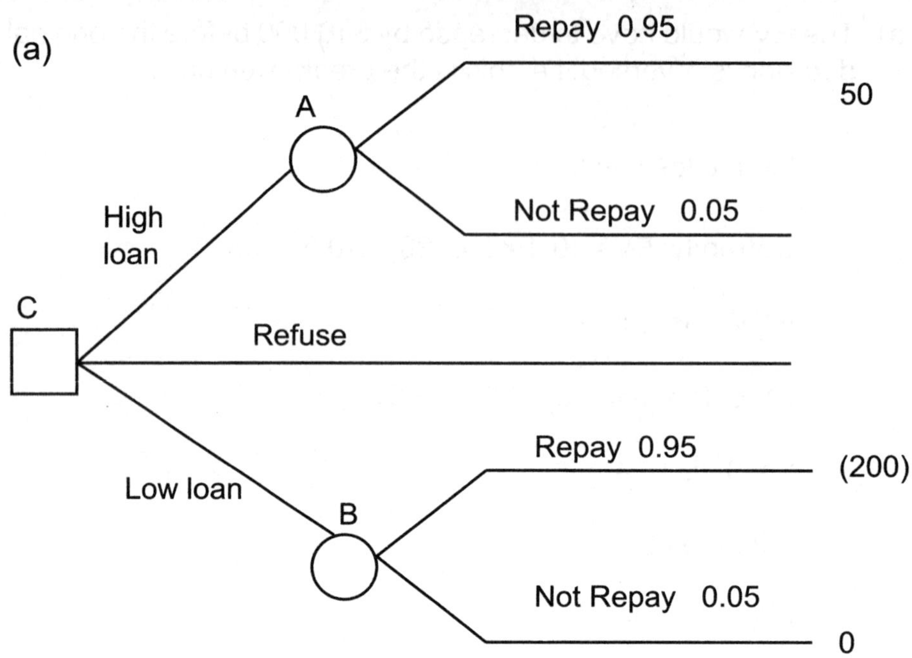

At points A and B calculate Expected Values;

At A EV = (0.95 × 50) + (0.05 × (200)) = **37.5**

At B EV = (0.95 × 20) + (0.05 × (20)) = **17.5**

At C compare the EVs of £37.5 and £17.5.

Recommendation; if a customer requests a loan give him/her a high loan limit.

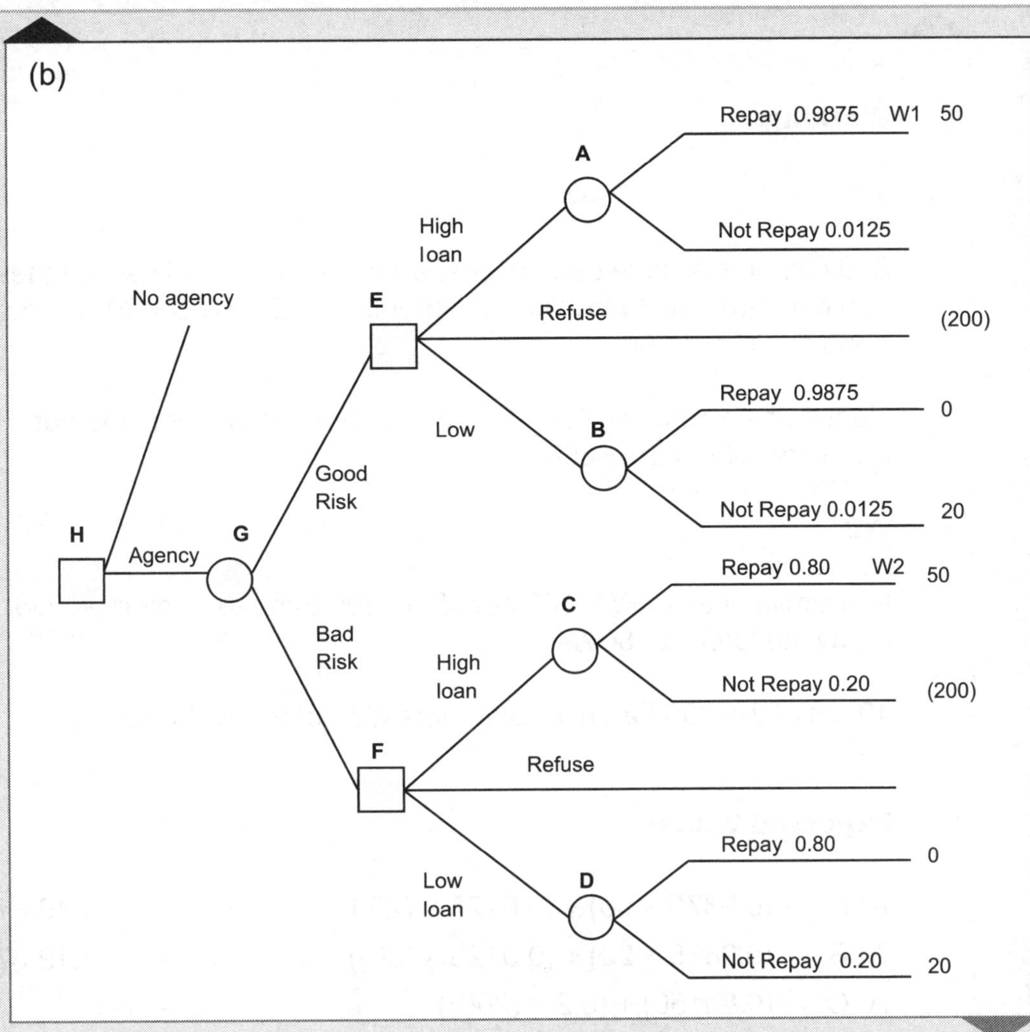
(b)
H
No agency
Agency
G
Good Risk
Bad Risk
E
High loan
Refuse
Low
A
Repay 0.9875 W1 50
Not Repay 0.0125
(200)
B
Repay 0.9875 0
Not Repay 0.0125 20
F
High loan
Refuse
Low loan
C
Repay 0.80 W2 50
Not Repay 0.20 (200)
D
Repay 0.80 0
Not Repay 0.20 20

Workings

W1

800 customers have been assessed as being a good risk. Of these 790 did repay the loan. This represents 98.75% (790 ÷ 800) of the good risk customers.

Hence, the remaining 1.25% of the good risk customers did not repay the loan. (10 ÷ 800).

W2

In a similar way to W1, 160 out of the 200 bad risk customers did repay the loan, i.e. 80%.

40 out of the 200 bad risk customers did not repay the loan, i.e. 20%.

Expected Values

At A	(0.9875 × 50) + (0.0125 × (200))	=	£46.875
At B	(0.9875 × 20) + (0.0125 × (30))	=	£19.375
At C	(0.8 × 50) + (0.2 × (200))	=	0
At D	(0.8 × 20) + (0.2 × (30))	=	£10.00

Decisions

At E compare A and B. Choose A, i.e. give customers a high loan

At F compare C and D. Choose D, i.e. give customers a low loan.

Expected Values

At G (0.8 × 46.875) + (0.2 × 10.00) = £39.5

Decision

At H compare "No agency" (return = £37.50) with the "agency" (return = £39.50)

The information from the agency is expected to increase profits by £2 per rating. This is the value of the information.

(c) Perfect information is a forecast that is 100% accurate. In the context of this problem it would be the credit rating agency providing an accurate forecast of the customer's ability to repay the loan.

If the new agency is approached;

Forecast	Decision	Outcome	Profit	Probability	Expected Value
Good risk	High loan	Repay	£50	0.95	47.50
Bad risk	Refuse loan	Nothing	£0	0.05	0
					£47.50

The expected return with perfect information	=	£47.50
The expected return with no information	=	(£37.50)
Therefore the value of the information is	=	£10.00

chapter

13

Basic investment appraisal techniques

Chapter learning objectives

Lead	Component
C1. Prepare information to support project appraisal.	(a) Explain the processes involved in making long-term decisions. (e) Explain the financial consequences of dealing with long-run projects, in particular the importance of accounting for the 'time value of money'.
C2. Evaluate project proposals.	(a) Evaluate project proposals using the techniques of investment appraisal. (b) Compare and contrast the alternative techniques of investment appraisal. (c) Prioritise projects that are mutually exclusive, involve unequal lives and/or are subject to capital rationing.

1 Session content diagram

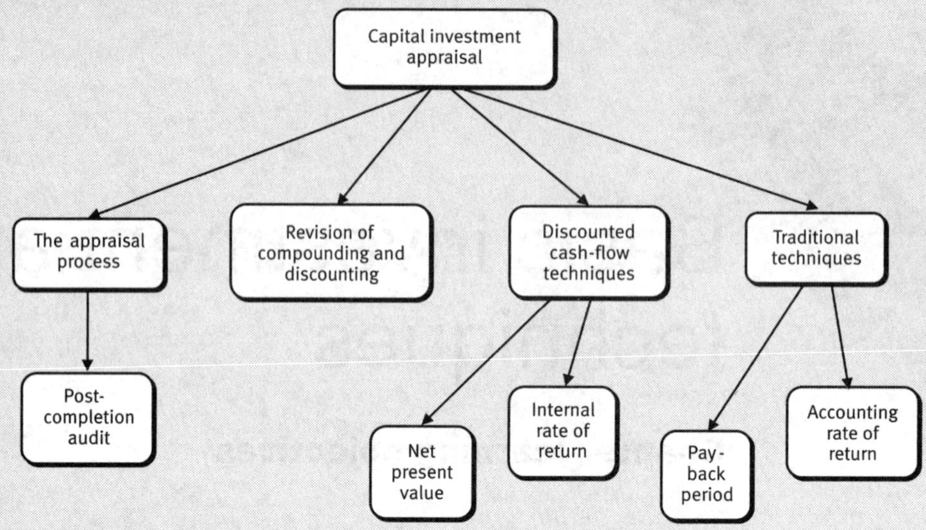

Introduction

Capital investment decisions normally represent the most important decisions that an organisation makes, since they commit a substantial proportion of a firm's resources to actions that are likely to be irreversible. Many different investment projects exist including; replacement of assets, cost-reduction schemes, new product/service developments, product/service expansions, statutory, environmental and welfare proposals, etc.

One characteristic of all capital expenditure projects is that the cash flows arise over the long term (a period usually greater than 12 months). Under this situation it becomes necessary to carefully consider the time value of money.

2 The time value of money

Money received today is worth more than the same sum received in the future, i.e. it has a **time value.**

Discounted cash flow (DCF) techniques take account of this time value of money when appraising investments.

The time value of money

There are three main reasons for the time value of money:

Potential for earning interest

If a capital investment is to be justified, it needs to earn at least a minimum amount of profit, so that the return compensates the investor for both the amount invested and also for the length of time before the profits are made. For example, if a company could invest $80,000 now to earn revenue of $82,000 in one week's time, a profit of $2,000 in seven days would be a very good return. However, if it takes four years to earn the money, the return would be very low.

Therefore money has a time value. It can be invested to earn interest or profits, so it is better to have $1 now than in one year's time. This is because $1 now can be invested for the next year to earn a return, whereas $1 in one year's time cannot. Another way of looking at the time value of money is to say that $1 in six years' time is worth less than $1 now.

Impact of inflation

In most countries, in most years prices rise as a result of inflation. Therefore funds received today will buy more than the same amount a year later, as prices will have risen in the meantime. The funds are subject to a loss of purchasing power over time.

Risk

The earlier cash flows are due to be received, the more certain they are – there is less chance that events will prevent payment. Earlier cash flows are therefore considered to be more valuable.

3 Compound interest

A sum invested today will earn interest. Compounding calculates the future (or **terminal value**) of a given sum invested today for a number of years.

To compound a sum, the figure is increased by the amount of interest it would earn over the period.

FORMULA FOR COMPOUNDING

$$V = X(1 + r)^n$$

Where
- V = Future value
- X = Initial investment (present value)
- r = Interest rate (expressed as a decimal)
- n = Number of time periods

Example 1

£100 is invested in an account for five years. The interest rate is 10% per annum. Calculate the value of the account after five years.

Example 2

£450 is invested in an account earning 6.25% interest p.a. Calculate the fund value after 12 years.

Example 3

£5000 is required in 10 years. £x is invested in an account earning 5% interest p.a. Calculate the value of £x.

4 Discounting

Discounting performs the opposite function to compounding. Compounding finds the future value of a sum invested now, whereas discounting considers a sum receivable in the future and establishes its equivalent value today. This value in today's terms is known as the **Present Value (PV).**

In potential investment projects, cash flows will arise at many different points in time. Calculating the present value of future flows will be a key technique in investment appraisal decisions.

FORMULAE FOR DISCOUNTING

	Present value = Future value x discount factor	LEARN
Where:	Discount factor = $\frac{1}{(1+r)^n}$ or $(1+r)^{-n}$	GIVEN
where:	r is the interest rate expressed as decimal n is the number of time periods	

$(1 + r)^{-n}$ can be looked up in discounting tables. It is known as the discount factor.

Example 4

Calculate how much should be invested now in order to have £250 in eight years' time? The account pays 12% interest per annum.

Example 5

Calculate the present value of £25,000 receivable in six years' time, if the interest rate is 10% p.a.

The cost of capital

In the above discussions we referred to the rate of interest. There are a number of alternative terms used to refer to the rate a firm should use to take account of the time value of money:

- cost of capital
- discount rate
- required return.

Whatever term is used, the rate of interest used for discounting reflects the cost of the finance that will be tied up in the investment.

5 Capital investment appraisal

Initial assumptions

(1) All cash inflows and outflows are known with certainty.

(2) Sufficient funds are available to undertake all profitable investments.

(3) There is zero inflation.

(4) There is zero taxation.

These assumptions are all considered in the next session.

Appraisal methods

There are four widely used appraisal methods:

(1) Net present value (NPV).

(2) Internal rate of return (IRR).

(3) The payback period.

(4) Accounting rate of return (ARR).

The NPV and IRR both consider the time value of money. They are discounted cash flow (DCF) techniques.

6 Net present value (NPV)

The net benefit or loss of benefit in present value terms from an investment opportunity.

The NPV represents the surplus funds (after funding the investment) earned on the project. This means that it telss us the impact on shareholder wealth. Therefore:

Decision criteria

- Any project with a positive NPV is viable.
- Projects with a negative NPV are not viable.
- Faced with mutually-exclusive projects, choose the project with the highest NPV.

What does the NPV actually mean?

Suppose, in an investment problem, we calculate the NPV of certain cash flows at 12% to be – $97, and at 10% to be zero, and yet at 8% the NPV of the same cash flows is + $108. Another way of expressing this is as follows.

- If the funds were borrowed at 12% the investor would be $97 out of pocket – i.e. the investment earns a yield below the cost of capital.
- If funds were borrowed at 10% the investor would break even – i.e. the investment yields a return equal to the cost of capital.
- If funds were borrowed at 8% the investor would be $108 in pocket – i.e. the investment earns a return in excess of the cost of capital.

In other words, a positive NPV is an indication of the surplus funds available to the investor now as a result of accepting the project.

Assumptions used in NPV & IRR

- All cash flows occur at the start or end of a year.

Although in practice many cash flows accrue throughout the year, for discounting purposes they are all treated as occurring at the start or end of a year. Note also that if today (T_0) is 01/01/20X0, the dates 31/12/20X1 and 01/01/20X2, although technically separate days, can be treated for discounting as occurring at the same point in time, i.e. at T_1.

- Initial investments occur at once (T_0), other cash flows start in one year's time (T_1).

In project appraisal, the investment needs to be made before the cash flows can accrue. Therefore, unless the examiner specifies otherwise, it is assumed that investments occur in advance. The first cash flows associated with running the project are therefore assumed to occur one year after the project begins, i.e. at T_1.

Example 6 – PROJECT APPRAISAL

Mickey Ltd is considering two mutually-exclusive projects with the following details:

Project A

Initial investment	£450,000				
Scrap value in year 5	£20,000				
Year:	1	2	3	4	5
Annual cash flows (£000)	200	150	100	100	100

Project B

Initial investment	£100,000					
Scrap value in year 5	£10,000					
Year:		1	2	3	4	5
Annual cash flows (£000)		50	40	30	20	20

Assume that the initial investment is at the start of the project and the annual cash flows are at the **end** of each year.

Required:

Calculate the Net Present Value for Projects A and B if the relevant cost of capital is 10%.

		Project A		Project B	
Year	**Discount factor 10%**	**Net cash flow** £000	**PV** £000	**Net cash flow** £000	**PV** £000
0					
1					
2					
3					
4					
5					

Calculate which project has the highest NPV.

Advantages	Disadvantages
• Does consider the time value of money	• Fairly complex
• It is a measure of absolute profitability	• Not well understood by non-financial managers
• Considers cash flows	• It may be difficult to determine the cost of capital
• It considers the whole life of the project	
• A company selecting projects on the basis of NPV maximisation should maximise shareholders wealth	

Advantages and disadvantages of NPV

When appraising projects or investments, NPV is considered to be superior (in theory) to most other methods. This is because it:

- considers the time value of money – discounting cash flows to PV takes account of the impact of interest, inflation and risk over time. (See later sessions for more on inflation and risk.) These significant issues are ignored by the basic methods of payback and annual rate of return (ARR)
- is an absolute measure of return – the NPV of an investment represents the actual surplus raised by the project. This allows a business to plan more effectively
- is based on cash flows not profits – the subjectivity of profits makes them less reliable than cash flows and therefore less appropriate for decision making. Neither ARR nor payback is an absolute measure
- considers the whole life of the project – methods such as payback only consider the earlier cash flows associated with the project. NPV takes account of all relevant flows associated with the project. Discounting the flows takes account of the fact that later flows are less reliable which ARR ignores
- should lead to maximisation of shareholder wealth. If the cost of capital reflects the investors' (i.e. shareholders') required return, then the NPV reflects the theoretical increase in their wealth. For a company, this is considered to be the primary objective of the business.

However, there are some potential drawbacks:

- It is difficult to explain to managers. To understand the meaning of the NPV calculated requires an understanding of discounting. The method is not as intuitive as techniques such as payback.
- It requires knowledge of the cost of capital. The calculation of the cost of capital is, in practice, more complex than identifying interest rates. It involves gathering data and making a number of calculations based on that data and some estimates. The process may be deemed too protracted for the appraisal to be carried out.
- It is relatively complex. For the reasons explained above, NPV may be rejected in favour of simpler techniques.

7 Internal rate of return (IRR)

This is the rate of return at which the project has a NPV of zero.

Decision criteria

- If the IRR is greater than the cost of capital the project should be accepted.
- Faced with mutually-exclusive projects choose the project with the higher IRR.

Further explanation of IRR

Using the NPV method, PVs are calculated by discounting cash flows at a given cost of capital, and the difference between the PV of costs and the PV of benefits is the NPV. In contrast, the IRR method of DCF analysis is to calculate the exact DCF rate of return that the project is expected to achieve.

If an investment has a positive NPV, it means it is earning more than the cost of capital. If the NPV is negative, it is earning less than the cost of capital. This means that if the NPV is zero, it will be earning exactly the cost of capital.

Conversely, the percentage return on the investment must be the rate of discount or cost of capital at which the NPV equals zero. This rate of return is called the IRR, or the DCF yield and if it is higher than the target rate of return then the project is financially worth undertaking.

Calculating the IRR (using linear interpolation)

The steps in linear interpolation are:

(1) Calculate two NPVs for the project at two different costs of capital

(2) Use the following formula to find the IRR:

FORMULA FOR IRR

$$IRR = L + \frac{N_L}{N_L - N_H} \times (H - L)$$

where:

L = Lower rate of interest

H = Higher rate of interest

N_L = NPV at lower rate of interest

N_H = NPV at higher rate of interest.

Example 6 - CONTINUED 1

(a) Calculate the internal rate of return of Project A.

		Project A	
Year	**Discount factors at ?%**	**Net cash flow £000**	**PV £000**
0		(450)	
1		200	
2		150	
3		100	
4		100	
5		120	

(b) Calculate the internal rate of return of Project B.

You are given the following:

At 10% the NPV was £33,310
At 20% the NPV is £8,510
At 30% the NPV is – £9,150

For examination purposes, the choice of rates to estimate the IRR is less important than your ability to perform the calculation to estimate it.

Calculating the IRR using a graph

The IRR may be calculated by a linear interpolation, i.e. by assuming a linear relationship between the NPV and the discount rate. Plotting a graph would give an approximate IRR, but the same point can also be found using a formula.

Step 1 Calculate two NPVs for the project at two different costs of capital. You can choose any costs of capital and get a fair result. However, it helps to find two costs of capital for which the NPV is close to 0, because the IRR will be a value close to them. Ideally, you should use one cost of capital where the NPV is positive and the other cost of capital where the NPV is negative, although this is not essential. YOu should not waste time in the exam

Step 2 Once the two NPVs have been calculated, they and their associated costs of capital can be used to calculate the IRR. In other words, we can estimate the IRR by finding the point where a line joining these points would cross the x-axis (the point where the NPV is zero) in a graph plotting the project NPV against various discount rates.

To calculate the exact IRR requires a more complex technique, best carried out using an Excel spreadsheet. This will not be expected in the exam.

IRR where there are annuities/perpetuities

(**Note:** This section should only be reviewed after annuities and perpetuities have been studied later in this chapter)

Calculating the IRR of a project with even cash flows

There is a simpler technique available, using annuity tables, if the project cash flows are annuities.

(1) Find the cumulative DF, Initial investment ÷ Annual inflow

(2) Find the life of the project, n.

(3) Look along the n year row of the cumulative DF until the closest value is found.

(4) The column in which this figure is found is the IRR.

Illustration – Calculating IRR of a project with even cash flows

Find the IRR of a project with an initial investment of $1.5 million and three years of inflows of $700,000 starting in one year.

Solution

NPV calculation:

		Cash flow	**DF (c) %**	**PV**
		$000		$000
Time				
0	Investment	(1,500)	1	(1,500)
1-3	Inflow	700	(b)	(a)
NPV				Nil

- The aim is to find the discount rate (c) that produces an NPV of nil.
- Therefore the PV of inflows (a) must equal the PV of outflows, $1,500,000.
- If the PV of inflows (a) is to be $1,500,000 and the size of each inflow is $700,000, the DF required (b) must be 1,500,000 ÷ 700,000 = 2.143.
- The discount rate (c) for which this is the 3-year factor can be found by looking along the 3-year row of the cumulative DFS shown in the annuity table.

- The figure of 2.140 appears under the 19% column suggesting an IRR of 19% is the closest.

Calculating the IRR of a project where the cash flows are perpetuities

$$\text{IRR of a perpetuity} = \frac{\text{Annual inflow}}{\text{Initial investment}} \times 100$$

Illustration – Calculating IRR where cash flows are perpetuities

Find the IRR of an investment that costs $20,000 and generates $1,600 for an indefinitely long period.

Solution

$$\text{IRR} = \frac{\text{Annual inflow}}{\text{Initial investment}} \times 100 = \frac{\$1{,}600}{\$20{,}000} \times 100 = 8\%$$

Advantages	Disadvantages
• Does consider the time value of money	• It is not a measure of absolute profitability
• As a percentage return it is easily understood by non-financial managers	• Interpolation only provides an estimate of the true IRR
• Considers cash flows	• Fairly complicated to calculate – although spreadsheets now have built-in programs
• It considers the whole life of the project	• The IRR of projects may conflict with the NPV. If this occurs the NPV must take precedence
• It can be calculated without reference to the cost of capital	
• A company selecting projects where the IRR exceeds the cost of capital should increase shareholders' wealth	

Advantages and disadvantages of IRR

Advantages:

- IRR considers the time value of money. The current value earned from an investment project is therefore more accurately measured. As discussed above this is a significant improvement over the basic methods.
- IRR is a percentage and therefore easily understood. Although managers may not completely understand the detail of the IRR, the concept of a return earned is familiar and the IRR can be simply compared with the required return of the organisation.
- IRR uses cash flows not profits. These are less subjective as discussed above.
- IRR considers the whole life of the project rather than ignoring later flows (which would occur with payback for example).
- IRR a firm selecting projects where the IRR exceeds the cost of capital should increase shareholders' wealth. This holds true provided the project cash flows follow the standard pattern of an outflow followed by a series of inflows, as in the investment examples above.

However there are a number of difficulties with the IRR approach:

- It is not a measure of absolute profitability. A project of $1,000 invested now and paying back $1,100 in a year's time has an IRR of 10%. If a company's required return is 6%, then the project is viable according to the IRR rule but most businesses would consider the absolute return too small to be worth the investment.
- Interpolation only provides an estimate (and an accurate estimate requires the use of a spreadsheet programme). The cost of capital calculation itself is also only an estimate and if the margin between required return and the IRR is small, this lack of accuracy could actually mean the wrong decision is taken.
- For example if the cost of capital is found to be 8% (but is actually 8.7%) and the project IRR is calculated as 9.2% (but is actually 8.5%) the project would be wrongly accepted. Note that where such a small margin exists, the project's success would be considered to be sensitive to the discount rate (see session 12 on risk).

- Non-conventional cash flows may give rise to no IRR or multiple IRRs. For example a project with an outflow at T0 and T2 but income at T1 could, depending on the size of the cash flows, have a number of different profiles on a graph (see below). Even where the project does have one IRR, it can be seen from the graph that the decision rule would lead to the wrong result as the project does not earn a positive NPV at any cost of capital.

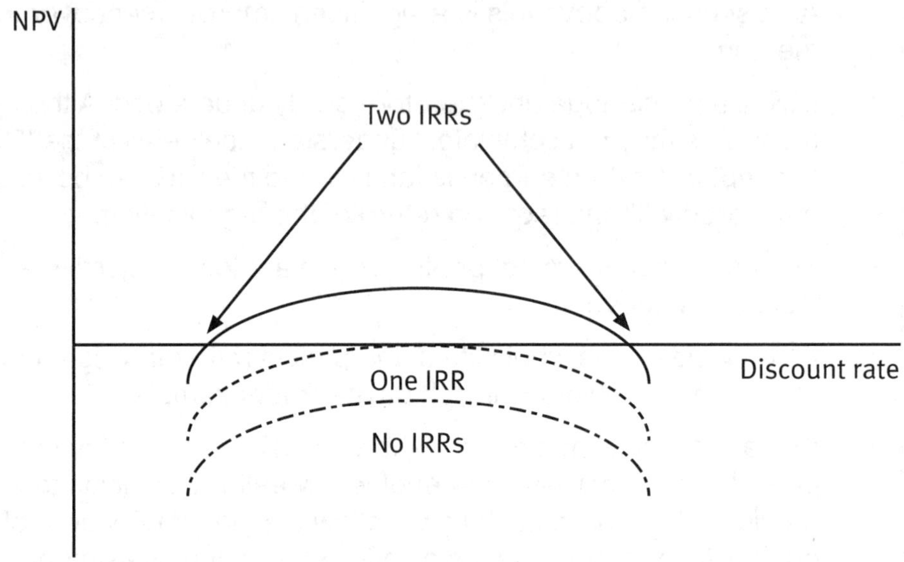

8 NPV versus IRR

Both NPV and IRR are investment appraisal techniques which discount cash flows and are superior to the basic techniques discussed in the previous session. However only NPV can be used to distinguish between two mutually-exclusive projects, as the diagram on the next page demonstrates.

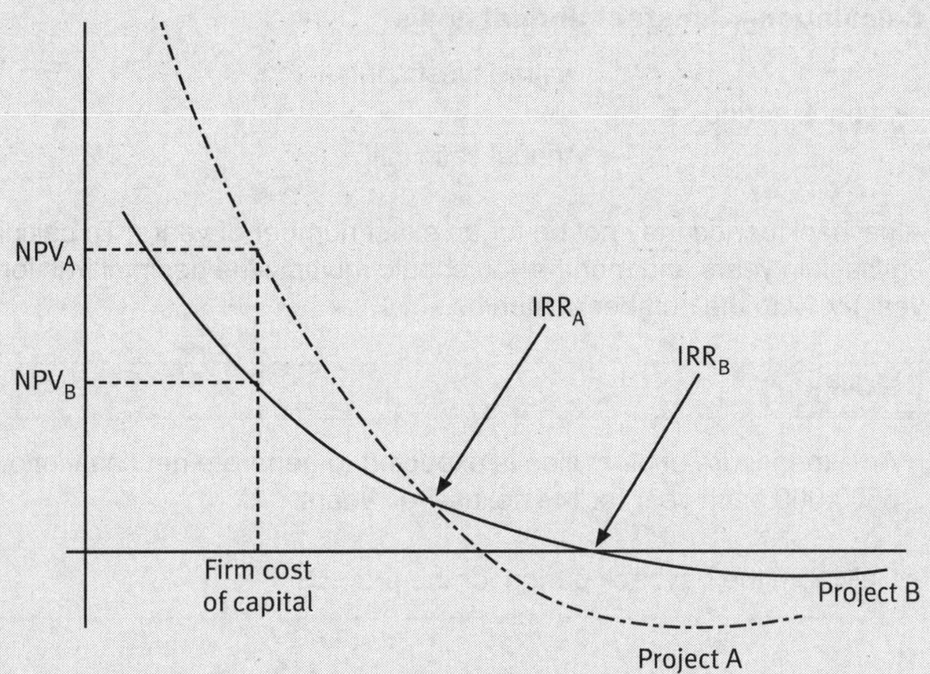

The profile of project A is such that it has a lower IRR and applying the IRR rule would prefer project B. However in absolute terms, A has the higher NPV at the company's cost of capital and should therefore be preferred.

NPV is therefore the better technique for choosing between projects.

The advantage of NPV is that it tells us the absolute increase in shareholder wealth as a result of accepting the project, at the current cost of capital. The IRR simply tells us how far the cost of capital could increase before the project would not be worth accepting.

9 The payback period

The payback period is the time a project will take to pay back the money spent on it. It is based on expected cash flows and provides a measure of liquidity.

This is the time which elapses until the invested capital is recovered. It considers cash flows only. Unlike DCF techniques, it is assumed that the **cash flows** occur evenly during the year.

Decision criteria

- Compare the payback period to the company's maximum return time allowed and if the payback is quicker the project should be accepted.
- Faced with mutually-exclusive projects choose the project with the quickest payback.

Calculation - Constant annual flows

$$\text{Payback period} = \frac{\text{Initial investment}}{\text{Annual cash inflow}}$$

A payback period may not be for an exact number of years. To calculate the payback in years and months you should multiply the decimal fraction of a year by 12 to the number of months.

Example 7

An expenditure of $2 million is expected to generate net cash inflows of $500,000 each year for the next seven years.

Calculate the payback period for the project?

Calculations - Uneven annual flows

However, if cash inflows are uneven (a more likely state of affairs), the payback has to be calculated by working out the cumulative cash flow over the life of a project

Example 6 - CONTINUED 2

Calculate which project should the company select if the objective is to minimise the payback period?

Calculate the discounted payback period for each project. Which project should now be selected?

Discounted payback

One of the major criticisms of using the payback period is that it does not take into account the time value of money. The discounted payback technique attempts to overcome this criticism by measuring the time required for the **present values** of the cash inflows from a project to equal the present values of the cash outflows.

The techniques is identical - but the present value of the cash flow is calculated before calculating the cummulative cash flow.

Advantages	Disadvantages
• Simple to understand	• Is not a measure of absolute profitability
• A project with a long payback periodtends to beriskier than one with a short payback period. Payback is a simple measure of risk	• Ignores the time value of money. **Note:** A discounted payback period may be calculated to overcome this problem
• Uses cash flows, not subjective accounting profits	• Does not take into account cash flows beyond the payback period
• Emphasises the cash flows in the earlier years	
• Firms selecting projects on the basis of payback periods may avoid liquidity problems	

Advantages and disadvantages of payback

Advantages

- Simplicity

As a concept, it is easily understood and is easily calculated.

- Rapidly changing technology

If new plant is likely to be scrapped in a short period because of obsolescence, a quick payback is essential.

- Improving investment conditions

When investment conditions are expected to improve in the near future, attention is directed to those projects that will release funds soonest, to take advantage of the improving climate.

- Payback favours projects with a quick return

It is often argued that these are to be preferred for three reasons.

  – Rapid project payback leads to rapid company growth – but in fact such a policy will lead to many profitable investment opportunities being overlooked because their payback period does not happen to be particularly swift.

- Rapid payback minimises risk (the logic being that the shorter the payback period, the less there is that can go wrong). Not all risks are related to time, but payback is able to provide a useful means of assessing time risk (and only time risk). It is likely that earlier cash flows can be estimated with greater certainty.
- Rapid payback maximises liquidity – but liquidity problems are best dealt with separately, through cash forecasting.

- Cash flows

Unlike ARR it uses cash flows, rather than profits, and so is less likely to produce an unduly optimistic figure distorted by assorted accounting conventions which might permit certain costs to be carried forward and not affect profit initially.

Disadvantages

- Project returns may be ignored – In particular, cash flows arising after the payback period are totally ignored.
- Timing ignored – Cash flows are effectively categorised as pre-payback or post-payback, but no more accurate measure is made. In particular, the time value of money is ignored.
- Lack of objectivity – There is no objective measure as to what length of time should be set as the minimum payback period. Investment decisions are therefore subjective.
- Project profitability is ignored – Payback takes no account of the effects on business profits and periodic performance of the project, as evidenced in the financial statements. This is critical if the business is to be reasonably viewed by users of the accounts.

10 Accounting rate of return (ARR)

The ARR method is also known as return on investment (ROI) or ROCE and has many different formulae depending on depreciation, stock valuation methods, etc.

The most common formula is:

$$\text{ARR} = \frac{\text{Average annual profit}}{\text{Average value of investment}}$$ **LEARN**

Important notes to the formula:

- The 'average annual profit' is after depreciation.
- Net cash flow is equivalent to 'profit before depreciation'.

Average annual profit = Net cash flow less depreciation

- The average value of the investment represents the average capital employed over the life of the project.

$$\text{Average value of investment} = \frac{\text{Initial investment plus residual value}}{2} \quad \textbf{LEARN}$$

Decision criteria

- The ARR for a project may be compared with the company's target return and if higher the project should be accepted.
- Faced with a choice of mutually-exclusive investments, the project with the highest ARR should be chosen.

Example 6 - CONTINUED 3

Project A

Initial investment		£450,000			
Scrap value in year 5		£20,000			
Year:	1	2	3	4	5
Annual cash flows (£000)	200	150	100	100	100

Project B

Initial investment	£100,000				
Scrap value in year 5	£10,000				
Year:	1	2	3	4	5
Annual cash flows (£000)	50	40	30	20	20

Required:

Calculate the ARR for each project, and indicate which project should be chosen.

Advantages	Disadvantages
• Simple to understand	• Ignores the time value of money
• Widely used and accepted	• Is not a measure of absolute profitability
• It can be obtained from readily available financial accounting data • It considers the whole life of the project	• Does not consider cash flows. Uses subjective accounting profits, which include depreciation

Advantages and disadvantages of ARR

Advantages

- Simplicity – As with the payback period, it is easily understood and easily calculated.
- Link with other accounting measures – Return on capital employed, calculated annually to assess a business or sector of a business (and therefore the investment decisions made by that business), is widely used and its use for investment appraisal is consistent with that. The ARR is expressed in percentage terms with which managers and accountants are familiar. However, neither this nor the preceding point necessarily justify the use of ARR.

Disadvantages

There are a number of specific criticisms of the ARR.

- It fails to take account of either the project life or the timing of cash flows (and time value of money) within that life.
- It will vary with specific accounting policies, and the extent to which project costs are capitalised. Profit measurement is thus ‘subjective’, and ARR figures for identical projects would vary from business to business.
- It might ignore working capital requirements.
- Like all rate of return measures, it is not a measurement of absolute gain in wealth for the business owners.
- There is no definite investment signal. The decision to invest or not remains subjective in view of the lack of an objectively set target ARR.
- It is concluded that the ARR does not provide a reliable basis for project evaluation.

11 NPV and IRR with equal cash flows

Discounting annuities

An annuity is a constant annual cash flow for a number of years.

When a project has equal annual cash flows the annuity factor may be used to calculate the NPV (and hence the IRR).

The **annuity factor** (AF) is the name given to the sum of the individual DF.

The PV of an annuity can therefore be quickly found using the formula:

PV = Annual cash flow × AF

Like with calculating a discount factor, the AF can be found using an annuity formula or annuity tables.

Annuity factor formula

The formula is:

$$AF = \frac{1-(1+r)^{-n}}{r}$$

For example, for a six-year annuity at 10%:

The AF

Formula or **Tables**

Formula

$$\frac{1-(1+r)^{-n}}{r}$$

$$= \frac{1-(1.1)^{-6}}{0.1}$$

$$=4.355$$

Tables

(given in examination)

You can simply find the AF from the annuity table by locating the DF at the 10% column and the six-year row, i.e. 4.355

Note: there is a small difference due to roundings.

Example 8 – ANNUITIES

(a) Pluto Ltd has been offered a project costing £50,000. The returns are expected to be £10,000 each year for seven years. Cost of capital is 10%. Calculate whether the project be accepted.

(b) Calculate the IRR of the project?

Discounting perpetuities

A perpetuity is an annual cash flow that occurs forever.

It is often described by examiners as a cash flow continuing 'for the foreseeable future'.

The PV of a perpetuity is found using the formula:

$$PV = \frac{\text{cashflow}}{r}$$

or

$$PV = \text{cashflow} \times \frac{1}{r}$$

$\frac{1}{r}$ is known as the perpetuity factor.

Example 9 – PERPETUITIES

An investment of £50,000 is expected to yield £5,670 per annum in perpetuity. Calculate the net present value of the investment opportunity if the cost of capital is 9%.

Annuities/perpetuities in advance

The use of annuity factors and perpetuity factors both assume that the first cash flow will be occuring in one year's time. If this is not the case, you will need to adjust your calculation.

Advanced annuities and perpetuities

Some regular cash flows may start now (at T_0) rather than in one years time (T_1).

Calculate the PV by ignoring the payment at T_0 when considering the number of cash flows and then adding one to the annuity or perpetuity factor.

Illustration – Advanced annuities and perpetuities

A 5-year $600 annuity is starting today. Interest rates are 10%. Find the PV of the annuity.

Solution

This is essentially a standard 4-year annuity with an additional payment at T_0. The PV could be calculated as follows:

	T_0		T_1	T_2	T_3	T_4
CF	600		600	600	600	600
	↓		↘	↓	↓	↙
PV	600	+	600 × 4-year 10% AF			

PV = 600 + 600 × 3.17 = 600 + 1902 = $2,502

The same answer can be found more quickly by adding 1 to the AF:

PV = 600 × (1 + 3.17) = 600 × 4.17 = $2,502.

Illustration – Advanced perpetuities

A perpetuity of $2,000 is due to commence immediately. The interest rate is 9%. What is the PV?

Solution

This is essentially a standard perpetuity with an additional payment at T_0. The PV could be calculated as follows:

T_0 T_1 T_2 T_3 T_4 ....

2,000 2,000 → ∞

PV (2000) + (2000 × 9% perpetuity formula)

Again, the same answer can be found more quickly by adding 1 to the perpetuity factor.

$$2000 \times \left(1 + \frac{1}{0.09}\right) = 2000 \times 12.11 = \$24{,}222$$

Annuities/perpetuities in arrears

Delayed annuities and perpetuities

Some regular cash flows may start later than T_1.

These are dealt with by:

(1) applying the appropriate factor to the cash flow as normal

(2) discounting your answer back to T_0.

Illustration – Delayed annuities and perpetuities

What is the PV of $200 incurred each year for four years, starting in three year's time, if the discount rate is 5%?

Solution

Method: A four-year annuity starting at T_3

(1-4)

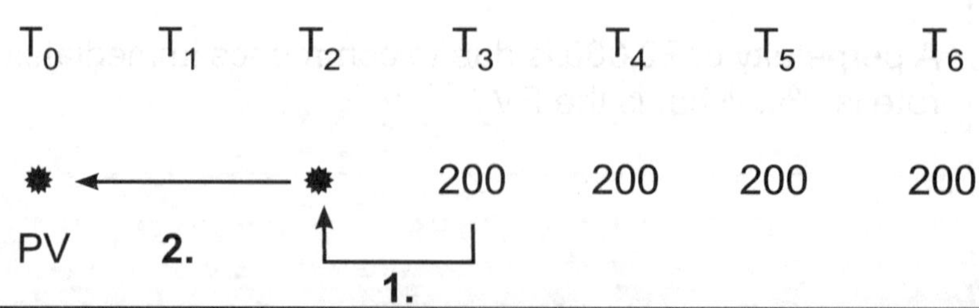

Step 1. Discount the annuity as usual

$200 \times$ 4yr 5% AF = $200 \times 3.456 = 709.2$

Note that this gives the value of the annuity at T_2

Step 2. Discount the answer back to T_0

$709.2 \times$ 2yr 5% DF = 709.2×0.907 = \$643

Annuity or perpetuity factors will discount the cash flows back to give the value one year before the first cash flow arose. For standard annuities and perpetuities this gives the present (T_0) value since the first cash flow started at T_1.

However for delayed cash flows, applying the factor will find the value of the cash flows one year before they began, which in this example is T_2. To find the PV, an additional calculation is required – the value must be discounted back to T_0.

Care must be taken to discount back the appropriate number of years. The figure here was discounted back two years because the first step gave the value at T_2. It can help to draw a timeline as above and mark on the effect of the first step (as shown with a 1. here) to help you remember.

12 The capital investment process

A decision making model for capital expenditure decisions is shown below:

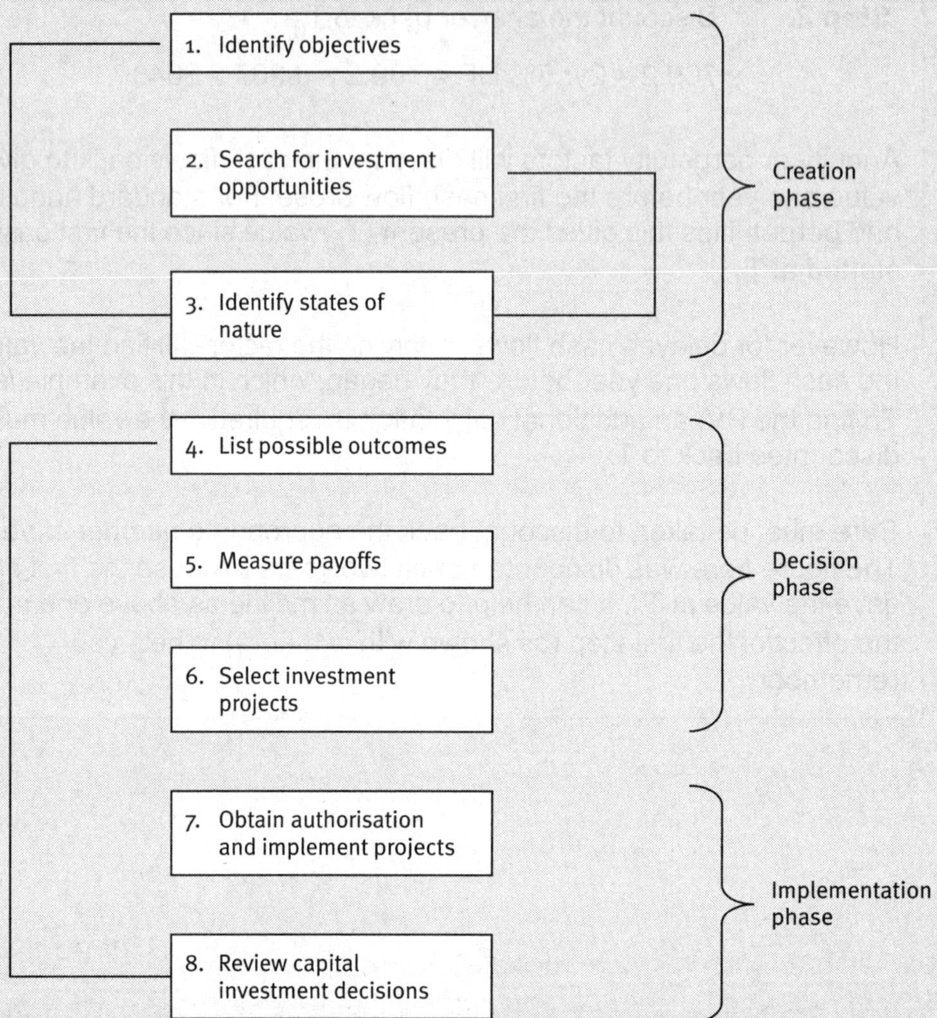

Notes to the diagram

Stage 1 indicates the objectives or goals of the organisation. Most organisations pursue a variety of goals, for example maximisation of profits, maximisation of sales, survival of the firm, achieving satisfactory profits and obtaining the largest share of the market. Achieving profit maximisation in the long term will ensure maximisation of the market value of the shareholders' wealth. The capital investment process seeks to achieve maximisation of wealth by maximising the net present value of future net cash inflows.

Stage 2 involves the search for investment opportunities. Without a proactive, deliberate search for creative projects and opportunities, even the most sophisticated evaluation techniques are worthless. A firm's prosperity is dependent upon its ability to create investment opportunities.

Stage 3 requires data to be gathered about possible future environments that may affect the outcomes of the project. Examples of states of nature include economic booms/recessions, high inflation, world shortages etc. It may be necessary to amend the company objectives (in the medium term at least) and/or to continue searching for new opportunities once the states of nature have been identified.

Stages 4, 5 and 6 are considered in detail in this session and Session 10. Examination questions typically involve listing the various alternatives open to a firm, identifying cash flows that are relevant to each opportunity, evaluating the value of these cash flows and finally recommending an optimum investment strategy.

Stage 7. It is essential to implement a sound system for approving capital investment proposals. Once approval has been obtained and initial outlays have been incurred the firm is often committed to the project for several years to come. Approval should not merely be a rubberstamping of the managers' proposals. A Capital Expenditure Committee should establish an approval procedure that both encourages managers to submit realistic, achievable proposals and ensures that the long-term objectives of the firm are being met.

Stage 8. The review stage is an important final step. This stage is usually achieved by carrying out a post-completion audit or appraisal. The audit is often initiated approximately 12 months into the investment project.

The capital expenditure committee

The Committee is usually responsible for overseeing the capital investment process. The functions of such a committee are to:

- co-ordinate capital expenditure policy;
- appraise and authorise capital expenditure on specific projects;
- review actual expenditure on capital projects against the budget (see next section).

In many organisations, multidisciplinary teams, or working parties, are set up to investigate individual proposals and report back to top management on their findings.

Such a team might comprise:

- project engineer;
- production engineer;
- management accountant;
- relevant specialist, e.g. personnel officer, for a project involving sports facilities or canteens, safety officers, etc.;
- economist.

Post-completion audit

The post-completion appraisal of projects provides a mechanism whereby experience gained from current and past projects can be fed into the organisation's decision-making process to aid decisions on future projects. In other words, it aids organisational learning. A post-completion appraisal reviews all aspects of an ongoing project in order to assess whether it has fulfilled its initial expectations. It is a forward-looking rather than a backward-looking technique. The task is often carried out by the Capital Expenditure Committee, or an appointed sub-committee. The committee would meet either annually, bi-annually, or if necessary, quarterly.

Benefits of post-completion audit

(1) If managers know in advance that projects are going to be subject to a post-completion appraisal they ensure that assumptions and plans for the project are more accurate and realistic.

(2) If an appraisal is carried out before the project life ends, and it is found that the benefits have been less than expected because of management inefficiency, then steps can be taken to improve efficiency.

(3) It might identify weaknesses in the forecasting techniques and the estimating techniques used to evaluate the project. The discipline and quality of forecasting for future investments can be improved.

(4) Managers may be motivated to achieve the forecast results if they are aware of a pending post-completion appraisal.

(5) The appraisal reveals the reliability and quality of contractors and suppliers involved in the project.

(6) The appraisal may highlight the reasons for success or failure in previous projects – thereby providing a learning experience for managers to aid better decision making in the future.

Problems with post-completion audits

(1) It may not be possible to identify separately the costs and benefits of any particular project.

(2) It can be a time-consuming and costly exercise.

(3) Applied punitively, post-completion appraisal may lead managers to becoming over-cautious and risk averse.

(4) The strategic effects of a capital investment project may take years to materialise and it may never be possible to identify and quantify them correctly.

(5) There are many uncontrollable factors in long-term investments. A post-completion appraisal will not help managers change these factors in the future.

13 Chapter summary

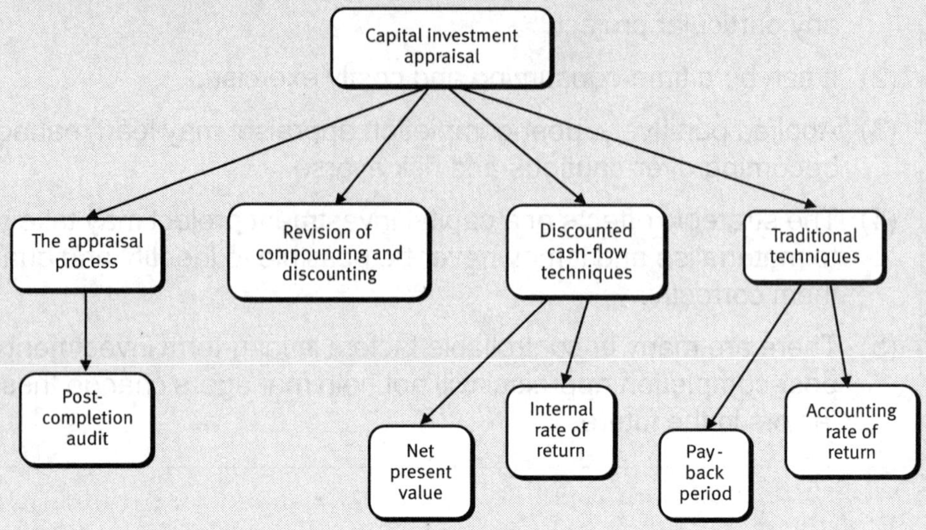

14 Practice questions

Test your understanding 1

An organisation is considering a capital investment in new equipment. The estimated cash flows are as follows.

Year	Cash flow
	$
0	(240,000)
1	80,000
2	120,000
3	70,000
4	40,000
5	20,000

The company's cost of capital is 9%.

Calculate the NPV of the project to assess whether it should be undertaken.

Test your understanding 2

A company is considering a project with a three-year life producing the following costs and revenues:

	£
Cost of machine	100,000
Depreciation of machine (for three years)	20,000 p.a.
Residual value of machine	40,000
Annual cost of direct labour	20,000
Annual charge for foreman (10% apportionment)	5,000
Annual cost of components required	18,000
Annual net revenues from machine	80,000
Cost of capital	20%

Identify which of the following is closest to the net present value of the machine:

A (£13,000)

B (£11,380)

C £11,610

D £22,370

(2 marks)

Test your understanding 3

A potential project's predicted cash flows give a NPV of $50,000 at a discount rate of 10% and –$10,000 at a rate of 15%.

Calculate the IRR.

Test your understanding 4

Identify the correct explanation of the internal rate of return - it is the interest rate that equates the present value of expected future net cash flows to:

A the initial cost of the investment outlay

B the depreciation value of the investment

C the terminal (compounded) value of future cash receipts

D the firm's cost of capital

(2 marks)

Test your understanding 5

A business undertakes high-risk investments and requires a minimum expected rate of return of 17% pa on its investments. A proposed capital investment has the following expected cash flows:

Year	$
0	(50,000)
1	18,000
2	25,000
3	20,000
4	10,000

(1) Calculate the NPV of the project if the cost of capital is 15%.

(2) Calculate the NPV of the project if the cost of capital is 20%.

(3) Use the NPVs you have calculated to estimate the IRR of the project.

(4) State, on financial grounds alone, whether this project should go ahead.

Test your understanding 6

Calculate the IRR of an investment of $50,000 if the inflows are:

(a) $5,000 in perpetuity

(b) $8,060 for eight years.

Test your understanding 7

£50,000 is to be spent on a machine having a life of five years and a residual value of £5,000. Operating cash inflows will be the same each year, except for year 1 when the figure will be £6,000. The accounting rate of return (ARR) is measured as average annual profit as a percentage of the initial investment. If the ARR is 30% then identify the payback period:

A 2.75 years

B 2.15 years

C 1.85 years

D 2.54 years

(4 marks)

Test your understanding 8

Goofy Ltd is considering a project, the estimated costs of which are £90,000. The returns are expected to be £20,000 p.a. for the first five years and £10,000 each year for the next five years. The assets may be sold at the end of the tenth year for £8,000. Cost of capital is 10%. Calcualte whether the project be accepted.

Test your understanding 9

£100,000 is deposited in a bank account paying 8% interest each year. Calculate the maximum sum that can be withdrawn from the account at the end of each year in perpetuity.

Test your understanding 10

In order to earn a perpetuity of £2,000 per annum calculate how much would need to be invested today. The account will pay 10% interest.

Test your understanding 11

A project has a normal pattern of cash flows (i.e. an initial outflow followed by several years of inflows).

Identify what would be the effects of an increase in the company's cost of capital on the internal rate of return (IRR) of the project and its discounted payback period (DPP)?

	IRR	DPP
A	Decrease	Decrease
B	Decrease	Increase
C	No change	Increase
D	No change	Decrease

(2 marks)

Test your understanding 12

MN plc has a rolling programme of investment decisions. One of these investment decisions is to consider mutually-exclusive investments A, B and C. The following information has been produced by the investment manager.

	Investment decision A £	**Investment decision B** £	**Investment decision C** £
Initial investment	105,000	187,000	245,000
Cash inflow for A: years 1 to 3	48,000		
Cash inflow for B: years 1 to 6		48,000	
Cash inflow for C: years 1 to 9			48,000
Net present value (NPV) at 10% each year	14,376	22,040	31,432
Ranking	3rd	2nd	1st
Internal rate of return (IRR)	17.5%	14%	13%
Ranking	1st	2nd	3rd

Required:

(a) Prepare a report for the management of MN plc which includes:

- a graph showing the sensitivity of the three investments to changes in the cost of capital;
- a statement of the reasons for differences between NPV and IRR rankings – use investment A to illustrate the points you make;
- a brief summary which gives MN plc's management advice on which project should be selected.

(18 marks)

(b) One of the directors has suggested using payback to assess the investments. Explain to him the advantages and disadvantages of using payback methods over IRR and NPV. Use the figures above to illustrate your answer.

(7 marks)

(Total: 25 marks)

Test your understanding 13

Calculate the PV of the following cash flows:

(1) A fifteen year annuity of $300 starting at once. Interest rates are 6%.

(2) A perpetuity of $33,000 commencing immediately. Interest rates are 22%.

Test your understanding 14

The financial director of A Co has prepared the following schedule to enable her to appraise a new project. Interest rates are 10%. She wants to calculate the PV of the cash flows using two different assumptions regarding the project duration.

The assumptions are as follows:

A That the real annual cash flow will be $250,000 from Year 4 for the foreseeable future.

B That the real annual cash flow will be $250,000 from Year 4 to Year 18.

					Assumption (a)	Assumption (b)
Year	T_0	T_1	T_2	T_3	T_4onwards	T_4-T_{18}
	$000	$000	$000	$000	$000	$000
Net cash flow	(2,000)	(440)	363	399	250	250

Requirement:

Calculate the NPV from the project under both assumptions.

Test your understanding answers

Example 1

$V = 100\ (1.10)^5 = £161.05$

Example 2

$V = 450(1.0625)^{12} = £931.45$

Example 3

$$x = \frac{5{,}000}{1.05^{10}} = £3{,}070$$

Example 4

$x = 250 \times 0.404 = £101$

Example 5

$PV = 25{,}000 \times 0.564 = £14{,}100$

Example 6 – PROJECT APPRAISAL

		Project A		Project B	
Year	**Discount factor**	**Cash flow** £000	**Present value** £000	**Cash flow** £000	**Present value** £000
0		(450)	(450)	(100)	(100)
1	0.909	200	181.8	50	45.45
2	0.826	150	123.9	40	33.04
3	0.751	100	75.1	30	22.53
4	0.683	100	68.3	20	13.66
5	0.621	120	74.52	30	18.63
		NPV =	73.62	NPV =	33.31

Example 6 - CONTINUED 1

(a)

		Project A	
Year	**Discount factors at 20%**	**Net cash flow £000**	**PV £000**
0	1.000	(450)	(450)
1	0.833	200	167
2	0.694	150	104
3	0.579	100	58
4	0.482	100	48
5	0.402	120	48
		NPV @ 20% =	(25)

$$IRR = L + \frac{N_L}{N_L - N_H} \times (H - L)$$

$$IRR = 10 + \frac{74}{74 - (-25)} \times (20 - 10)$$

$$IRR = 10 + \frac{74}{99} \times (10)$$

$$IRR = 10 + (0.747 \times 10)$$

IRR = 17.5%

(b) **Project B**

At 10% the NPV was £33,310
At 20% the NPV is £8,510
At 30% the NPV is – £9,15

$$IRR = 10 + \frac{33,310}{33,310 - (-9,150)} \times (30 - 10)$$

$$IRR = 10 + \frac{33,310}{42,460} \times (20)$$

$$IRR = 10 + (0.785 \times 20)$$

IRR = 25.7%

Example 7

Calculation - constant annual flows

$$\text{Payback Period} = \frac{\$2m}{\$\ 500,000}$$

Payback Period = 4 years

Example 6 - CONTINUED 2

Project A	Cashflow	Cummulative cash flow
Year 0	(450)	(450)
Year 1	200	(250)
Year 2	150	(100)
Year 3	100	0

Payback period = 3 years

Project B		
Year 0	(100)	(100)
Year 1	50	(50)
Year 2	40	(10)
Year 3	30	20

Payback period = 3 years
(or 2 years and 4 months)

Example 6 - CONTINUED 3

	Project A	Project B
	£000	£000
Total profit before depreciation (total operating cash)	650	160
Less total depreciation	(430)	(90)
Total profit after depreciation	220	70
÷ number of years	5	5
Average annual profit	44	14
Average value of investment	235	55
Accounting rate of return	18.7%	25.5%

Conclusion: the firm should select project B

Project A	NPV:	£73,620
	IRR:	17.5%
	Payback period:	3 years
	Discounted payback period:	just over 4 years
	ARR:	18.7%
Project B	NPV:	£33,310
	IRR:	25.7%
	Payback period:	2 years and 4 months
	Discounted payback period:	just under 3 years
	ARR:	25.5%

Example 8 – ANNUITIES

(a)

Year	Cash flow £	Discount factor	Present value £
0	(50,000)		(50,000)
1–7	10,000	4.868	48,680
			1,320

(b) £10,000 × annuity factor = £50,000

Annuity factor = 5

Using tables and a life of seven years, the closest annuity factor to 5 is 5.033. This means the IRR is approximately 9%

Example 9 – PERPETUITIES

NPV = (£50,000) + £5,670 ÷ 0.09 = £13,000

Test your understanding 1

Year	Cash flow	DF at 9%	PV
	$		$
0	(240,000)	1.000	(240,000)
1	80,000	0.917	73,360
2	120,000	0.842	101,040
3	70,000	0.772	54,040
4	40,000	0.708	28,320
5	20,000	0.650	13,000
NPV			+ 29,760

The PV of cash inflows exceeds the PV of cash outflows by $29,760, which means that the project will earn a DCF return in excess of 9%, i.e. it will earn a surplus of $29,760 after paying the cost of financing. It should therefore be undertaken.

Test your understanding 2

Revenue – components – labour = £80,000 – £18,000 – £20,000 = £42,000

Year	Cash flow £000		Discount factor	Present value
0	Initial cost	(100)		(100)
1 - 3	Annual cash	42	2.106	88.452
3	Residual	40	0.579	23.16
				11.612

Net present value = £11,612

Answer C

Test your understanding 3

$$IRR = 10\% + \frac{50,000}{50,000-(-10,000)} \times (15\%-10\%) = 14.17\%$$

Test your understanding 4

At the IRR, PV of future net cash flows = initial capital outlay.

Answer A

Test your understanding 5

Year	**Cash flow**	**DF @ 15%**	**PV @ 15%**	**DF @ 20%**	**PV @ 20%**
	$		$		$
0	(50,000)	1.000	(50,000)	1.000	(50,000)
1	18,000	0.870	15,660	0.833	14,994
2	25,000	0.756	18,900	0.694	17,350
3	20,000	0.658	13,160	0.579	11,580
4	10,000	0.572	5,720	0.482	4,820
NPV			+ 3,440		(1,256)

The IRR is above 15% but below 20%.

Using the interpolation method:

(1) The NPV is + 3,440 at 15%.

(2) The NPV is – 1,256 at 20%.

(3) The estimated IRR is therefore:

$$\text{IRR} = 15\% + \frac{3{,}440}{3{,}440 - (-1{,}256)} \times (20 - 15)\%$$

$$= 15\% + 3.7\%$$

$$= 18.7\%$$

(4) The project is expected to earn a DCF return in excess of the target rate of 17%, so on financial grounds (ignoring risk) it is a worthwhile investment.

Test your understanding 6

$$\text{(a) IRR} = \frac{\text{Annual inflow}}{\text{Initial investment}} \times 100 = \frac{\$5{,}000}{\$50{,}000} \times 100 = 10\%$$

(b) NPV calculation

		Cash flow	DF(c) %	PV
		$		$
Time				
0	Investment	(50,000)	1	(50,000)
1-8	Inflow	8,060	(b)	(a)
			NPV	Nil

- The aim is to find the discount rate (c) that produces an NPV of nil.
- Therefore the PV of inflows (a) must equal the PV of outflows, $50,000.
- If the PV of inflows (a) is to be $50,000 and the size of each inflow is $8,060, the DF required must be 50,000 ÷ 8,060 = 6.20.
- The discount rate (c) for which this is the 8-year factor can be found by looking along the 8-year row of the cumulative DFS shown in the annuity table.
- The figure of $6.210 appears under the 6% column suggesting an IRR of 6% is the closest.

Test your understanding 7

Average annual profit = £50,000 × 30%	£15,000
	× 5 yrs
Total profit	£75,000
Add back depreciation	£45,000
	———
Total cash	£120,000
Less year 1 cash flow	(6,000)
	———
	£114,000
Cash per annum (yrs 2–5) 114 / 4	£28,500
Outlay	£50,000
Cash inflow after 2 years 6,000 + 28,500	£34,500
Still required	£15,500
Proportion of year 3 to gain balance of cash =	15,500 ÷ 28,500 = 0.54
Hence payback period =	2.54 years

Answer D

Test your understanding 8

Year	Cash flow £	Discount factor	Present value £
0	(90,000)		(90,000)
1 - 5	20,000 p.a	3.791	75,820
6 - 10	10,000 p.a.	2.354	23,540
10	8,000	0.386	3,088
			———
			12,448
			———

Test your understanding 9

Maximum withdrawal = £100,000 × 0.08 = £8,000 per annum in perpetuity.

Test your understanding 10

Initial investment required = £2,000 ÷ 0.10 = £20,000.

Test your understanding 11

The IRR will be unaffected by the cost of capital. As the discount rate increases future cash flow reduce in present value terms, therefore the discounted payback period will increase.

Answer C

Test your understanding 12

(a)

To:	The Management
From:	The Management Accountant
Subject:	Investment projects A, B and C
Date:	1 July 2006

The investment manager has analysed three mutually-exclusive investment opportunities A, B and C. The financial benefits from these opportunities are illustrated below in diagrammatical form.

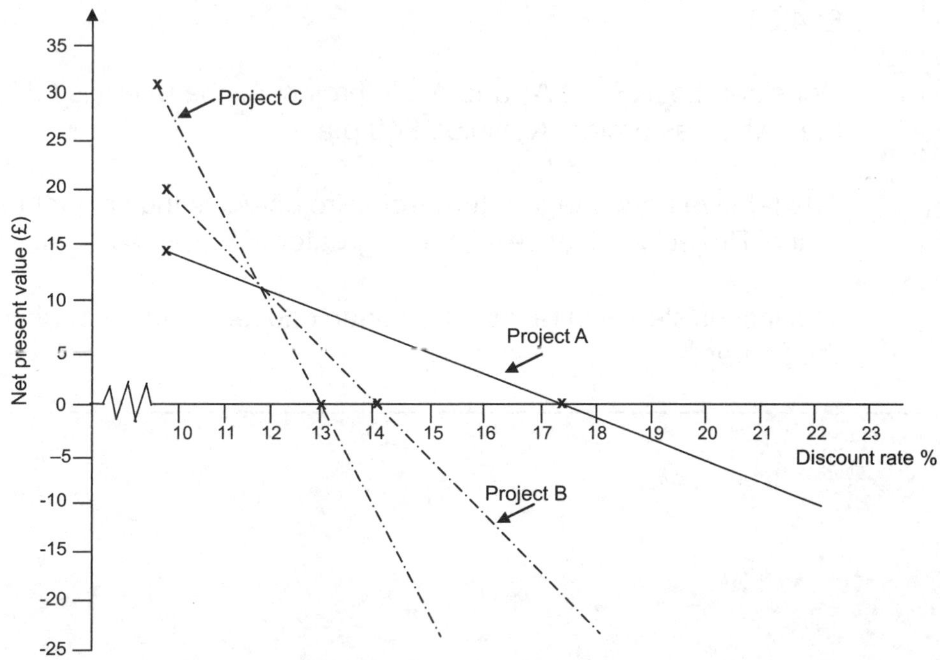

Reasons for differences between NPV and IRR rankings

There are two main reasons that NPV and IRR rankings differ:

(1) The magnitude of the cash flows.

(2) The timing of the cash flows.

Magnitude of cash flows

Project A_1	**Year**		**Cash flow**
			£
	0	17.5%	
	1	3 years	
	2	just over 4 years	
	3	18.7%	

Project A_2	**Year**	**Cash flow**
		£
	0	(105)
	1	49
	2	49
	3	49

The cash flows in Project A_1 are approximately 1,000 times bigger than those in Project A_2. Hence the NPV of Project A_1 will be approximately 1,000 times bigger than the NPV of Project A_2. The NPV of Project A_1 is £14,376, but the NPV of A_2 will be just over £14.38.

Consider the IRRs of A_1 and A_2. In project A_2 the return is £48,000 p.a., whereas project A_2 yields £49 p.a.

The relative percentage return from Project A_2 is thus higher than that of Project A_1. Hence A_2 has a greater IRR than A_1.

The inconsistency in ranking has been caused by the magnitude of the figures.

Timing of cash flows

The actual time periods when the cash is generated can produce conflicting results.

Again consider two projects.

Project A_1	**Year**	**Cash flow** £
	0	(105,000)
	1	48,000
	2	48,000
	3	48,000

Project A_2	**Year**	**Cash flow** £
	0	(105,000)
	1	130,000
	2	0
	3	0

The NPV of Project A_2 is £13,170 (130 × 0.909 – 105).

This NPV is lower than the NPV of Project A_1.

The magnitude of the cash sums is very similar in both projects.

If we consider how the NPVs of the two projects reduce as the discount rate rises.

The NPV of A_1 will fall rapidly as the cash flows in the years 2 and 3 very quickly reduce in present value terms. The NPV of this project becomes zero at a 17.5% discount rate.

The cash in Project A_2 is all received in the first year. This cash sum is only £130,000, compared to cash in flows of £144,000 in Project A_1. However the value of the year 1 cash flow remains strong even as the discount rate rises.

Indeed, at a discount rate of 17.5% the NPV of A_2 is still positive at £5,630 (130 × 1/1.175 – 105).

Hence the IRR of Project A_2 MUST be greater than 17.5%.

Again there has been a conflict in the rankings, this time because of the timing of the cash flows.

These examples should illustrate that it is just as important to consider WHEN the cash flows arise as to consider HOW MUCH the cash flows are. It is very important to obtain cash in the early years of a project whilst it holds a high present value.

Comparison of opportunities A, B and C

The capital outlay in Project C is much greater than the other two projects. Cash inflows are generated for 9 years.

At a low cost of capital this project is worth the most to the company. The cash in years 6-9 maintains a high value when discount rates are low.

However, this project is very sensitive to increases in discount rates. As the cost of capital rises the NPV of Project C declines rapidly. This is illustrated in the graph at the beginning of the report.

Project A is less sensitive to increases in discount rates. All its cash is received in years 1 to 3. These maintain a strong value as the discount rate increases. Project A could be said to be the least risky of the three choices if interest rates are volatile.

Which project should be selected?

The company has a cost of capital of 10%. At this rate Project C produces an NPV of £31,432. This is of higher benefit to MN plc than either projects A or B. Hence this project should be selected.

Assumptions: cash flows are known and certain. The cost of capital is known. Taxation and inflationary aspects have been ignored.

If MN plc is very risk averse, Project A may be considered as its NPV is more robust to increases in the cost of capital than projects B or C.

If you require any further information on this matter, please do not hesitate to contact me.

Signed: Management Accountant

(b) The payback period is the time that elapses before the initial cash outlay is recovered.

The paybacks in the example are:

Project A:	2 years 2 months
Project B:	3 years 10 months
Project C:	5 years 1 month

Advantages of payback

(1) *Exposure to risk*. It is widely recognised that long-term forecasting is less reliable than short-term forecasts. Projects with short paybacks tend to be less risky than projects with long paybacks. A project with a one-year payback is less risky than a project with a 10-year payback. Management can have very little confidence in forecasts of events ten years from now.

(2) *Liquidity*. Investment opportunities often require significant capital outlay. It may be important to recover this capital expenditure quickly for the company to maintain a strong position. Payback illustrates how quickly the capital can be recovered.

(3) *Simple measure*. The payback period is not a complicated measure. Technical expertise is not required to understand the meaning of payback.

(4) *Not subjective*. Payback period uses cash flows. Some investment appraisal methods use the rather more subjective measure of accounting profit (the accounting rate of return).

Disadvantages of payback

(1) The time value of money is ignored. Each of the projects being considered by MN plc generates £48,000. Payback period fails to recognise that as time elapses the present value of this cash diminishes. It would be possible to overcome this problem by calculating a discounted payback period.

(2) Cash flows after the payback are ignored. Option C has a payback of a little over five years. This information does not reveal that Project C continues to generate cash for four further years.

(3) Not a measure of absolute profitability. Payback fails to indicate HOW MUCH each project is worth. It seems naïve to select a project on the basis of payback without considering the amount of benefit received.

In the example Project A has a payback of just over two years, however its NPV is only £14,376.

Project C yields an NPV of £31,432 – more than double A's NPV. Payback period ignores this fact.

Test your understanding 13

(1) This is a standard 14-year annuity with one additional payment at T_0.

Step 1: Look up the 14-year AF ⇨

AF = 9.295

Step 2: Add 1 ⇨ 9.295 + 1 = 10.295

Step 3: Calculate the PV ⇨300 × 10.295 = $3,088.50

(2) This is simply a standard perpetuity with one additional payment at T_0.

Step 1: Calculate the perpetuity factor ⇨ 1/0.22 = 4.545

Step 2: Add 1 ⇨ 4.545 + 1 = 5.545

Step 3: Calculate the PV ⇨ 33,000 × 5.545 = $182,982

Test your understanding 14

					Assumption (a)	Assumption (b)
Year	T_0	T_1	T_2	T_3	T_4onwards	T_4- T_{18}
	\$000	\$000	\$000	\$000	\$000	\$000
Net cash flow	(2,000)	(440)	363	399	250	250
Perpetuity factor (here discounts the cash flow to T_3)					1 ÷ 0.1 = 10	
AF (here discounts the cash flow to T_3)						15-yr 10% AF =7.606
DFs @ 10%	1.000	0.909	0.826	0.751	0.751	0.751
PV	(2,000)	(400)	300	300	1,878	1,428
NPV (a)					78	
NPV (b)						(372)

chapter

14

Further aspects of investment appraisal

Chapter learning objectives

Lead	Component
C1. Prepare information to support project appraisal.	(b) Apply the principles of relevant cash flow analysis to long-run projects that continue for several years. (c) Calculate project cash flows, accounting for tax and inflation, and apply perpetuities to derive 'end of project' value where appropriate. (d) Apply activity-based costing techniques to derive approximate 'long-run' product or service costs appropriate for use in strategic decision making. (f) Apply sensitivity analysis to cash flow parameters to identify those to which net present value is particularly sensitive. (g) Prepare decision support information for management, integrating financial and non-financial considerations.

1 Session content diagram

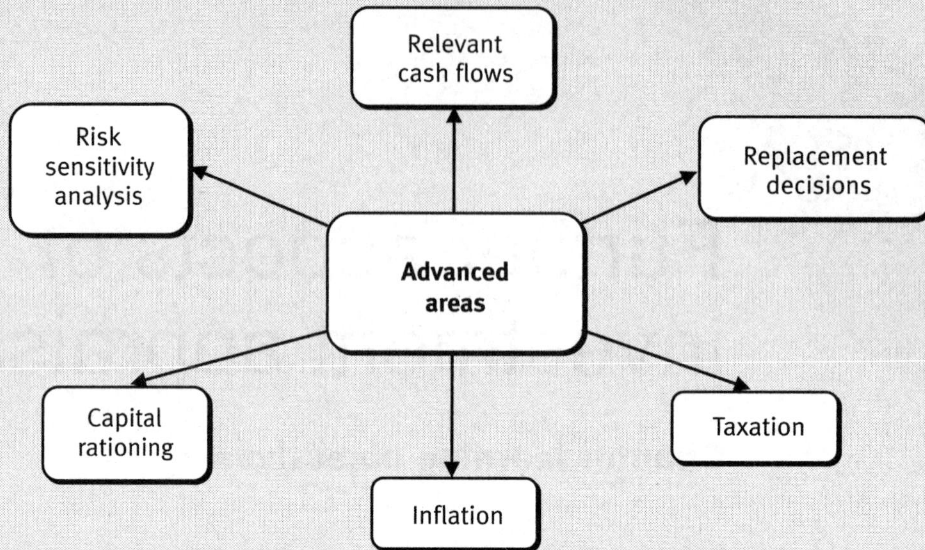

2 NPV and sensitivity analysis

Investment appraisal often involves a degree of uncertainty and risk, This may be dealt with in a number of ways:

- Adding a risk premium to the discount rate
- Payback period
- Sensitivity analysis - explored further here
- Probability distribution
- Monte Carlo Simulation

Further details

- **Adding a risk premium to the discount rate**

  A premium may be added to the usual discount rate to provide a safety margin. Marginally profitable projects (perhaps the riskiest) are less likely to have a positive NPV. The premium may vary from project to project to reflect the different levels of risk.

- **Payback period**

  Estimates of cash flows several years ahead are quite likely to be inaccurate and unreliable. It may be difficult to control capital projects over a long period of time. Risk may be limited by selecting projects with short payback periods.

- **Sensitivity charts**

  These diagrams illustrate how the NPV is affected by changes in one of the input parameters. The charts have been examined frequently in the management accounting examinations. Typical charts may show:

  NPV vs. discount rate,

  NPV vs. level of activity,

  NPV vs. change in variable cost per unit,

  NPV vs. change in selling price.

  The NPV should be plotted on the y-axis and the other parameter on the x-axis. Calculate two NPVs at two different levels (e.g. low demand and high demand) and then plot the two points. Draw the relationship assuming linearity.

- **Probability distribution**

  A probability distribution of expected cash flows may be determined and hence the expected NPV (EV) may be found together with risk analysis, e.g. best possible outcome, worst possible outcome, probability of a negative NPV, etc. A more sophisticated measure of risk is to calculate the standard deviation. This considers the degree of dispersion of the different possible NPVs around the expected NPV. The greater the spread of outcomes around the expected NPV, the higher the potential risk. The coefficient of variation should be calculated to compare projects. This was considered in an earlier Lesson.

- **Monte Carlo Simulation**

  Actual possible cash flows are considered together with the predicted probability. The simulation run will generate various combinations of actual possible cash flows and calculate the associated NPV. The computer generation of the events will reflect the probability of the event occurring. This may be done with the help of random numbers. The simulation package will usually be run several times to illustrate to managers the full range of actual possible outcomes. Simulations should reveal potential problem areas and areas of risk.

Sensitivity analysis in NPV questions typically involves posing 'what if' questions. The NPV is recalculated under different conditions, e.g. what would happen if demand fell by 10%, how would the result be affected if variable costs are 5% higher, etc.

Alternatively, we may wish to discover the maximum possible change in one of the parameters before the opportunity becomes non-viable.

This maximum possible change is often expressed as a percentage:

$$\text{Sensitivity margin} = \frac{\text{NPV}}{\text{PV of flow under consideration}}$$

LEARN

This formula works for total cash flows. It cannot be used for individual units, selling prices, variable cost per unit, etc. Have a go at the following example.

Example 1 – SENSITIVITY ANALYSIS

BJS Ltd is considering investing £120,000 in equipment that has a life of 15 years. Its final scrap value is £25,000.

The equipment will be used to produce 15,000 deluxe pairs of rugby boots per annum, generating a contribution of £2.75 per pair. Specific fixed costs are estimated at £18,000 per annum. The firm has a 15 % cost of capital.

Requirements:

(a) Calculate the NPV of the project.

(b) Calculate the sensitivity of your NPV to the:
   (i) initial investment;
   (ii) annual contribution;
   (iii) annual fixed costs.

(c) Draw a diagram to illustrate the sensitivity of the project to the annual demand.

(d) Use your diagram to identify the minimum annual sales required to ensure that the project at least breaks even.

Advantages and disadvantages of sensitivity analysis

Strengths of sensitivity analysis

- No complicated theory to understand.
- Information will be presented to management in a form which facilitates subjective judgement to decide the likelihood of the various possible outcomes considered.
- Identifies areas which are crucial to the success of the project. If the project is chosen, those areas can be carefully monitored.
- Indicates just how critical are some of the forecasts which are considered to be uncertain.

Weaknesses of sensitivity analysis

- It assumes that changes to variables can be made independently, e.g. material prices will change independently of other variables. This is unlikely. If material prices went up the firm would probably increase selling price at the same time and there would be little effect on NPV. A technique called simulation (see later) allows us to change more than one variable at a time.
- It only identifies how far a variable needs to change. It does not look at the probability of such a change. In the above analysis, sales volume appears to be the most crucial variable, but if the firm were facing volatile raw material markets a 65% change in raw material prices would be far more likely than a 29% change in sales volume.
- It is not an optimising technique. It provides information on the basis of which decisions can be made. It does not point directly to the correct decision.

3 Relevant cash flows

Investment decisions, like all other decisions, should be analysed in terms of cash flows that can be directly attributable to them. This has many implications:

Sunk costs

A sunk cost has already been incurred and therefore will not be relevant to the investment decision.

Opportunity cost

As in all decision making, opportunity costs are relevant, and should be included in investment decisions.

Fixed costs

Should be treated as a whole, and only where relevant. This means that fixed overheads that are "absorbed"/ "charged"/ "allocated"/ "apportioned" to a project should be ignored. Only extra/incremental changes in fixed overheads should be included in discounted cash flow calculations.

Depreciation

Depreciation is not a cash flow, and so should **never** be included in a discounted cash-flow calculation. The only investment appraisal technique that will include depreciation is ARR, which is rarely examined.

Further details

Costs to ignore

- Depreciation – this is not a cash flow and any depreciation charges should be excluded from DCF calculations. If profit figures after depreciation have been provided, the profit needs to be increased by adding back the depreciation.
- Apportioned fixed costs – the cost of producing an item may include an apportionment of factory-wide fixed costs using some standard basis for absorption. These should be excluded; fixed costs may appear in a DCF calculation, but only if it is known that they will increase as a result of accepting a project.
- Book values of assets – these fall into the same category as depreciation, they are not cash flows and must be ignored.
- Interest payments – in most cases it can be assumed that the cost of interest has been taken into account by the discounting process. Interest payments should be ignored since to do otherwise would be 'double counting'.
- Sunk costs – any sums that have already been spent or committed and cannot be influenced by the investment decision should be ignored.

Cash flows to include

The cash flows that should be included are those which are specifically incurred as a result of the acceptance or non-acceptance of the project. In some cases, these may be opportunity costs.

When deciding what figure should be included in any DCF calculation it sometimes helps to tabulate for a particular element of cost.

Cash flow if project accepted	-	Cash flow if project rejected	= Relevant cash flow

Example 2

A mining operation uses skilled labour costing $4 per hour, which generates a contribution, after deducting these labour costs, of $3 per hour.

A new project is now being considered that requires 5,000 hours of skilled labour. There is a shortage of the required labour. Any used on the new project must be transferred from normal working. Calculate the relevant cost of using the skilled labour on the project. Calculate the contribution cash flow that is lost if the labour is transferred from normal working

Activity 2

Suppose the facts about labour are as above, but there is a surplus of skilled labour already employed (and paid) by the business which is sufficient to cope with the new project. The presently idle men are being paid full wages.

Calculate the contribution cash flow that is lost if the labour is transferred to the project from doing nothing.

More on opportunity costs

If there are scarcities of resources to be used on projects (e.g. labour, materials, machines), then consideration must be given to revenues that could have been earned from alternative uses of the resources.

Opportunity cost is the value of the benefit sacrificed when one course of action is chosen in preference to an alternative. The opportunity cost is represented by the forgone potential benefit from the best rejected course of action.

For example, the skilled labour that is needed on the new project might have to be withdrawn from normal production causing a loss in contribution. This is obviously relevant to the project appraisal. The cash flows of a single department or division cannot be looked at in isolation. It is always the effects on cash flows of the whole organisation that must be considered.

Example

A new contract requires the use of 50 tons of metal ZX81. This metal is used regularly on all the firm's projects. There are 100 tons of ZX81 in stock at the moment that were bought for $200 per ton. The current purchase price is $210 per ton, and the metal could be disposed of for net scrap proceeds of $150 per ton. With what cost should the new contract be charged for the ZX81?

Solution

The use of the material in stock for the new contract means that more ZX81 must be bought for normal workings. The cost to the organisation is therefore the money spent on purchase, no matter whether existing stock or new stock is used on the contract. Assuming that the additional purchases are made in the near future, the relevant cost to the organisation is current purchase price, i.e.:

50 tons * $210 = $10,500

Example

Suppose the organisation has no use for the ZX81 in stock. What is the relevant cost of using it on the new contract?

Solution

Now the only alternative use for the material is to sell it for scrap. To use 50 tons on the contract is to give up the opportunity of selling it for:

50 * $150 = $7,500

The contract should therefore be charged with this amount.

Example

Suppose that there is no alternative use for the ZX81 other than a scrap sale, but that there is only 25 tons in stock.

Solution

The relevant cost of the 25 tons in stock is $150 per ton. The organisation must then purchase a further 25 tons, and assuming this is in the near future, it will cost $210 per ton.

The contract must be charged with:

	$
25 tons @ $150	3,750
25 tons @ $210	5,250
	9,000

Relevant costs and the decision to abandon

During our initial consideration of project appraisals, it was noted that past costs were irrelevant to any decision regarding the future of a project. This remains true for those occasions when the company has already started a project and wishes to establish whether it should continue with it, or whether it should abandon the project part way through its life.

The only relevant costs are future costs: these will be compared with future revenues to decide the viability of abandonment. Management is often reluctant to take a decision to abandon a project half-way through, as it is often considered to reflect a poor past decision; however true this may be, it would be even worse to compound the error by making another poor decision. Projects must, therefore, be kept constantly under review.

Factors in the decision to abandon

The following considerations must be taken into account in deciding whether to continue or abandon a project:

- the costs, and cost cash flows, of proceeding with the project
- the revenues, and revenue cash flows, associated with the project
- revenues that would arise if the project were abandoned
  - other projects, which may be:
    alternatives to the project under consideration
    more profitable uses of funds tied up in the project under review.

Each of these factors must be consciously assessed at each stage of the project's life and, if it is seen that abandoning the project would be more beneficial than proceeding with it, then an abandonment decision must be made.

4 Dealing with taxation

Taxation may have a significant impact on the viability of a capital investment project. Taxation payments and savings in tax payments are clearly cash flows associated with the project. They are relevant, and should be considered in a DCF analysis.

There are two types of taxation that we need to deal with:

(1) corporation tax;

(2) capital allowances, also known as tax depreciation.

A detailed knowledge of tax is not required for this paper. Assumptions and simplifications will be made. These will usually be set out clearly in each examination question. It is important to follow the instructions for the treatment of tax in the question being attempted. Any assumptions that you make must also be clearly stated.

Corporation tax

Typical assumptions are:

(1) Net cash flows from the project should be considered as the taxable profits arising from the project. Depreciation is not an allowable deduction. It may be necessary to make adjustments for depreciation.

(2) Timing of the payments: corporation tax may be payable in the year following the one in which the taxable profits are made. The examiner may state that the tax payable must be made in four quarterly instalments – two in the year of the profit arising, and two instalments in the following year. (The payments are due in months 7, 10, 13 and 16 from the start of the accounting period.) Always read the question carefully.

The corporation tax rate will be given in the question.

The impact of taxation on cash flows

Taxation has the following effects on an investment appraisal problem:

- Project cash flows will give rise to taxation which itself has an impact on project appraisal. Normally we assume that tax paid on operating flows is due one year after the related cash flow. However, it is possible for alternative assumptions to be made and so you should read any examination question carefully to ascertain precisely what assumptions are made in the question.
- Organisations benefit from being able to claim capital allowances – a tax deductible alternative to depreciation. The effect of these is to reduce the amount of tax that organisations are required to pay. Again it is important to read any examination question carefully in order to identify what treatment is expected by the examiner. A common assumption is that WDAs at 25% pa are receivable.

Note that the **WDAs are not cash flows** and to calculate the tax impact we have to multiply each year's WDA by the corporation tax rate. The effect of a WDA is on the amount of tax payable, which is the relevant cash flow.

In dealing with these tax effects it is always assumed that:

- where a tax loss arises from the project, there are sufficient taxable profits elsewhere in the organisation to allow the loss to reduce any relevant (subsequent) tax payment (and it may therefore be treated as a cash inflow) and that the company has sufficient taxable profits to obtain full benefit from capital allowances.

In practice, the effects of taxation are complex, and are influenced by a number of factors including the following:

- the taxable profits and tax rate
- the company's accounting period and tax payment dates
- capital allowances
- losses available for set-off

but many of these issues are ignored or simplified for the purposes of NPV investment appraisal.

Capital allowances or tax depreciation

Capital allowances are used to reduce taxable profits, and the consequent reduction in a tax payment should be treated as a cash saving arising from the acceptance of the project.

Writing-down allowances

In this examination writing-down allowances are generally allowed on the cost of plant and machinery at the rate of 25% on a reducing balance basis. It may also be possible to claim allowances on the costs of installation, such as labour and overhead costs of removing an old machine and levelling the area for the new machine. Remember to state your assumptions.

Balancing allowance (or charge)

When the plant is eventually sold, there may be a difference between the reducing balance amount and the selling price of the asset. An appropriate adjustment must be made to ensure that the company receives allowances equal to the total allowance allowed (i.e. purchase price less final value)

Always assume 'short-life asset' treatment on sale of the asset.

Timing of the tax savings associated with capital allowances

It is likely that the corporation tax will be paid in four quarterly instalments. Hence, the benefit of tax saved because of capital allowances is received when the corporation tax should have been paid. Thus, half the tax is saved in the current year, and half is saved in the year following:

Capital allowances

If a business buys a capital asset in one year and sells it several years later, the total tax relief it will receive is the tax on the cost of the asset less its eventual disposal value.

For example, if a business buys equipment for $100,000 in Year 0 and disposes of it in Year 5 for $20,000, it will receive tax relief on the net cost of $80,000. If the rate of corporation tax is 30%, the reduction in tax payments over the five years would be 30% × $80,000 = $24,000.

Balancing allowances are given as a final deduction to ensure the full fall in value has been allowed. Balancing charges occur where the total WDAs claimed exceed the fall in value of the asset. The excess claimed is treated as a taxable amount in the year of disposal.

Example 3 – CAPITAL ALLOWANCES

An asset is purchased for £50,000. At the end of the fourth year it will be sold for £10,000. Writing-down allowances are 25 per cent reducing balance and corporation tax is 30 per cent.

Corporation tax is payable in months 7, 10, 13 and 16 of the year in which the profit arises.

Required:

(a) Calculate the capital allowances each year and the associated corporation tax saving.

(b) Illustrate the timing of the tax savings calculated in part (a).

For tax purposes care must be taken to identify the exact time of asset purchase.

- Assets are assumed to be bought at T_0.
- This could be the very end of an accounting period (e.g. 31/21/X1) or the start of another (e.g.1/1/X2).
- There is no distinction between these dates for discounting, but there is for tax.

Asset bought at the start of an accounting period:

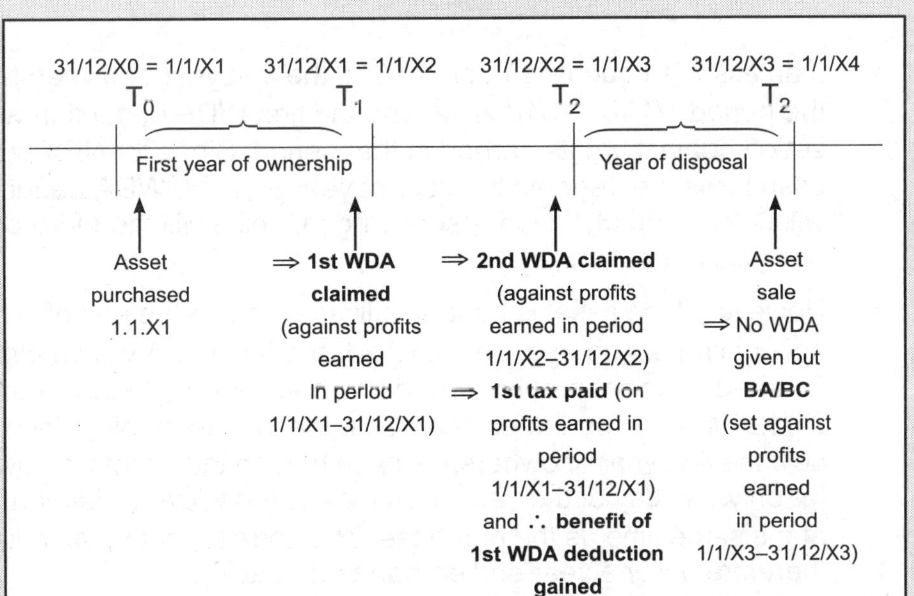

Asset bought at the end of an accounting period:

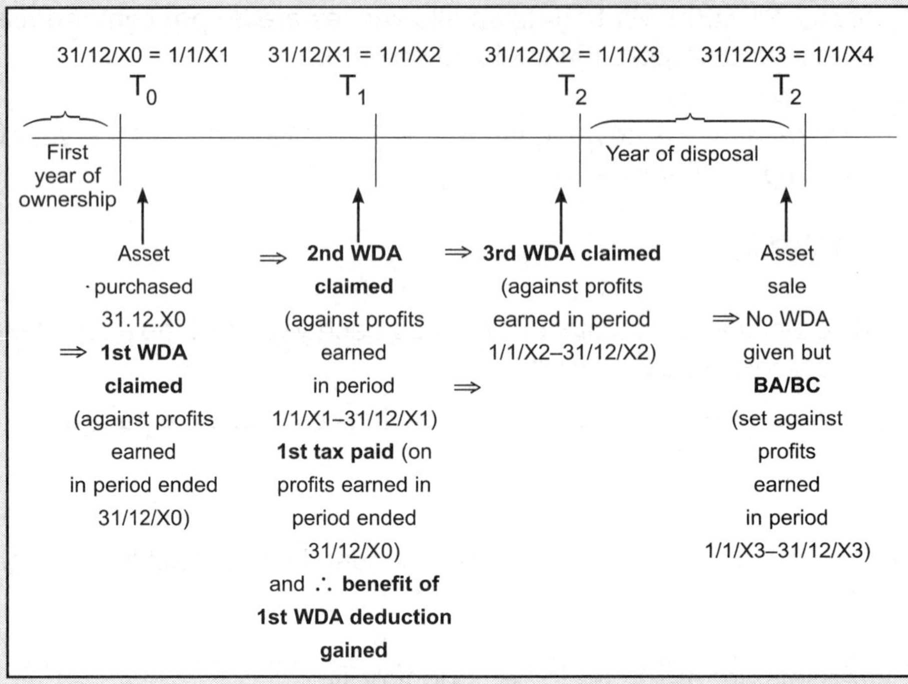

Timing of asset purchase and sale

Although the total value of WDAs will not alter, the timing of the asset purchase affects how much of the total fall in value is claimed in each tax year. Because of the time value of money, the later the deductions are taken, and the corresponding tax relief claimed, the less worthwhile the WDAs will be.

- If an asset is bought at T_0 on 1/1/X2, the first year of ownership is the period 1/1/X2 – 31/12/X2, and the first WDA deduction will be set off against profits earned in that period. Since for NPV purposes cash flows are deemed to occur at year end, the WDA deduction will be claimed at T_1. Corresponding tax relief will therefore occur one year later at T_2.
- However, if the asset is bought, still at T_0, but at the end of an accounting period, e.g. on 31/12/X1, the first WDA will be allowed for set-off against profits earned in the accounting period 1/1/X1 – 31/12/X1 (i.e. a period earlier that in the past example) since this is now the first year of ownership, even though the asset was owned for only one day of the year. This means the WDA is claimed at T_0, at the same time as the purchase. The corresponding tax relief will therefore occur a year earlier than before at T_1.

Example 4

An asset is bought on the first day of the year for $10,000 and will be used on a project for four years after which it will be disposed of on the final day of year 4. Tax is payable at 30%, one year in arrears, and capital allowances are available at 25% reducing balance.

Required:

(a) Calculate the WDA and hence the tax savings for each year if the proceeds on disposal of the asset are $2,500.

(b) Calculate how your answer change if the asset was bought on the last day of the previous accounting period.

5 Working capital

The next example has an investment of working capital included in it.

The treatment of working capital is as follows:

- It is treated as an investment at the start of the project, like any other investment. Any additional working capital requirements are invested when required. **Only *the change* in working capital is treated as a cash flow**.
- Working capital does not qualify for tax relief – so is ignored in the capital allowance calculations.
- At the end of the project the working capital is 'released'. This is treated as a cash inflow at the end of the project, equal to the total investment in working capital (unless told otherwise).

Example 5

Camp plc has produced and marketed sleeping bags for several years. The sleeping bags are much heavier than some of the modern sleeping bags being introduced to the market. The company is concerned about the effect this will have on its sales.

Camp Plc are considering investing in new technology that would enable them to produce a much lighter and more compact sleeping bag. The new machine will cost £250,000 and is expected to have a life of four years with a scrap value of £10,000. In addition an investment of £35,000 in working capital will be required initially.

The following forecast annual trading account has been prepared for the project:

	£
Sales	200,000
Material	(40,000)
Labour	(30,000)
Variable overheads	(10,000)
Depreciation	(20,000)
Annual profit	**100,000**

The company's cost of capital is 10%. Corporation tax is charged at 30% and is payable quarterly, in the 7th and 10th months of the year in which the profit is earned and the 1st and 4th month of the following year. A writing-down allowance of 25% on reducing balance is available on capital expenditure.

Requirement:

Calculate whether Camp plc should invest in the new technology.

6 Proforma layout for calculations

NPV with tax – Example pro forma

(for 2 Year Project)

	Year 0	Year 1	Year 2	Year 3
	£	£	£	£
Revenue		X	X	
Costs		(X)	(X)	
		—	—	
Net cash flow		X	X	
Tax on net cash flow		(X)	(X)	(X)
Investment	(X)			
Scrap value			X	
Tax saved (capital allowances)		X	X	X
Working capital	(X)		X	
Net cash flows	(X)	X	X	X
Discount factor	1.00	x	x	x
Present value	PV	PV	PV	PV

In the examination, for a short life project, with cash flows inflating at different rates, it is best to set the NPV calculation out with the cash flows down the side and the time across the top.

7 Dealing with inflation

The cost of capital is also known as the cost of money. It is the cost of obtaining capital funds. In simple terms this represents interest payable on a loan, or perhaps interest foregone by removing funds from an investment account in order to sink them into a capital project.

Remember: the cost of money represents the going interest rate.

If money is invested in an account, it will earn interest. However, inflation will have the effect of reducing the value of the return. By deflating the future cash (money) we can find the real return from the investment, i.e. the return at today's prices.

Remember: inflation reduces the value of future cash.

Example 6 – REAL RATE OF RETURN

£1,000 is invested in an account that pays 10% interest per annum. Inflation is currently 7% per annum.

Calculate the real return on the investment.

8 The impact of inflation on cash flows

Where cash flows have not been increased for expected inflation they are known as **current cash flows**, or **real cash flows**.

Where cash flows have been increased to take account of expected inflation they are known as **money cash flows**, or **nominal cash flows**. Remember, if they do take inflation into account, they represent expected flows of money, hence the term 'money cash flows'.

You can assume that cash flows you are given in the exam are the money cash flows unless told otherwise.

If the examiner specifies that the cash flows are in current terms you will generally need to put these in money terms before you can discount them (although see "other methods of dealing with inflation" below).

- For example if the question tells you that sales for the next 3 years are £100 in current terms but are expected to inflate by 10%, then what he actually means is that the sales will be:

Year 1: £110
Year 2: £121 } ie these are the cash flows in money terms
Year 3: £133.10

Make sure you read the question carefully. Sometimes you will be given the cash flows in Year 1 terms with subsequent inflation.

- For example if the question says "Sales will be £100 in the first year, but are then going to inflate by 10% for the next two years", then the sales will be:

Year 1: £100
Year 2: £110 } compare these to the previous example – make sure
Year 3: £121 you understand why they are different!

FORMULA

To find the real rate of return:

$$(1+r)=\frac{(1+m)}{(1+i)}$$

LEARN

The impact of inflation can be dealt with in two different ways - both methods give the same NPV.

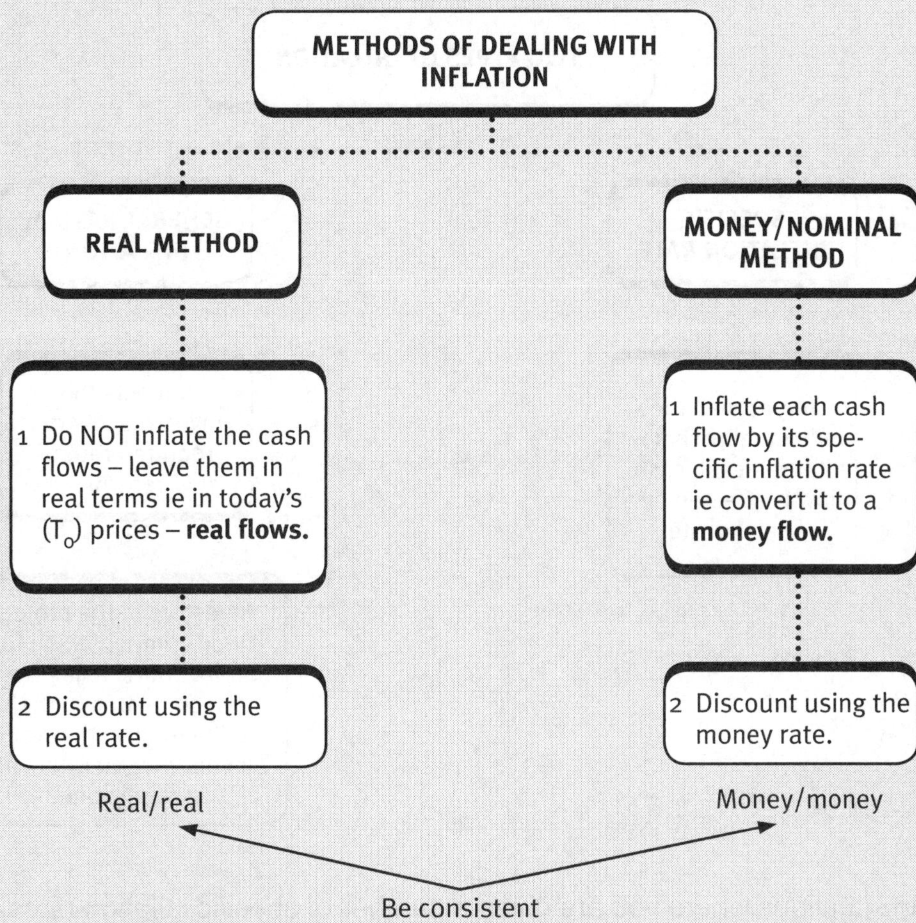

Example 7 – NPV AND INFLATION

Storm Ltd is evaluating project X which requires an initial investment of £50,000. Expected net cash flows are £20,000 per annum for 4 years at today's prices. However these are expected to rise by 5.5% per annum because of inflation. The firm's cost of capital is 15%. Calculate the NPV by:

(a) discounting money cash flows;

(b) discounting real cash flows.

9 Specific and general inflation rates

The TYUs given above had all cash flows inflating at the general rate of inflation. In practice, inflation does not affect all costs to the same extent. In some investment appraisal questions you may be given information on more than one inflation rate. In these situations you will have information on both specific inflation rates and general inflation rates.

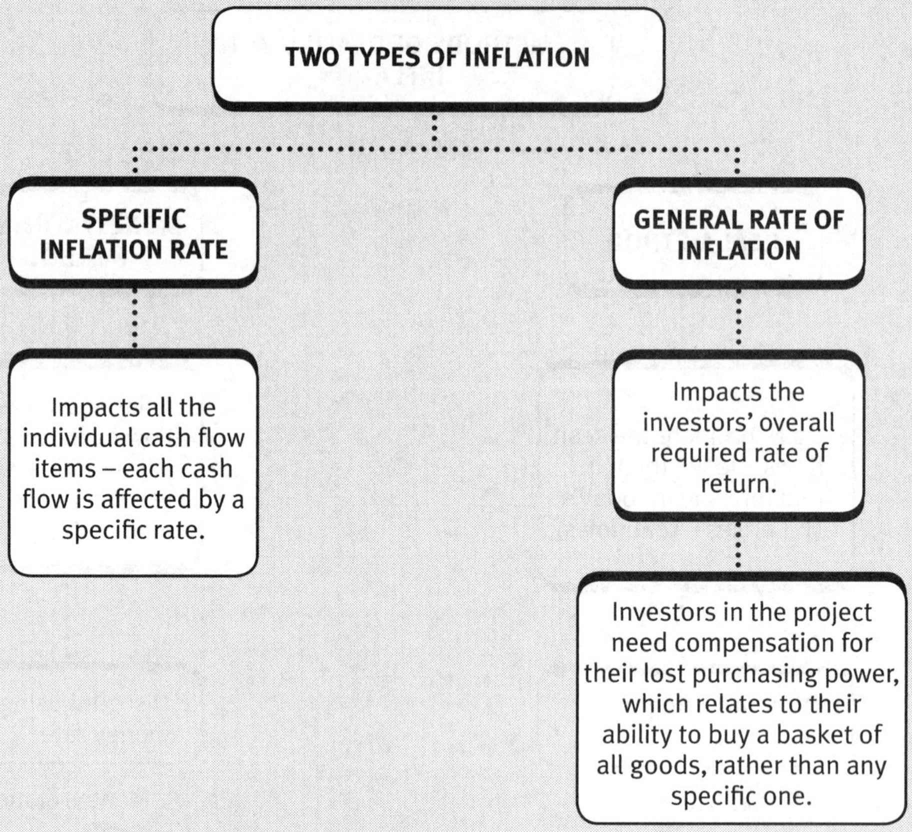

In situations where you are given a number of specific inflation rates, the real method outlined above cannot be used.

The following gives a useful summary of how to approach examination questions.

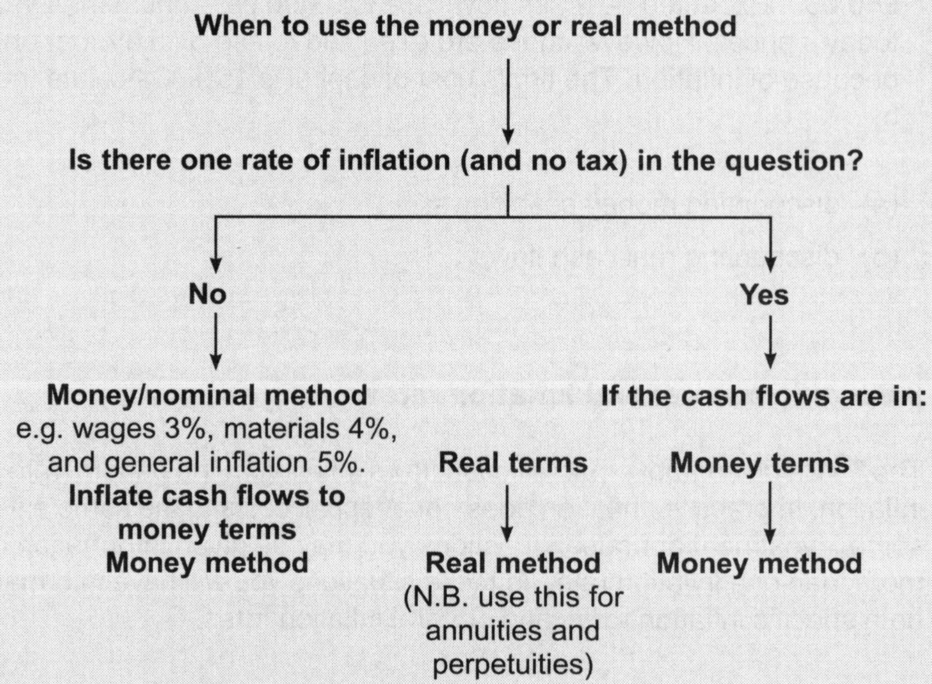

If a question contains both tax and inflation, it is advisable to use the money method.

Specific and general inflation rates

If there is one rate of inflation in the question both the real and money method will give the same answer. However it is easier to adjust one discount rate, rather than all the cash flows over a number of years. This is particularly true where the cash flows are annuities. The real method is the only possible method where they are perpetuities.

Although it is theoretically possible to use the real method in questions incorporating tax, it is extremely complex. It is therefore much safer (and easier) to use the money/nominal method in all questions where tax is taken into account.

To use the real method when cash flows inflate at different rates (specific rates) is extremely complex and would involve a lot of calculations. It is therefore advisable to always use the money method in these situations. This involves:

- inflating the cash flows at their specific inflation rates
- discounting using the money rate

Very often the money rate will not be given in the question but will need to be calculated. This should be done using the real rate and the general inflation rate.

Example 8

Thunder plc has just developed a new product to be called the Lightening and is now considering whether to put it into production. The following information is available:

(i) Costs incurred in the development of Lightening amount to £480,000.

(ii) Production of Lightening will require the purchase of new machinery at a cost of £2,400,000 payable immediately. This machinery is specific to the production of Lightening and will be obsolete and valueless when production ceases. The machinery has a production life of four years and a production capacity of 30,000 units per annum.

(iii) Production costs of Lightening (at year 1 prices) are estimated as follows:

	£
Direct material	8.00
Direct labour	12.00
Variable overheads	12.00

In addition, fixed production costs (at year 1 prices), including straight-line depreciation on plant and machinery, will amount to £800,000 per annum.

(iv) The selling price of Lightening will be £80.00 per unit (at year 1 prices). Demand is expected to be 25,000 units per annum for the next four years.

(v) The retail price index is expected to be at 5% per annum for the next four years and the selling price of Lightening is expected to increase at the same rate. Annual inflation rates for production costs are expected to be as follows:

	%
Direct material	4
Direct labour	10
Variable overheads	4
Fixed costs	5

(vi) The company's cost of capital in money terms is expected to be 15%.

You may ignore the effects of taxation.

Unless otherwise specified all costs and revenues should be assumed to arise at the end of each year.

Requirement:

Calcualte whether Thunder plc should produce Lightening on the basis of the information above.

(15 marks)

Deflation

Many western economies have very low rates of inflation at present and some are even experiencing deflation. Deflation may also apply to certain hi-tech materials which get considerably cheaper when they go into mass production.

Deflation may affect business decision making in several ways:

- Investing in projects that have long payback periods may require some courage.
- Borrowing to finance the purchase of assets that are going to fall in value may also require some courage: money rates will be low, but real rates are higher.
- It may be difficult to reduce some costs – especially wages – in line with deflation.
- Consumers may defer purchasing decisions if they anticipate that prices will fall.

10 Dealing with questions with both tax and inflation

Combining tax and inflation in the same question does not make it any more difficult than keeping them separate.

Questions with both tax and inflation are best tackled using the money method.

- Inflate costs and revenues, where necessary, before determining their tax implications.
- Ensure that the cost and disposal values have been inflated (if necessary) before calculating WDAs.
- Always calculate working capital on these inflated figures, unless given.
- Use a post-tax money discount rate.

Example 9

Ackbono Co is considering a potential project with the following forecasts:

	Now	T_1	T_2	T_3
Initial investment ($million)	(1,000)			
Disposal proceeds ($million)				200
Demand (millions of units)		5	10	6

The initial investment will be made on the first day of the new accounting period.

The selling price per unit is expected to be $100 and the variable cost $30 per unit. Both of these figures are given in today's terms.

Tax is paid at 30%, one year after the accounting period concerned.

WDA's are available at 25% reducing balance.

The company has a real required rate of return of 6.8%.

General inflation is predicted to be 3% pa but the selling price is expected to inflate at 4% and variable costs by 5% pa

Calculate the NPV of the project.

N.B. work in $ millions.

11 Capital asset replacement decisions

As the title suggests, this section considers the need to replace old, worn out capital assets within a firm.

There are two distinct types of decisions to consider:

(1) Considering mutually-exclusive options with unequal lives.

(2) Calculating an optimum replacement cycle.

We shall consider each in turn.

Mutually-exclusive options with unequal lives

Companies considering the replacement of an asset may be faced with alternatives where the life spans of the various machines differ, but the asset is required for the foreseeable future. The options must be evaluated over a comparable number of years.

Example 10 – REPLACEMENT DECISION

Donald Ltd is considering replacing an asset with one of two possible machines:

Machine X	Initial cost	£120,000
	Life	3 years
	Running costs	£20,000 p.a.
	Residual value	£10,000
Machine Y	Initial cost	£60,000
	Life	2 years
	Running costs	Year 1 : £40,000
		Year 2 : £35,000
	Residual value	nil

The machines will be required into the foreseeable future. The company's cost of capital is 10%.

Required:

Calculate which machine should be purchased.

Method and answer guide

Firstly calculate the NPV of costs:

		Machine X		Machine Y	
Year	**Discount factor**	**Cash flow** £000	**Present value** £000	**Cash flow** £000	**Present value** £000
0					
1	0.909				
2	0.826				
3	0.751				

It is not appropriate to compare these two NPVs. Machine X shows three years of costs whereas Machine Y only has two years worth of costs. Remember that the machines are needed into the foreseeable future, so do not pick the cheapest single purchase. The machine will be replaced many times over the next few years. Because of this we need to find a way of comparing the costs over an equal time period (not unequal years).

In order to compare like with like we will calculate an **equivalent annual cost**. This is similar to an average annual cash flow. Once both machines' costs have been annualised the cheapest machine can be chosen by comparing annual costs.

FORMULA

$$\text{Equivalent annual cost} = \frac{\text{PV of costs}}{\text{Annuity factor for year n}}$$

LEARN

where n is the machine life time

Machine X:

EAC =

Machine Y:

EAC =

Now select the cheapest option.

Optimum replacement cycles

Companies purchasing new plant and machinery must decide how often to replace them. Generally, as machinery ages its residual value decreases and the annual running costs increase. However, companies are unlikely to want to replace assets too frequently because of the capital outlay associated with the purchase.

In the next section we shall calculate the optimum replacement cycle in order to minimise long-term costs.

Factors in replacement decisions

The factors to be considered include the following:

- Capital cost of new equipment – the higher cost of equipment will have to be balanced against known or possible technical improvements.

- Operating costs – operating costs will be expected to increase as the machinery deteriorates over time. This is referred to as operating inferiority, and is the result of:
  - increased repair and maintenance costs
  - loss of production due to 'down-time' resulting from increased repair and maintenance time
  - lower quality and quantity of output.
- Resale value – the extent to which old equipment can be traded in for new.
- Taxation and investment incentives.
- Inflation – both the general price level change, and relative movements in the prices of inputs and outputs.

Example 11 – REPLACEMENT CYCLE

A supermarket is trying to determine the optimal replacement policy for its fleet of delivery vehicles. The total purchase price of the fleet is £220,000.

The running costs and scrap values of the fleet at the end of each year are:

	Year 1	**Year 2**	**Year 3**	**Year 4**	**Year 5**
Running costs	£110,000	£132,000	£154,000	£165,000	£176,000
Scrap value	£121,000	£88,000	£66,000	£55,000	£25,000

The supermarket's cost of capital is 12% per annum.

Ignore taxation and inflation.

Identify at the end of which year the supermarket should replace its fleet of delivery vehicles:

A Year 1

B Year 2

C Year 3

D Year 4

E Year 5

(4 marks)

Method of solution

(1) Consider each possible replacement cycle in turn: 1 year, 2 year, 3 year etc.

(2) Calculate the PV of costs for each cycle.

(3) Divide this PV by the annuity factor to find the equivalent annual cost.

(4) Select the replacement cycle with the lowest equivalent annual cost.

				Replacement cycle							
	Discount	**1 year**		**2 years**		**3 years**		**4 years**		**5 years**	
Year	**factor**	**Cash**	**PV**	**Cash**	**PV**	**Cash**	**PV**	**Cash**	**PV**	**Cash**	**PV**
0								(220)	(220)	(220)	(220)
1	0.893							(110)	(98.2)	(110)	(98.2)
2	0.797							(132)	(105.2)	(132)	(105.2)
3	0.712							(154)	(109.6)	(154)	(109.6)
4	0.636							(110)	(70)	(165)	(104.9)
5	0.567									(151)	(85.6)
PV of costs									(603.0)		(723.5)
Annuity factor									3.037		3.605
Equivalent annual cost									(198.6)		(200.7)

Limitations of replacement analysis

The replacement analysis model assumes that the firm replaces like with like each time it needs to replace an existing asset.

However this assumption ignores

- changing technology - machines fast become obsolete and can only be replaced with a more up-to-date model which will be more efficient and perhaps perform different functions
- inflation - the increase in price over time increases the cost structure of the different assets, meaning that the optimal replacement cycle can vary over time
- change in production plans - firms cannot predict with accircacy the market environment they will be facing in the future and whether they will even need to make use of the asset at that time.

12 Capital rationing

If investment funds are unlimited then all projects with a positive NPV should be undertaken. Capital rationing occurs when insufficient funds are available to undertake all beneficial projects.

The term soft capital rationing is often used to refer to situations where for various reasons the firm internally imposes a budget ceiling on the amount of capital expenditure. If the capital is restricted because of external constraints such as the inability to obtain funds from the financial markets, the term hard capital rationing is used. The type of rationing imposed on a firm will not, however, affect our analysis.

The objective of all capital rationing exercises is the maximisation of the total NPV of the chosen projects' cash flows at the cost of capital. Thus it becomes necessary to rank projects to enable the optimum combination to be undertaken.

Underlying assumptions:

- Individual projects are divisible. The resulting NPV will be pro-rated. For example, if only 25% of the capital is available for a project only 25% of its NPV will be earned.
- Annual cash flows cannot be delayed or brought forward.

Single-period capital rationing

As the title suggests this is where capital funds are restricted in just one period (year 0). Essentially the decision aims to maximise NPV given a single limiting factor. As with other decisions with one scarce resource, the opportunities should be ranked according to NPV per £1 invested. This measure is called the profitability index or cost-benefit ratio.

$$\text{Profitability index} = \frac{\text{NPV}}{\text{Initial Investment}}$$

LEARN

The optimal investment plan is determined by:

(1) calculating a PI for each project

(2) ranking the projects according to their PI

(3) allocating funds according to the projects' rankings until they are used up.

Example 12 – CAPITAL RATIONING

A company may undertake any of the following investment projects.

Project	Investment required £000	Net present value £000
A	3,400	850
B	2,750	825
C	2,000	720
D	3,400	680
E	860	430
F	950	400
G	1,250	350

In the next budget period there is only £9 million available for capital expenditure projects. Each project is divisible.

Required:

(a) If the company ranks the projects according to highest NPVs, which projects will be undertaken? Calculate the total NPV.

(b) If the company selects projects according to their profitability index, calculate which projects will be undertaken. Calculate the total NPV now.

Indivisible projects

In these circumstances, the objective can only be achieved by selecting from amongst the available projects on a trial and error basis. Because of the problem of indivisibility this may leave some funds unutilised.

Example

PQ has $50,000 available to invest. Its cost of capital is 10%. The following indivisible projects are available:

Project	Initial outlay $	Return p.a. to perpetuity $
1	20,000	1,500
2	10,000	1,500
3	15,000	3,000
4	30,000	5,400
5	25,000	4,800

Solution

The first stage is to calculate the NPV of the projects.

Project	Initial outlay $	PV of cash flows $	NPV $
1	20,000	15,000	(5,000)
2	10,000	15,000	5,000
3	15,000	30,000	15,000
4	30,000	54,000	24,000
5	25,000	48,000	23,000

The approach is then one of considering all possible combinations of projects under the investment limit of $50,000.

The optimum selection of projects is as follows:

Project	Initial outlay $	NPV $
2	10,000	5,000
3	15,000	15,000
5	25,000	23,000
	50,000	43,000
Unused funds	Nil	
Funds available	50,000	

Multiple-period capital rationing

It is likely that there is a capital expenditure ceiling each and every year. When capital is limited in several years we now have to deal with several limiting factors. The investment decision must now be solved using linear programming.

More than two projects

You are not likely to be asked to solve such problems numerically, but you may need to know that they require a mathematical technique known as linear programming to solve these situations.

Conditions for linear programming

However, it may be defined so as to be suitable for a linear programming approach. For linear programming to be suitable, the following conditions must apply:

- The proportions undertaken of each of the projects available are the variables.
- Projects are assumed to be divisible.
- There are only two projects being considered. If there are more than two projects, then the simplex technique is required. A solution would be provided in the form of a final simplex tableau which would require interpretation.
- NPVs are linearly related to the proportion of each project accepted.

- Cash limits year by year form the constraints.
- The objective is to maximise the NPV of cash flows at the cost of capital.

13 ABC in longer term decisions

The role of ABC

Activity-based costing (ABC) has been discussed in an earlier chapter. In this section we briefly discuss the role of ABC in longer-term decision making.

ABC systems are primarily designed to furnish management with cost information relating to an organisation's products. However, the production of this information is not an end in itself. Indeed it is the use to which such activity-based information is put that represents its real purpose and its value should be assessed against this end-result.

An ABC system produces historic information relating to its products or service provision which is of much assistance to management in analysing and explaining an organisation's profitability. However, many commentators including Robert Kaplan and Robin Cooper have viewed ABC as supporting major areas of strategic decision making with organisations, these being:

- decisions concerning product pricing strategy
- changes to the range and mix of products via the promotion and discontinuance of current lines, and
- new product development.

When ABC information is used in the above ways then it will underpin policy decisions of senior management and will therefore have a significant influence upon the longer-term prosperity of an organisation. Advocates of the use of ABC for strategic decision making maintain that its value lies in greater accuracy attaching to product costing which in turn increases the degree of reliability of cost information used for the above purposes. They further maintain that the use of ABC may give an indication of the long-term variable cost of products which arguably is the most relevant cost information for use in decisions of the above type. Given the inherent uncertainty involved in strategic decision making, management may use ABC information in decision-modelling and sensitivity analysis to assist in the making of such decisions.

The end product of an ABC system is an estimate of the historic cost of each of an organisation's products. However, strategic decision making involves future time periods and thus it is future outlay costs that need to be taken into consideration as opposed to historic costs. Therefore, it is arguable that the results obtained from an ABC system should only be used as a starting point in the determination of cost information that is aimed at assisting in the making of longer-term decisions. This is especially the case if ABC based product costs are viewed as estimates of longer term product costs as 'nothing is forever' and historic costs are susceptible to substantial change since all factors of production become variable in the longer term.

Any cost information which has been produced based on past activities must be used with caution with regard to longer-term decisions. Even so, ABC information may provide a sound starting point for the preparation of cost information to be used in strategic decision making. It has been argued that a significant advantage of ABC over conventional costing systems lies in its suitability for strategic decision making. Kaplan has argued that for decisions of a strategic nature a long-term perspective is usual and maintains that an ABC system gives product cost information which matches this requirement particularly well. This is evidenced by his assertion that 'conventional notions of fixed and variable costs are ignored because, for the purposes of product cost analysis, the time period is long enough to warrant treatment of virtually all costs as variable'.

14 Qualitative factors

The emphasis in this chapter has been on investment appraisal as a computational exercise: known numbers are inserted into formulae and a numerical result is produced. But, in reality, investment decisions are also influenced by many qualitative factors that must also be borne in mind in the investment appraisal exercise.

Qualitative factors

Consider the typical example of the proposed purchase of a new machine in a manufacturing plant. The machine offers both quantitative and qualitative costs and benefits, as below.

Quantitative costs include:

- the purchase price of the machine
- installation and training costs.

Quantitative benefits include:

- lower direct labour costs
- lower scrap costs and items requiring rework
- lower stock costs.

Qualitative costs include:

- increased noise level
- lower morale if existing staff have to be made redundant.

Qualitative benefits include:

- reduction in product development time
- improved product quality and service
- increase in manufacturing flexibility.

Because the qualitative factors are difficult to state in numerical terms, they are conventionally ignored in the investment appraisal exercise. However such an approach is flawed. If a question asks you to carry out a DCF analysis and then comment on what you have done, be certain to point out the qualitative factors that could additionally be brought into the decision.

15 Chapter summary

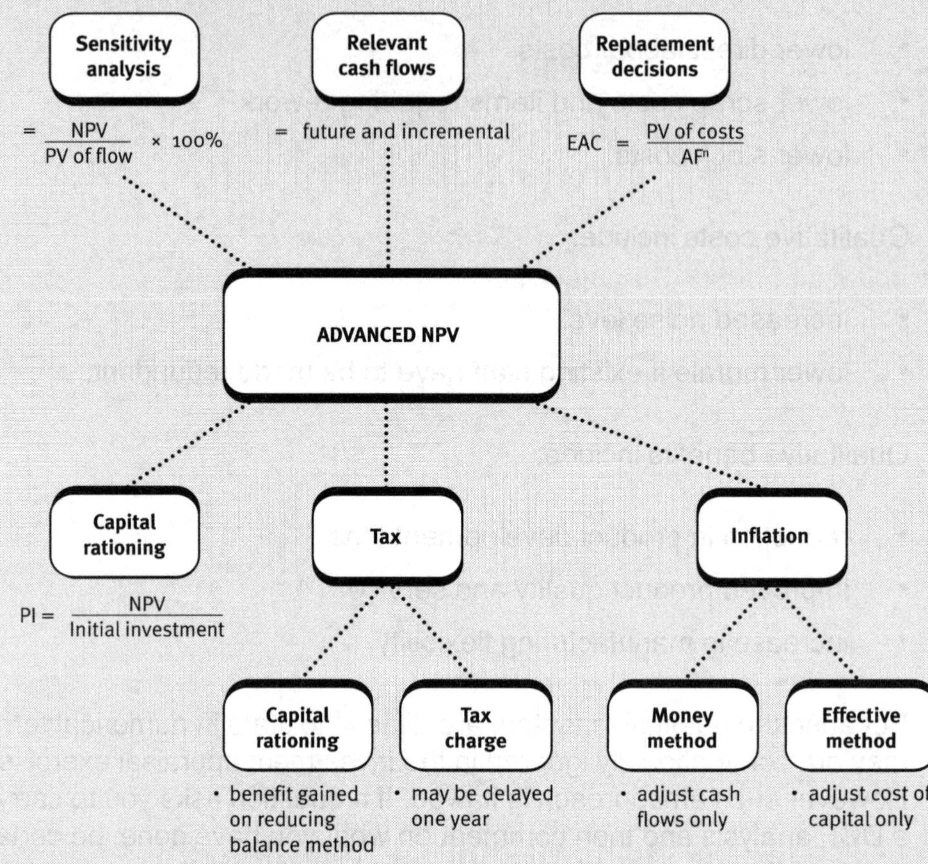

16 Practice questions

Test your understanding 1

Bacher Co is considering investing \$500,000 in equipment to produce a new type of ball. Sales of the product are expected to continue for three years, at the end of which the equipment will have a scrap value of \$80,000. Sales revenue of \$600,000 pa will be generated at a variable cost of \$350,000. Annual fixed costs will increase by \$40,000.

(a) **Calculate whether, on the basis of the estimates given, the project should be undertaken, assuming that all cash flows occur at annual intervals and that Bacher Co has a cost of capital of 15%.**

(b) **Calculate the percentage changes required in the following estimates for the investment decision to change:**

(i) initial investment

(ii) scrap value

(iii) selling price

(iv) unit variable cost

(v) annual fixed cost

(vi) sales volume

(vii) cost of capital.

Test your understanding 2

The management of a company are making a decision on whether or not to purchase a new piece of plant and machinery which costs £100,000. The new machine will generate a net cash flow of £30,000 each year for four years. At the end of the fourth year it will be sold for £20,000. The company's cost of capital is 5%. Writing-down allowances are 25% reducing balance and corporation tax is 30%. Corporation tax is payable quarterly, in the seventh and tenth months of the year in which the profit is earned, and in the first and fourth months of the following year.

Required:

Calculate the net present value of the project and advise management.

Test your understanding 3

Dralin Co is considering an investment of $460,000 in a non-current asset expected to generate substantial cash inflows over the next five years. Unfortunately the annual cash flows from this investment are uncertain, but the following probability distribution has been established:

Annual cash flow ($)	Probability
50,000	0.3
100,000	0.5
150,000	0.2

At the end of its five-year life, the asset is expected to sell for $40,000. The cost of capital is 5%.

Calculate whether the investment should be undertaken.

Test your understanding 4

Smith has decided to increase its productive capacity to meet an anticipated increase in demand for its products. The extent of this increase in capacity has still to be determined, and a management meeting has been called to decide which of the following two mutually exclusive proposals – A or B – should be undertaken.

The following information is available:

	Proposal A	Proposal B
	$	$
Capital expenditure		
Buildings	50,000	100,000
Plant	200,000	300,000
Installation	100,000	15,000
Net Income		
Annual pre-depreciation profits (note (1))	70,000	95,000
Other relevant income and expenditure		
Sales promotion (note (2))	-	15,000
Plant scrap value	10,000	15,000
Buildings disposable value (note (3))	30,000	60,000
Working capital required over the project life	50,000	65,000

Notes:

(1) The investment life is ten years.

(2) An exceptional amount of expenditure on sales promotion of $15,000 will have to be spent in year 2 of proposal B.This has not been taken into account in calculating pre-depreciation profits.

(3) It is the intention to dispose of the buildings in ten years' time.

Using an 8% discount rate, you are required to calculate which of the two alternatives should be chosen.

Test your understanding 5

Lincoln plc is considering the production of a new product, Plasticoats, in order to extend the wide range of existing products.

It is intended that production should start on 1 January 2007, and should continue for three years, after which time it is expected that demand for Plasticoats will cease.

The directors of Lincoln plc have made estimates in relation to the production and sale of Plasticoats as follows:

(1) 100,000 Plasticoats will be produced and sold in each of the three years.

(2) The selling price per Plasticoat will be £24 during 2007, but will increase in 2008 and 2009 at the same rate as Retail Price Index. The RPI is expected to rise at an annual compound rate of 6%.

(3) Plasticoats produced in each year will be all sold during the same year. Production will entail the use of the following resources:

(i) **Materials:** Each Plasticoat will require 2 kgs of Plastic and 1 kg of Oats. Plastic is used regularly by Lincoln plc, on many different products, whereas Oats can be used only in the production of Plasticoats. If not used to produce Plasticoats, Oats must be sold. Lincoln currently has in its warehouse 200,000 kgs of Plastic, and 120,000 kg of Oats. All of the Plastic was bought at a price of £1 per kg, all of the Oats at a price of 80p per kg. Current (January 2007) selling prices of the two materials are Plastic 75p per kg; Oats 60p per kg. Current buying prices are Plastic £1.20 per kg; Oats £1.10 per kg.

Both Plastic and Oats must be bought and paid for at the beginning of the year in which they are to be used in production, and both the market selling and buying prices of the two materials are expected to rise at an annual compound rate of 7%.

(ii) **Labour:** Each Plasticoat requires half an hour of highly skilled labour, currently (1 January 2007) paid £8 per hour, and 1 hour of unskilled labour, currently paid £5 per hour. Labour costs, both skilled and unskilled, are expected to increase at an annual compound rate of 10% over the life of Plasticoats. During 2007 only, Lincoln expects to have available 150,000 surplus hours of unskilled labour. It does not intend to lay off any of its workers.

Skilled labour, however, is in short supply, a situation which the directors expect to persist for both 2007 and 2008, but not for 2009. By switching skilled labour to the production of Plasticoats, net contributions of £5 per hour for 2007 and £6 per hour for 2008 must be foregone elsewhere in the firm.

(iii) **Overheads:** Lincoln plc allocates overheads to production by the use of a predetermined rate. The estimated current (1 January 2007) overhead cost per unit for Plasticoats is

	£
Allocated central costs	1.60
Depreciation of machinery	0.20
Variable overheads	1.00
TOTAL	**2.80**

Central costs and variable overheads are expected to rise at the same rate as the Retail Price Index.

(iv) **Machinery:** The machinery to be used in producing Plasticoats is already owned, and has a net book value of £100,000. The depreciation charge of 20p per Plasticoat is based on an estimated resale value at the end of 2009 of £40,000 (i.e. annual straight-line depreciation over the next three years is (£100,000 – £40,000) ÷ 3, which equals £20,000 and represents a cost of 20p for each of the 100,000 Plasticoats expected to be produced each year). The current resale value of the machinery is £180,000. The machinery is presently used for the production of one of Lincoln's other products. Lincoln will rent replacement machinery for three years with identical productive capacity for an initial payment of £100,000 on 1 January 2007 and three annual rental payments of £70,000 to be paid at the end of each year, to maintain production of the other product.

Assume that all receipts and payments (excluding materials cost, initial payment on rented machinery and proceeds from sale of machinery) arise on the last day of the year to which they relate, and that all prices change annually at midnight on 31 December for the following year. Lincoln's cost of capital is 8%

Required:

Calculate whether Lincoln plc should undertake production of Plasticoats.

Test your understanding 6

A company has a money cost of capital of 21% per annum. The inflation rate is currently estimated at 9% per annum.

Identify the real cost of capital:

A 9%

B 11%

C 12%

D 14%

(2 marks)

Test your understanding 7

A company is considering investing £1,000,000 in launching a new product. The project will incur annual fixed costs of £60,000. The investment capital will be sold at the end of the project life, seven years from now, for £50,000. The product is expected to generate a unit contribution of £12.50. The company has a cost of capital of 8%.

Identify the minimum annual sales required to make the project viable:

A 19,720 units

B 101,824 units

C 87,467 units

D 22,143 units

(3 marks)

Test your understanding 8

W is considering investing in a new machine which has a capital cost of $25,000. It has an estimated life of four years and a residual value of $5,000 at the end of four years. The machine qualifies for tax depreciation at the rate of 25% per year on a reducing balance basis.

An existing machine would be sold immediately for $8,000 if the new machine were to be bought. The existing machine has a tax written down value of $3,000.

The existing machine generates annual net contribution of $30,000. This is expected to increase by 40% if the new machine is purchased.

W pays corporation tax on its profits at the rate of 30%, with half of the tax being payable in the year that the profit is earned and half in the following year. The company's after tax cost of capital is 15% per year.

Calculate whether the investment is worthwhile.

Test your understanding 9

A company is considering a cost-saving project. This involves purchasing a machine costing $7,000, which will result in annual savings (in real terms) on wage costs of $1,000 and on material costs of $400.

The following forecasts are made of the rates of inflation each year for the next five years:

Wage costs	10%
Material costs	5%
General prices	6%

The cost of capital of the company, in real terms, is 8.5%.

Calculate the NPV of the project, assuming that the machine has a life of five years and no scrap value.

Test your understanding 10

Storm Co is evaluating Project X, which requires an initial investment of $50,000. Expected net cash flows are $20,000 pa for four years at today's prices. However these are expected to rise by 5.5% pa because of inflation. The firm's cost of capital is 15%.

Calculate the NPV by:

(a) discounting money cash flows

(b) discounting real cash flows.

Test your understanding 11

Leo is contemplating spending £400,000 on new machinery. This will be used to produce a revolutionary type of lock, for which demand is expected to last three years. Equipment will be bought on 31 December 2005 and revenue from the sale of locks will be receivable on the 31 December 2006, 2007 and 2008. Labour costs for the three years, payable in arrears, are estimated at £500,000 per annum in current terms. These figures are expected to rise at the rate of 10% per annum.

Materials required for the three years are currently in stock. They originally cost £300,000; they would cost £500,000 at current prices although Leo had planned to sell them for £350,000. The sales revenue from locks in the first year is projected at £900,000. This figure will rise by 5% per annum over the product's life.

If Leo has a money cost of capital of 13%, identify the net present value of the project (to the nearest £000)

A (£130,000)

B (£23,000)

C £52,000

D £126,000

(4 marks)

Test your understanding 12

A contract is due to be commenced immediately. In one year's time it will require material XG. Price data relating to XG are as follows:

	£
Cost now	7,800
Cost in one year's time	8,800

The cost of storing XG for one year is £110, payable in one year's time.

If the cost of capital were 10% per annum, identify the present value of the cost of using material XG, assuming the contractor wished to maximise net present value:

A £7,800

B £7,900

C £7910

D £8,000

(1 mark)

Test your understanding 13

November 2007

In early November 2007, R Ltd considered manufacturing a new product called Sparkle. Up to that time £750,000 had been spent on researching the product. The company estimated that it would take two further years to develop Sparkle to the point of production and by that time it would probably have a lead of 18 months over its chief competitor. R Ltd expected to launch Sparkle on 1 November 2009 and to produce and sell 100,000 units in the first year if £1.5 million was spent on pre-launch advertising. During the first year of production, R Ltd planned to spend £750,000 on advertising; this level of expenditure would be maintained each year.

From the second year onwards, the market was expected to increase to between 160,000 and 200,000 units. Once the competitor entered the market, it was thought that the competitor would win 50% market share very quickly because of its reputation.

The development and engineering costs of Sparkle were estimated to be £6 million, £2 million of which would be incurred in the first year of development, 2007/08. A special piece of equipment costing £500,000 would be required for production and this was to be installed in the month prior to the commencement of manufacture.

R Ltd planned to set a selling price of £249 a unit on the basis that variable manufacturing and distribution costs were expected to be £122 per unit. The company normally sets selling prices so that the contribution/sales ratio is 50% or slightly more. The fixed administrative and space costs that relate to the product, and which would be incurred from the commencement of production, were estimated to be £7.5 million per annum. It was also estimated that working capital of £2.5 million would be needed at the start of production in November 2009.

The product was expected to have a life span of about five years, at which time the equipment would be scrapped as having no value. The company estimated its cost of capital to be 12% per annum.

November 2010

Development of Sparkle took six months longer than planned. This was largely because it proved necessary to employ two extra members of staff in the engineering department for the technical aspects of the product development.

The engineering department did not have a budget for this in year 1 (2007/08) and so employment was delayed until the start of the second year, November 2008, when the budget for the extra funds had been approved. This caused the planned expenditure on development for year 2 to be spread over the 18 month period from the start of year 2 to the middle of year 3. The two new members of staff were employed at salaries of £45,000 each and employment costs were estimated to be 100% of the first year's salary. As a result, production started six months late in May 2010, the pre-launch costs were delayed accordingly and only 55,000 units were sold in the year November 2009 to October 2010.

As expected, the competitor has decided to enter the market and is launching its rival product Glitter this month, November 2010.

R Ltd now predicts the market for 2010/11 to be 150,000 units and its share of this to be 50%. Thereafter the market size will be as forecast previously, i.e. between 160,000 and 200,000 units each year, and the product life cycle will stop at the same date as planned previously. The monetary value of all expenditures and revenues to date has been very close to the estimates and there is no reason to revise future forecasts in this respect.

Required:

Using the case of Sparkle in the scenario:

(a) Calculate the net present value of the project as perceived at the beginning of November 2007, when R Ltd decided to manufacture Sparkle. State clearly any assumptions you make.

(11 marks)

(b) Calculate the revised net present value of the whole project as perceived at the beginning of November 2010.

(8 marks)

(c) Describe the position revealed by the figures you have calculated in (a) and (b) and on the events which have taken place. Identify what the company should do now?

(6 marks)

(Total: 25 marks)

Test your understanding 14

A landowner in Scotland proposes to develop a number of ski runs down the side of a mountain. The runs will be approximately 5 km long, dropping 1,000 metres from the mountain's summit to a car park. Two alternative strategies (each giving the same capacity) are being considered for the development.

- *Low investment*, involving the construction of a series of tows to haul skiers from the car park to the summit: the initial cost of constructing the tows will be £250,000 and tow motors will have to be replaced after five years at a cost of £50,000; operating costs will be £90,000 per year (fixed) and £3.50 per skier (variable).
- *High investment*, involving the construction of a cable-car system giving a non-stop ride to the summit: the initial cost of constructing the lift will be £1,200,000; operating costs will be £30,000 per year (fixed) and £1 per skier (variable).

The Regional Tourist Board will subsidise the initial construction cost of the development (using either strategy) by providing a loan for half the value of the initial construction cost. The loan is at an interest rate of 4% repayable over six years on an annuity basis. The Tourist Board requires (as a condition of the loan) that a flat fee of £8 is charged for each skier towed/ lifted to the summit.

The number of skiers using the runs will be dependent on the quality of snow cover. The better the snow cover, then the more runs it will be possible to open and the longer the runs will be able to stay open. The landowner forecasts that in any 10-year period, and assuming an £8 fee, the seasons will be as follows:

Quality of snow cover	Number of seasons	Number of skiers
Good	3	60,000
Moderate	4	40,000
Poor	3	5,000

The landowner has stated:

> 'Although the quality of snow cover is unpredictable for any one year, we can determine the expected outcome for an average year using probabilities and base our investment appraisal and business plan on that.'

A business adviser has commented on this statement as follows:

> 'The whole problem about winter sports in Scotland is the variability and unpredictability of snow cover. On average conditions are as good as any in Europe. However, if your first three seasons are poor then this could have a devastating effect on project viability.'

The landowner's cost of money is 12% per annum and in appraising investments he considers cash flows over a 10-year period only.

Required:

Identify for the landowner which strategy he should adopt (low or high investment) on the basis of the expected value methodology he advocates, and assuming an £8 fee.

(5 marks)

Test your understanding answers

Example 1 – SENSITIVITY ANALYSIS

(a)

Year		Cash flow £	15% discount factor	Present Value
0	Investment	(120,000)		(120,000)
1–15	Contribution	41,250	5.847	241,189
1–15	Fixed costs	(18,000)	5.847	(105,246)
15	Scrap value	25,000	0.123	3,075
				19,018

Net Present Value = £19,018

(b)

(i) If the capital outlay were to rise by more than £19,018 the project would cease to be viable. As a percentage increase this is:

$$\text{Sensitivity margin} = \frac{£19,018}{£120,000} \times 100\% = 15.85\ \%$$

(ii) If the PV of contribution were to fall by more than £19,018 the project would cease to be viable. As a percentage change this is:

$$\text{Sensitivity margin} = \frac{£19,018}{£241,189} \times 100\% = 7.89\ \%$$

(iii) If the PV of fixed costs were to rise by more than £19,018 the project would cease to be viable. As a percentage increase this is:

$$\text{Sensitivity margin} = \frac{£19,018}{£105,246} \times 100\% = 18.07\ \%$$

(c) Let annual demand be 10,000 units.

Annual contribution is then £27,500

Year		Cash flow £	15% discount factor	Present Value
0	Investment	(120,000)		(120,000)
1–15	Contribution	27,500	5.847	160,792.5
1–15	Fixed costs	(18,000)	5.847	(105,246)
15	Scrap value	25,000	0.123	3,075
				61,378.5

Now plot NPV versus demand.

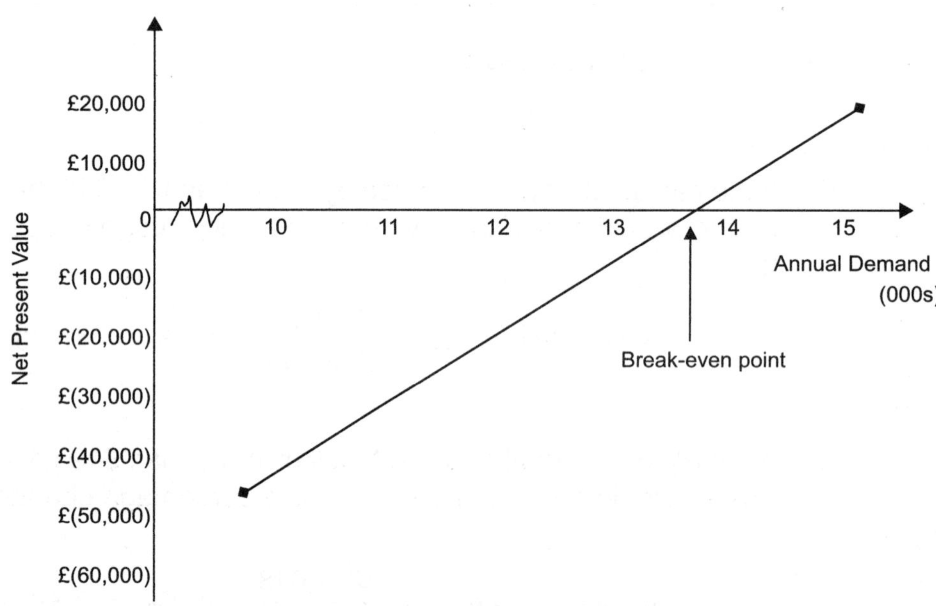

(d) Taking a reading from the graph the break-even point appears to be at about 13,800 units.

The break-even point may also be calculated:

PV of contribution can fall to £222,171 before NPV becomes negative.

Annual cash amount	=	£222,171 ÷ 5.847 = £37,997
Let 'x' be minimum sales level		
Annual contribution	=	£2.75 x = £37,997
Therefore	x =	13,817 units

Example 2

	$
Contribution per hour lost from normal working	3
Add back: labour cost per hour that is not saved	4
	7

The contract should be charged with 5,000 x $7 = $35,000

Activity 2

Nothing. The relevant cost is zero.

Example 3 – CAPITAL ALLOWANCES

(a)

Initial cost: £50,000 Selling price: £10,000 Total capital allowances: £40,000

Year	Reducing balance	Capital allowance at 25%	Tax saved at 30%
	£50,000		
1	£37,500	£12,500	£3,750
2	£28,125	£9,375	£2,813
3	£21,094	£7,031	£2,109
4	£10,000	£11,093	£3,328

Scrap value

(b)

Year	Cash benefit received	Total
1	£1,875	**£1,875**
2	£1,875 + £1,407	**£3,282**
3	£1,406 + £1,055	**£2,461**
4	£1,054 + £1,664	**£2,718**
5	£1,664	**£1,664**

Example 4

(a)

Time		**$**	**Tax saving @ 30%**	**Timing of tax relief**
T_0	Initial investment	10,000		
T_1	WDA @ 25%	(2,500)	750	T_2
	Written down value	7,500		
T_2	WDA @ 25%	(1,875)	563	T_3
	Written down value	5,625		
T_3	WDA @ 25%	(1,406)	422	T_4
	Written down value	4,219		
T_4	Sale proceeds	(2,500)		
T_4	BA	1,719	516	T_5

Note:

- total WDAs = 2,500 + 1,875 + 1,406 + 1,719 = 7,500 = fall in value of the asset
- total tax relief = 750 + 563 + 422 + 516 = 2251 ≈ 7,500 × 30% (WDAs x tax rate)

(b) The asset is still bought at time T0 but falls into the previous accounting period for tax purposes. The overall value of WDAs claimed and therefore the total tax saving remains unchanged, but the timing and amount of the individual amounts will alter. Because of the time value of money, this will impact the final NPV.

Time			Tax saving @ 30%	Timing of relief
		$	$	
T_0	Initial investment	10,000		
T_0	WDA @ 25%	(2,500)	750	T_1
	Written down value	7,500		
T_1	WDA @ 25%	(1,875)	563	T_2
	Written down value	5,625		
T_2	WDA @ 25%	(1,406)	422	T_3
	Written down value	4,219		
T_3	WDA @ 25%	(1,055)	317	T_4
		3,164		
T_4	Sale proceeds	(2,500)		
T_4	BA	664	199	T_5

Note:

- total WDAs = 2,500 + 1,875 + 1,406 + 1,055 + 664 = 7,500 = fall in value of the asset
- total tax relief = 750 + 563 + 422 + 317 + 199 = 2251 ≈ 7,500 x 30% (WDAs x tax rate)

Example 5

Corporation tax

Depreciation is not an allowable expense.

Therefore, taxable profit = £100,000 + £20,000 = £120,000 p.a.

Corporation tax at 30% = £36,000 p.a.

Half payable in current year, half payable in year following.

Capital allowances

Capital cost:	£250,000
Scrap value:	£10,000
Total capital allowances:	£240,000

Year	Reducing balance	Capital allowance	Tax saved (30%)	Benefit received	Total cash benefit
1	£187,500	£62,500	£18,750	£9,375	**£9,375**
2	£140,625	£46,875	£14,063	£9,375 + £7,032	**£16,407**
3	£105,469	£35,156	£10,547	£7,031 + £5,274	**£12,305**
4	£10,000	£95,469	£28,641	£5,273 + £14,321	**£19,594**
5				£14,320	**£14,320**

Yr	Asset £	Profits £	Corporation tax £	WDA benefit £	Total net cash £	Discount factor	Present value £
0	(285,000) *				(285,000)		(285,000)
1		120,000	(18,000)	9,375	111,375	0.909	101,240
2		120,000	(36,000)	16,407	100,407	0.826	82,936
3		120,000	(36,000)	12,305	96,305	0.751	72,325
4	45,000 *	120,000	(36,000)	19,594	148,594	0.683	101,489
5			(18,000)	14,320	(3,680)	0.621	(2,285)
						NPV =	**70,703**

* working capital of £35,000 is injected in Year 0 and then released in Year 4.

Example 6 – REAL RATE OF RETURN

After 1 year £1,000 will have compounded up to £1,000 × 1.10 = £1,100.

Now deflate this figure to find the real return on the investment:

£1,100 ÷ 1.07 = £1,028

Therefore, the £1,000 has increased by 2.8% in real terms. This is the real rate.

Example 7 – NPV AND INFLATION

(a) **Discounting money cash flow at the money rate**

Year	Money cash flow £	Discount rate 15%	Present value £
0	(50,000)		(50,000)
1	21,100	0.870	18,357
2	22,261	0.756	16,829
3	23,485	0.658	15,453
4	24,776	0.572	14,172
		NPV =	**14,811**

(b) **Discounting the real cash flows at the real rate**

Calculate the real rate.

$$(1+r)=\frac{(1+m)}{(1+i)}$$

$$(1+r)=\frac{(1+0.15)}{(1+0.055)}$$

$$(1+r)=1.0900$$

$$\therefore\ r = 0.09,\ \text{i.e. } 9\%$$

Year	Real cash flow	Discount rate	Present value
	£	9%	£
0	(50,000)		(50,000)
1-4	20,000 p.a.	3,240	64,800
		NPV =	**14,800**

Example 8

Notes:

£480,000 development cost is a sunk cost.

Depreciation is not a cash flow and should be excluded form the fixed costs.

Depreciation = £2,400,000 + 4 years = £600,000 p.a.

Therefore relevant fixed cost = £800,000 – £600,000 = £200,000.

Year 1 cash flows are:

		£000
Revenue	25,000 × £80	2,000 – rises at 5%
Direct material	25,000 × £8	200 – rises at 4%
Direct labour	25,000 × £12	300 – rises at 10%
Variable overheads	25,000 × £12	300 – rises at 4%
Fixed costs		200 – rises at 5%

Year	0	1	2	3	4
	£000				
Capital	(2,400)				
Revenue		2,000	2100	2205	2315
Direct material		(200)	(208)	(216)	(225)
Direct labour		(300)	(330)	(363)	(399)
Variable OH		(300)	(312)	(324)	(337)
Fixed cost		(200)	(210)	(221)	(232)
Net cash flow	(2,400)	1000	1040	1081	1122
15% disc. factor		0.870	0.756	0.658	0.572
Present value	**(2,400)**	**870**	**786**	**711**	**642**

The net present value is £609,000.

Therefore the company should invest in the project.

Example 9

$ millions	T_0	T_1	T_2	T_3	T_4
Sales **(W1)**		520	1082	675	
Variable costs **(W1)**		(158)	(331)	(208)	
Net trading inflows		362	751	467	
Tax payable (30%)			(109)	(225)	(140)
Initial investment	(1,000)				
Scrap proceeds				200	
Tax relief on WDAs **(W2)**			75	56	109
Net cash flows	(1,000)	362	717	498	(31)
DF @ 10% **(W3)**	1	0.909	0.826	0.751	0.683
PV	(1,000)	329	592	374	(21)
				NPV	274

W1: revenue and costs

Revenue and costs need to be expressed in money terms.

e.g. revenue at T_2 = \$10m × 100 × (1.04)2 = \$1,081.6m.

2 years

W2: WDAs

Time		$m	Tax saving	Timing of tax relief
			$m	
T_0	Initial investment	1000		
T_1	WDA @ 25%	(250)	75	T_2
	Written down value	750		
T_2	WDA @ 25%	(188)	56	T_3
	Written down value	562		
	Sale proceeds	(200)		
T_3	BA	362	109	T_4

W3: Discount rate

(1+i) = (1+r) × (1+h) = 1.068 × 1.03 = 1.10, giving a money rate (i) – 10%.

Example 10 – REPLACEMENT DECISION

Machine X:

NPV of one life cycle	= £162,210
EAC	= £162,210 ÷ 2.487
	= £65,223 p.a.

Machine Y:

NPV of one life cycle	= £125,270
EAC	= £125,270 ÷ 1.736
	= £72,160 p.a.

Machine X is the cheapest.

Example 11 – REPLACEMENT CYCLE

		Replacement Cycle									
	Discount	**1 year**		**2 year**		**3 year**		**4 year**		**5 year**	
Year	**Factor**	**Cash**	**PV**	**Cash**	**PV**	**Cash**	**PV**	**Cash**	**PV**	**Cash**	**PV**
0		(220)	(220)	(220)	(220)	(220)	(220)	(220)	(220)	(220)	(220)
1	0.893	11	9.8	(110)	(98.2)	(110)	(98.2)	(110)	(98.2)	(110)	(98.2)
2	0.797			(44)	(35.1)	(132)	(105.2)	(132)	(105.2)	(132)	(105.2)
3	0.712					(88)	(62.6)	(154)	(109.6)	(154)	(109.6)
4	0.636							(110)	(70.0)	(165)	(104.9)
5	0.567									(151)	(85.6)
			(210.2)		(353.3)		(486.0)		(603.0)		(723.5)
÷ Annuity factor			÷ 0.893		÷ 1.690		÷ 2.402		÷ 3.037		÷ 3.605
			———		———		———		———		———
Equivalent annual cost			(235.4)		(209.1)		(202.3)		(198.6)		(200.7)
			———		———		———		———		———

Note: in the year of sale, net cash flow is SCRAPLESS RUNNING COST

∴ Most economical replacement cycle is four years.

Answer D

Example 12 – CAPITAL RATIONING

Project	Investment Required £000	Net Present Value £000	NPV ranking	Profitability Index	Index ranking
A	3,400	850	1	0.25	6
B	2,750	825	2	0.30	4
C	2,000	720	3	0.36	3
D	3,400	680	4	0.20	7
E	860	430	5	0.50	1
F	950	400	6	0.42	2
G	1,250	350	7	0.28	5

(a)

Project	Investment £000	NPV £000
A	3,400	850
B	2,750	825
C	2,000	720
D	850	170 *
TOTAL	9,000	2,565

* NPV has been pro-rated: (850/3,400) × 680

(b)

Project	Investment £000	NPV £000
E	860	430
F	950	400
C	2,000	720
B	2,750	825
G	1,250	350
A	1,190	297.50*
TOTAL	9,000	3,022.50

* (1,190/3,400) × 850

Test your understanding 1

Although part (a) could be completed most efficiently by finding the PV of net annual inflows ($600,000 – $350,000 – $40,000), i.e. of $210,000, part (b) would be most effectively negotiated if the separate PVs were found.

NPV calculation

Time		**Cash flow**	**15% DF**	**PV**
		$000		$000
0	Equipment	(500)	1.000	(500)
1-3	Revenue	600	2.283	1,370
1-3	Variable costs	(350)	2.283	(799)
1-3	Fixed costs	(40)	2.283	(91)
3	Scrap value	80	0.658	53
NPV ($000)				33

The project should, on the basis of these estimates, be accepted.

(a) **Sensitivity analysis**

(i) Initial investment

For the decision to change, the NPV must fall by $33,000. For this to occur, the cost of the equipment must rise by $33,000.

This is a rise of: $\frac{33}{500} \times 100 = 6.6\%$

(ii) Scrap value

If the NPV is to fall by $33,000, the PV of scrap proceeds must fall by $33,000. The PV of scrap proceeds is currently $53,000. It must fall by: 33÷53 × 100 = 62.26%, say 62.

(iii) Selling price

If sales price varies, sales revenue will vary (assuming no effect on demand). If the NPV of the project is to fall by $33,000, the selling price must fall by:

$$\frac{33}{1,370} \times 100 = 2.4\%$$

(iv) Unit variable cost

The project's NPV must fall by $33,000 therefore the PV of the variable costs must rise by $33,000. Since the PV of variable costs is $799,000, a rise of $33,000 is an increase of:

$$\frac{33}{799} \times 100 = 4.1\%$$

(v) Annual fixed costs

Since the PV of fixed costs is $91,000, a rise of $33,000 is an increase of:

$$\frac{33}{91} \times 100 = 36\%$$

(vi) Sales volume

If sales volume falls, revenue and variable costs fall (contribution falls). If the NPV is to fall by $33,000, volume must fall by:

$$\frac{33}{1,370 - 799} \times 100 = 5.8\%$$

(vii) Cost of capital

If NPV is to fall, cost of capital must rise. The figure which the cost of capital must rise to, that gives an NPV of zero, is the project's IRR.

NPV ($000) = − 500 + [210 × 2.210] + [80 × 0.624] = 14 The IRR is a little more than 17%, possibly 18%, but the formula can be used.

$$\text{IRR} \approx 15 + \frac{33}{33 - 14} \times (17 - 15)$$

≈ 18.47%, say 18.50%

To find the IRR, which is probably not much above 15%, the NPV at 17% can be found using the summarised cash flows.

The cost of capital would have to increase from 15% to 18½% before the investment decision changes

Test your understanding 2

Before you start a table of cash flows sort out corporation tax and capital allowance benefits.

Corporation tax

30% of net cash flows (profits), i.e.30% of £30,000 = £9,000.

Half is payable in the year of the profit, and half in the year following, i.e.:

Year	Corporation tax
1	£4,500
2	£9,000
3	£9,000
4	£9,000
5	£4,500

Capital allowances

Capital cost: £100,000

Scrap value: £20,000

Total capital allowances: £80,000

Year	Reducing balance	Capital allowance	Tax saved (30%)	Benefit received	Total cash benefit
1	£75,000	£25,000	£7,500	£3,750	£3,750
2	£56,250	£18,750	£5,625	£3,750 + £2,813	£6,563
3	£42,188	£14,062	£4,219	£2,812 + £2,110	£4,922
4	£20,000	£22,188	£6,656	£2,109 + £3,328	£5,437
5				£3,328	£3,328

Scrap value

Now you can calculate the net cash flow each year, and discount:

Yr	Asset £	Profits £	Corporation tax £	WDA benefit £	Total net cash £	Discount factor	Present value £
0	(100,000)				(100,000)		(100,000)
1		30,000	(4,500)	3,750	29,250	0.952	27,846
2		30,000	(9,000)	6,563	27,563	0.907	25,000
3		30,000	(9,000)	4,922	25,922	0.864	22,397
4	20,000	30,000	(9,000)	5,437	46,437	0.823	38,218
5			(4,500)	3,328	(1,172)	0.784	(919)
						NPV =	**12,542**

Test your understanding 3

Expected annual cash flows are:

Annual cash flow (x)	Probability (p)	PV
50,000	0.3	15,000
100,000	0.5	50,000
150,000	0.2	30,000
		95,000

NPV calculation:

Time	Cash flow	DF 5%	PV
	$		$
0	(460,000)	1.000	(460,000)
1-5	95,000	4.329	411,255
5	40,000	0.784	31,360
		NPV =	(17,385)

As the ENPV is negative, the project should not be undertaken.

An alternative approach would be to calculate three separate NPVs and then combine them, giving the following figures:

Annual cash flow	Probability	NPV
		$
$		
50,000	0.3	(212,190)
100,000	0.5	4,260
150,000	0.2	220,710

ENPV = 0.3 × (-212,190) + 0.5 × 4,260 + 0.2 × (220,710) = (17,385)

Even though the ENPV is negative these figures show that there is a 70% chance of the project giving a positive NPV. Some investors may consider the project acceptable on this basis.

Test your understanding 4

Since the decision has been made to increase capacity (i.e. 'to do nothing' is not an alternative), the easiest approach is to discount the incremental cash flows.

The tabular approach of the previous chapter is still appropriate particularly as the project lasts for ten years (other forms of presentation will appear later).

Time		*A*	*B*	*B - A*	*8%*	PV
		$000	*$000*	*$000*	*DF/AF*	$000
0	Capital expenditure	(260)	(415)	(155)	1	(155)
0	Working capital	(50)	(65)	(15)	1	(15)
2	Promotion	-	(15)	(15)	0.857	(13)
1-10	Net income	70	95	25	6.710	168
10	Scrap proceeds	40	75	35	0.463	16
10	Working capital	50	65	15	0.463	7
	Net present value					8

The present value of proposal B exceeds that of proposal A by $8,000 at 8% and therefore proposal B is preferred.

Assumptions

- The disposal value of buildings is realistic and all other figures have been realistically appraised.
- Expenditure on working capital is incurred at the beginning of the project life and recovered at the end.
- Adequate funds are available for either proposal.
- All cash flows occur annually in arrears.

Test your understanding 5

Year	1.1.07	31.12.07	31.12.08	31.12.09
	0	1	2	3
	£000	£000	£000	£000
Inflows				
Revenues		2,400	2,544	2,696.64
Outflows				
Materials:				
Plastic	240	256.80	274.776	
Oats	72	94.16	125.939	
Labour:				
Unskilled		nil	550	605
Skilled		650	740	484
Overheads		100	106	112.36
Machinery	100	70	70	70
Total Outflows	412	1,170.96	1,886.715	1271.36
Net Cash Flows	(412)	1,229.04	677.285	1,425.28
Discount factor		0.926	0.857	0.794
Present Value	(412)	1,138.09	580.433	1,131.67

Net Present Value = £2,438,193 > 0 so accept

Workings:

Plastic	200,000 kg × £1.20	= £240,000
	£240,000 × 1.07	= £256,800
Oats	Opportunity cost of 120,000 kg × 60p	= £72,000
	80,000 kg × £1.10 × 1.07	= £94,160
	100,000 kg × £1.10 × 1.07 × 1.07	= £125,939
Labour		
Unskilled	nil	
	100,000 hrs × £5 × 1.10	= £550,000
	£550,000 × 1.10	= £605,000
Skilled	100,000 × 0.5 × (£8 + £5)	= £650,000
	100,000 × 0.5 × (£8.80 + £6)	= £740,000
	100,000 × 0.5 × £8 × 1.102	= £484,000

Test your understanding 6

1.21 ÷ 1.09 = 1.11

Answer B

Test your understanding 7

Year	**Cash flow** £000		**Discount factor**	**Present Value** £000
0	Initial cost	(1,000)		(1,000)
1–7	Fixed costs	(60)	5.206	(312.36)
7	Residual	50	0.583	29.15
				(1,283.21)

PV of annual contribution required:	£1,283,210
Annuity factor years 1 – 7	÷ 5.206
Annual contribution required	£246,486.75
Contribution per unit	÷ £12.50
Minimum number of units	19,719 units

Answer A

Test your understanding 8

(W1) The incremental increase in contribution earned as a result of using the new machine is $30,000 x 40% = $12,000 per year.

(W2) Tax due/paid on incremental contribution earned:

Year	**Incr. Contibution**	**Tax due (30%)**	**Year tax paid**				
			1	**2**	**3**	**4**	**5**
1	12,000	3,600	1,800	1,800			
2	12,000	3,600		1,800	1,800		
3	12,000	3,600			1,800	1,800	
4	12,000	3,600				1,800	1,800
5	12,000	3,600					
			1,800	3,600	3,600	3,600	1,800

(W3) Tax depreciation/ tax relief

Existing machine

The sale of the existing machine leads to a balancing charge of $8,000 – $3,000 = $5,000. Tax payable on this is $5,000 ´ 30% = $1,500. Assume this is paid half in year 0 and half in year 1.

New machine

Year	**Bal b/f**	**Tax depr (25%)**	**Tax relief (30%)**	**Year relief received**				
				1	**2**	**3**	**4**	**5**
1	25,000	6,250	1,875	937	938			
2	18,750	4,688	1,406		703	703		
3	14,063	3,515	1,055			528	527	
4	10,547	5,547 *	1,664				832	832
				937	1,641	1,231	1,359	832

* Disposal = $5,000 when the TWDV was $10,547. Therefore the Balancing allowance = $5,547.

All figures **$**	Year 0	Year 1	Year 2	Year 3	Year 4	Year 5
Incremental contribution (W1)		12,000	12,000	12,000	12,000	
Capital	(25,000)				5,000	
Tax paid (W2)		(1,800)	(3,600)	(3,600)	(3,600)	(1,800)
Tax paid on existing machine (W3)	(750)	(750)				
Tax relief on new machine (W3)		937	1,641	1,231	1,359	832
Net cash flow	(25,750)	10,387	10,041	9,631	14,759	(968)
DCF @ 15%	1	0.870	0.756	0.658	0.572	0.497
Present values	(25,750)	9,037	7,591	6,337	8,442	(4.81)

Net present value = $5,176

The net present value is positive and therefore it is worthwhile purchasing the machine.

Test your understanding 9

Since the question contains both specific and general inflation rates, the money method should be used

Step 1

The money method needs to be calculated using the information provided on the real rate of return and the general rate of inflation

(1 + i) = (1 + r)(1 + h)

(1 + i) = (1.085)(1.06)

i = 15%

Step 2

Inflate the cash flows using the specific inflation rates and discount using the money rate calculated above.

	T_0	T_1	T_2	T_3	T_4	T_5
	$	$	$	$	$	$
Investment	(7,000)					
Wages savings (inflating @ 10%)		1,100	1,210	1,331	1,464	1,610
Materials savings (inflating @ 5%)		420	441	463	486	510
Net cash flow	(7,000)	1,520	1,651	1,794	1,950	2,120
PV factor @ 15%	1.000	0.870	0.756	0.658	0.572	0.497
PV of cash flow	(7,000)	1,322	1,248	1,180	1,115	1,054

Therefore NPV = $(1,081) which suggests the project is not worthwhile.

Test your understanding 10

Discounting the money cash flows at the money rate - the money method

Discounting money cash flow at the money rate: The cash flows at today's prices are inflated by 5.5% for every year to take account of inflation and convert them into money flows. They are then discounted using the money cost of capital.

The money cash flows are therefore:

Time	Working	Money cash flow
		$
0	(50,000)	= (50,000)
1	20,000 × 1.055	= 21,100
2	$20,000 \times (1.055)^2$	= 22,261
3	$20,000 \times (1.055)^3$	= 23,485
4	$20,000 \times (1.055)^4$	= 24,776

Note: The question simply refers to the 'firm's cost of capital'. You can assume this is the money rate – if you are given a real rate the examiner will always specify.

Time	Money cash flow	Discount rate	PV
	$	15%	$
0	(50,000)	1	(50,000)
1	21,100	0.870	18,357
2	22,261	0.756	16,829
3	23,485	0.658	15,453
4	24,776	0.572	14,172
		NPV =	14,811

Discounting the real cash flows at the real rate - the real method.

Calculate the real rate by removing the general inflation from the money cost of capital:

$$(1+r) = \frac{(1+i)}{(1+h)}$$

$$(1+r) = \frac{(1+1.15)}{(1.055)}$$

$$(1+r) = 1.09$$

Therefore $r = 0.09$ i.e. 9.%

The real rate can now be applied to the real flows without any further adjustments.

Year	Real cash flow	Discount rate	PV
	$	**9%**	$
0	(50,000)	1	(50,000)
1-4	20,000	3.240	64,800
		NPV =	14,800

Note: Differences due to rounding.

Test your understanding 11

All cash flows shown are money cash (£000)

Year	Capital	Labour	Material	Revenue	Net cash	13% factors	Present value
0	(400)		(350)		(750)		(750)
1		(550)		900	350	0.885	310
2		(605)		945	340	0.783	266
3		(665.5)		992	326.5	0.693	226
						NPV =	52

Net Present Value = £52,000

Answer C

Test your understanding 12

If buy now PV of costs = £7,800 + £110 × 0.909 = £7,900

If buy in one year, PV of costs = £8,800 × 0.909 = £8,000

Therefore, buy XG now

Answer B

Test your understanding 13

(a) ***Examination tip**: Set up a table of cash flows. Keep all workings separate from this table.*

Year	Date	Advertising £000	Capital costs £000	Contribution £000	Working capital £000	Net cash flow £000	12% discount factor £000	Present value £000
0	1.11.07							
1	1.11.08		(2,000)			(2,000)	0.893	(1,786)
2	1.11.09	(1,500)	(4,500)		(2,500)	(8,500)	0.797	(6,775)
3	1.11.10	(750)		12,700		11,950	0.712	8,508
4	1.11.11	(750)		17,145		16,395	0.636	10,427
5	1.11.12	(750)		11,430		10,680	0.567	6,056
6	1.11.13	(750)		11,430		10,680	0.507	5,415
7	1.11.14	(750)		11,430	2,500	13,180	0.452	5,957
								27,803
				Less PV of fixed costs: 7,500 × (4.564 – 1.690)				(21,555)
								—
				Net present value				6,24
								—

Production:

Year		
1	100,000	units
2	135,000	units*
3	90,000	
4	90,000	
5	90,000	
*(160 + 200)/2	180	
1st 6 months	90	
2nd 6 months	45	(50% because of competitor)
Total for year	135	

Contribution per unit: £249 – £122 = £127

***Examination tip**: Stating assumptions is very important in this question.*

Assumptions:

- The amount already spent is not relevant – it is a sunk cost.
- The sales figures are the average of the range and the competitor takes 50% of market share after 18 months of sales.
- The equipment has no scrap value after five years.
- Working capital is released immediately production ceases.
- Inflation has been ignored.

Conclusion: the NPV is £6,248,000. Hence the project should be accepted.

(b)

Year	Date	Fixed cost £000	Advertising £000	Capital costs £000	Contribution £000	Working capital £000	Net cash flow £000	12% discount factor £000	Present value £000
0	1.11.07								
1	1.11.08			(2,000)			(2,000)	0.893	(1,786)
2	1.11.09			(2,847)		(2,500)	(2,847)	0.797	(2,269)
3	1.11.10	(3,750)	(1,875)	(1,923)	6,985		(3,063)	0.712	(2,181)
4	1.11.11	(7,500)	(750)		9,525		1,275	0.636	811
5	1.11.12	(7,500)	(750)		11,430		3,180	0.567	1,803
6	1.11.13	(7,500)	(750)		11,430		3,180	0.507	1,612
7	1.11.14	(7,500)	(750)		11,430	2,500	5,680	0.452	2,567
									———
					Net present value				558
									———

Development costs:

Year		
1		= £2m
2	2/3 of £4m = £2.667m + £0.180	= £2.847m
3	1/3 of £4m = £1.333m + £0.090 + £0.5m	= £1.923m

Salary costs in Year 2: £180,000

Salary costs in Year 3: £90,000

Advertising in Year 3: £1.5m + £0.375 (50% of £750,000) = £1.875m

Production:

Year		
3	55,000 units @ £127	= £6.985m
4	150,000 × 50% @ £127	= £9.525m
5	90,000 units @ £127	= £11.430m

(c) The project is extremely sensitive to the sales in early years of the life cycle. These have been severely reduced due to the delay in the project (55,000 v 100,000 in Year 3) and the reduced total sales in Year 4 (down 30,000 units). This second reduction may also be attributable to the delay in product launch.

This large loss in profits is due to a budget constraint which involves a very small increase in the total development budget. The need for and the effects of not spending this small increase should have been made clear early on to avoid this ludicrous situation. If the sales figures in the remaining years are at the lower bound of the forecast, the project may well make a loss.

As the major cash outflows have already taken place (development, operating equipment and pre-launch marketing) the project should continue to reap the positive cash flows forecast for the next four years. The company can attempt to improve the size of the future positive cash flows by:

– finding ways to compete with its competitor that holds 50% of the market share;
– further develop the product or market to extend the life cycle of the project;
– an ongoing cost-reduction exercise.

Test your understanding 14

(a) **Low investment**

Year		Cash flow £000	12% discount factor	Present value
0	Initial cost	(250)	1.000	(250)
5	Replacement of motors	(50)	0.567	(28.35)
1–10	Fixed costs	(90)	5.650	(508.50)
1–10	Contribution (W1)	159.75	5.650	902.6
0	Loan	125	1.000	125.0
1–6	Loan repayment (W2)	(23.8)	4.111	(97.8)
				142.9

High investment

Year		Cash flow £000	12% discount factor	Present value
0	Initial cost	(1,200)	1.000	(1,200)
1–10	Fixed costs	(30)	5.650	(169.5)
1–10	Contribution (W1)	248.5	5.650	1,404.0
0	Loan	600	1.000	600
1–6	Loan repayment (W2)	(114.5)	4.111	(470.7)
				163.8

Workings:

(W1) Expected values

Expected demand = 0.3 × 60 + 0.4 × 40 + 0.3 × 5 = 35,500 skiers

Low investment: Contribution per annum = (£8 – £3.50) × 35,500 = £159,750

High investment: Contribution per annum = (£8 – £1) × 35,500 = £248,500

(W2) Annuity

Initial loan = PV of repayments

PV of repayments = £x per annum × annuity factor

Low investment

£125,000 = £X × 5.242 (annuity factor, year 6, 4%)

∴ £X = £23,800

High investment

£600,000 = £X × 5.242

∴ £X = £114,500

Low investment: NPV	= £142,900
High investment: NPV	= £163,800

∴ Adopt high investment strategy.

chapter

15

Working capital management

Chapter learning objectives

Lead	Component
E1. Analyse the working capital position and identify areas for improvement.	(a) Explain the importance of cash flow and working capital management. (b) Interpret working capital ratios for business sectors.

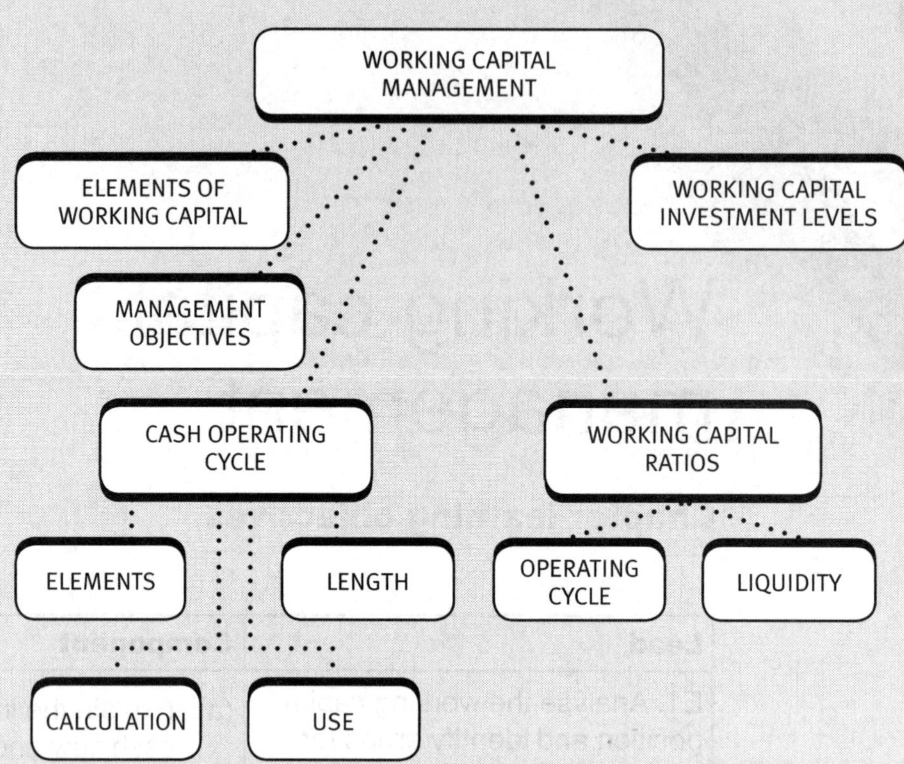

1 The elements of working capital

Working capital is the capital available for conducting the day-to-day operations of an organisation; normally the excess of current assets over current liabilities.

Working capital management is the management of all aspects of both current assets and current liabilities, to minimise the risk of insolvency while maximising the return on assets.

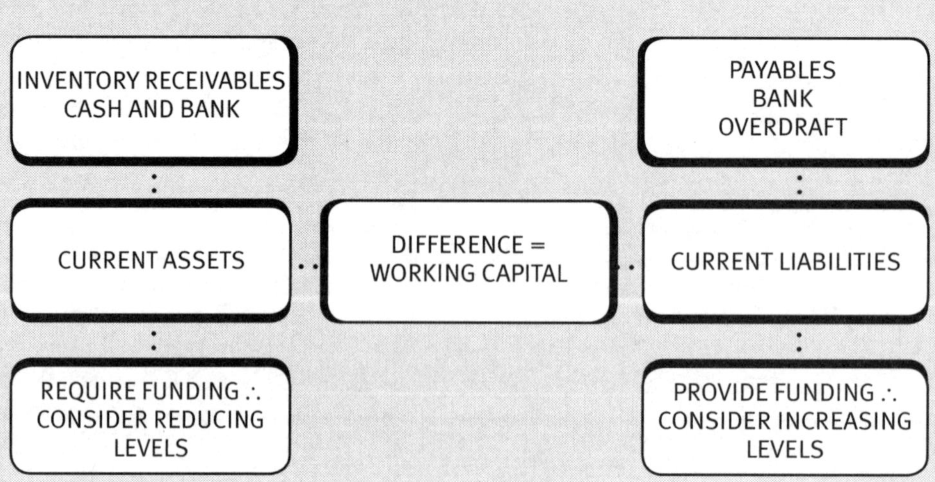

Investing in working capital has a cost, which can be expressed either as:

- the cost of funding it, or
- the opportunity cost of lost investment opportunities because cash is tied up and unavailable for other uses.

Working capital and cash flows

Working capital is an investment which affects cash flows.

- When inventory is purchased, cash is paid to acquire it.
- Receivables represent the cost of selling goods or services to customers, including the costs of the materials and the labour incurred.
- The cash tied up in working capital is reduced to the extent that inventory is financed by trade payables. If suppliers give a firm time to pay, the firm's cash flows are improved and working capital is reduced.

2 The objectives of working capital management

The main objective of working capital management is to get the balance of current assets and current liabilities right.

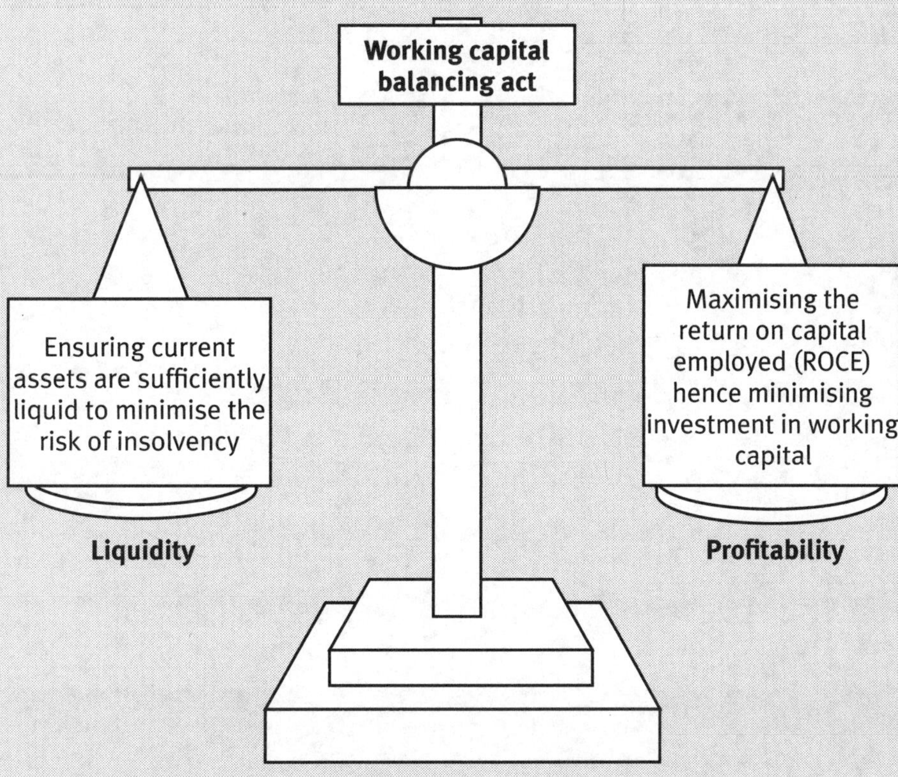

This can also be seen as the trade-off between cash flow versus profits.

Current assets are a major balance sheet item and are especially significant to smaller firms. Mismanagement of working capital is therefore a common cause of business failure, e.g.:

- inability to meet bills as they fall due
- demands on cash during periods of growth being too great (overtrading)
- overstocking.

The trade-off between liquidity and profitability and its role in determining a business' overall investment in working capital is fundamental to your understanding of working capital management for the examination.

Example 1 - LIQUIDITY VERSUS PROFITABILITY

Fill in the blanks in the table to identify the advantages of having more or less working capital.

Advantages of keeping it high ↑		↓ Advantages of keeping it low
	INVENTORY	
	+	
	RECEIVABLES	
	+	
	CASH	
	=	
	CURRENT ASSETS	
	–	
	TRADE PAYABLES	
	=	
	WORKING CAPITAL	

Profitability v liquidity

The decision regarding the level of overall investment in working capital is a cost/benefit trade-off – **liquidity versus profitability**, or **cash flow versus profits**.

Cash flow versus profit

It is worth while stressing the difference between cash flow and profits. Cash flow is as important as profit. Unprofitable companies can survive if they have liquidity. Profitable companies can fail if they run out of cash to pay their liabilities (wages, amounts due to suppliers, overdraft interest, etc.).

Some examples of transactions that have this 'trade-off' effect on cash flows and on profits are as follows:

(a) Purchase of non-current assets for cash. The cash will be paid in full to the supplier when the asset is delivered; however profits will be charged gradually over the life of the asset in the form of depreciation.

(b) Sale of goods on credit. Profits will be credited in full once the sale has been confirmed; however the cash may not be received for some considerable period afterwards.

(c) With some payments such as tax there may be a significant timing difference between the impact on reported profit and the cash flow.

Clearly, cash balances and cash flows need to be monitored just as closely as trading profits. The need for adequate cash flow information is vital to enable management to fulfil this responsibility.

Profitability versus liquidity

Liquidity in the context of working capital management means having enough cash or ready access to cash to meet all payment obligations when these fall due. The main sources of liquidity are usually:

- cash in the bank
- short-term investments that can be cashed in easily and quickly
- cash inflows from normal trading operations (cash sales and payments by receivables for credit sales)
- an overdraft facility or other ready source of extra borrowing.

The basis of the trade off is where a company is able to improve its profitability but at the expense of tying up cash. For example:

- Receiving a bulk purchase discount (improved profitability) for buying more inventory than is currently required (reduced liquidity)
- Offering credit to customers (attracts more customers so improves profitability but reduces liquidity)

Sometimes, the opposite situation can be seen where a company can improve its liquidity position but at the expense of profitability. For example. offering an early settlement discount to customers.

Aggressive versus defensive approach

A firm choosing to have a lower level of working capital than rivals is said to have an **'aggressive'** approach, whereas a firm with a higher level of working capital has a **'defensive'** approach.

Overtrading

Healthy trading growth typically produces:

- increased profitability
- the need to increase investment in non-current assets and working capital.

If the business does not have access to sufficient capital to fund the increase, it is said to be "overtrading". This can cause serious trouble for the business as it is unable to pay its business creditors.

Typical indicators of overtrading

- A rapid increase in turnover
- A rapid increase in the volume of current assets
- Most of the increase in assets being financed by credit
- A dramatic drop in the liquidity ratios (see next section)

Solutions to overtrading

Overtrading can be a very serious risk, especially if there is a possibility that the bank will withdraw its overdraft facility. The solution to a problem of overtrading is either:

- to raise more long-term capital, in the form of new shares or loans, or
- to ensure that the profit from trading is more than the net increase in inventories plus receivables less trade payables, or
- to improve working capital management, so that there is a reduction in the inventory holding period or a reduction in the average time for customers to pay.

3 Working capital ratios – liquidity

Two key measures, the current ratio and the quick ratio, are used to assess short-term liquidity. Generally a higher ratio indicates better liquidity.

Current ratio

Measures how much of the total current assets are financed by current liabilities.

$$\text{Current ratio} = \frac{\text{Current assets}}{\text{Current liabilities}}$$

A measure of 2:1 means that current liabilities can be paid twice over out of existing current assets.

Quick (acid test) ratio

The quick or acid test ratio:

- measures how well current liabilities are covered by liquid assets
- is particularly useful where inventory holding periods are long.

$$\text{Quick ratio (acid test)} = \frac{\text{Current assets - Inventory}}{\text{Current liabilities}}$$

A measure of 1:1 means that the company is able to meet existing liabilities if they all fall due at once.

Typical targets

These liquidity ratios are a guide to the risk of cash flow problems and insolvency. If a company suddenly finds that it is unable to renew its short-term liabilities (for instance if the bank suspends its overdraft facilities) there will be a danger of insolvency unless the company is able to turn enough of its current assets into cash quickly.

In general, high current and quick ratios are considered 'good' in that they mean that an organisation has the resources to meet its commitments as they fall due. However, it may indicate that working capital is not being used efficiently, for example that there is too much idle cash that should be invested to earn a return.

Current ratio

The 'ideal' current ratio is commonly considered to be about 2.0 times (or 2:1). However, a 'safe' current ratio varies widely between different types of business, because businesses in different industries have differing operating cash flow patterns. It is more useful to look at changes in the current ratio over time, or for a company to compare its current ratio with the current ratios of other companies in the same industry.

When the current ratio is less than 1.0 (1:1), this means that the business has more current liabilities than it has current assets. This could be an indication of liquidity problems. However, companies in certain industries can operate successfully with low current ratios, without any liquidity problems. For example, a supermarket has no receivables because all its sales are for cash, and its inventory holding period is often much shorter than the time it takes to pay its suppliers. As a result, unless the supermarket holds on to its spare cash, its current liabilities will usually be larger than its current assets.

Quick ratio

Although the 'ideal' quick ratio is considered to be 1.0 times (1:1), this is a broad guideline. As explained above, 'safe' minimum working capital ratios differ between different types of industry. For example, a supermarket is likely to have both a low current ratio and a very low quick ratio.

To monitor liquidity, changes in the quick ratio over time should be assessed, or comparisons should be made with other companies in the same industry.

Note on overdrafts

Some companies use an overdraft as part of their long-term finance, in which case the current and quick ratios may appear worryingly low. In such questions you could suggest that the firm reschedule the overdraft as a loan. Not only would this be cheaper but it would also improve liquidity ratios.

4 The cash operating cycle

The elements of the operating cycle

The cash operating cycle is the length of time between the company's outlay on raw materials, wages and other expenditures and the inflow of cash from the sale of goods.

The faster a firm can 'push' items around the cycle the lower its investment in working capital will be.

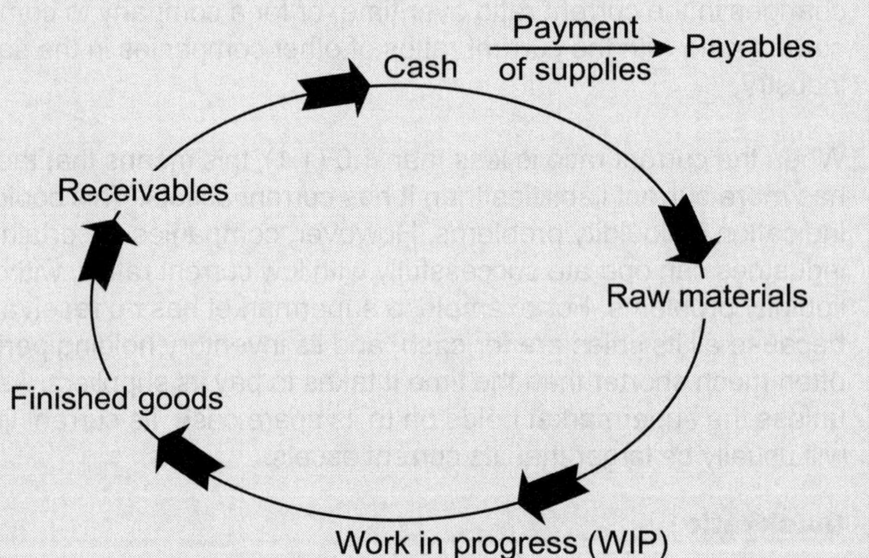

TIME LINE

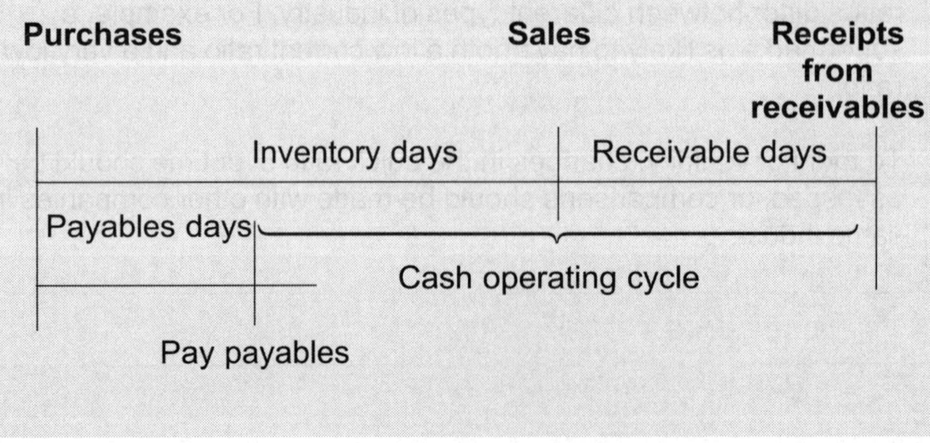

The cash operating cycle

The cash operating cycle reflects a firm's investment in working capital as it moves through the production process towards sales. The investment in working capital gradually increases, first being only in raw materials, but then in labour and overheads as production progresses. This investment must be maintained throughout the production process, the holding period for finished goods and up to the final collection of cash from trade receivables.

(**Note:** The net investment can be reduced by taking trade credit from suppliers.)

Calculation of the cash operating cycle

For a manufacturing business, the cash operating cycle is calculated as:

Raw materials holding period	x
Less: payables' payment period	(x)
WIP holding period	x
Finished goods holding period	x
Receivables' collection period	x
	x

For a wholesale or retail business, there will be no raw materials or WIP holding periods, and the cycle simplifies to:

Inventory holding period	x
Less: payables' payment period	(x)
Receivables' collection period	x
	x

The cycle may be measured in days, weeks or months and it is advisable, when answering an exam question, to use the measure used in the question.

Example 2 - CASH OPERATING CYCLE

A company has provided the following information:

Receivables collection period	56 days
Raw material inventory holding period	21 days
Production period (WIP)	14 days
Suppliers' payment period	42 days
Finished goods holding period	28 days

Calculate the length of the operating cycle

Factors affecting the length of the operating cycle

Length of the cycle depends on:

- liquidity versus profitability decisions
- management efficiency
- industry norms, e.g. retail versus construction.

The optimum level of working capital is the amount that results in no idle cash or unused inventory, but that does not put a strain on liquid resources.

The length of the cycle

The length of the cycle depends on how the balancing act between liquidity and profitability is resolved, the efficiency of management and the nature of the industry.

The optimum level is the amount that results in no idle cash or unused inventory, but that does not put a strain on liquid resources. Trying to shorten the cash cycle may have detrimental effects elsewhere, with the organisation lacking the cash to meet its commitments and losing sales since customers will generally prefer to buy from suppliers who are prepared to extend trade credit, and who have items available when required.

Additionally, any assessment of the acceptability or otherwise of the length of the cycle must take into account the nature of the business involved.

A supermarket chain will tend to have a very low or negative cycle – they have very few, if any, credit customers, they have a high inventory turnover and they can negotiate quite long credit periods with their suppliers.

A construction company will have a long cycle – their projects tend to be long-term, often extending over more than a year, and whilst progress payments may be made by the customer (if there is one), the bulk of the cash will be received towards the end of the project.

The amount of cash required to fund the operating cycle will increase as either:

- the cycle gets longer
- the level of activity/sales increases.

This can be summed up as follows:

Activity/sales	**Length of cycle**	**Funds needed increase proportionate to:**
Stays constant =	Increases ↑	Days in cycle
Increase ↑	Stays constant =	Sales

Where level of activity (sales) is constant and the number of days of the operating cycle increase the amount of funds required for working capital will increase in approximate proportion to the number of days.

Where the cycle remains constant but activity (sales) increase the funds required for working capital will increase in approximate proportion to sales.

By monitoring the operating cycle the manager gains a macro view of the relative efficiency of the working capital utilisation. Further it may be a key target to reduce the operating cycle to improve the efficiency of the business.

5 Working capital ratios – operating cycle

The periods used to determine the cash operating cycle are calculated by using a series of working capital ratios.

The ratios for the individual components (inventory, receivables and payables) are normally expressed as the number of days/weeks/months of the relevant income statement figure they represent.

Illustration – Working capital ratios - operating cycle

X plc has the following figures from its most recent accounts:

	$m
Receivables	4
Trade payables	2
Average raw material inventory	1
Average WIP inventory	1.3
Average finished goods inventory	2
Sales (80% on credit)	30
Materials usage	20
Materials purchases (all on credit)	18
Production cost	23
Cost of sales	25

Required:

Calculate the relevant working capital ratios. Round your answers to the nearest day.

Raw material inventory holding period

The length of time raw materials are held between purchase and being used in production.

Calculated as:

$$= \frac{\text{Average inventory held}}{\text{Material usage}} \times 365$$

$$= \frac{(\text{Opening inventory} + \text{closing inventory}) \div 2}{\text{Material usage}} \times 365$$

NB. Where usage cannot be calculated, purchases gives a good approximation.

Solution 1 to Illustration

$$\frac{\$1m}{\$20m} \times 365 = 18 \text{ days}$$

WIP holding period

The length of time goods spend in production.

Calculated as:

$$= \frac{\text{Average WIP}}{\text{Production cost}} \times 365$$

NB. Where production cost cannot be calculated, cost of goods sold gives a good approximation.

Solution 2 to Illustration

$$\frac{\$1.3m}{\$23m} \times 365 = 21 \text{ days}$$

Finished goods inventory period

The length of time finished goods are held between completion or purchase and sale.

Calculated as:

$$= \frac{\text{Average finished goods in inventory}}{\text{Cost of goods sold}} \times 365$$

For all inventory period ratios, a low ratio is usually seen as a sign of good working capital management. It is very expensive to hold inventory and thus minimum inventory holding usually points to good practice.

Solution 3 to Illustration

$$\frac{\$2m}{\$25m} \times 365 = 29 \text{ days}$$

Inventory turnover

For each ratio, the corresponding turnover ratio can be calculated as:

$$\text{Inventory turnover (no of times)} = \frac{\text{Cost}}{\text{Average inventory held}}$$

Generally this is less useful in the examination.

Using finished goods information from illustration 1:

$$\text{Inventory turnover} = \frac{\$25m}{\$2m} = 12.5 \text{ times}$$

Thus finished goods inventory turns round/is turned into sales 12.5 times in the year.

Trade receivables days

The length of time credit is extended to customers.

Calculated as:

$$= \frac{\text{Average receivables}}{\text{Credit sales}} \times 365$$

Generally shorter credit periods are seen as financially sensible but the length will also depend upon the nature of the business.

Solution 4 to Illustration

$$\frac{\$4m}{\$30m \times 80\%} \times 365 = 61 \text{ days}$$

Interpreting trade receivables collection periods

Businesses which sell goods on credit terms specify a credit period. Failure to send out invoices on time or to follow up late payers will have an adverse effect on the cash flow of the business. The receivables collection period measures the average period of credit allowed to customers.

In general, the shorter the collection period the better because receivables are effectively 'borrowing' from the company. Remember, however, that the level of receivables reflects not only the ability of the credit controllers but also the sales and marketing strategy adopted, and the nature of the business. Any change in the level of receivables must therefore be assessed in the light of the level of sales.

Trade payables days

The average period of credit extended by suppliers.

Calculated as:

$$= \frac{\text{Average payables}}{\text{Credit purchases}} \times 365$$

Solution 5 to Illustration

$$\frac{\$2m}{\$18m} \times 365 = 41\text{days}$$

Complications in calculations

There are differences in the way that the ratio might be calculated:

- Total purchases for the year should be used where possible. If the figure for purchases is not available, the cost of sales in the year should be used instead.
- The figure for purchases excludes any sales tax recoverable, whereas the carrying amount for payables includes sales tax. To make a like-for-like comparison, it might be appropriate to add recoverable sales tax back into purchases, or remove the sales tax element from trade payables. However, this is not usually done.

- Where available, the average trade payables during the year should be used, normally calculated as the average of the trade payables at the beginning and the end of the year. However, if you wish to compare the average payment period in the most recent year and the previous year, and you only have figures for the two years, it will be necessary to use the end-of-year trade payables rather than an average value for the year.

Generally, increasing payables days suggests advantage is being taken of available credit but there are risks:

- losing supplier goodwill
- losing prompt payment discounts
- suppliers increasing the price to compensate.

The operating cycle

The ratios can then be brought together to produce the cash operating cycle.

	Days
Raw material inventory days	18
Trade payables days	(41)
WIP period	21
Finished goods inventory days	29
Receivables days	61
Length of cash operating cycle	88

The cash operating cycle tells us it takes X plc 88 days between paying out for material inventories and eventually receiving cash back from customers.

As always this must then be compared with prior periods or industry average for meaningful analysis.

Working capital turnover

Working capital turnover

One final ratio that relates to working capital is the working capital turnover ratio and is calculated as:

$$\frac{\text{Sales revenue}}{\text{Net working capital}}$$

This measures how efficiently management is utilising its investment in working capital to generate sales and can be useful when assessing whether a company is overtrading.

It must be interpreted in the light of the other ratios used.

Additional points for calculating ratios

The ratios may be needed to provide analysis of a company's performance or simply to calculate the length of the operating cycle.

There are a few simple points to remember which will be of great use in the examination:

- Where the period is required in days, the multiple in the ratios is 365, for months the multiple is 12, or 52 for weeks.
- If you are required to compare ratios between two balance sheets, it is acceptable to base each holding period on balance sheet figures, rather than an average, in order to see whether the ratio has increased or decreased.
- For each ratio calculated above, the corresponding turnover ratio can be calculated by inverting the ratio given and removing the multiple.
- When using the ratios to appraise performance, it is essential to compare the figure with others in the industry or identify the trend over a number of periods.
- Ratios have their limitations and care must be taken because:
  - the balance sheet values at a particular time may not be typical
  - balances used for a seasonal business may not represent average levels, e.g. a fireworks manufacturer
  - ratios can be subject to window dressing/manipulation
  - ratios concern the past (historic) not the future
  - figures may be distorted by inflation and/or rapid growth.

From an examination point of view, calculating the ratios is only the start – interpretation is the key to a good answer. Try to build a cumulative picture, e.g. the current ratio looks good until we find out from calculating the inventory holding period that there are high levels of illiquid inventory.

Do not be afraid to point out further information that may be required to provide a better interpretation of your calculations, e.g. the company credit policy, industry benchmarks, etc.

6 Working capital investment levels

The working capital ratios shown above can be used to predict the future levels of investment (the balance sheet figure) required. This is done by re-arranging the formulas. For example:

$$\text{Trade receivables balance} = \frac{\text{Trade receivables days}}{365} \times \text{Credit sales}$$

Example 3 - WORKING CAPITAL INVESTMENT LEVELS

X plc has the following expectations for the forthcoming period.

	$m
Sales	10
Materials	(6)
Other costs	(2)
Profit	2

The following working capital ratios are expected to apply.

Inventory days	30 days
Receivables days	60 days
Payables days	40 days

Required:

Calculate the working capital requirement.

Working capital investment levels

Working capital investment levels

The level of working capital required is affected by the following factors:

(1) The nature of the business, e.g. manufacturing companies need more inventory than service companies.

(2) Uncertainty in supplier deliveries. Uncertainty would mean that extra inventory needs to be carried in order to cover fluctuations.

(3) The overall level of activity of the business. As output increases, receivables, inventory, etc. all tend to increase.

(4) The company's credit policy. The tighter the company's policy the lower the level of receivables.

(5) The length of the operating cycle. The longer it takes to convert material into finished goods into cash the greater the investment in working capital

(6) The credit policy of suppliers. The less credit the company is allowed to take, the lower the level of payables and the higher the net investment in working capital.

7 Chapter summary

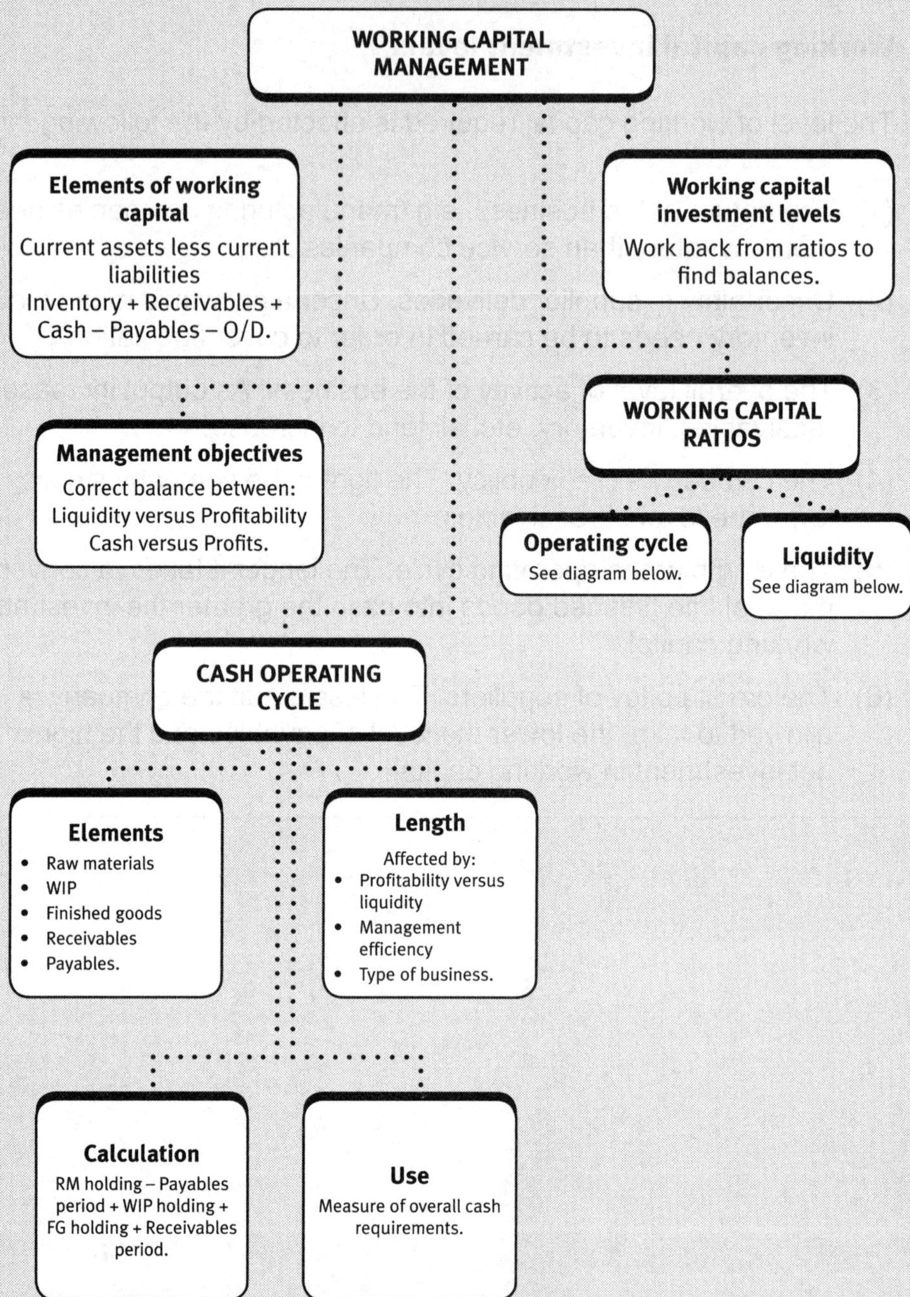

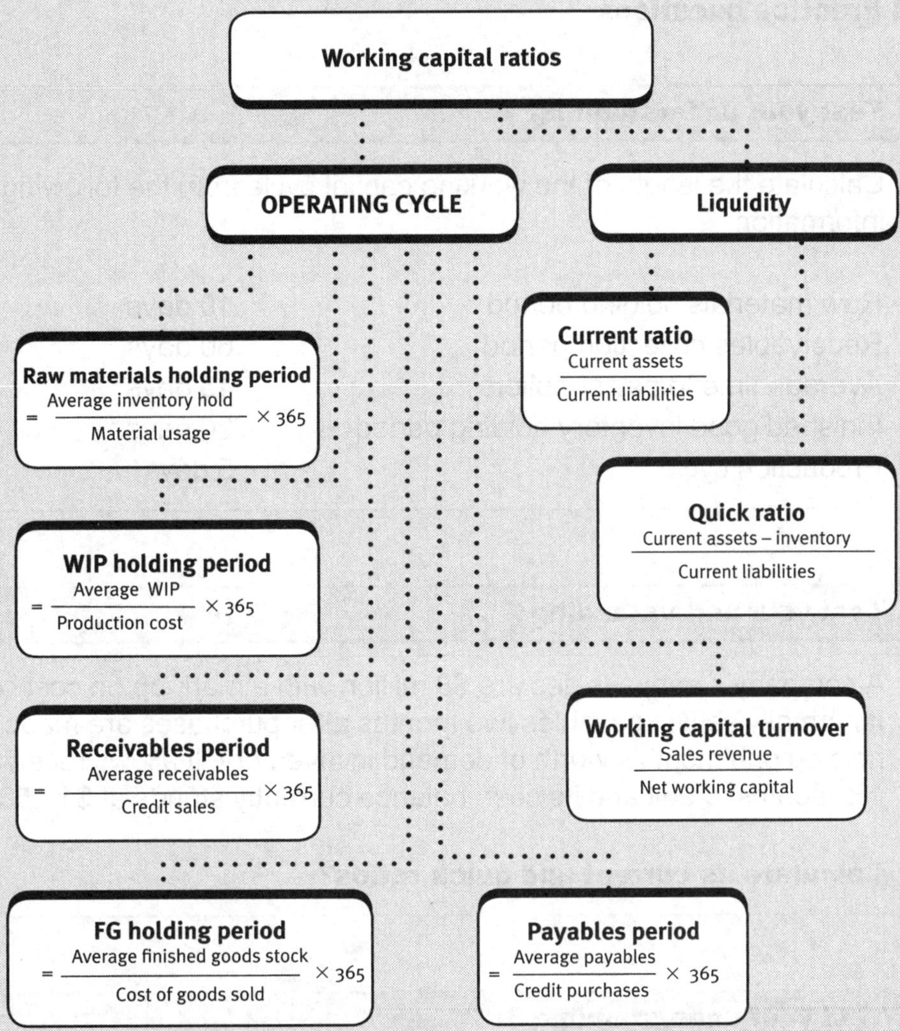
Working capital ratios
OPERATING CYCLE
Liquidity
Current ratio
Current assets
Current liabilities
Quick ratio
Current assets – inventory
Current liabilities
Raw materials holding period
= Average inventory hold / Material usage × 365
WIP holding period
= Average WIP / Production cost × 365
Receivables period
= Average receivables / Credit sales × 365
Working capital turnover
Sales revenue
Net working capital
FG holding period
= Average finished goods stock / Cost of goods sold × 365
Payables period
= Average payables / Credit purchases × 365

8 Practice questions

Test your understanding 1

Calculate the length of the working capital cycle from the following information:

Raw materials holding period	10 days
Receivables collection period	60 days
Average time to pay suppliers	45 days
Finished good inventory holding period	20 days
Production cycle	5 days

Test your understanding 2

A company's annual sales are $8 million with a mark-up on cost of 60%. It normally settles payables two months after purchases are made, holding one month's worth of demand in inventory. It allows receivables 1½ months' credit and its cash balance currently stands at $1,250,000.

Calculate its current and quick ratios?

Test your understanding 3

A company has a quick (or acid test) ratio of 0.80:1. State whether the quick ratio would increase or decrease in each of the following situations.

(Take each situation individually, not together.)

(a) it receives payment of an amount owed by a trade customer.

(b) it sells an item of inventory at a loss

(c) it pays an invoice from a trade supplier.

Test your understanding 4

Marlboro Co estimates the following figures for the coming year.

Sales - all on credit	$3,600,000
Average receivables	$306,000
Gross profit margin *	25% on sales
Finished goods	$200,000
Work in progress	$350,000
Raw materials (balance held)	$150,000
Trade payables	$130,000

Inventory levels are constant.

* Raw materials are 80% of cost of sales - all on credit.

Required:

Calculate the cash operating cycle.

Test your understanding 5

Identify which of the following transactions will result in an increase in working capital:

A Writing off a debt as uncollectable

B Paying the invoice of a trade supplier

C Selling goods on credit at a profit

D Buying inventory for cash

Test your understanding 6

Appraisal of working capital management

You have been given the following information for a company:

Summarised balance sheets(statements of financial position) at 30 June

	20X7		20X6	
	$000	$000	$000	$000
Non-current assets (carrying value)		130		139
Current assets:				
Inventory	42		37	
Receivables	29		23	
Bank	3		5	
		74		65
Total assets		204		204
Equity and liabilities				
Ordinary share capital (50 cent shares)		35		35
Share premium account		17		17
Revaluation reserve		10		-
Profit and loss account		31		22
		93		74
Non-current liabilities				
5% secured loan notes		40		40
8% Preference shares ($1 shares)		25		25
Current liabilities				
Trade payables	36		55	
Taxation	10		10	
		46		65
Total equity and liabilities		204		204

Summarised income statements for the year ended 30 June

	20X7		20X6	
	$000	$000	$000	$000
Sales		209		196
Opening inventory	37		29	
Purchases	162		159	
	199		188	
Closing inventory	42		37	
		157		151
Gross profit		52		45
Finance costs	2		2	
Depreciation	9		9	
Sundry expenses	14		11	
		25		22
Operating profit		27		23
Taxation		10		10
Profit after taxation		17		13
Dividends:				
Ordinary shares	6		5	
Preference shares	2		2	
		8		7
Retained profit		9		6

Required:

(a) Calculate the liquidity ratios in 20X6 and 20X7

(b) Calculate the length of the cash operating cycle in 20X6 and 20X7

(c) State whether the working capital is being managed effectively

Test your understanding 7

The following data relate to Mugwump Co, a manufacturing company.

Sales revenue for year:	$1,500,000
Costs as percentage of sales:	30%
Direct materials	
Direct labour	25%
Variable overheads	10%
Fixed overheads	15%
Selling and distribution	5%

Average statistics relating to working capital are as follows:

- receivables take 2½ months to pay
- raw materials are in inventory for three months
- WIP represents two months' half-produced goods
- finished goods represent one month's production
- credit is taken

– Materials	2 months
– Direct labour	1 week
– Variable overheads	1 month
– Fixed overheads	1 month
– Selling and distribution	½ month

WIP and finished goods are valued at the cost of material, labour and variable expenses.

Calculate the working capital requirement of Mugwump Co assuming that the labour force is paid for 50 working weeks in each year.

Test your understanding 8

Brash is a medium-sized company producing a range of engineering products. Recently its sales have risen rapidly. It is now early in Year 3, and a summary of the company's performance and financial position in Years 1 and 2 are set out below:

Summary income statements for the year ended 31 December

	Year 1	Year 2
	$000	$000
Sales	12,000	16,000
Cost of sales	7,000	9,150
Operating profit	5,000	6,850
Interest	200	250
Profit before taxation	4,800	6,600
Taxation	1,000	1,600
Profit after taxation	3,800	5,000

		Year 1		Year 2
		$000		$000
Non-current assets		9,000		12,000
Current assets				
Inventory	1,400		2,200	
Receivables	1,600		2,600	
Cash	1,500		100	
		4,500		4,900
Total assets		13,500		16,900
Ordinary shares (50c each)		3,000		3,000
Accumulated profit		6,500		9,500
		9,500		12,500
Non-current liabilities (10% loan)		2,000		2,000
Current liabilities				
Trade payables	1,500		2,000	
Other payables	500		200	
Bank overdraft	0		200	
		2,000		2,400
		13,500		16,900

Required:

Explain why Brash might be overtrading, by identifying how the company is showing four symptoms of overtrading.

Test your understanding 9

Hottubes Co is a small company specialising in the supply of high quality amplifier do-it-yourself kits for sale to Hi-Fi enthusiasts. These include superior electronic components, circuit boards and detailed instructions. Promotion is carried out through adverts in electronics and Hi-Fi magazines. The company buys most of its components from a specialist supplier in Hong Kong and the remainder from a few local suppliers.

The CEO (and founder) is very proud of the company's performance and recently made the following comment.

'We have excellent products as seen in the recent rave reviews in a major consumer electronics magazine. Our business has grown rapidly over recent years and we have good profitability. We also have good liquidity with current assets easily covering current liabilities. This is partly due to improved credit control over receivables. However, our Hong Kong supplier demands payment at the end of each month for all items shipped in that month…'

As with many other small businesses, Hottubes uses its bank overdraft to finance working capital and has no other longer term funding. The current overdraft rate is 1.0% per month on the monthly outstanding balance.

Extracts from the management accounts for the last two years are as follows.

31 December

	20X2	**20X1**
	$000	$000
Sales	1,024	640
Cost of sales	640	400
Other expenses	132	81
Inventories		
Components	300	208
Finished kits	220	96
Trade receivables	320	204
Trade payables	135	104
Other payables	31	30
Corporation tax due	63	40
Purchases for the year	776	490
Bank overdraft	180	100

Requirement:

Prepare briefing notes for a meeting with the CEO calculating the company's working capital position and identify areas for improvement. Include in your answer a calculation of the cash operating cycle and any other calculations you feel are appropriate.

(Total: 15 marks)

Test your understanding answers

Example 1 - LIQUIDITY VERSUS PROFITABILITY

Advantages of keeping it high		**Advantages of keeping it low**
Few stockouts		Less cash tied up in inventory
Bulk purchase discounts Reduced ordering costs	**INVENTORY**	Lower storage costs Flexibility
	+	
Customers like credit – ∴ profitable as attracts more sales	**RECEIVABLES**	Less cash tied up Less chance of irrecoverable debts Reduced costs of credit control
	+	
Able to pay bills on time Take advantage of unexpected opportunities Avoid high borrowing costs	**CASH**	Can invest surplus to earn high returns Less vulnerable to takeover
	=	
	CURRENT ASSETS	
Preserves own cash – cheap source of finance	– **TRADE PAYABLES**	Lose prompt payment discounts Loss of credit status Less favourable supplier treatment
	=	
	WORKING CAPITAL	

Example 2 - CASH OPERATING CYCLE

	Days
Raw materials inventory holding period	21
Less: suppliers' payment period	(42)
WIP holding period	14
Finished goods holding period	28
Receivables' collection period	56
Operating cycle (days)	77

Example 3 - WORKING CAPITAL INVESTMENT LEVELS

We need to use the ratios to calculate balance sheet values in order to construct the projected working capital position.

				$m
Inventory	=	30 ÷ 365	× $6m	= 0.49
Receivables	=	60 ÷ 365	× $10m	1.64
Trade payables	=	40 ÷ 365	× $6m	= (0.66)
Working capital required				1.47

Test your understanding 1

	Days
Raw materials holding period	10
Production cycle	5
Finished good inventory holding period	20
Receivables collection period	60
	95
Average time to pay suppliers	(45)
Working capital cycle	50

Test your understanding 2

Step 1 Calculate annual cost of sales, using the cost structure.

	%	$m
Sales	160	8
Cost of sales (COS)	100	5
Gross profit	60	3

Step 2 Calculate payables, receivables and inventory.

20X6 20X5

$$\text{Payables} = \frac{2}{12} \times \text{annual COS} = \frac{2}{12} \times \$5\text{m} = \$0.833\text{m}$$

$$\text{Receivables} = \frac{1.5}{12} \times \text{annual sales} = \frac{1.5}{12} \times \$8\text{m} = \$1\text{m}$$

$$\text{Inventory} = \frac{1}{12} \times \text{annual COS} \quad \frac{1}{12} \times \$5\text{m} = \$0.417\text{m}$$

Step 3 Calculate the ratios.

$$\text{Current ratio} = \frac{\text{Inventory + receivables + cash}}{\text{Payables}} = \frac{0.417 + 1 + 1.25}{0.833} = 3.2$$

$$\text{Quick ratio} = \frac{\text{Receivables + cash}}{\text{Payables}} = \frac{1 + 1.25}{0.833} = 2.7$$

Test your understanding 3

(a) There is no change in the quick ratio. There is no change in current assets excluding inventory, and no change in current liabilities. The effect of the transaction is to reduce receivables and increase cash by the same amount.

(b) The quick ratio will rise higher than 0.80:1. The sale of the inventory, even at a loss, will result in an increase in either receivables or cash. Inventory is not included in the calculation of the quick ratio; therefore the reduction in inventory is irrelevant. Since current assets excluding inventory increase and current liabilities are unchanged, the quick ratio must increase.

(c) The quick ratio will fall. There will be an equal decrease in cash and trade payables.

It may be easier to understand by making up some numbers. Say the current assets (without inventories) were $80,000 and current liabilities were $100,000 to begin with. If a $30,000 supplier invoice was paid then the new balances would be $50,000 of current assets and $70,000 of current liabilities. The quick ratio would have lowered to ($50,000/$70000) 0.714:1.

Test your understanding 4

Income statement

	$	$
Turnover		3,600,000
Cost of sales		
Materials - 80% (given)	2,160,000	
Other (balancing figure)	540,000	
		2,700,000
Gross profit - 25% (given)		900,000

Cash operating cycle

Raw materials holding period

$$\frac{\$150,000}{\$2,160,000} \times 365 = 25 \text{ days}$$

Trade payables days

$$\frac{\$130,000}{\$2,160,000} \times 365 = (22) \text{ days}$$

WIP holding days

$$\frac{\$350,000}{\$2,700,000} \times 365 = 48 \text{ days}$$

Finished goods holding period

$$\frac{\$200,000}{\$2,700,000} \times 365 = 27 \text{ days}$$

Receivables collection period

$$\frac{\$306,000}{\$3,600,000} \times 365 = 31 \text{ days}$$

109 days

Test your understanding 5

The correct answer is **C**

Items B and D result in no change in working capital. Item B results in an equal reduction in both cash and trade payables. Item D results in an increase in inventory but an equal decrease in cash. Writing off a receivable (item A) reduces working capital, because there is a reduction in receivables but no reduction in current liabilities. Selling goods on credit reduces inventory but increases receivables by a larger amount (= the gross profit on the sale); therefore total working capital increases by the amount of the gross profit.

Test your understanding 6

The current ratio:

20X7		**20X6**	
$\frac{74}{46}$	= 1.6	$\frac{65}{65}$	= 1.0

The quick (or acid test) ratio:

20X7		**20X6**	
$\frac{32}{46}$	= 0.7	$\frac{28}{65}$	= 0.4

Both of these ratios show an improvement. The extent of the change between the two years seems surprising and would require further investigation. It would also be useful to know how these ratios compare with those of a similar business, since typical liquidity ratios for supermarkets, say, are quite different from those for heavy engineering firms.

In 20X7 current liabilities were well covered by current assets. Liabilities payable in the near future are 70% covered by cash and receivables (a liquid asset, close to cash).

To better understand the liquidity ratios we can then look at each individual component of working capital:

The inventory holding period:

20X7

$$\frac{(\frac{1}{2}(37 + 42) \times 365 \text{ days})}{157} = 92 \text{ days}$$

20X6

$$\frac{(\frac{1}{2}(29 + 37) \times 365 \text{ days})}{151} = 80 \text{ days}$$

The inventory holding period has lengthened. In general, the shorter the stock holding period the better. It is very expensive to hold stock and thus minimum stock holding usually points to good management.

The current ratio calculation now seems less optimistic, considering the holding period for inventory of 92 days. Inventory that takes nearly four months to sell is not very liquid! It would be better to focus attention on the acid test ratio.

Receivables days:

	20X7	**20X6**
Average daily sales	$\frac{\$209,000}{365} = \$573$	$\frac{\$196,000}{365} = \$537$
Closing trade receivables	$29,000	$23,000
Receivables days	$\frac{\$29,000}{\$573} = 51 \text{ days}$	$\frac{\$23,000}{\$537} = 43 \text{ days}$

Or more quickly:

20X7

$$\frac{29,000}{209,000} \times 365 \text{ days} = 50.6 \text{ days}$$

20X6

$$\frac{23,000}{196,000} \times 365 = 42.8 \text{ days}$$

Compared with 20X6, the receivables collection period has worsened in 20X7. It would be important to establish the company policy on credit allowed. If the average credit allowed to customers was, say, 30 days, then something is clearly wrong. Further investigation might reveal delays in sending out invoices or failure to 'screen' new customers.

This situation suggests yet a further review of the liquidity ratios. The acid test ratio ignores inventory but still assumes receivables are liquid. If debt collection is a problem then receivables too are illiquid and the company could struggle to pay its current liabilities were they all to fall due in a short space of time.

Payables days:

	20X7		20X6	
Average daily purchases	$162,000 / 365	= $444	$159,000 / 365	= $436
Closing trade receivables	$36,000		$55,000	
Payables' payment period	81 days		126 days	

Or more quickly:

20X6

$$\frac{36,000}{162,000} \times 365 \text{ days} = 81.1 \text{ days}$$

20X6

$$\frac{55,000}{159,000} \times 365 = 126.3 \text{ days}$$

The payables' payment period has reduced substantially from last year. It is, however, in absolute terms still a high figure. Often, suppliers request payment within 30 days. The company is taking nearly three months. Trade creditors are thus financing much of the working capital requirements of the business, which is beneficial to the company.

A high level of creditor days may be good in that it means that all available credit is being taken, but there are three potential disadvantages of taking extended credit:

- Future supplies may be endangered.
- Availability of cash discounts is lost.
- Suppliers may quote a higher price for the goods knowing the company takes extended credit.

Additionally when viewed alongside the previous ratios calculated, this might suggest a cash flow problem causing suppliers to be left unpaid.

Length of the operating cycle:

	20X7 days	20X6 days
Inventory holding period	92	80
+		
Receivables' collection period	51	43
–		
Payables' payment period	(81)	(126)
=		
Cash operating cycle	62 days	(3 days)

Our example shows that, in 20X7, there is approximately a 62-day gap between paying cash to suppliers for goods, and receiving the cash back from customers. However, in 20X6, there was the somewhat unusual situation where cash was received from the customers, on average, more than 3 days before the payment to suppliers was needed.

Test your understanding 7

1. Costs incurred

	$
Direct materials 30% of $1,500,000	450,000
Direct labour 25% of $1,500,000	375,000
Variable overheads 10% of $1,500,000	150,000
Fixed overheads 15% of $1,500,000	225,000
Selling and distribution 5% of $1,500,000	75,000

2. Average value of current assets

	$	$
Finished goods 1/12 × $975,000		81,250
Raw materials 3/12 × $450,000		112,500
WIP:		
(2 months @ half produced –		
1 month equivalent cost)		
Materials		
1/12 × $450,000	37,500	
Labour 1/12 × $375,000	31,250	
Variable overheads 1/12 × $150,000	12,500	
		81,250
Receivables 2 ½ /12 × $1,500,000		312,500
		587,500

3. Average value of current liabilities

Materials 2/12 × $450,000	75,000	
Labour 1/50 × $375,000	7,500	
Variable overheads 1/12 × $150,000	12,500	
Fixed overheads 1/12 × $225,000	18,750	
Selling and distribution 1/24 × $75,000	3,125	
		(116,875)

4. Working capital required	470,625

Test your understanding 8

Sales increased by 33.3% between Year 1 and Year 2, but total working capital (= current assets minus current liabilities) remained the same, at $2,500,000. Companies that increase their sales without a sufficient increase in working capital might be at risk of overtrading (or 'under-capitalisation').

The liquidity position has deteriorated between Year 1 and Year 2. At the end of Year 1, the current ratio was 2.25:1 and at the end of Year 2 it was 2.04:1 (4,900:2,400). At the end of Year 2, the quick ratio was 1.55:1 and at the end of Year 2 it was 1.13:1 (2,700:2,400). A worsening liquidity position, in spite of being profitable, is also a sign of overtrading.

The worsening liquidity is also evident in the decline in the cash position, from a cash balance of $1,500,000 at the end of Year 1 to a negative net balance of $100,000 at the end of Year 2.

The average time for customers to pay was 49 days in Year 1 (365 days × 1,600/12,000). This had risen to about 59 days in Year 2 ((365 days × 2,600/16,000). Allowing customers a longer time to pay can also be a sign of overtrading, because a company might have to offer more generous credit terms in order to achieve growth in sales.

Test your understanding 9

Tutorial note: detailed discussions of receivables, payables and inventories policies are covered in later chapters. However, you should still be able to use some common sense to comment on the reasonableness of Hottubes' figures, especially given the description of its products, customers, suppliers and market.

Briefing Notes

(1) **Introduction – the profitability v liquidity trade-off**

- Sales have grown 60% over the last year, reflecting increasing customer awareness of a quality product.
- However, the overdraft has increased by $80,000 suggesting that there may be problems with working capital management.
- Has growth been pursued at the expense of liquidity?
- Over-trading is common in small companies with high growth.

(2) **Overview – Liquidity ratios**

- Current ratio is 2.05 and growing. This is >1 and, viewed in isolation, suggests that there are few short term liquidity problems (as indicated by the CEO).
- However, the quick ratio is only 0.78. This is <1 suggesting potential problems.
- In particular the company would struggle to repay its overdraft should the bank recall the facility for any reason.
- The current ratio appears healthy only because of the very high levels of inventory.

(3) **Overview – The cash operating cycle**

- The operating cycle has increased from 282 to 317 days and seems excessively high at over ten months.
- This means that more funds are tied up in working capital and is a concern, given the high growth rates of Hottubes.
- New business will result in increased cash outflows with resulting increased inflows delayed a further ten months. This is likely to result in the overdraft increasing in the short term.

(4) **Specific issues – Receivables**

- Credit control does appear to have improved as receivables days has fallen from 116 to 114 days.
- However, this still seems excessively high given that most customers are individual enthusiasts and not major corporations.
- Given the specialist nature of the product would it be possible to insist on payment up front before kits are despatched? It is unlikely that such a policy would lose sales. There is no reason for the firm to offer credit.
- Note: even halving receivables would free up $160,000 cash – this would reduce the overdraft significantly.

(5) **Specific issues – Inventories**

- Hottubes is holding over 4 months' worth of kits and the figure seems to be rising.
- It is difficult to justify why such high kit inventory levels are being held. Presumably the production period is quite short (components simply need to be placed in boxes) and, in any case, customers will probably be happy to wait for kits should there be production delays.
- The holding period of components has fallen but, as with kits, seems excessive. The time period could be justified if certain components are rare and difficult to source but there is no suggestion that the Hong Kong supplier could not send additional components at short notice if the need arose (e.g. by airmail?)

(6) **Specific issues – Payables**

- Hottubes is currently taking two months to pay suppliers. This seems high given the Hong Kong supplier's insistence that goods are paid for in the month they are shipped.
- While delaying payment is good for Hottubes' liquidity, there is a danger that the Hong Kong supplier will respond through some or all of the following:
  - Price rises.
  - Refusing to supply.
  - Refusing to allow further credit.
  - Sending Hottubes lower grade components.
- It appears that Hottubes is dependent on the supplier for its competitive advantage and would thus be advised to ensure this relationship does not deteriorate due to late payment.

(7) **Specific issues - Overdraft**

- Hottubes is dependent on its overdraft for financing. Unless working capital policies change, the overdraft looks set to increase.
- The firm should do detailed cash flow forecasts to identify how large it will grow, to ensure that any limits are not breached.
- The possibility of consolidating part of the overdraft into a loan should also be considered.

Appendix – Key Figures

	20X2	**20X1**
Receivables credit period	114	116
Components holding period	141	155
Finished kits holding period	125	88
Trade payables period	(63)	(77)
Length of operating cycle	317	282
Current ratio(840/409 and 508/274)	2.05	1.85
Quick ratio(320/409 and 204/274)	0.78	0.74

chapter

16

Working capital management – inventory control

Chapter learning objectives

Lead	Component
E1. Analyse the working capital position and identify areas for improvement.	(g) Analyse the impacts of alternative policies for stock management.

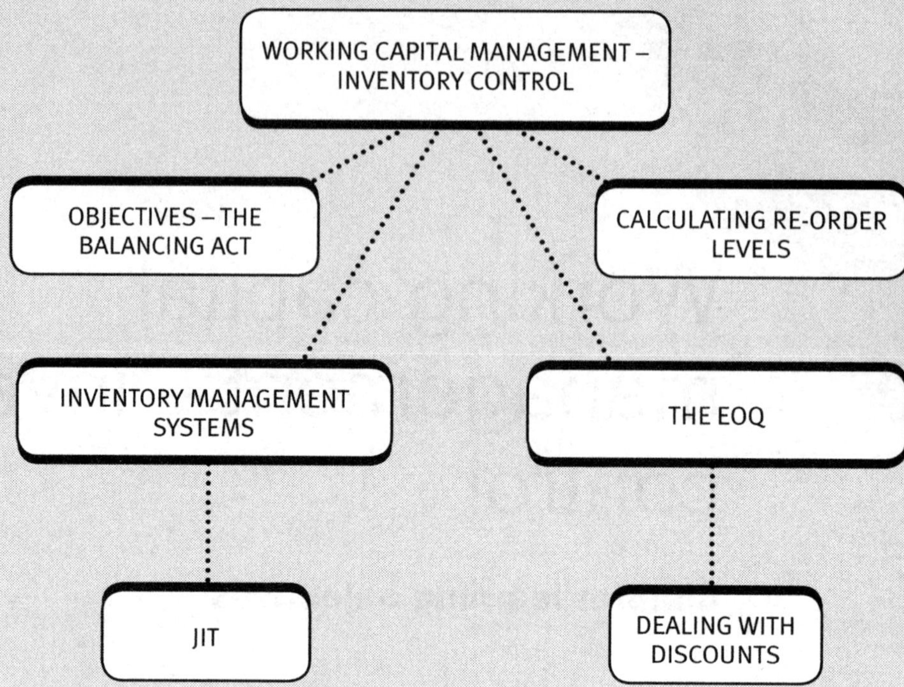

1 The objectives of inventory management

Inventory is a major investment for many companies. Manufacturing companies can easily be carrying inventory equivalent to between 50% and 100% of the revenue of the business. It is therefore essential to reduce the levels of inventory held to the necessary minimum.

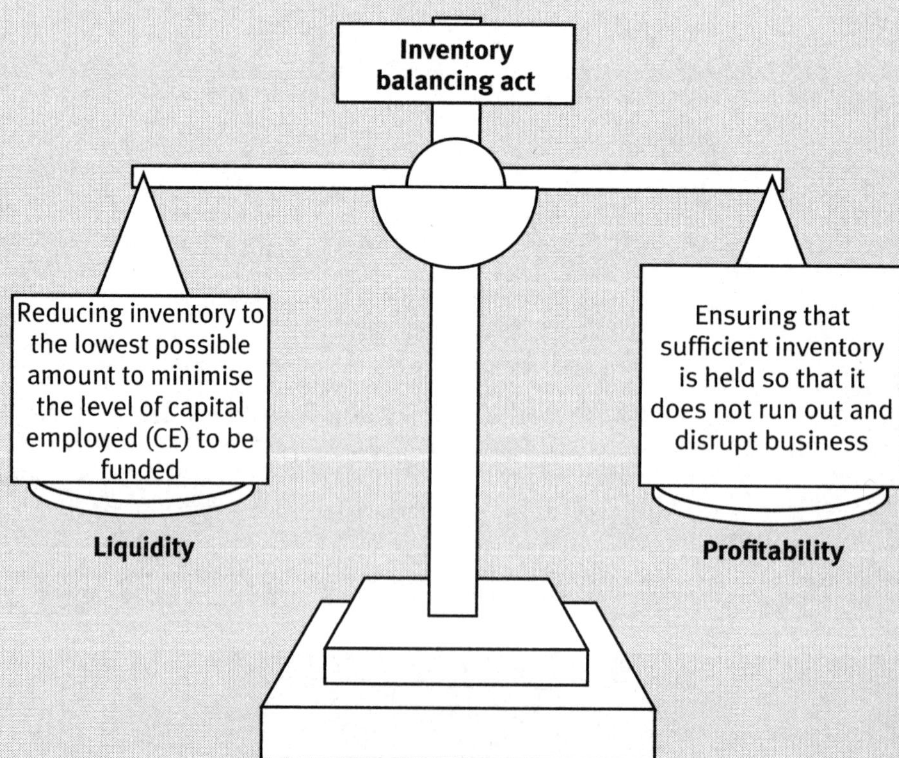

Costs of high inventory levels

Keeping inventory levels high is expensive owing to:

- purchase costs
- holding costs:
  - storage
  - stores administration
  - risk of theft/damage/obsolescence.

Costs of high inventory levels

Carrying inventory involves a major working capital investment and therefore levels need to be very tightly controlled. The cost is not just that of purchasing the goods, but also storing, insuring, and managing them once they are in inventory.

Purchase costs: once goods are purchased, capital is tied up in them and until sold on (in their current state or converted into a finished product), the capital earns no return. This lost return is an opportunity cost of holding the inventory.

Storage and stores administration: in addition, the goods must be stored. The company must incur the expense of renting out warehouse space, or if using space they own, there is an opportunity cost associated with the alternative uses the space could be put to. There may also be additional requirements such as controlled temperature or light which require extra funds.

Other risks: once stored, the goods will need to be insured. Specialist equipment may be needed to transport the inventory to where it is to be used. Staff will be required to manage the warehouse and protect against theft and if inventory levels are high, significant investment may be required in sophisticated inventory control systems.

The longer inventory is held, the greater the risk that it will deteriorate or become out of date. This is true of perishable goods, fashion items and high-technology products, for example.

Costs of low inventory levels

If inventory levels are kept too low, the business faces alternative problems:

- stockouts:
  - lost contribution
  - production stoppages
  - emergency orders
- high re-order/setup costs
- lost quantity discounts.

Costs of low inventory levels

Stockout: if a business runs out of a particular product used in manufacturing it may cause interruptions to the production process – causing idle time, stockpiling of work-in-progress (WIP) or possibly missed orders. Alternatively, running out of goods held for onward sale can result in dissatisfied customers and perhaps future lost orders if custom is switched to alternative suppliers. If a stockout looms, the business may attempt to avoid it by acquiring the goods needed at short notice. This may involve using a more expensive or poorer quality supplier.

Re-order/setup costs: each time inventory runs out, new supplies must be acquired. If the goods are bought in, the costs that arise are associated with administration – completion of a purchase requisition, authorisation of the order, placing the order with the supplier, taking and checking the delivery and final settlement of the invoice. If the goods are to be manufactured, the costs of setting up the machinery will be incurred each time a new batch is produced.

Lost quantity discounts: purchasing items in bulk will often attract a discount from the supplier. If only small amounts are bought at one time in order to keep inventory levels low, the quantity discounts will not be available.

The challenge

The objective of good inventory management is therefore to determine:

- the optimum re-order level – how many items are left in inventory when the next order is placed, and
- the optimum re-order quantity – how many items should be ordered when the order is placed

for all material inventory items.

In practice, this means striking a balance between holding costs on the one hand and stockout and re-order costs on the other.

The balancing act between liquidity and profitability, which might also be considered to be a trade-off between holding costs and stockout/re-order costs, is key to any discussion on inventory management.

Terminology

Other key terms associated with inventory management include:

- lead time – the lag between when an order is placed and the item is delivered
- buffer inventory – the basic level of inventory kept for emergencies. A buffer is required because both demand and lead time will fluctuate and predictions can only be based on best estimates.

Ensure you can distinguish between the various terms used: re-order level, re-order quantity, lead time and buffer inventory.

2 Economic order quantity (EOQ)

For businesses that do not use just in time (JIT) inventory management systems (discussed in more detail below), there is an optimum order quantity for inventory items, known as the EOQ.

The challenge

The aim of the EOQ model is to minimise the total cost of holding and ordering inventory.

EOQ explanation

To minimise the total cost of holding and ordering inventory, it is necessary to balance the relevant costs. These are:

- the variable costs of holding the inventory
- the fixed costs of placing the order

Holding costs

The model assumes that it costs a certain amount to hold a unit of inventory for a year (referred to as C_H in the formula). Therefore, as the average level of inventory increases, so to will the total annual holding costs incurred.

Because of the assumption that demand per period is known and is constant (see below), conclusions can be drawn over the average inventory level in relationship to the order quantity.

When new batches or items of inventory are purchased or made at periodic intervals, the inventory levels are assumed to exhibit the following pattern over time.

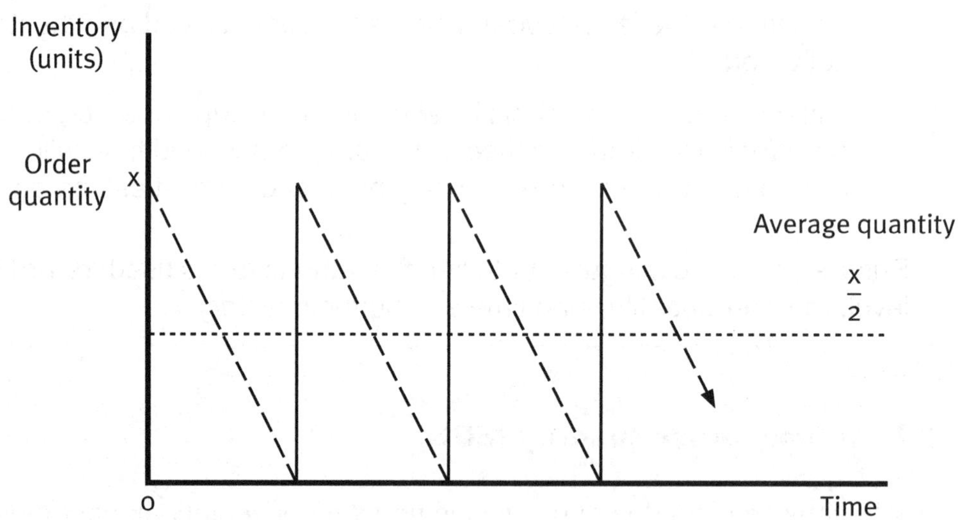

If x is the quantity ordered, the annual holding cost would be calculated as:

Holding cost per unit × Average inventory:

$$C_H \times \frac{x}{2}$$

We therefore see an upward sloping, linear relationship between the re-order quantity and total annual holding costs.

Ordering costs

The model assumes that a fixed cost is incurred every time an order is placed (referred to as C_O in the formula). Therefore, as the order quantity increases, there is a fall in the number of orders required, which reduces the total ordering cost.

If D is the annual expected sales demand, the annual order cost is calculated as:

Order cost per order × no. of orders per annum.

$$C_O \times \frac{D}{x}$$

However, the fixed nature of the cost results in a downward sloping, curved relationship.

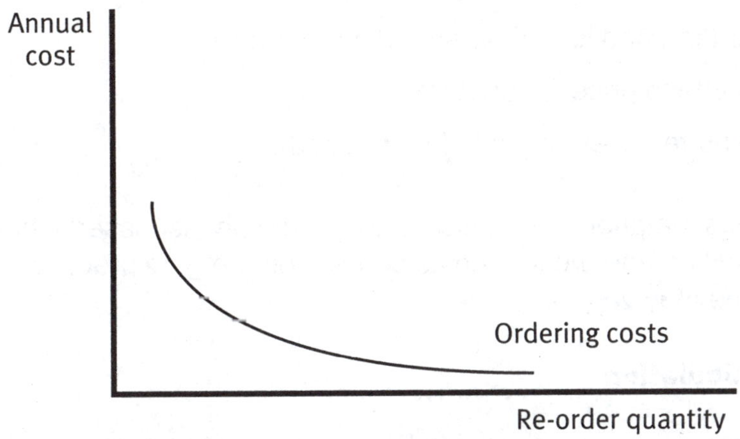

Because you are trying to balance these two costs (one which increases as re-order quantity increases and one which falls), total costs will always be minimised at the point where the total holding costs equals the total ordering costs. This point will be the economic order quantity.

When the re-order quantity chosen minimises the total cost of holding and ordering, it is known as the EOQ.

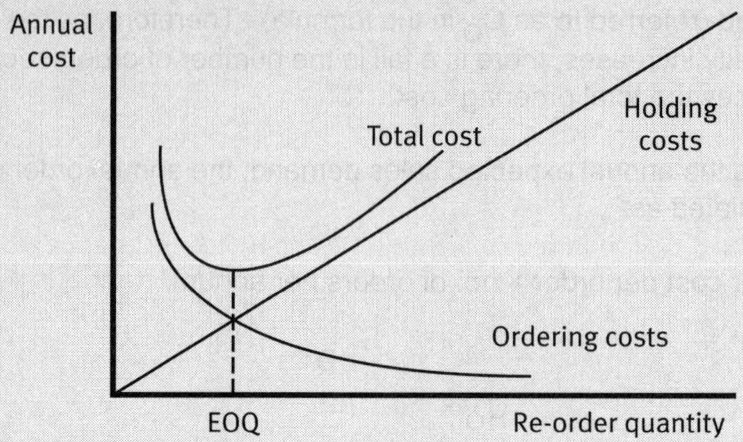

Assumptions

The following assumptions are made:

- demand and lead time are constant and known
- purchase price is constant
- no buffer inventory held (not needed).

These assumptions are critical and should be discussed when considering the validity of the model and its conclusions, e.g. in practice, demand and/or lead time may vary.

The calculation

The EOQ can be more quickly found using a formula (given in the examination):

$$EOQ = \sqrt{\frac{2C_O D}{C_H}}$$

where:

C_O = cost per order

D = annual demand

C_H = cost of holding one unit for one year.

Example 1

A company requires 1,000 units of material X per month. The cost per order is $30 regardless of the size of the order. The holding costs are $2.88 per unit pa.

Required:

Investigate the total cost of buying the material in quantities of 400, 500, or 600 units at one time. Identify the cheapest option.

Apply the EOQ formula to prove your answer is correct.

Dealing with quantity discounts

Discounts may be offered for ordering in large quantities. If the EOQ is smaller than the order size needed for a discount, should the order size be increased above the EOQ?

To work out the answer you should carry out the following steps:

Step 1: Calculate EOQ, ignoring discounts.

Step 2: If the EOQ is below the quantity qualifying for a discount, calculate the total annual inventory cost arising from using the EOQ.

Step 3: Recalculate total annual inventory costs using the order size required to just obtain each discount.

Step 4: Compare the cost of Steps 2 and 3 with the saving from the discount, and select the minimum cost alternative.

Step 5: Repeat for all discount levels.

Example 2

W Co is a retailer of barrels. The company has an annual demand of 30,000 barrels. The barrels cost $12 each. Fresh supplies can be obtained immediately, with ordering and transport costs amounting to $200 per order. The annual cost of holding one barrel in stock is estimated to be $1.20.

A 2% discount is available on orders of at least 5,000 barrels and a 2.5% discount is available if the order quantity is 7,500 barrels or above.

Required:

Calculate the EOQ ignoring the discount and calculate if it would change once the discount is taken into account.

Criticisms of EOQ

The EOQ model can be criticised in several ways:

- It is based on simplifying assumptions, such as constant and predictable material usage rates.
- It will not indicate the optimal purchase quantity when there are price discounts for buying in larger quantities.
- It ignores the problem of managing stock-outs.
- It is inconsistent with the philosophy of just-in-time management and total quality management.

3 Calculating the re-order level (ROL)

Known demand and lead time

Having decided how much inventory to re-order, the next problem is when to re-order. The firm needs to identify a level of inventory which can be reached before an order needs to be placed.

The **ROL** is the quantity of inventory on hand when an order is placed.

When demand and lead time are known with certainty the ROL may be calculated exactly, i.e. ROL = demand in the lead time.

Example 3

Using the data for W Co, assume that the company adopts the EOQ as its order quantity and that it now takes two weeks for an order to be delivered.

Calculate how frequently will the company place an order? Calculate how much inventory will it have on hand when the order is placed?

Buffer stock

Setting the reorder level so high means that in effect there is a buffer stock. Buffer stock is a quantity of inventory that should not usually be needed, but that might be needed if actual demand during the supply lead time exceeds the average demand.

	Units
Reorder level: (Maximum demand per day, in units x maximum re-order lead time)	X
(Average demand per day, in units x average re-order lead time)	Y
Buffer Stock	X - Y

Buffer stock has a cost. The annual cost of holding buffer stock is the amount of the buffer stock multiplied by the annual holding cost for one unit of the inventory item.

ROL with variable demand or variable lead time

When lead time and demand are known with certainty, ROL = demand during lead time. Where there is uncertainty, an optimum level of buffer inventory must be found.

This depends on:

- variability of demand
- cost of holding inventory
- cost of stockouts.

You will not be required to perform this calculation in the examination.

Inventory warning levels

Two warning levels might also be used, to indicate when the quantity of an item in inventory is either:

- higher than should be expected, or
- below the buffer stock level.

If the quantity of inventory goes above the maximum level or below the minimum level, the inventory manager should monitor the position carefully, and where appropriate take control measures.

The **maximum inventory level** should be:

- Reorder level
- Plus reorder quantity
- Minus [Minimum demand per day/week, in units] × [Minimum re-order lead time].

The maximum inventory level will occur when a new order has just been delivered by the supplier, the order has been delivered within the minimum lead time, and demand has been at a minimum during the lead time.

The **minimum inventory level** should be the buffer stock level:

- Reorder level
- Minus [Average demand per day/week, in units] × [Average re-order lead time].

4 Centralised versus decentralised purchasing

An organisation might have several locations, departments or group companies that each use the same raw materials and components. These might all be located within the same country, or they might be scattered across the world and geographically remote from each other.

In such cases, a policy decision must be made about whether to have centralised or decentralised purchasing of materials.

- With centralised purchasing, all materials are purchased by the same central purchasing department. Purchases prices and quantities are decided centrally and inventory levels are also monitored and controlled centrally.

- With decentralised purchasing, the authority to purchase materials is delegated to several operating units within the organisation, each with its own buying department or buying managers. Purchases prices and quantities are decided locally and the local management is also responsible for inventory management at a local level.

Advantages and disadvantages

Advantages of centralised purchasing

- A centralised buyer is able to order in larger quantities, and might be able to negotiate lower prices for bulk purchase orders.
- A centralised buyer might have a wider network of suppliers than a local buyer would have, and should be able to ensure that the best available prices are identified.
- It is easier to enforce common quality standards for purchased materials.
- With centralised buying, it should also be easier to manage inventory levels efficiently. The buyer should have access to information about the current inventory quantities at all locations in the organisation, and where appropriate can arrange for inventory to be transferred from one location to another, without having to purchase additional quantities.
- In an organisation whose operating units are all within a fairly small geographical area, it should also be possible to operate with a single centralised stores department as well as a centralised purchasing department. It should be much easier to control inventory levels with a central store than with several localised stores.
- Decisions about taking early settlement discounts can be co-ordinated and taken on a global basis, taking due account of the cash flow position of the organisation as a whole.

Disadvantages of centralised purchasing

- Local buying managers should be able to develop stronger relationships with local suppliers, possibly ensuring greater reliability of supply.
- A local buying manager might be much more flexible, and able to take advantage of temporary low prices locally that a central buying manager might not notice.
- A local manager can respond to inventory shortages more quickly than a centralised buying team. New materials can often be ordered and delivered much more quickly when the buying is done locally: central buyers might be slow and bureaucratic.
- Buying and inventory control are important aspects of operational and financial management. If authority is delegated to operating units (investment centres) within an organisation, it is appropriate that the responsibility for buying and inventory management should also be delegated.

5 Chapter summary

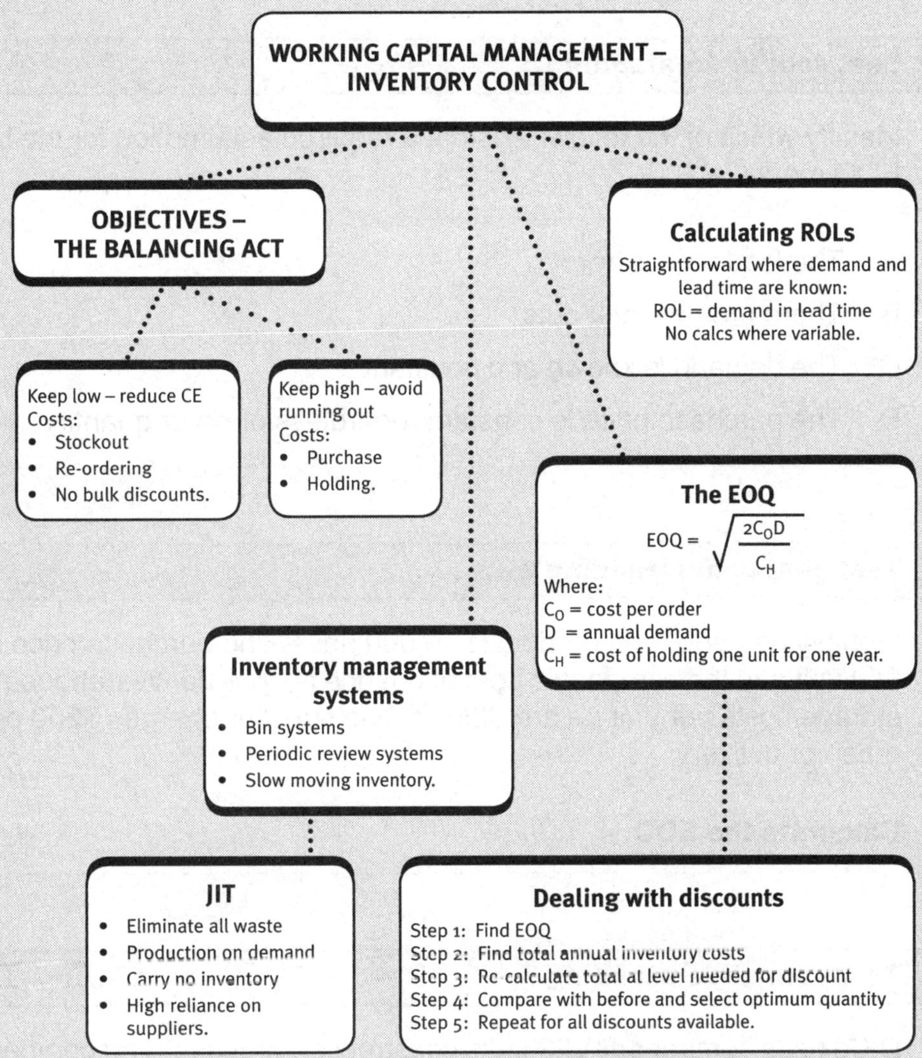

6 Practice questions

Test your understanding 1

Identify which of the following is not a required assumption for the basic EOQ model?

A The lead time is zero

B There are no stock-outs

C The demand is known and constant

D The purchase price is constant regardless of order quantity

Test your understanding 2

Monthly demand for a product is 10,000 units. The purchase price is $10/unit and the company's cost of finance is 15% pa. Warehouse storage costs per unit pa are $2/unit. The supplier charges $200 per order for delivery.

Calculate the EOQ.

Test your understanding 3

D Co uses component V22 in its construction process. The company has a demand of 45,000 components pa. They cost $4.50 each. There is no lead time between order and delivery, and ordering costs amount to $100 per order. The annual cost of holding one component in inventory is estimated to be $0.65.

A 0.5% discount is available on orders of at least 3,000 components and a 0.75% discount is available if the order quantity is 6,000 components or above.

Calculate the optimal order quantity.

Test your understanding 4

Using the data relating to D Co (previous question), and ignoring discounts, assume that the company adopts the EOQ as its order quantity and that it now takes three weeks for an order to be delivered.

(a) Calculate how frequently will the company place an order

(b) Calculate how much inventory will it have on hand when the order is placed

Test your understanding 5

A company has estimated that for the coming season weekly demand for components will be 80 units. Suppliers take three weeks on average to deliver goods once they have been ordered and a buffer inventory of 35 units is held.

If the inventory levels are reviewed every six weeks, calculate how many units will be ordered at a review where the count shows 250 units in inventory.

Test your understanding 6

(a) Explain why the net present value (NPV) method of investment appraisal is thought to be superior to other approaches. **(7 marks)**

(b) Hexicon Inc manufactures and markets automatic washing machines. Among the many hundreds of components which it purchases each year from external suppliers for assembling into the finished article are drive belts, of which it uses 40,000 units pa. It is considering converting its purchasing, delivery and inventory control of this item to a just-in-time system. This will raise the number of orders placed but lower the administrative and other costs of placing and receiving orders. If successful, this will provide the model for switching most of its inwards supplies on to this system. Details of actual and expected ordering and carrying costs are given in the table below.

		Actual	Proposed
C_O =	Ordering cost per order	$100	$25
P =	Purchase cost per item	$2.50	$2.50
C_H =	Inventory holding cost (as a percentage of the purchase cost)	20%	20%

To implement the new arrangements will require 'one-off' reorganisation costs estimated at $4,000 which will be treated as a revenue item for tax purposes. The rate of corporation tax is 33% and Hexicon can obtain finance at 12%. The effective life span of the new system can be assumed to be eight years.

Required:

(i) Calculate the effect of the new system on the economic order quantity (EOQ).

(ii) Calculate whether the new system is worthwhile in financial terms.

(12 marks)

(c) You are required to briefly explain the nature and objectives of JIT purchasing agreements concluded between components users and suppliers.

(6 marks)

(Total: 25 marks)

Test your understanding answers

Example 1

	Order quantity		
	400 units	**500 units**	**600 units**
Average inventory	200	250	300
No. of orders pa	30	24	20
	$	$	$
Holding cost – average units × $2.88	576	720	864

	Order quantity		
	400 units	500 units	600 units
Ordering cost – no. of orders × $30	900	720	600
Total cost	1,476	1,440	1,464

Therefore the best option is to order 500 units each time.

Note that this is the point at which total cost is minimised and the holding costs and order costs are equal.

Solution using the formula:

$$EOQ = \sqrt{\frac{2C_OD}{C_H}}$$

$C_O = 30$

$D = 1{,}000 \times 12 = 12{,}000$

$C_H = 2.88$

$$EOQ = \sqrt{\frac{2 \times 30 \times 12{,}000}{2.88}} = 500$$

Example 2

Step 1 Calculate EOQ, ignoring discounts.

$$EOQ = \sqrt{\frac{2C_OD}{C_H}}$$

$C_O = 200$

$D = 30{,}000$

$C_H = 1.20$

$$EOQ = \sqrt{\frac{2 \times 200 \times 30{,}000}{1.2}} = 3{,}162$$

Step 2 As this is below the level for discounts, calculate total annual inventory costs.

Total annual costs for the company will comprise holding costs plus re-ordering costs.

= (Average inventory $\times C_H$) + (Number of re-orders pa $\times C_O$)

$$= \frac{3{,}162}{2} \times \$1.20 + \frac{30{,}000}{3{,}162} \times \$200$$

= \$1,897.20 + \$1,897.53

= \$3,794.73

= \$3,795

Step 3 Recalculate total annual inventory costs using the order size required to just obtain the discount.

At order quantity 5,000, total costs are as follows.

= (Average inventory × C_H) + (Number of re-orders pa × C_O)

$$= \frac{5,000}{2} \times \$1.20 + \frac{30,000}{5,000} \times \$200$$

= $3,000 + $1,200

= $4,200

	$
Extra costs of ordering in batches of 5,000 (4,200 – 3,795)	(405)
Less: Saving on discount 2% × $12 × 30,000	7,200
Step 4 Net cost saving	6,795

Hence batches of 5,000 are worthwhile.

Step 3 (again)

At order quality 7,500, total costs are as follows:

= (Average inventory × C_H) + (Number of re-orders pa × C_O)

$$= \frac{7,500}{2} \times \$1.20 + \frac{30,000}{7,500} \times \$200$$

= $4,500 + $800

= $5,300

Extra costs of ordering in batches of 7,500 (5,300 - 4,200)	(1,100)
Less: Saving on extra discount (2.5% - 2%) × 30,000)	1,800
Step 4 Net cost saving (again)	700

So a further cost saving can be made on orders of 7,500 units.

Note: If Step 1 produces an EOQ at which a discount would have been available, and the holding cost would be reduced by taking the discount, i.e. where C_H is based on the purchase price × the cost of finance, the EOQ must be recalculated using the new C_H before the above steps are followed.

Example 3

- Annual demand is 30,000. The original EOQ is 3,162. The company will therefore place an order once every

  3,162 ÷ 30,000 × 365 days = 38 days

- The company must be sure that there is sufficient inventory on hand when it places an order to last the two weeks' lead time. It must therefore place an order when there is two weeks' worth of demand in inventory:

  i.e. ROL 2 ÷ 52 × 30,000 = 1,154 units

Test your understanding 1

The correct answer is **A**.

The EOQ model assumes a known and constant order lead time. The lead time does not have to be zero.

Test your understanding 2

$$EOQ = \sqrt{\frac{2C_oD}{C_H}}$$

$C_O = 200$

$D = 10,000 \times 12 = 120,000$

$C_H = (10 \times 0.15) + 2 = 3.5$

$$EOQ = \sqrt{\frac{2 \times 200 \times 120,000}{3.5}} = 3,703$$

Test your understanding 3

Step 1

$$EOQ = \sqrt{\frac{2C_OD}{C_H}}$$

$C_O = 100$

$D = 45,000$

$C_H = 0.65$

$$EOQ = \sqrt{\frac{2 \times 100 \times 45,000}{0.65}} = $$ 3,721, which would qualify for a 0.5% discount

Step 2

Total annual costs for the company will comprise holding costs plus re-ordering costs.

= (Average inventory × C_H) + (Number of re-orders pa × C_O)

$$=\left(\frac{3{,}721}{2} \times \$0.65\right) + \left(\frac{45{,}000}{3{,}721} \times \$100\right)$$

= $2,419

Step 3

At order quantity 6,000, total costs are as follows.

(6,000 × $0.65/2) + (45,000 × $100 ÷ 6,000) = $2,700

	$
Extra costs of ordering in batches of 6,000 (2,700 – 2,419)	(281)
Less: Saving on extra discount	
(0.75% – 0.5%) × $4.5 × 45,000	506.25

Step 4

Net cost saving	225.25

So a saving can be made on orders of 6,000 units.

Test your understanding 4

(a) Annual demand is 45,000. The original EOQ is 3,721.

The company will therefore place an order once every

3,721 ÷ 45,000 × 365 days = 30 days

(b) The company must be sure that there is sufficient inventory on hand when it places an order to last the three weeks' lead time. It must therefore place an order when there is three weeks' worth of demand in inventory:

3/52 × 45,000 = 2,596 units

Test your understanding 5

Demand per week is 80 units. The next review will be in six weeks by which time 80 × 6 = 480 units will have been used.

An order would then be placed and during the lead time – three weeks – another 80 × 3 = 240 units will be used.

The business therefore needs to have 480 + 240 = 720 units in inventory to ensure a stockout is avoided. Since buffer inventory of 35 units is required, the total number needed is 755 units.

Since the current inventory level is 250 units, an order must be placed for 755 – 250 = 505 units.

Test your understanding 6

(a) **Use of NPV**

The following reasons may be cited for using the net present value (NPV) method of investment appraisal:

- Compared to accounting rate of return (ARR), it discounts real cash flows as opposed to accounting profits which are affected by non-cash items.
- Compared to measuring internal rate of return (IRR), the NPV method only gives one solution. In some circumstances, (when there are a number of outflows occurring at different times), multiple IRR solutions are possible.
- Compared to the payback method, NPV considers all of the cash flows of a project.
- By using a discount rate it measures the opportunity cost of the money invested by a person in a project.
- The interest rate used can be increased/decreased depending upon the level of perceived risk in the investment.
- The NPV of a project can be shown to be equal to the increase in the value of shareholder's equity in the company. Thus the method is consistent with the objective of shareholder wealth maximisation.

(b) **Economic order quantity:**

(i)

The present EOQ is $\sqrt{\dfrac{2C_OD}{C_H}} = \sqrt{\dfrac{2 \times 100 \times 40{,}000}{20\% \times 2.50}}$ = 4,000 units/order

The revised EOQ is $\sqrt{\dfrac{2C_OD}{C_H}} = \sqrt{\dfrac{2 \times 25 \times 40{,}000}{20\% \times 2.50}}$ = 2,000 units/order

From this it can be seen that the EOQ is halved.

(ii) The number of orders has increased from (40,000 ÷ 4,000) 10 orders to (40,000 ÷ 2,000) 20 orders. However, ordering costs are reduced by:

(10 × $100) – (20 × $25) = $500 per annum

Average inventories have also reduced from 2,000 units (4,000 ÷ 2) to 1,000 units (2,000 ÷ 2). Consequently carrying costs have reduced by 20% × $2.50 × 1,000 = $500 per annum.

Total inventory costs are thereby reduced by $1,000 per annum (before tax).

Assuming that Hexicon Inc pays tax in the same year as it earns profits, the present value of the proposal is found by comparing the outflow cost with the discounted after-tax savings over the eight-year life of the proposal (using a 12% discount rate). The after-tax savings are $1,000 × 67% = $670.

Discounted savings:

Year	**Narrative**	**Cash flow**	**DF @ 12%**	**PV**
		$		$
1 - 8	After tax savings	670	4.968	3,329
0	Cost of reorganisation	(4,000)	1.000	(4,000)
0	Tax saving (assume same year: 33% × $4,000)	1,320	1.000	1,320
	Net benefit			649

As the present value of the proposal is positive, it is worthwhile.

(c) **JIT**

The main objective of Just In Time (JIT) purchasing is to match the delivery of components from suppliers to their usage in production. If this is achieved there are significant benefits to be gained by both the supplier and the customer.

The customer is likely to use only one supplier for each component and to build up a relationship with the supplier which encourages communication thus enabling the supplier to benefit from advanced production planning and economies of scale. To enhance this relationship, the customer makes a long-term commitment to future orders.

The supplier guarantees to deliver goods of an appropriate quality in accordance with an agreed delivery schedule. The benefit to the customer is thereby a reduction (or elimination) of inventory holding and significant cost savings. These arise in both holding costs and also in materials handling, because goods are transferred directly from goods inwards to production.

chapter

17

Working capital management – cash control

Chapter learning objectives

Lead	Component
E1. Analyse the working capital position and identify areas for improvement.	(c) Analyse cash-flow forecasts over a twelve-month period. (d) Discuss measures to improve a cash forecast situation.

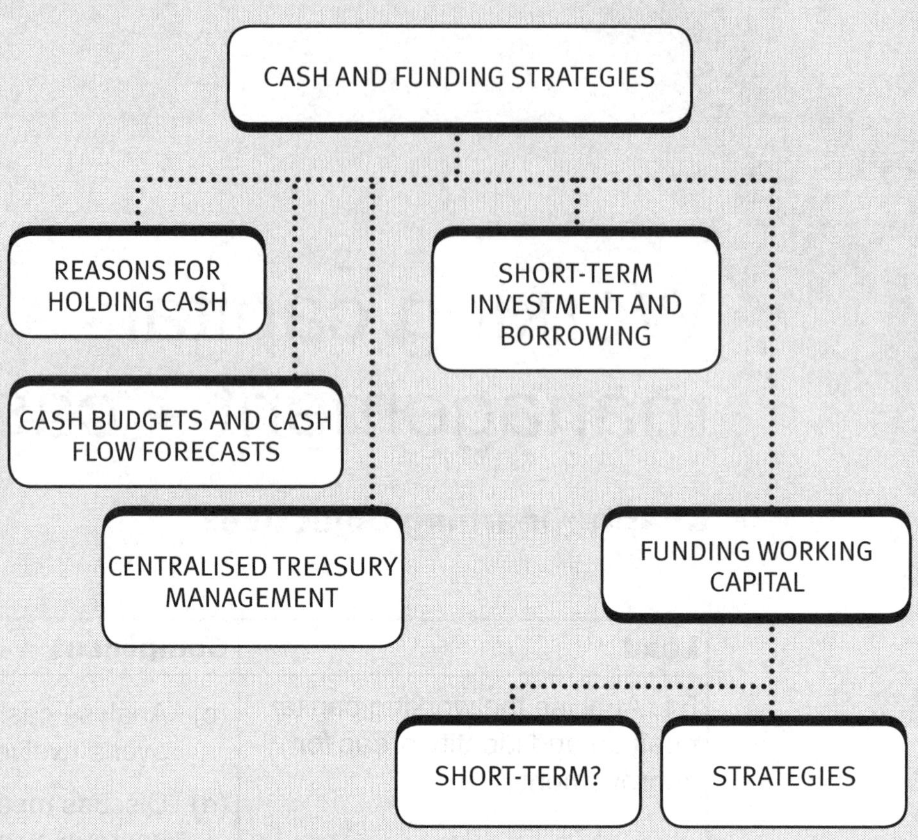

1 Reasons for holding cash

Although cash needs to be invested to earn returns, businesses need to keep a certain amount readily available. The reasons include:

- transactions motive
- precautionary motive
- investment motive.

Failure to carry sufficient cash levels can lead to:

- loss of settlement discounts
- loss of supplier goodwill
- poor industrial relations
- potential liquidation.

Reasons for holding cash

Cash is required for a number of reasons:

Transactions motive – cash required to meet day-to-day expenses, e.g. payroll, payment of suppliers, etc.

Precautionary motive – cash held to give a cushion against unplanned expenditure (the cash equivalent of buffer inventory).

Speculative motive – cash kept available to take advantage of market investment opportunities.

The cost of running out of cash depends on the firm's particular circumstances but may include not being able to pay debts as they fall due which can have serious operational repercussions:

- settlement discounts for early payment are unavailable
- trade suppliers refuse to offer further credit, charge higher prices or downgrade the priority with which orders are processed
- if wages are not paid on time, industrial action may well result, damaging production in the short-term and relationships and motivation in the medium-term
- the court may be petitioned to wind up the company if it consistently fails to pay bills as they fall due.

Once again therefore the firm faces a balancing act:

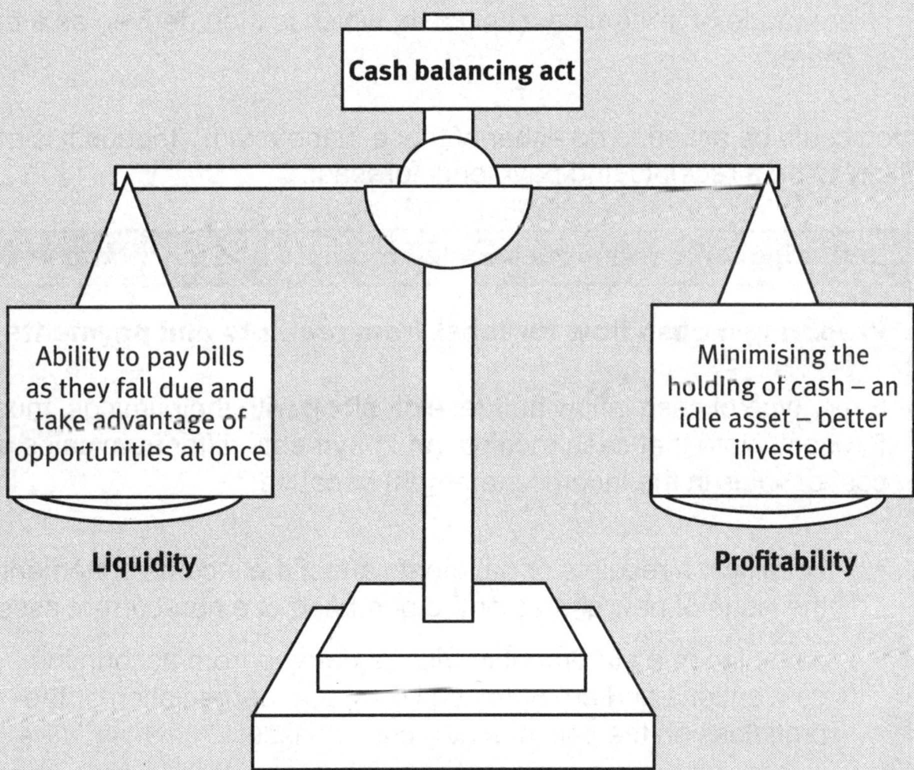

Remember to consider the four motives for holding cash and the liquidity/profitability trade-off in a question that asks for a discussion of cash management.

2 Cash budgets and cash flow forecasts

A **cash forecast** is an estimate of cash receipts and payments for a future period under existing conditions.

A **cash budget** is a commitment to a plan for cash receipts and payments for a future period after taking any action necessary to bring the forecast into line with the overall business plan.

Cash budgets are used to:

- assess and integrate operating budgets
- plan for cash shortages and surpluses
- compare with actual spending.

Cash forecasts can be prepared based on:

- Receipts and payments forecast. This is a forecast of cash receipts and payments based on predictions of sales and cost of sales and the timings of the cash flows relating to these items.
- Balance sheet (statement of financial position) forecast. This is a forecast derived from predictions of future balance sheets. Predictions are made of all items except cash, which is then derived as a balancing figure.

You could be asked to do either of these in the exam - though it is most likely to be a receipts and payments forecast.

Preparing forecasts from planned receipts and payments

Preparing a cash flow forecast from receipts and payments

Every type of cash inflow and receipt, along with their timings, must be forecast. Note that cash receipts and payments differ from sales and cost of sales in the income statement because:

- not all cash receipts or payments affect the income statement, e.g. the issue of new shares or the purchase of a non-current asset
- some income statement items are derived from accounting conventions and are not cash flows, e.g. depreciation or the profit/loss on the sale of a non-current asset
- the timing of cash receipts and payments does not coincide with the income statement accounting period, e.g. a sale is recognised in the income statement when the invoice is raised, yet the cash payment from the receivable may not be received until the following period or later.

The following approach should be adopted for examination questions.

Step 1 – Prepare a proforma

Month:	1 $	2 $	3 $	4 $
Receipts (few lines)				
Sub total				
Payments (Many lines)				
Sub total				
Net cash flow				
Balance brought down				
Balance carried down				

Step 2 – Fill in the simple figures

Some payments need only a small amount of work to identify the correct figure and timing and can be entered straight into the proforma. These would usually include:

- wages and salaries
- fixed overhead expenses
- dividend payments
- purchase of non-current assets.

Step 3 – Work out the more complex figures

The information on sales and purchases can be more time consuming to deal with, e.g.:

- timings for both sales and purchases must be found from credit periods
- variable overheads may require information about production levels
- purchase figures may require calculations based on production schedules and inventory balances.

Example 1 - FORECAST CASH RECEIPTS

The forecast sales for an organisation are as follows:

	January	February	March	April
	$	$	$	$
Sales	6,000	8,000	4,000	5,000

All sales are on credit and receivables tend to pay in the following pattern:

	%
In month of sale	10
In month after sale	40
Two months after sale	45

The organisation expects the rate of irrecoverable debts to be 5%.

Calculate the forecast cash receipts from receivables in April.

Example 2 - FORECAST CASH PAYMENTS

A manufacturing business makes and sells widgets. Each widget requires two units of raw materials, which cost $3 each. Production and sales quantities of widgets each month are as follows:

Month	Sales and production units
December (actual)	50,000
January (budget)	55,000
February (budget)	60,000
March (budget)	65,000

In the past, the business has maintained its inventories of raw materials at 100,000 units. However, it plans to increase raw material inventories to 110,000 units at the end of January and 120,000 units at the end of February. The business takes one month's credit from its suppliers.

Calculate the forecast payments to suppliers each month, for raw material purchases.

Example 3 - FULL CASH FLOW FORECAST

The following budgeted income statement has been prepared for Quest Company for the four months January to April Year 1:

	January	February	March	April
	$000	$000	$000	$000
Sales	60.0	50.0	70.0	60.0
Cost of production	50.0	55.0	32.5	50.0
(Increase)/decrease in inventory	(5.0)	(17.5)	20.0	(5.0)
Cost of sales	45.0	37.5	52.5	45.0
Gross profit	15.0	12.5	17.5	15.0
Administration and selling overhead	(8.0)	(7.5)	(8.5)	(8.0)
Net profit before interest	7.0	5.0	9.0	7.0

The working papers provide the following additional information:

- 40% of the production cost relates to direct materials. Materials are bought in the month prior to the month in which they are used. 50% of purchases are paid for in the month of purchase. The remainder are paid for one month later.
- 30% of the production cost relates to direct labour which is paid for when it is used.
- The remainder of the production cost is production overhead. $5,000 per month is a fixed cost which includes $3,000 depreciation. Fixed production overhead costs are paid monthly in arrears. The remaining overhead is variable. The variable production overhead is paid 40% in the month of usage and the balance one month later.
- The administration and selling costs are paid quarterly in advance on 1 January, 1 April, 1 July and 1 October. The amount payable is $15,000 per quarter.
- Trade payables on 1 January Year 1 are expected to be:
  – Direct materials: $10,000
  – Production overheads: $11,000

- All sales are on credit. 20% of receivables are expected to be paid in the month of sale and 80% in the following month. Unpaid trade receivables at the beginning of January were $44,000.
- The company intends to purchase capital equipment costing $30,000 in February which will be payable in March.
- The bank balance on 1 January Year 1 is expected to be $5,000 overdrawn.

Required:

Prepare a cash budget for each of the months January to March Year 1 for Quest Company.

Preparing forecasts from a statement of financial position

Preparing a cash flow forecast from a balance sheet(Statement of financial position)

Used to predict the cash balance at the end of a given period, this method will typically require forecasts of:

- changes to non-current assets (acquisitions and disposals)
- future inventory levels
- future receivables levels
- future payables levels
- changes to share capital and other long-term funding (e.g. bank loans)
- changes to retained profits.

3 Using spreadsheets in cash forecasting

Many businesses prepare cash budgets and cash forecasts using a computer and spreadsheet software such as Excel®.

Spreadsheets are useful for cash forecasting for several important reasons:

- They **save time** in preparing forecasts. When the basic 'model' has been constructed, it is a relatively simple task to insert figures into the model, and leave it to the model to produce the completed forecast. The model, once established, can then be used whenever a new forecast is required.

- They are extremely useful for **sensitivity analysis**. When there is uncertainty in the forecast, the assumptions for the forecast can be changed and an alternative forecast produced. This allows management to consider a range of different possible outcomes, without needing much time or effort.
- Cash flow forecasts **can be consolidated**. For example, if the same spreadsheet model is used to prepare cash forecasts for each division or region in the company, a spreadsheet model can also automatically produce a consolidated cash flow forecast for the company as a whole.

More details

Sensitivity analysis

When budgets are prepared, there are a very large number of assumptions and estimates, for example the estimated sales each month, the estimates of costs, assumptions about when receivables will pay and when suppliers will be paid, and so on. Any of these estimates and assumptions could turn out to be inaccurate.

One of the enormous benefits of using spreadsheets to prepare a cash budget is that it is very easy to carry out sensitivity analysis.

Sensitivity analysis involves asking 'What if…?' questions, and finding out by how much the expected results will change if some of the forecasts or assumptions are altered.

For example, what if sales are 10% less than predicted, or what if capital expenditure is double the amount forecast? Depending on what the results of the analysis show, management might decide to take action to reduce the potential risks.

Consolidation

As well as being of assistance in preparing cash flow forecasts for individual business units, a computerised spreadsheet package may also be used to consolidate individual forecasts into one overall forecast for the organisation as a whole.

Individual forecasts may be prepared by:

- the various group companies
- individual operating units, e.g. branches of a retail store
- individual cost centres, e.g. stores, purchasing, production, service centres
- individual budget holders, e.g. marketing.

If all the individual forecasts are prepared using the same spreadsheet software, it will be possible for these to be uploaded to a central computer, programmed to produce a consolidated forecast.

4 Measures to improve a cash forecast situation

Introduction

An initial cash forecast might predict an unsatisfactory cash flow situation. The forecast might indicate that the company will have a cash deficit that cannot be met by existing short-term borrowing arrangements, such as a bank overdraft facility.

When this situation occurs, action will need to be taken to manage future cash flows in order to improve the forecast position. The nature of this management action will depend upon the answers to the following questions:

- Does the forecast indicate a continuing trend of an increasing surplus or an increasing cash deficit, or do net monthly balances move between surplus and deficit on a seasonal basis?
- What size of cash surpluses are forecast (if any) and for how long will they be available?
- Are the forecast cash deficits within the current overdraft facility?
- Which cash flows are to some extent discretionary, either in size or timing?

Cash deficits can arise from:

- Basic trading factors underlying the business, such as falling sales or increasing costs. To correct these, normal business measures need to be taken. Sales may be improved by increased marketing activity or revised pricing policies. Cost cutting exercises may also be necessary.

- Short-term deficiencies in the working capital cycle, such as an exceptionally long average holding period for inventory or a long average time to pay by credit customers.

Possible decisions that could be taken to deal with forecast short-term cash deficits include:

- additional short-term borrowing
- negotiating a higher overdraft limit with the bank
- the sale of short-term investments, if the company has any
- using different forms of financing to reduce cash flows in the short term, such as leasing instead of buying outright
- changing the amount of discretionary cash flows, deferring expenditures or bringing forward revenues. For example:
  - reducing the dividend to shareholders
  - postponing non-essential capital expenditure
  - bringing forward the planned disposal of non-current assets
  - reducing inventory levels, perhaps incorporating 'just-in-time' techniques (although this will take time to implement)
  - shortening the operating cycle by reducing the time taken to collect receivables, perhaps by offering a discount or using a factor or invoice discounting. (The management of trade receivables is dealt with more fully in a later chapter.)
  - shortening the operating cycle by delaying payment to payables.

Dealing with surpluses

If the forecast shows cash surpluses, these will be dealt with according to their size and duration. Management should consider a policy for how surplus cash should be invested so as to achieve a return on the money, but without investing in items where the risk of a fall in value is considered too high. The interest or other return earned can be used to improve the overall cash position. Care must be taken to ensure these investments can be realised as needed, to fund forecast deficits.

Where long-term cash surpluses are forecast, management might consider other possible uses of the surpluses, such as paying a higher dividend or repaying loans and other debts.

5 Chapter summary

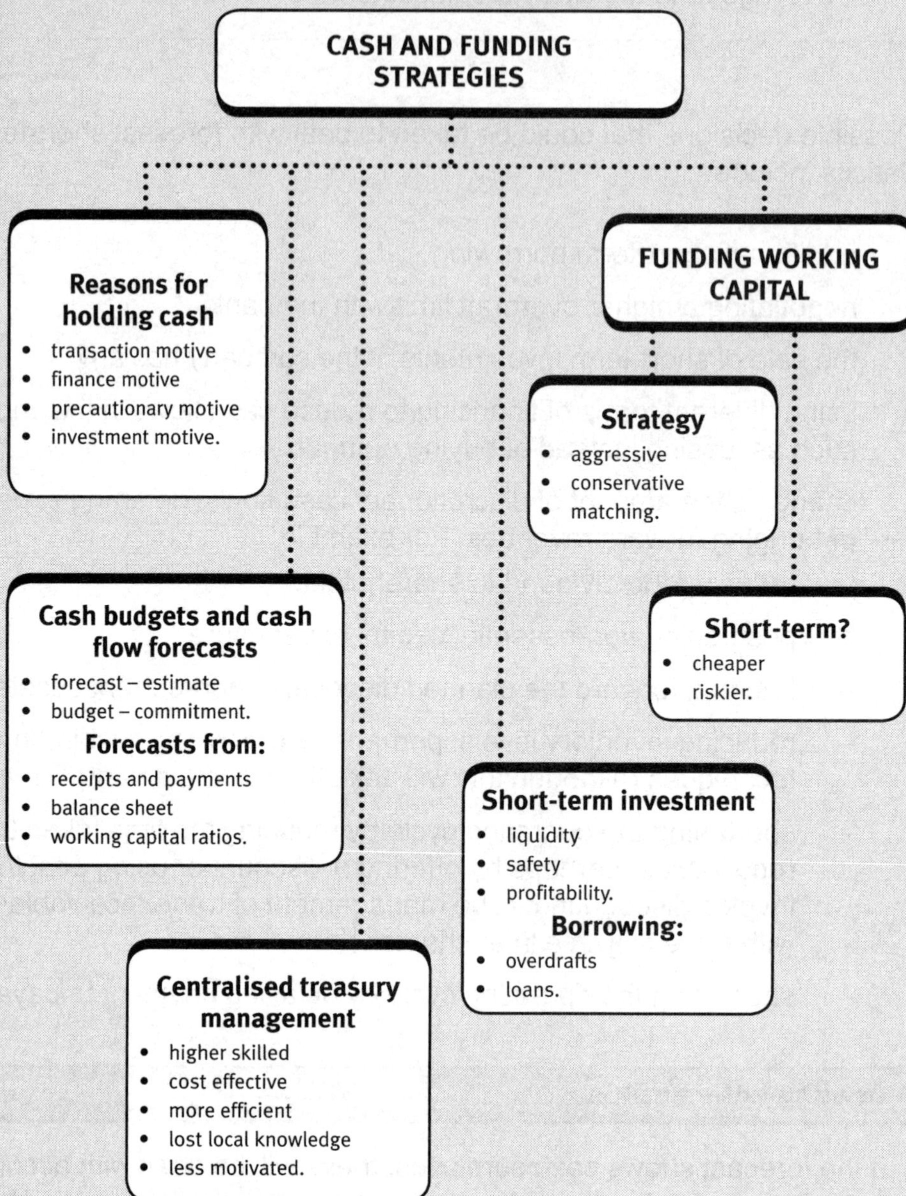

6 Practice questions

Test your understanding 1

A business has estimated that 10% of its sales will be cash sales, and the remainder credit sales. It is also estimated that 50% of credit customers will pay in the month following sale, 30% two months after sale, 15% three months after sale and bad debts will be 5% of credit sales.

Total sales figures are as follows:

Month	$
October	80,000
November	60,000
December	40,000
January	50,000
February	60,000
March	90,000

Required:

Prepare a month-by-month budget of cash receipts from sales for the months January to March.

Test your understanding 2

Winters Company expects 75% of sales to be collected in the month of sale, 20% in the month following and 5% to be bad debts. At 31 December 20X4, $50,000 of December's sales are still outstanding receivables.

Identify receipts in January from sales in December:

A 10,000

B 20,000

C 37,500

D 40,000

Test your understanding 3

A company sells a range of services, all on credit. Customers on average pay as follows:

	%
In month after sale	30
Two months after sale	65

The organisation expects a bad debt rate of 5%.

At 1 January Year 2, opening trade receivables were $322,200, before deducting any allowance for doubtful debts. Sales in December Year 1 were $213,000.

Required:

Calculate the receipts from the opening trade receivables in January Year 2 and in February Year 2

(5 marks)

Test your understanding 4

You are given the following budgeted information about an organisation:

	January	February	March
Opening inventory in units	100	150	120
Closing inventory in units	150	120	180
Sales in units	400	450	420

The cost of materials is $2 per unit. 40% of purchases are paid for immediately in cash. 60% of purchases are on credit and are paid two months after the purchase.

Required:

Calculate the budgeted payments in March for purchases of materials.

(5 marks)

Test your understanding 5

In the near future a company will purchase a manufacturing business for $315,000, this price to include goodwill ($150,000), equipment and fittings ($120,000), and inventory of raw materials and finished goods ($45,000).

A delivery van will be purchased for $15,000 as soon as the business purchase is completed. The delivery van will be paid for in the second month of operations.

The following forecasts have been made for the business following purchase:

I Sales (before discounts) of the business's single product, at a mark-up of 60% on production cost will be:

Month	1	2	3	4	5	6
($000)	96	96	92	96	100	104

25% of sales will be for cash; the remainder will be on credit, for settlement in the month following that of sale. A discount of 10% will be given to selected credit customers, who represent 25% of gross sales.

II Production cost will be $5 per unit. The production cost will be made up of:

Raw materials	$2.50
Direct labour	$1.50
Fixed overhead	$1.00

III Production will be arranged so that closing inventory at the end of any month is sufficient to meet sales requirements in the following month. A value of $30,000 is placed on the inventory of finished goods, which was acquired on purchase of the business. This valuation is based on the forecast of production cost per unit given in (ii) above.

IV The single raw material will be purchased so that inventory at the end of a month is sufficient to meet half of the following month's production requirements. Raw material inventory acquired on purchase of the business ($15,000) is valued at the cost per unit that is forecast as given in (ii) above. Raw materials will be purchased on one month's credit.

V Costs of direct labour will be met as they are incurred in production.

VI The fixed production overhead rate of $1.00 per unit is based upon a forecast of the first year's production of 150,000 units. This rate includes depreciation of equipment and fittings on a straight-line basis over the next five years. Fixed production overhead is paid in the month incurred.

VII Selling and administration overheads are all fixed, and will be $208,000 in the first year. These overheads include depreciation of the delivery van at 30% pa on a reducing balance basis. All fixed overheads will be incurred on a regular basis, and paid in the month incurred, with the exception of rent and rates. $25,000 is payable for the year ahead in month one for rent and rates.

A **Prepare a monthly cash flow forecast. You should include the business purchase and the first four months of operations following purchase.**

B **Calculate the inventory, receivables, and payables balances at the end of the four-month period. Describe briefly the liquidity situation.**

Test your understanding 6

Thorne Co values, advertises and sells residential property on behalf of its customers. The company has been in business for only a short time and is preparing a cash budget for the first four months of 2006. Expected sales of residential properties are as follows.

	2005	**2006**	**2006**	**2006**	**2006**
Month	December	January	February	March	April
Units sold	10	10	15	25	30

The average price of each property is $180,000 and Thorne Co charges a fee of 3% of the value of each property sold. Thorne Co receives 1% in the month of sale and the remaining 2% in the month after sale. The company has nine employees who are paid on a monthly basis. The average salary per employee is $35,000 per year. If more than 20 properties are sold in a given month, each employee is paid in that month a bonus of $140 for each additional property sold.

Variable expenses are incurred at the rate of 0.5% of the value of each property sold and these expenses are paid in the month of sale. Fixed overheads of $4,300 per month are paid in the month in which they arise. Thorne Co pays interest every three months on a loan of $200,000 at a rate of 6% per year. The last interest payment in each year is paid in December.

An outstanding tax liability of $95,800 is due to be paid in April. In the same month Thorne Co intends to dispose of surplus vehicles, with a net book value of $15,000, for $20,000. The cash balance at the start of January 2006 is expected to be a deficit of $40,000.

Required:

Prepare a monthly cash budget for the period from January to April 2006. Your budget must clearly indicate each item of income and expenditure, and the opening and closing monthly cash balances.

(10 marks)

Test your understanding 7

Zed Co has the following balance sheet(Statement of financial position) at 30 June 20X3:

	$	$
Non-current assets:		
Plant and machinery		192,000
Current assets:		
Inventory	16,000	
Receivables	80,000	
Bank	2,000	
		98,000
Total assets		290,000
Equity and liabilities:		
Issued share capital		216,000
Retained profits		34,000
		250,000
Current liabilities		
Trade payables	10,000	
Dividend payable	30,000	
		40,000
Total equity and liabilities		290,000

(a) The company expects to acquire further plant and machinery costing $8,000 during the year to 30 June 20X4.

(b) The levels of inventories and receivables are expected to increase by 5% and 10% respectively by 30 June 20X4, due to business growth.

(c) Trade payables and dividend liabilities are expected to be the same at 30 June 20X4.

(d) No share issue is planned, and retained profits for the year to 30 June 20X4 are expected to be $42,000.

(e) Plant and machinery is depreciated on a reducing balance basis, at the rate of 20% pa, for all assets held at the balance sheet date.

Prepare a balance sheet forecast as at 30 June 20X4, and identify what the cash balance or bank overdraft will be at that date.

Test your understanding 8

Identify which of the following is unsuitable as a cash flow to be deferred to avoid a temporary cash shortage:

A Replacement of office furniture

B Investment in a short-term cash deposit

C Investment in a long-term strategic expansion

D Dividend payment (deferral agreed by the shareholders)

Test your understanding answers

Example 1 - FORECAST CASH RECEIPTS

Cash from:		$
April sales:	10% × $5,000	500
March sales:	40% × $4,000	1,600
February sales:	45% × $8,000	3,600
		5,700

Example 2 - FORECAST CASH PAYMENTS

When inventories of raw materials are increased, the quantities purchased will exceed the quantities consumed in the period.

Figures for December are shown because December purchases will be paid for in January, which is in the budget period.

Quantity of raw material purchased in units:

		Material (@ 2 units per widget)			
	Units of widgets produced	**December**	**January**	**February**	**March**
	Units	Units	Units	Units	Units
December	50,000	100,000			
January	55,000		110,000		
February	60,000			120,000	
March	65,000				130,000
Increase in inventories		–	10,000	10,000	–
Total purchase quantities		100,000	120,000	130,000	130,000
At $3 per unit		300,000	360,000	390,000	390,000

Having established the purchases each month, we can go on to budget the amount of cash payments to suppliers each month. Here, the business will take one month's credit.

	January	February	March
	$	$	$
Payment to suppliers	300,000	360,000	390,000

At the end of March, there will be payables of $390,000 for raw materials purchased, which will be paid in April.

Example 3 - FULL CASH FLOW FORECAST

We can take each item of cash flow in turn, and use workings tables to calculate what the monthly cash flows are.

(W1) Cash from sales

	Total sales	Cash reciepts January	Cash receipts February	Cash Receipts March
	$	$	$	$
Opening receivables		44,000	-	-
January	60,000	12,000	48,000	-
February	50,000	-	10,000	40,000
March	70,000	-	-	14,000
		56,000	58,000	54,000

(W2) Payments for materials purchases

Material purchases are made in the month prior to the month in which they are used, so the starting point for working out materials purchases and payments for the purchases is the production costs in each month.

	January $	**February** $	**March** $	**April** $
Total cost of production	50,000	55,000	32,500	50,000
Material cost of production (40%)	20,000	22,000	13,000	20,000
Purchases in the month	22,000	13,000	20,000	unknown

Payments are made 50% in the month of purchase and 50% in the following month. The trade payables at 1 January will all be paid in January, since these represent 50% of material purchases in December.

	Purchases $	**January** $	**February** $	**March** $
Opening payables for materials		10,000		
January	22,000	11,000	11,000	-
February	13,000	-	6,500	6,500
March	20,000	-	-	10,000
Total payments		21,000	17,500	16,500

(W3) Payments for overheads

In this example, we have to separate fixed and variable overheads. Total overhead costs are 30% of production costs (100% -40% direct materials -30% direct labour).

	January $	February $	March $
Total cost of production	50,000	55,000	32,500
Overhead cost of production (30%)	15,000	16,500	9,750
Fixed costs	(5,000)	(5,000)	(5,000)
Variable overhead costs	10,000	11,500	4,750

Of the monthly fixed overhead costs of $5,000, $3,000 is depreciation which is not a cash expenditure. Monthly fixed cost cash expenditure is therefore $2,000.

The opening balance of unpaid overhead costs at the beginning of January must consist of $2,000 fixed overheads and $9,000 (the balance) variable overheads. All these costs should be paid for in January. Variable overheads are paid 40% in the month of expenditure and 60% the following month.

Fixed overheads	Cost $	January $	February $	March $
Opening payables for fixed overheads		2,000		
January	2,000	-	2,000	-
February	2,000	-	-	2,000
March	2,000	-	-	-
Total payments		2,000	2,000	2,000

Variable overheads	Cost $	January $	February $	March $
Opening payables for variable overheads		9,000		
January	10,000	4,000	6,000	-
February	11,500	-	4,600	6,900
March	4,750	-	-	1,900
Total payments		13,000	10,600	8,800

The other items of cash flow are straightforward, although it is important to notice that the payments for administration and selling overheads are paid quarterly, and the cash payment ($15,000) is not the same as the total overhead cost for the quarter. Presumably there are depreciation charges within the total costs given.

Payments for direct labour are 30% of direct labour costs (= 30% of production costs) in the month.

The cash budget can be prepared as follows:

	January $	February $	March $
Receipts			
From sales	56,000	58,000	54,000
Payments			
Capital expenditure	-	-	30,000
For direct materials	21,000	18,000	16,500
For direct labour	15,000	10,500	9,750
For fixed production overheads	2,000	2,000	2,000
For variable production overheads	13,000	14,875	8,800
For admin/selling overhead	15,000	–	–
Total outflow	66,000	72,750	67,050
Net cash flow for month	(10,000)	11,400	(13,050)
Opening balance	(5,000)	(15,000)	(3,600)
Closing balance	(15,000)	(3,600)	(16,650)

Analysis

The company will be overdrawn throughout the three-month period, therefore it is essential that it should have access to borrowings to cover the shortfall. The bank might already have agreed an overdraft facility, but this should be at least $16,650 and ideally higher, to allow for the possibility that the actual cash flows will be even worse than budgeted.

Test your understanding 1

Sales month	Total sales $	Cash reciepts January $	Cash receipts February $	Cash receipts March $
October	80,000	10,800	-	-
November	60,000	16,200	8,100	-
December	40,000	18,000	10,800	5,400
January	50,000	5,000	22,500	13,500
February	60,000	-	6,000	27,000
March	90,000	-	-	9,000
Total Receipts		50,000	47,400	54,900

Test your understanding 2

The correct answer is **D.**

$50,000 represents 25% of December sales (100% – 75%).

Total sales in December were therefore $5,000/25% = $200,000.

Expected amount to be received in January = 20% × $200,000 = $40,000.

Test your understanding 3

The trade receivables at the beginning of January Year 2 represent 100% of sales in December Year 1 and the unpaid receivables for sales in November Year 1. They can be analysed as follows:

	$
Total trade receivables	322,200
Consisting of:	
100% of sales for December Year 1	(213,000)
Unpaid amounts for sales in November Year 1	109,200

The unpaid amounts from November Year 1 represent 70% of total sales in that month, because 30% pay in the month following sale (December Year 1).

It therefore follows that total sales in November Year 1 were $109,200/70% = $156,000.

Sales month	**Total sales**		**Cash receipts January**		**Cash receipts February**
	$		$		$
November	156,000	65%	101,400	-	-
December	213,000	30%	63,900	65%	138,450
			165,300		138,450

Test your understanding 4

Purchases	January units	February units	March units
Sales qquantity	400	450	420
Less:opening inventory	(100)	(150)	(120)
Add: closing inventory	150	120	180
Production in units = units purchased	450	420	480
Cost of purchase @ $2 per unitr	*$900*	$840	$960

Payments in March		$
For January purchases	(60% of $900)	540
For March purchases	(40% of $960)	384
Total payments for materials		924

Test your understanding 5

A **Monthly cash budget**

	Month 1	Month 2	Month 3	Month 4
	$	$	$	$
Cash inflows:				
Cash sales	24,000	24,000	23,000	24,000
Credit sales		72,000	72,000	69,000
Less: Discounts		(2,400)	(2,400)	(2,300)
Total inflow	24,000	93,600	92,600	90,700
Cash outflows:				
Purchases **(W1)**	–	44,375	29,375	30,625
Labour **(W1)**	27,000	17,250	18,000	18,750
Production overhead **(W2)**	10,500	10,500	10,500	10,500
Selling and administration overhead **(W3)**	39,875	14,875	14,875	14,875
Purchase of business	315,000	–	–	–
Purchase of van	–	15,000	–	–
Total outflow	392,375	102,000	72,750	74,750
Net cash flow for month	(368,375)	(8,400)	19,850	15,950
Opening balance	0	(368,375)	(376,775)	(356,925)
Closing balance	(368,375)	(376,775)	(356,925)	(340,975)

Workings (W1)

	Month 1	Month 2	Month 3	Month 4	Month 5	Month 6
Sales ($)	96,000	96,000	92,000	96,000	100,000	104,000
Sales units	12,000	12,000	11,500	12,000	12,500	13,000
+ Closing inventory	12,000	11,500	12,000	12,500	13,000	
– Opening inventory	6,000	12,000	11,500	12,000	12,500	13,000
Production (units)	18,000	11,500	12,000	12,500	13,000	
Raw material usage (Production × $2.50)	45,000	28,750	30,000	31,250	32,500	
+ Closing inventory	14,375	15,000	15,625	16,250		
– Opening inventory	15,000	14,375	15,000	15,625		
Purchases (one month delay)	44,375	29,375	30,625	31,875		
Labour cost (production × $1.50)	27,000	17,250	18,000	18,750		

(W2) – Production overheads

	$
Annual overheads (150,000 × $1)	150,000
Depreciation (120,000/5)	(24,000)
	126,000
Monthly cash outflow (126,000/12)	10,500

(W3) – Selling and administration overheads

Annual overheads	$
	208,000
Depreciation (15,000 × 0.3)	(4,500)
	203,500
Less: Rent and rates in month 1	25,000
Monthly cash outflow – months 2, 3, 4 (178500/12)	178,500
Month 1: 25,000 + 14,875	14,875
	39,875

B **Closing balances:**

Inventory:	$
Finished goods (12,500 × $5)	62,500
Raw materials	16,250
	78,750
Receivables:	
Month 4 credit sales (96,000 × 0.75)	72,000
Less: Discount (10% × 0.25 × 96,000)	(2,400)
	69,600
Payables	31,875

Apart from the purchase of the business, which will require separate long-term finance, the cash flow forecast suggests that there will be sufficient cash inflows to meet the cash outflows on an ongoing basis. The current assets and receivables provide sufficient funds to cover the payables.

Test your understanding 6

Cash budget for Thorne Co:

	January	February	March	April
Receipts	$	$	$	$
Cash fees	18,000	27,000	45,000	54,000
Credit fees	36,000	36,000	54,000	90,000
Sale of assets				20,000
Total receipts	54,000	63,000	99,000	164,000
Payments				
Salaries	26,250	26,250	26,250	26,250
Bonus			6,300	12,600
Expenses	9,000	13,500	22,500	27,000
Fixed overheads	4,300	4,300	4,300	4,300
Taxation				95,800
Interest			3,000	
Total payments	39,550	44,050	62,350	165,950
Net cash flow	14,450	18,950	36,650	(1,950)
Opening balance	(40,000)	(25,550)	(6,600)	30,050
Closing balance	(25,550)	(6,600)	30,050	28,100

Workings

Month	**December**	**January**	**February**	**March**	**April**
Units sold	10	10	15	25	30
Sales value ($000)	1,800	1,800	2,700	4,500	5,400
Cash fees at 1% ($)	18,000	18,000	27,000	45,000	54,000
Credit fees at 2% ($)	36,000	36,000	54,000	90,000	108,000
Variable costs at 0·5% ($)		9,000	13,500	22,500	27,000

Monthly salary cost = (35,000 × 9)/12 = $26,250

Bonus for March = (25 – 20) × 140 × 9 = $6,300 Bonus for April = (30 – 20) × 140 × 9 = $12,600.

Test your understanding 7

Zed Co – Balance sheet (Statement of financial position) at 30 June 20X4

	$	$	$
Non-current assets:			
Plant and machinery[(192,000 + 8,000) × 80%]			160,000
Current assets:			
Inventory (16,000 × 105%)		16,800	
Receivables (80,000 × 110%)		88,000	
Bank (balancing figure)		67,200	
			172,000
Total assets			332,000
Equity and liabilities			
Issued share capital			216,000
Retained profits (34,000 + 42,000)			76,000
			292,000
Current liabilities:			
Trade payables		10,000	
Dividend payable		30,000	
			40,000
Total equity and liabilities			332,000

The forecast is that the bank balance will increase by $65,200 (i.e. $67,200 – $2,000). This can be reconciled as follows:

	$	$
Retained profit		42,000
Add: Depreciation (20% of ($192,000 + $8,000))		40,000
		82,000
Less: Non-current asset acquired		(8,000)
		74,000
Increase in inventory	800	
Increase in receivables	8,000	
		(8,800)
Increase in cash balance		65,200

Test your understanding 8

The correct answer is **B**.

A short-term deposit is a cash equivalent. Deferring the transfer of cash to a short-term deposit will not deal with the problem of a temporary cash shortage, because it will usually be possible to withdraw the cash from deposit on demand, for the loss of some or all of the interest.

chapter

18

Working capital management – accounts receivable and payable

Chapter learning objectives

Lead	Component
E1. Analyse the working capital position and identify areas for improvement.	(e) Analyse trade debtor and creditor information. (f) Analyse the impacts of alternative debtor and creditor policies.

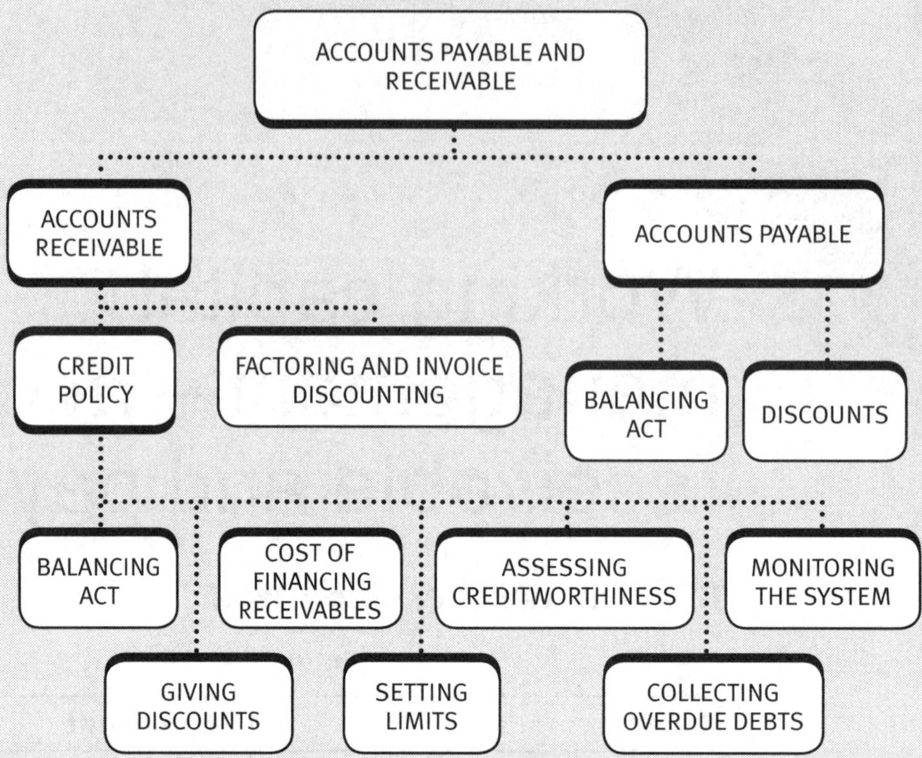

1 Accounts receivable – establishing a credit policy

The balancing act

Management must establish a credit policy. The optimum level of trade credit extended represents a balance between two factors:

- profit improvement from sales obtained by allowing credit
- the cost of credit allowed.

Why have a credit policy?

A firm must establish a policy for credit terms given to its customers. Ideally the firm would want to obtain cash with each order delivered, but that is impossible unless substantial settlement (or cash) discounts are offered as an inducement. It must be recognised that credit terms are part of the firm's marketing policy. If the trade or industry has adopted a common practice, then it is probably wise to keep in step with it.

A lenient credit policy may well attract additional customers, but at a disproportionate increase in cost.

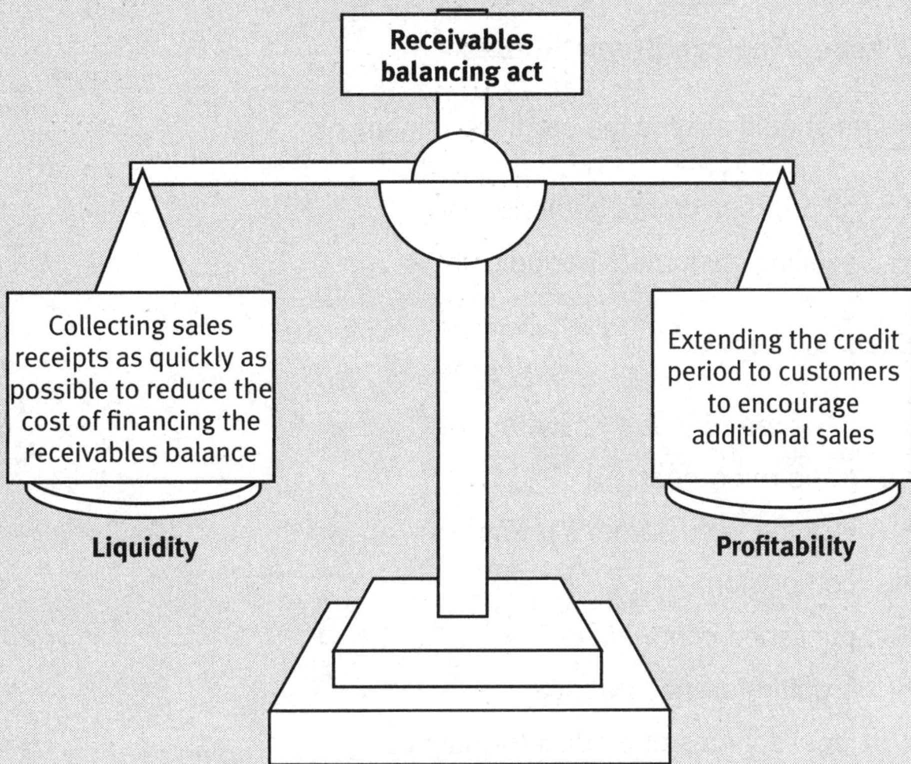

Remember this trade-off is a key factor in determining the company's working capital investment.

For accounts receivable, the company's policy will be influenced by:

- demand for products
- competitors' terms
- risk of irrecoverable debts
- financing costs
- costs of credit control.

Receivables management has four key aspects:

(1) Assessing creditworthiness.

(2) Setting credit limits.

(3) Invoicing promptly and collecting overdue debts.

(4) Monitoring the credit system.

This is a useful structure to adopt for examination questions that ask about the management of receivables.

2 Assessing creditworthiness

A firm should assess the creditworthiness of:

- all new customers immediately
- existing customers periodically.

Information may come from:

- bank references
- trade references
- visit to the customer's premises
- competitors
- published information
- credit reference agencies
- legal sources of credit information
- company sales records
- credit scoring
- credit rating (large corporate customrs only).

Assessing creditworthiness

To minimise the risk of irrecoverable debts occurring, a company should investigate the creditworthiness of all new customers (credit risk), and should review that of existing customers from time to time, especially if they request that their credit limit should be raised. Information about a customer's credit rating can be obtained from a variety of sources.

These include:

- Bank references – A customer's permission must be sought. These tend to be fairly standardised in the UK, and so are not perhaps as helpful as they could be.
- Trade references – Suppliers already giving credit to the customer can give useful information about how good the customer is at paying bills on time. There is a danger that the customer will only nominate those suppliers that are being paid on time.
- Visit to the customer's premises – A sales representative might visit the business premises of the customer. A visit will provide information about the actual 'physical' operations and assets of the customer, and might provide some reassurance that the customer's business has substance.

- Competitors – in some industries such as insurance, competitors share information on customers, including creditworthiness.
- Published information – The customer's own annual accounts and reports will give some idea of the general financial position of the company and its liquidity.
- Credit reference agencies – Agencies such as Dunn & Bradstreet publish general financial details of many companies, together with a credit rating. They will also produce a special report on a company if requested. The information is provided for a fee.
- Legal sources of credit information – Instead of using a credit reference agency, a company might check available legal records itself to find out whether the customer has a history of insolvency or non-payment. For example, in the UK information can be obtained from the Register of County Court Judgements and from the Individual Insolvency Register.
- Company's own sales records – For an existing customer, the sales ledgers will show how prompt a payer the company is, although they cannot show the ability of the customer to pay.
- Credit scoring – Indicators such as family circumstances, home ownership, occupation and age can be used to predict likely creditworthiness. This is useful when extending credit to the public where little other information is available. A variety of software packages is available which can assist with credit scoring.
- Large corporate customers only: credit rating – Very large companies might have a credit rating from one of the major credit rating agencies, Moody's and Standard & Poors. A supplier might use a company's credit rating to decide how much credit to allow, without having to carry out a detailed credit check itself.

3 Setting credit limits

Credit limits should be set to reflect both the:

- amount of credit available
- length of time allowed before payment is due.

The ledger account should be monitored to take account of orders in the pipeline as well as invoiced sales, before further credit is given.

Managing existing customers

A company might have a system for monitoring the credit status of existing customers. If the customer appears to be a lower credit risk than initially thought, the company might be prepared to offer a higher credit limit. If the customer's credit status does not improve, a request for more credit from the customer should be refused.

The credit status of existing customers should be based on:

- the customer's payment record and history of prompt or late payments, and
- any new information that is obtained about the customer, for example from its most recent annual financial statements.

Example

A company might group its existing customers into six categories, as follows:

Customer categories

	Financially strong	*Financially stable*	*Financially weak*
Prompt payer	Category A	Category B	Category C
Late payer	Category D	Category E	Category F

The amount of credit offered to the customer (and possibly also the payment terms) would vary according to the category of the customer. If a customer moves from one category to a stronger category, a higher credit limit would be allowed if required.

4 Invoicing and collecting overdue debts

A credit period only begins once an invoice is received so prompt invoicing is essential. If debts go overdue, the risk of default increases, therefore a system of follow-up procedures is required:

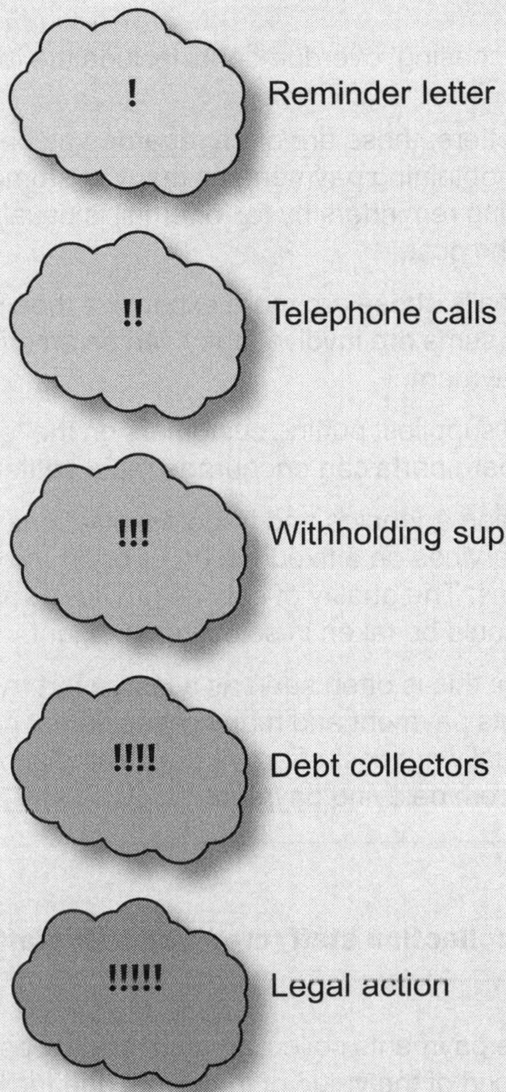

Invoicing and collecting overdue debts

The longer a debt is allowed to run, the higher the probability of eventual default. A system of follow-up procedures is required, bearing in mind the risk of offending a valued customer to such an extent that their business is lost.

Techniques for 'chasing' overdue debts include the following:

- Reminder letters: these are often regarded as being a relatively poor way of obtaining payment, as many customers simply ignore them. Sending reminders by fax or email is usually more productive than using the post.
- Telephone calls: these are more expensive than reminder letters but where large sums are involved they can be an efficient way of speeding payment.
- Withholding supplies: putting customers on the 'stop list' for further orders or spare parts can encourage rapid settlement of debts.
- Debt collection agencies and trade associations: these offer debt collection services on a fixed fee basis or on 'no collection no charge' terms. The quality of service provided varies considerably and care should be taken in selecting an agent.
- Legal action: this is often seen as a last resort. A solicitor's letter often prompts payment and many cases do not go to court. Court action is usually not cost effective but it can discourage other customers from delaying payment.

Motivating debt collection staff (credit control staff): collection targets

If employees in the payments collection team are to operate effectively, they need to be convinced of the value of their work and their contribution to the objectives of the organisation. One way of improving performance and increasing staff motivation might be to set collection targets. A collection target is a target for the amount of payments to collect for trade receivables within a given period of time. Targets can be set for:

- individual members of the collection team, and
- the credit control team as a whole.

Targets for collection will not be a motivator, however, unless performance is assessed and individuals are rewarded (with a bonus) on the basis of meeting or exceeding targets.

Example 1 - COLLECTION TARGETS

At the end of March, the trade receivables of M were as follows:

		$
From March sales	(100% of sales in the month)	1,200,000
From February sales	(70% of sales in the month)	700,000
From January sales	(30% of sales in the month)	270,000
		2,170,000

This represents an average of 60 days' sales outstanding, made up as follows:

		Days
From March sales	(100% x 31 days)	31
From February sales	(70% x 28 days)	20
From January sales	(30% x 31 days)	9
		60

The company wants to reduce its average days sales outstanding from 60 days to 50 days by the end of April. Sales in April are expected to be $1,100,000, all on credit. It intends to do this by aiming to collect payments of the oldest outstanding receivables.

Requirement:

Calculate the collection target that should be set for staff.

5 Monitoring the system

The position of receivables should be regularly reviewed as part of managing overall working capital and corrective action taken when needed. Methods include:

- age analysis
- ratios
- statistical data.

Monitoring the system

Management will require regular information to take corrective action and to measure the impact of giving credit on working capital investment. Typical management reports on the credit system will include the following points.

- Age analysis of outstanding debts.

  The analysis shows for how long the current trade receivables have been outstanding. The information can help management to decide on its policies or tactics for trying to collect overdue payments. For example, management might decide that it is not worth the effort for the moment to try collecting debts over four months old, and the immediate collection effort should focus instead on debts between three and four months old.

  The analysis might also list the unpaid amounts within each time band, so that the collection staff know which specific customers and unpaid debts they should be working on.
- Ratios, compared with the previous period or target, to indicate trends in credit levels and the incidence of overdue and irrecoverable debts.
- Statistical data to identify causes of default and the incidence of irrecoverable debts among different classes of customer and types of trade.

6 Accounts receivable - calculations

Costs of financing receivables

Key working:

$$\text{Finance cost} = \text{Receivable balance} \times \text{Interest (overdraft) rate}$$

$$\downarrow$$

$$\text{Receivable balance} = \text{Sales} \times \frac{\text{Receivable days}}{365}$$

Example 2 - COST OF FINANCING RECEIVABLES

Paisley Co has sales of $20 million for the previous year, receivables at the year end were $4 million, and the cost of financing receivables is covered by an overdraft at the interest rate of 12% pa.

Required:

(a) calculate the receivables days for Paisley

(b) calculate the annual cost of financing receivables.

Early settlement discounts

Cash discounts are given to encourage early payment by customers. The cost of the discount is balanced against the savings the company receives from having less capital tied up due to a lower receivables balance and a shorter average collection period. Discounts may also reduce the number of irrecoverable debts.

The calculation of the annual cost can be expressed as a formula:

$$\text{Annual cost of discount} = \left[1 + \frac{\text{discount}}{\text{amount left to pay}}\right]^{\text{no.of periods}} - 1$$

$$\text{where no. of periods} = \frac{365 / 52 / 12}{\text{no. of days / weeks / months earlier the money is received.}}$$

Notice that the annual cost calculation is always based on the amount left to pay, i.e. the amount net of discount.

If the cost of offering the discount exceeds the rate of overdraft interest then the discount should not be offered.

Example 3 - EARLY SETTLEMENT DISCOUNTS

Paisley Co has sales of $20 million for the previous year, receivables at the year end of $4 million and the cost of financing receivables is covered by an overdraft at the interest rate of 12% pa. It is now considering offering a cash discount of 2% for payment of debts within 10 days. Calculate whether the new policy should be introduced if 40% of customers will take up the discount?

7 Accounts receivable - factoring

Factoring is the outsourcing of the credit control department to a third party.

The debts of the company are effectively sold to a factor (normally owned by a bank). The factor takes on the responsibility of collecting the debt for a fee. The company can choose some or all of the following three services offered by the factor:

(1) debt collection and administration – recourse or non-recourse

(2) financing

(3) credit insurance.

These are of particular value to:

- smaller firms
- fast growing firms.

Make sure you can discuss the various services offered and remember that non-recourse factoring is more expensive as the factor bears the costs of any irrecoverable debts.

More details

Debt collection and administration – the factor takes over the whole of the company's sales ledger, issuing invoices and collecting debts.

Financing provision – in addition to the above, the factor will advance up to 80% of the value of a debt to the company; the remainder (minus finance costs) being paid when the debts are collected. The factor becomes a source of finance. Finance costs are usually 1.5% to 3% above bank base rate and charged on a daily basis.

Credit insurance – the factor agrees to insure the irrecoverable debts of the client. The factor would then determine to whom the company was able to offer credit.

Some companies realise that, although it is necessary to extend trade credit to customers for competitive reasons, they need payment earlier than agreed in order to assist their own cash flow. Factors exist to help such companies.

Factoring is most suitable for:

- small and medium-sized firms which often cannot afford sophisticated credit and sales accounting systems, and

- firms that are expanding rapidly. These often have a substantial and growing investment in inventory and receivables, which can be turned into cash by factoring the debts. Factoring debts can be a more flexible source of financing working capital than an overdraft or bank loan.

Factoring is primarily designed to allow companies to accelerate cash flow, providing finance against outstanding trade receivables. This improves cash flow and liquidity.

Factoring can be arranged on either a 'without recourse' basis or a 'with recourse' basis.

- When factoring is without recourse or 'non-recourse', the factor provides protection for the client against irrecoverable debts. The factor has no 'comeback' or recourse to the client if a customer defaults. When a customer of the client fails to pay a debt, the factor bears the loss and the client receives the money from the debt.
- When the service is with recourse ('recourse factoring'), the client must bear the loss from any irrecoverable debt, and so has to reimburse the factor for any money it has already received for the debt.

Credit protection is provided only when the service is non-recourse and this is obviously more costly.

Typical factoring arrangements

Administration and debt collection

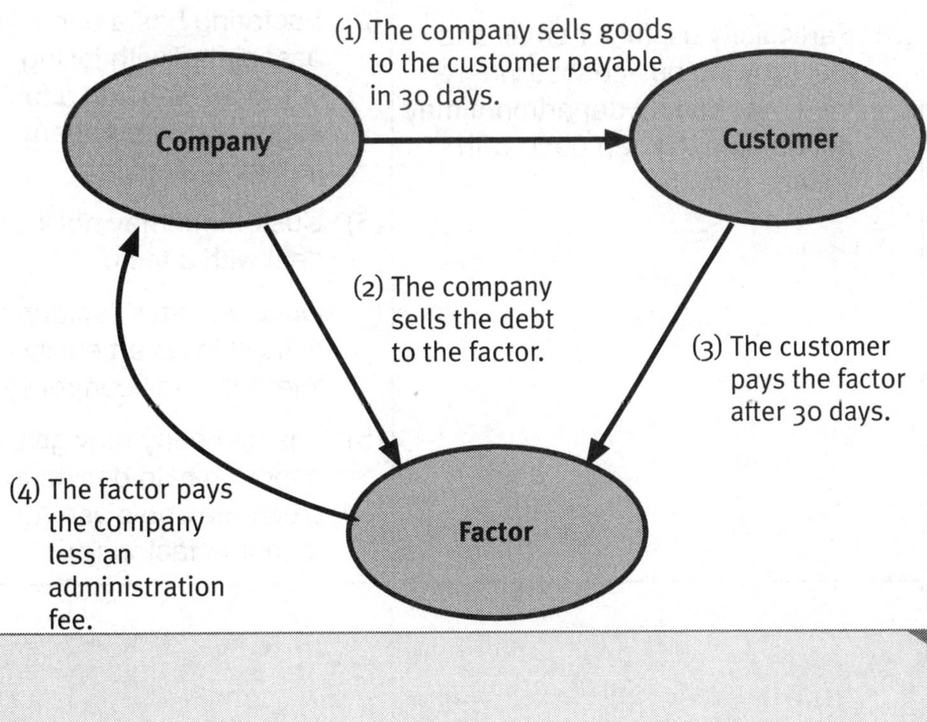

Including financing

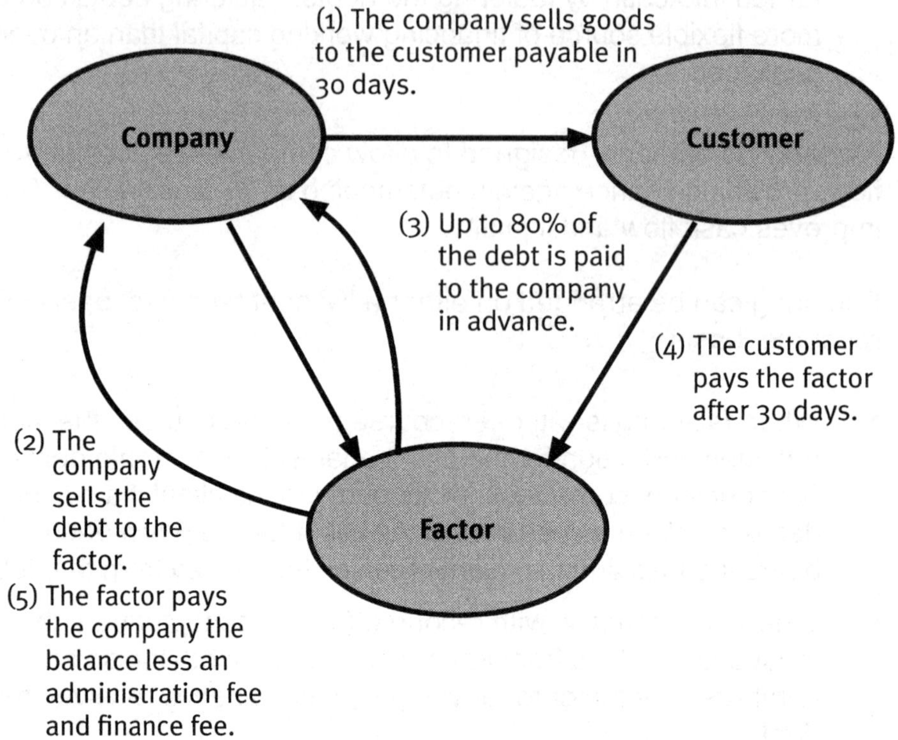

Advantages	Disadvantages
(1) Saving in administration costs. (2) Reduction in the need for management control. (3) Particularly useful for small and fast growing businesses where the credit control department may not be able to keep pace with volume growth.	(1) Likely to be more costly than an efficiently run internal credit control department. (2) Factoring has a bad reputation associated with failing companies; using a factor may suggest your company has money worries. (3) Customers may not wish to deal with a factor. (4) Once you start factoring it is difficult to revert easily to an internal credit control system. (5) The company may give up the opportunity to decide to whom credit may be given (non-recourse factoring).

Benefits and problems with factoring

The benefits of factoring are as follows.

- A business improves its cash flow, because the factor provides finance for up to 80% or more of debts within 24 hours of the invoices being issued. A bank providing an overdraft facility secured against a company's unpaid invoices will normally only lend up to 50% of the invoice value. (Factors will provide 80% or so because they set credit limits and are responsible for collecting the debts.)
- A factor saves the company the administration costs of keeping the sales ledger up to date and the costs of debt collection.
- A business can use the factor's credit control system to assess the creditworthiness of both new and existing customers.
- Non-recourse factoring is a convenient way of obtaining insurance against irrecoverable debts.

Problems with factoring.

- Although factors provide valuable services, companies are sometimes wary about using them. A possible problem with factoring is that the intervention of the factor between the factor's client and the debtor company could endanger trading relationships and damage goodwill. Customers might prefer to deal with the business, not a factor.
- When a non-recourse factoring service is used, the client loses control over decisions about granting credit to its customers.
- For this reason, some clients prefer to retain the risk of irrecoverable debts, and opt for a 'with recourse' factoring service. With this type of service, the client and not the factor decides whether extreme action (legal action) should be taken against a non-payer.
- On top of this, when suppliers and customers of the client find out that the client is using a factor to collect debts, it may arouse fears that the company is beset by cash flow problems, raising fears about its viability. If so, its suppliers may impose more stringent payment terms, thus negating the benefits provided by the factor.
- Using a factor can create problems with customers who may resent being chased for payment by a third party, and may question the supplier's financial stability.

Example 4 - FACTORING ARRANGEMENTS

Edden is a medium-sized company producing a range of engineering products, which it sells to wholesale distributors. Recently, its sales have begun to rise rapidly due to economic recovery. However, it is concerned about its liquidity position and is looking at ways of improving cash flow.

Its sales are $16 million pa, and average receivables are $3.3 million (representing about 75 days of sales).

One way of speeding up collection from receivables is to use a factor.

Required:

Cacualte the relative costs and benefits of using the factor in each of the following scenarios.

(a) The factor will operate on a service-only basis, administering and collecting payment from Edden's customers. This is expected to generate administrative savings of $100,000 each year.

The factor has undertaken to pay outstanding debts after 45 days, regardless of whether the customers have actually paid or not. The factor will make a service charge of 1.75% of Edden's turnover. Edden can borrow at an interest rate of 8% pa.

(b) It is now considering a factoring arrangement with a different factor where 80% of the book value of invoices is paid immediately, with finance costs charged on the advance at 10% pa.

Suppose that this factor will charge 1% of sales as their fee for managing the sales ledger, that there will be administrative savings of $100,000 as before, but that outstanding balances will be paid after 75 days (i.e. there is no change in the typical payment pattern by customers this time).

8 Accounts receivable – invoice discounting

Invoice discounting is a method of raising finance against the security of receivables without using the sales ledger administration services of a factor.

While specialist invoice discounting firms exist, this is a service also provided by a factoring company. Selected invoices are used as security against which the company may borrow funds. This is a temporary source of finance, repayable when the debt is cleared. The key advantage of invoice discounting is that it is a confidential service, and the customer need not know about it.

In some ways it is similar to the financing part of the factoring service without control of credit passing to the factor.

Ensure you can explain the difference between factoring and invoice discounting, and the situations where one may be more appropriate than the other.

Invoice discounting

Typical arrangement

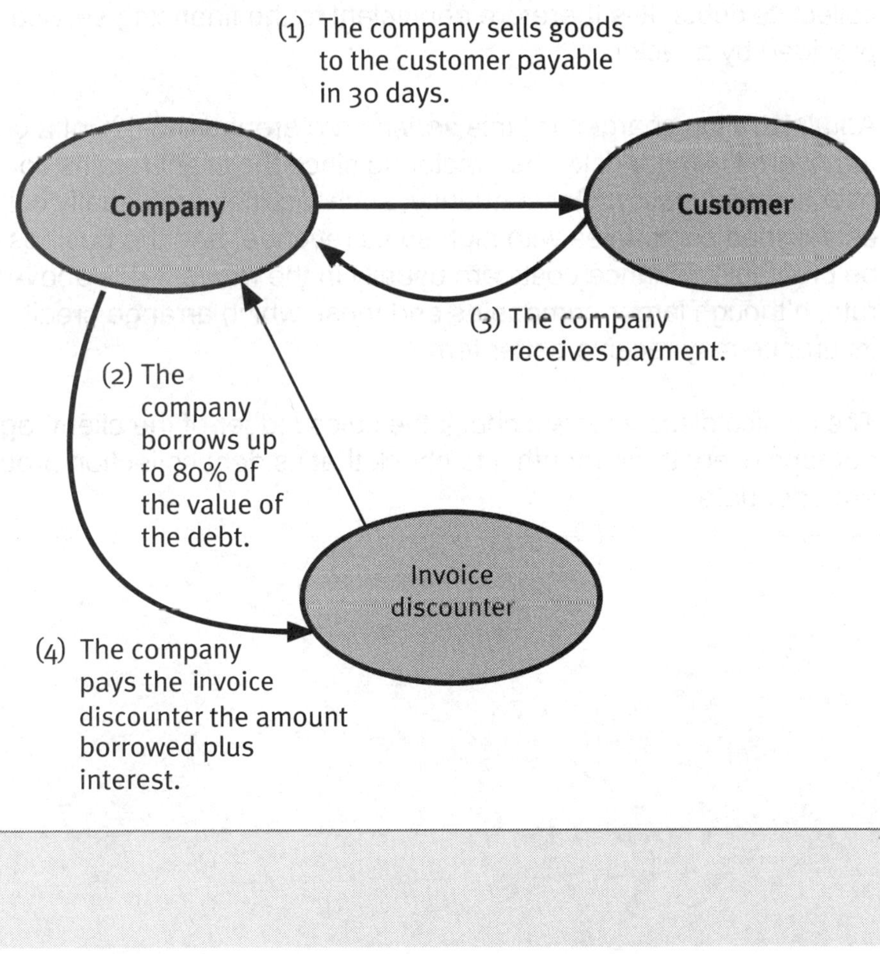

Invoice discounting is a method of raising finance against the security of receivables without using the sales ledger administration services of a factor. With invoice discounting, the business retains control over its sales ledger, and confidentiality in its dealings with customers. Firms of factors will also provide invoice discounting to clients.

The method works as follows:

- The business sends out invoices, statements and reminders in the normal way, and collects the debts. With 'confidential invoice discounting', its customers are unaware that the business is using invoice discounting.
- The invoice discounter provides cash to the business for a proportion of the value of the invoice, as soon as it receives a copy of the invoice and agrees to discount it. The discounter will advance cash up to 80% of face value.
- When the business eventually collects the payment from its customer, the money must be paid into a bank account controlled by the invoice discounter. The invoice discounter then pays the business the remainder of the invoice, less interest and administration charges.

Invoice discounting can help a business that is trying to improve its cash flows, but does not want a factor to administer its sales ledger and collect its debts. It is therefore equivalent to the financing service provided by a factor.

Administration charges for this service are around 0.5-1% of a client's turnover. It is more risky than factoring since the client retains control over its credit policy. Consequently, such facilities are usually confined to established companies with high sales revenue, and the business must be profitable. Finance costs are usually in the range 3-4% above base rate, although larger companies and those which arrange credit insurance may receive better terms.

The invoice discounter will check the sales ledger of the client regularly, perhaps every three months, to check that its debt collection procedures are adequate.

Illustration of the invoice discounting process

Illustration – Invoice discounting

At the beginning of August, Basildon plc sells goods for a total value of $300,000 to regular customers but decides that it requires payment earlier than the agreed 30-day credit period for these invoices.

A discounter agrees to finance 80% of their face value, i.e. $240,000, at an interest cost of 9% pa.

The invoices were due for payment in early September, but were subsequently settled in mid-September, exactly 45 days after the initial transactions. The invoice discounter's service charge is 1% of invoice value. A special account is set up with a bank, into which all payments are made.

The sequence of cash flows is:

August	Basildon receives cash advance of $240,000.	
Mid-September	Customers pay $300,000.	
	Invoice discounter receives the full $300,000 paid into the special bank account.	
	Basildon receives the balance payable, less charges, i.e.	
	Service fee = 1% × $300,000 =	$3,000
	Finance cost = 9% × $240,000 × 45/365 =	$2,663
	Total charges	$5,663
	Basildon receives:	
	Balance of payment from customer	$60,000
	Less charges	$5,663
		$54,337
Summary $300,000 invoiced	Total receipts by Basildon: $240,000 + $54,337	$294,337
	Invoice discounter's fee and interest charges	$5,663

9 Accounts payable – managing trade credit

Trade credit is the simplest and most important source of short-term finance for many companies.

Again it is a balancing act between liquidity and profitability.

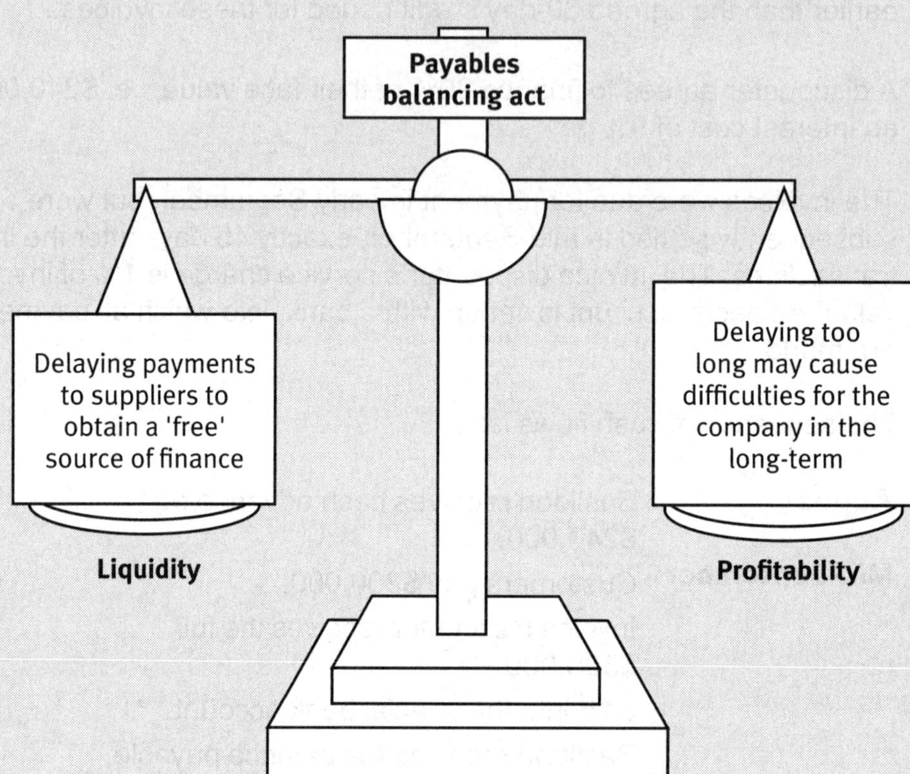

By delaying payment to suppliers companies face possible problems:

- supplier may refuse to supply in future
- supplier may only supply on a cash basis
- there may be loss of reputation
- supplier may increase price in future.

Trade credit is normally seen as a 'free' source of finance. Whilst this is normally true, it may be that the supplier offers a discount for early payment. In this case delaying payment is no longer free, since the cost will be the lost discount.

In the examination, you need to be able to calculate the cost of this discount foregone.

Trade payables

Under **trade credit** a firm is able to obtain goods (or services) from a supplier without immediate payment, the supplier accepting that the firm will pay at a later date.

Trade credit periods vary from industry to industry and each industry will have what is a generally accepted norm which would be from seven days upwards. The usual terms of credit range from four weeks to the period between the date of purchase and the end of the month following the month of purchase.

However, considerable scope for flexibility exists and longer credit periods are sometimes offered, particularly where the type of business activity requires a long period to convert materials into saleable products, e.g. farming.

A proportion of the firm's suppliers will normally offer **settlement discounts** which should be taken up where possible by ensuring that special clearing treatment is given where settlement discount is allowed. However, if the firm is short of funds, it might wish to make maximum use of the credit period allowed by suppliers regardless of the settlement discounts offered.

It is a mistake to reduce working capital by holding on to creditors' money for a longer period than is allowed as, in the long-term, this will affect the supplier's willingness to supply goods and raw materials, and cause further embarrassment to the firm.

Favourable credit terms are one of several factors which influence the choice of a supplier. Furthermore, the act of accepting settlement discounts has an opportunity cost, i.e. the cost of finance obtained from another source to replace that not obtained from creditors.

Whilst trade credit may be seen as a source of **free credit** , there will be **costs** associated with extending credit taken beyond the norm – lost discounts, loss of supplier goodwill, more stringent terms for future sales.

In order to compare the cost of different sources of finance, all costs are usually converted to a rate per annum basis. The cost of extended trade credit is usually measured by loss of discount, but the calculation of its cost is complicated by such variables as the number of alternative sources of supply, and the general economic conditions.

Certain assumptions have to be made concerning (a) the maximum delay in payment which can be achieved before the supply of goods is withdrawn by the supplier, and (b) the availability of alternative sources of supply.

Example 5 - ACC. PAYABLE: DISCOUNT FOR EARLY PAYMENT

One supplier has offered a discount to Box Co of 2% on an invoice for $7,500, if payment is made within one month, rather than the three months normally taken to pay. If Box's overdraft rate is 10% pa, calculate if it is financially worthwhile for them to accept the discount and pay early?

Age analysis of payables

The value of an age analysis of trade payables is probably less obvious than the value of an age analysis of trade receivables. However, management needs to be aware of:

- the total amount payable to suppliers
- when the money will be payable
- the amounts payable to each individual supplier, and how close this is to the credit limit available from the supplier
- whether the company is failing to pay its trade suppliers on time.

10 Chapter summary

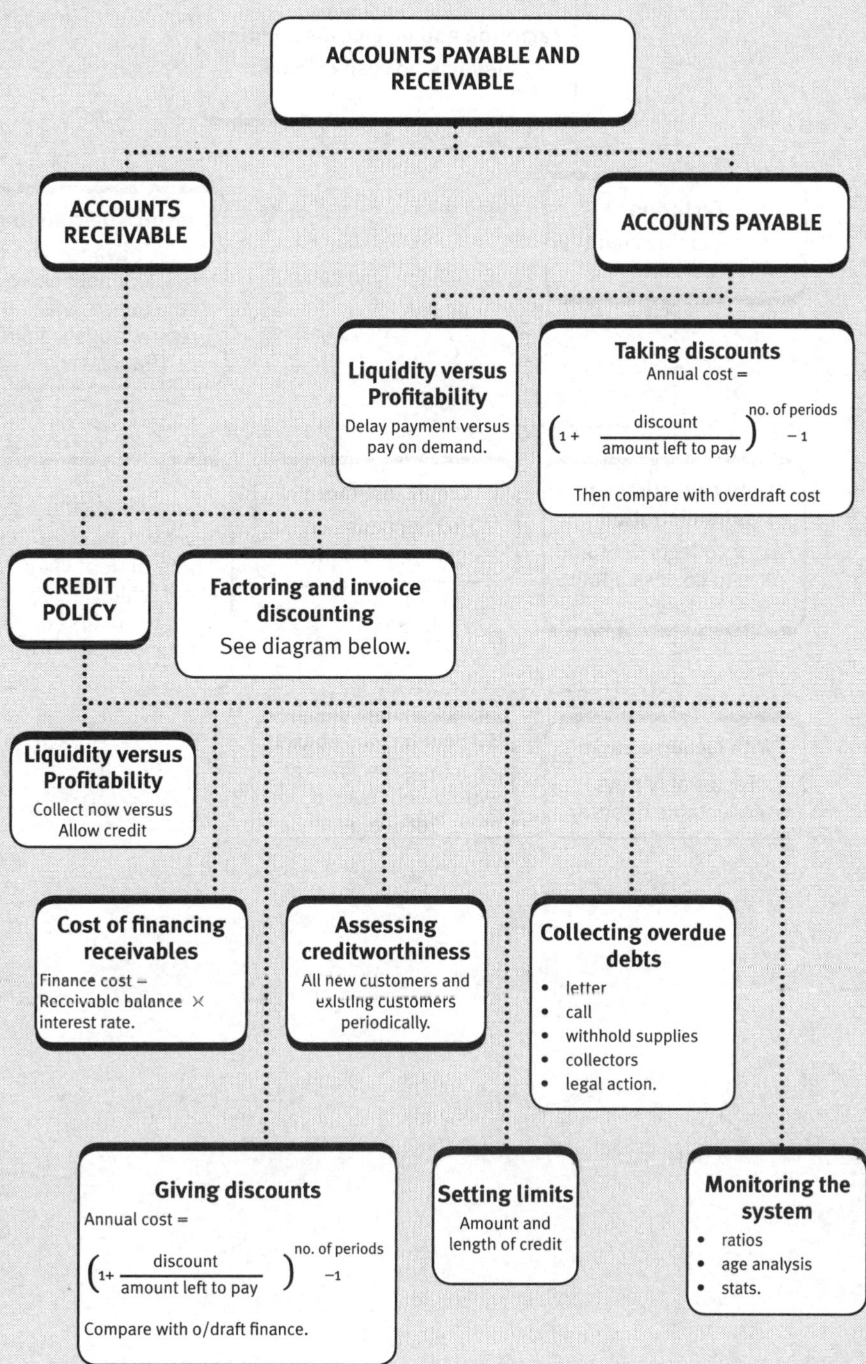

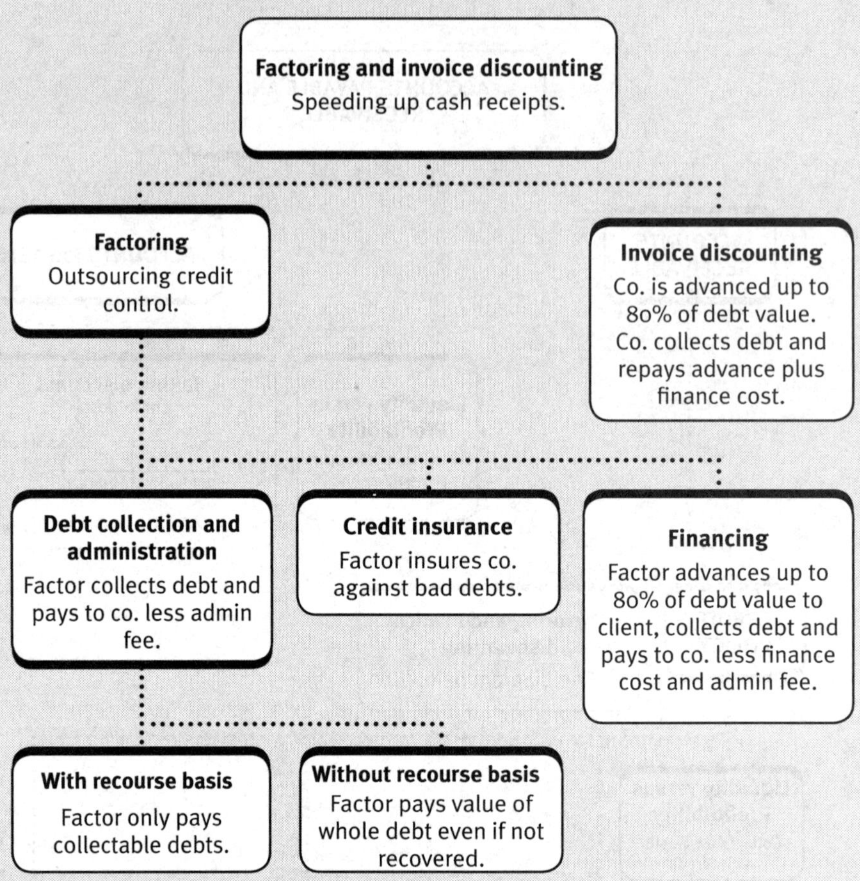
Factoring and invoice discounting
Speeding up cash receipts.
Factoring
Outsourcing credit control.
Invoice discounting
Co. is advanced up to 80% of debt value. Co. collects debt and repays advance plus finance cost.
Debt collection and administration
Factor collects debt and pays to co. less admin fee.
Credit insurance
Factor insures co. against bad debts.
Financing
Factor advances up to 80% of debt value to client, collects debt and pays to co. less finance cost and admin fee.
With recourse basis
Factor only pays collectable debts.
Without recourse basis
Factor pays value of whole debt even if not recovered.

11 Practice questions

Test your understanding 1

Identify which of the following occurs first in the credit cycle:

A Deliver goods

B Accept order

C Send invoice

D Send statement

Test your understanding 2

A company expects credit sales of $110,000 in July, rising by $10,000 each month for the next two months. Outstanding trade receivables at the beginning of July were $165,000, representing all of June sales and 22 days of May sales. Sales in June were $95,000.

The company wishes to reduce the average days sales outstanding to 45 days by the end of July and 40 days by the end of August.

On the assumption that the target should be to collect first the receivables that have been unpaid for the longest time, calculate the collection targets for:

(a) July, and

(b) August.

Test your understanding 3

List five methods of carrying out a credit check on a potential new customer, before deciding whether to give credit and if so, what the credit limit should be.

Test your understanding 4

A company is considering a change in its credit policy. It has estimated that if credit terms are extended from 30 days to 60 days, total annual sales will increase by 10% from the current level of $12 million. It has been estimated that as a consequence of the change in credit terms and the higher sales volume, bad debts would increase from 2% to 3% of sales. The company's cost of capital is 8%.

The increase in sales would not affect annual fixed costs. The contribution to sales ratio is 40%.

Required:

Calculate the effect of the change in credit policy on the annual profit before taxation. Assume a 360-day year of 30 days each month.

Test your understanding 5

A company is offering a cash discount of 2.5% to receivables if they agree to pay debts within one month. The usual credit period taken is three months.

Calculate the effective annualised cost of offering the discount and should it be offered, if the bank would loan the company at 18% pa?

Test your understanding 6

Calculate the equivalent annual cost of the following credit terms: 1.75% discount for payment within three weeks; alternatively, full payment must be made within eight weeks of the invoice date. Assume there are 50 weeks in a year.

Test your understanding 7

Marton Co produces a range of specialised components, supplying a wide range of customers, all on credit terms. 20% of revenue is sold to one firm. Having used generous credit policies to encourage past growth, Marton Co now has to finance a substantial overdraft and is concerned about its liquidity.

Marton Co borrows from its bank at 13% pa interest. No further sales growth in volume or value terms is planned for the next year.

In order to speed up collection from customers, Marton Co is considering two alternative policies:

Option one

Factoring on a non-recourse basis, the factor administering and collecting payment from Marton Co's customers. This is expected to generate administrative savings of $200,000 pa and to lower the average receivable collection period by 15 days. The factor will make a service charge of 1% of Marton Co's revenue and also provide credit insurance facilities for an annual premium of $80,000.

Option two

Offering discounts to customers who settle their accounts early. The amount of the discount will depend on speed of payment as follows.

Payment within 10 days of despatch of invoices 3%

Payment within 20 days of despatch of invoices 1.5%

It is estimated that customers representing 20% and 30% of Marton Co's sales respectively will take up these offers, the remainder continuing to take their present credit period.

Extracts from Marton Co's most recent accounts are given below:

	($000)
Sales (all on credit)	20,000
Cost of sales	(17,000)
Operating profit	3,000

Current assets:	
inventory	2,500
receivables	4,500
cash	Nil

Calculate the relative costs and benefits in terms of annual profit before tax of each of the two proposed methods of reducing receivables, and identify the most financially advantageous policy.

Test your understanding answers

Example 1 - COLLECTION TARGETS

- If no money is collected at all during April, the days sales outstanding would increase from 60 days to 90 days (= 60 days + 30 days in April).
- If days sales outstanding is reduced to 50 days, representing the most recent sales, these will be the sales in April and 20 days of sales in March.
- To reach the target of 50 days by collecting the oldest unpaid receivables, the company must collect 40 days of sales, representing:

	Days	$
From March sales *	11	425,806
From February sales	20	700,000
From January sales	9	270,000
		1,395,806

* March amount calculated as (11/31 x $1,200,000)

The collection target for April should therefore be $1,395,806, probably rounded up to $1,400,000.

Note: In this example, the collection target focuses on the trade receivables that have been unpaid for the longest time. A different policy could be followed, such as chasing the customers who are most likely to pay early, or chasing customers who are overdue with their payment by only one or two weeks.

Example 2 - COST OF FINANCING RECEIVABLES

Solution

(a) Receivables days = $4m ÷ $20m × 365 = 73 days

(b) Cost of financing receivables = $4m × 12% = $480,000.

Example 3 - EARLY SETTLEMENT DISCOUNTS

Discount as a percentage of amount paid = 2 ÷ 98 = 2.04%

Receivables days are 73 per illlustration1, so:

Saving is 63 days (dropping from 73 days to 10) and there are 365 ÷ 63 = 5.794 periods in a year

Annualised cost of discount % is

$(1 + 0.0204)^{5.794} - 1 = 0.1241 = 12.41\%$.

The overdraft rate is 12%.

It would be marginally cheaper to borrow the money from the bank rather than offer the discount.

Example 4 - FACTORING ARRANGEMENTS

(a) **Reduction in receivables days = 75 - 45 = 30 days**

Reduction in receivables	= 30 ÷ 365 × \$16m	= \$1,315,068
Saving in finance cost	= (8% × \$1,315,068)	= \$105,205
		say \$105,000
Administrative savings		= \$100,000
Service charge	= (1.75% × \$16m)	= \$280,000

Summary

	$
Service charge	(280,000)
Finance cost saved by reducing receivables	105,000
Administration costs saved	100,000
Net annual cost of the service	(75,000)

Edden will have to balance this cost against the security offered by improved cash flows and greater liquidity.

(b)	Costs offactoring	Savings
	$	$
Sales ledger administration 1% × $16m	160,000	
Administration cost savings		100,000
Cost of factor finance 10% × 80% × $3.3m	264,000	
Overdraft finance costs 8% × 80% × $3.3m saved		211,200
Total	424,000	311,200
Net cost of factoring	112,800	

As before the firm will have to balance this cost against the security offered by improved cash flows and greater liquidity.

Example 5 - ACC. PAYABLE: DISCOUNT FOR EARLY PAYMENT

Discount saves 2% of $7,500 =$150

Financed by overdraft for extra two months in order to pay early:

Cost = $10\% \times \frac{2}{12} \times \$7{,}500$ = ($125)

Net saving = $25

It is worth accepting the discount.

Alternatively :

Discount as a percentage of amount paid = $\frac{150}{7{,}350}$ = 2.04%

Saving is 2 months and there are $\frac{12}{2}$ = 6 periods in a year

Annualised cost of not taking the discount (and therefore borrowing from the supplier) is: $(1+0.0204)^6 - 1$ = 0.1288 = 12.88%

The overdraft rate is 10%.

It would be cheaper to borrow the money from the bank to pay early and accept the discount.

Test your understanding 1

The correct answer is **B**.

The supplier accepts an order before delivering the goods, sending an invoice and subsequently sending a statement.

Test your understanding 2

Target receivables

End of July	**Days**		$
July sales	31		110,000
June sales (balance)	14	(14/30 x $95,000)	44,333
	45		154,333

End of August	**Days**		$
August sales	31		120,000
July sales (balance)	9	(9/31 x $110,000)	31,935
	40		151,935

Target collections

	July $	**August** $
Receivables at the beginning of the month	165,000	154,533
Sales in the month	110,000	120,000
	275,000	274,333
Receivables at the end of the month	(154,333)	(151,935)
Target collections in the month	120,667	122,398

Test your understanding 3

Choose 5 from the following list:

- bank references
- trade references
- visit to the customer's premises
- competitors
- published information
- credit reference agencies
- legal sources of credit information
- company sales records
- credit scoring
- credit rating (large corporate customrs only).

Test your understanding 4

	Without the new credit policy	With the new credit policy
Annual sales	$12,000,000	$13,200,000
Average trade receivables	$1,000,000 ($12m x 30/360)	$2,200,000 ($13.2m x 60/360)
Increase in trade receivables		$1,200,000
Bad debts	$240,000 (= 2%)	$396,000 (= 3%)
Increase in bad debts		$156,000
Increase in annual sales		$1,200,000

	$	$
Increase in annual contribution (40%)		480,000
Increase in bad debts	156,000	
Increase in interest cost of receivables (8% x $1,200,00)	96,000	
		(252,000)
Net iIncrease in profit before tax		228,000

Test your understanding 5

Discount as a percentage of amount paid = 2.5/97.5 = 2.56%

Saving is 2 months and there are 12/2 = periods in a year.

Annualised cost of discount % is

$(1+0.0256)^6 - 1 = 0.1638 = 16.38\%$.

The loan rate is 18%.

It would therefore be worthwhile offering the discount.

Test your understanding 6

Step 1

Work out the discount available and the amount due if the discount were taken.

Discount available on a $100 invoice = 1.75% × $100 = $1.75.

Amount due after discount = $100 × $1.75 = $98.25

Step 2

The effective interest cost of not taking the discount is:

1.75 ÷ 98.25 = 0.0178

for an 8 – 3 = five-week period.

Step 3

Calculate the equivalent annual rate. There are ten five-week periods in a year.

The equivalent interest annual rate is $(1 + 0.018)^{10} - 1 = 0.195$ or 19.5%.

Test your understanding 7

The relative costs and benefits of each option are calculated as follows:

Option 1 – Factoring

Reduction in receivables days	=15 days	
Reduction in receivables	= 15 ÷ 365 × $20m =	$821,916
Effect on profit before tax:		
Finance cost saving	= (13% × $821,916) =	$106,849
Administrative savings	=	$200,000
Service charge	= (1% × $20m) =	($200,000)
Insurance premium	=	($80,000)
Net profit benefit	=	$26,849

Option 2 – The discount

With year-end receivables at $4.5 million, the receivables collection period was: $4.5m ÷ $20m × 365 = 82 days.

The scheme of discounts would change this as follows:

10 days for 20% of customers

20 days for 30% of customers

82 days for 50% of customers

Average receivables days become:

(20% × 10) + (30% × 20) + (50% × 82) = 49 days

Hence, average receivables would reduce from the present $4.5 million to:

49 × $20m ÷ 365 = $2,684,932

Finance cost saving = 13% × ($4.5m – $2.685m) = $235,950

The cost of the discount:

(3% × 20% × $20m) + (1.5% × 30% × $20rn) = ($210,000)

The net benefit to profit before tax : $25,950

The figures imply that factoring is marginally the more attractive, but this result relies on the predicted proportions of customers actually taking up the discount and paying on time. It also neglects the possibility that some customers will insist on taking the discount without bringing forward their payments. Marton Co would have to consider a suitable response to this problem.

Conversely, the assessment of the value of using the factor depends on the factor lowering Marton Co's receivables days. If the factor retains these benefits for itself, rather than passing them on to Marton Co, this will raise the cost of the factoring option. The two parties should clearly specify their mutual requirements from the factoring arrangement on a contractual basis.

chapter

19

Short-term finance and investments

Chapter learning objectives

Lead	Component
E2. Identify short-term funding and investment opportunities.	(a) Identify sources of short-term funding. (b) Identify alternatives for investment of short-term cash surpluses. (c) Identify appropriate methods of finance for trading internationally.

1 Session content diagram

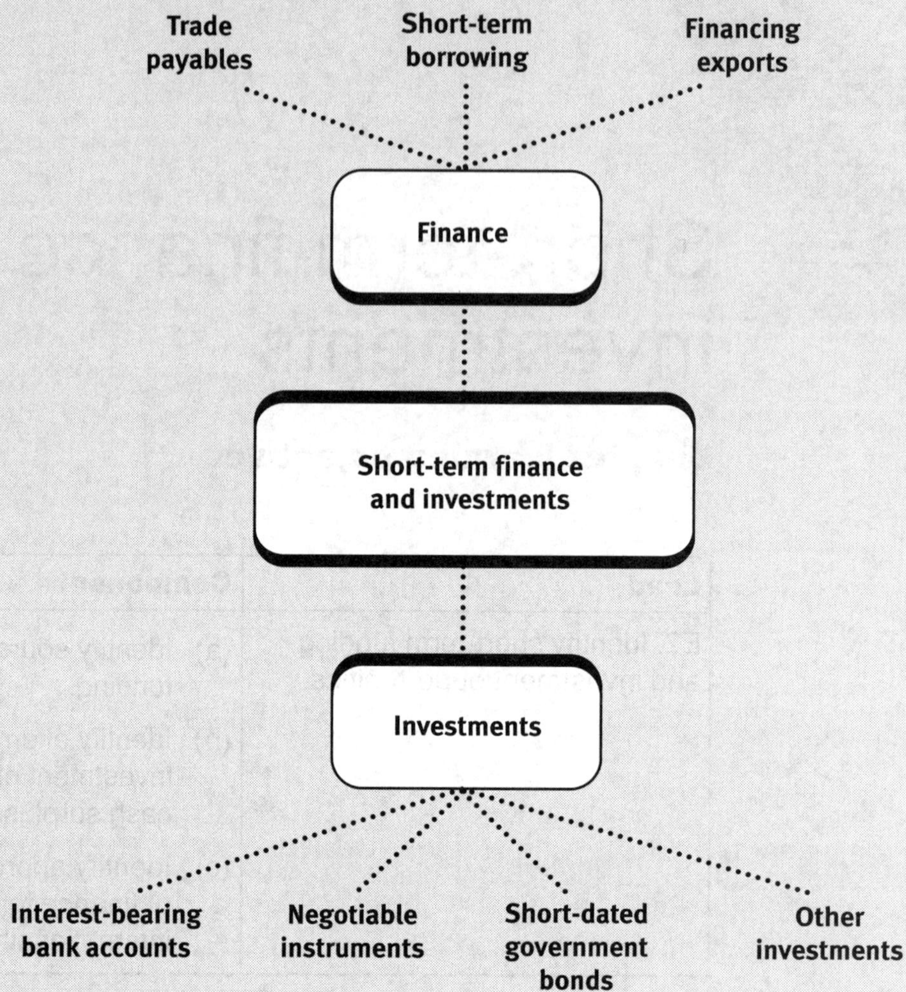

2 Short-term finance

Current liabilities should not be allowed to increase to a level where the cash position and liquidity of the company are at risk. This requires careful management of short-term finance.

The main sources of short-term funding are:

- trade payables
- bank overdrafts and short-term loans
- possibly, using trade receivables to borrow from a factor or invoice discounter (covered in an earlier chapter).

Trade payables as a source of short-term funds

Suppliers are a source of short-term finance because they provide goods (inventory) on credit. In some cases, suppliers might not be paid until after the goods they have supplied have been re-sold. This occurs, for example, in supermarkets. A supermarket might re-sell the goods provided by a supplier many days before the supplier is eventually paid.

It is a well-established business practice that trade credit should be agreed, which means that suppliers should finance the business of their customers to some extent.

The amount of trade credit varies from one industry to another, and can also vary with changes in economic conditions. However, if normal credit terms are 30 days, and a company purchases, say, $1,200,000 of goods on credit each year, it should be financed by $100,000 of trade credit on average.

A huge attraction of trade credit is that it has no interest cost. Unlike banks, trade suppliers do not charge interest on debts.

Benefits of paying suppliers late	Potential problems when paying suppliers late
• alleviates cash flow difficulties	• loss of any settlement discount
• cash can earn a return whilst still in the paying company's account	• could obtain a poor credit rating
	• supplier may stop further supplies
	• supplier may increase future selling prices to compensate
	• could face legal action from the suplier

Short-term borrowing

Short-term cash requirements can also be funded by borrowing from the bank. There are two main sources of bank lending:

- bank overdraft
- bank loans.

Bank overdrafts are mainly provided by the clearing banks and are an important source of company finance.

Advantages	Disadvantages
• Flexibility	• Repayable on demand
• Only pay for what is used,so cheaper	• May require security
	• Variable finance costs

Bank loans are a contractual agreement for a specific sum, loaned for a fixed period, at an agreed rate of interest. They are less flexible and more expensive than overdrafts but provide greater security.

Short term borrowing

Finance costs on bank loans and overdrafts are normally variable, i.e. they alter in line with base rates. Fixed rate loans are available, but are less popular with firms (and providers of finance).

Bank overdrafts

A common source of short-term financing for many businesses is a bank overdraft. These are mainly provided by the clearing banks and represent permission by the bank to write cheques even though the firm has insufficient funds deposited in the account to meet the cheques.

An overdraft limit will be placed on this facility, but provided the limit is not exceeded, the firm is free to make as much or as little use of the overdraft as it desires. The bank charges interest on amounts outstanding at any one time, and the bank may also require repayment of an overdraft at any time.

The advantages of overdrafts are the following.

- Flexibility – they can be used as required.
- Cheapness – interest is only payable on the finance actually used, usually at 2-5% above base rate (and all loan interest is a tax deductible expense).

The disadvantages of overdrafts are as follows.

- Overdrafts are legally repayable on demand. Normally, however, the bank will give customers assurances that they can rely on the facility for a certain time period, say six months.
- Security is usually required by way of fixed or floating charges on assets or sometimes, in private companies and partnerships, by personal guarantees from owners.
- Interest costs vary with bank base rates. This makes it harder to forecast and exposes the business to future increases in interest rates.

Overall, bank overdrafts are one of the most important sources of short-term finance for industry.

Bank loans

A bank loan represents a formal agreement between the bank and the borrower, that the bank will lend a specific sum for a specific period (one to seven years being the most common). Interest must be paid on the whole of this sum for the duration of the loan.

This source is, therefore, liable to be more expensive than the overdraft and is less flexible but, on the other hand, there is no danger that the source will be withdrawn before the expiry of the loan period. Interest rates and requirements for security will be similar to overdraft lending.

Comparison of bank loans and overdrafts

Consider a company that requires a maximum of $600 over the next four months. However, it is only halfway through month four that it actually requires the full amount.

The difference can be shown as follows:

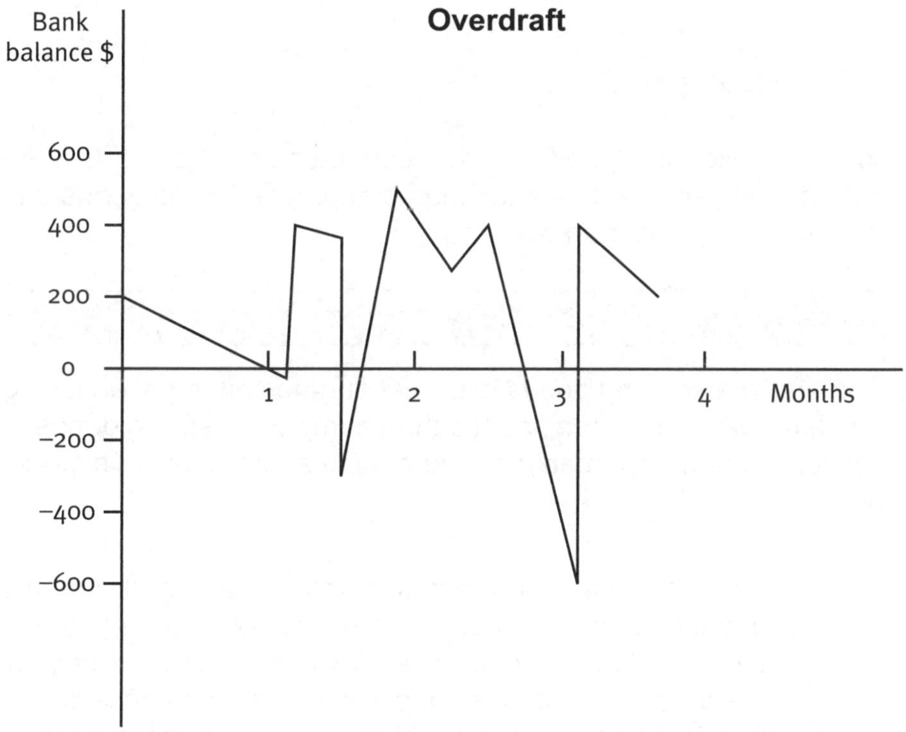

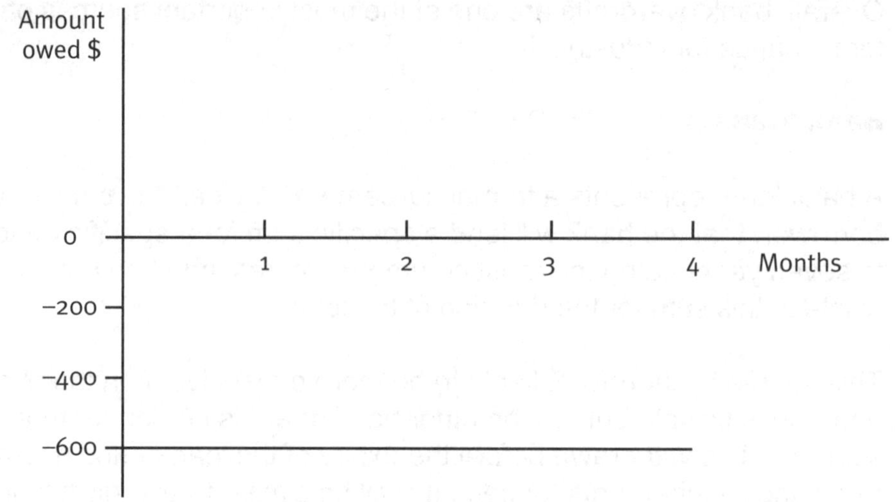

If an overdraft is used, the company will pay interest on the maximum amount part way through month 4. For the remainder of the period it will pay interest on an overdraft of substantially less than that, or it will pay no interest at all as it has a positive bank balance. If it borrows $600 by way of a bank loan at the beginning of the four months, it must pay interest for four months on the amount borrowed, despite the fact that it rarely requires the full sum.

3 Financing exports

Companies exporting goods to other countries often have much greater problems with credit and finance than companies selling goods and services to domestic markets.

Export risks

Companies exporting goods to other countries often have much greater problems with credit and finance than companies selling goods and services to domestic markets. The particular problems of exporters can be:

- The credit risk. There might be inadequate credit information about foreign customers. If payment from a foreign customer is overdue, it might be difficult to try to collect the money due to the geographical distance, different time zones and lack of familiarity with the legal system in the customer's country.
- The long time that may elapse between supplying goods to a foreign buyer and receiving payment: this problem is particularly severe when goods are sent by ship to a distant country.

- Due to this long time period between supply and payment, an exporter might have cash flow difficulties, and could need short-term finance to support its export operations.
- Foreign exchange control restrictions in the buyer's country, and weak domestic currency in the buyer's country. It might be difficult to obtain payment from the buyer due to the weakness of the domestic currency in the buyer's country.
  - The government of the country might impose restrictions on payments by its nationals to foreign suppliers in a 'hard' currency such as US dollars. This makes it difficult for the exporter to invoice the buyer in a hard currency.
  - The exporter might be unwilling to invoice the customer in the customer's own currency, because it might lose much of its value even within the trade credit period.

Several methods are available for dealing with the problems of financing exports and controlling the credit risk. These include:

- documentary credits
- bills of exchange
- export factoring
- forfaiting.

Financial instruments

Documentary credits (irrevocable letters of credit)

Business transactions between businesses in some countries are carried out on normal commercial terms. For example, trading between companies in the European Union is carried out mainly on normal credit terms, although a foreign currency might be involved for either the buyer or seller.

Trading between other countries, however, is more complex, particularly when it will take a considerable time to ship the goods from the exporter's country to the importer. The exporter might want payment as soon as possible, but the importer needs to be satisfied before paying that the exporter has complied with the terms of the sale agreement.

The problem of guaranteeing payment can be overcome by using an irrevocable letter of credit, also called an irrevocable documentary credit. A letter of credit is an undertaking given by its issuer that payment will be guaranteed for the exporter, provided that the exporter complies with certain specific requirements within a specified time limit.

The specific requirements relate mainly to the provision of satisfactory documentation for the exports, such as valid shipping documents and insurance documents, and valid import or export licences. The exporter must provide these as evidence that goods of the proper quantity and description are being shipped in the agreed manner, and are properly insured. This gives comfort to the buyer that the goods will be delivered as ordered.

The letter of credit is provided not by the importer, but by a bank on behalf of the importer. It might be issued by a bank in the importer's country, and confirmed by another bank in the exporter's country. A confirmed irrevocable letter of credit therefore provides payment guarantees to the exporter from two banks, thereby minimising the credit risk. Once issued, the irrevocable letter of credit cannot be revoked and cancelled. However, it ceases to apply if the exporter fails to comply with any of the specified terms and conditions.

An irrevocable letter of credit is arranged as follows:

- The importer asks a bank in its country to provide an irrevocable letter of credit for an import transaction. The exporter might require the letter of credit also to be confirmed by another bank in its own country.
- The letter of credit is issued, and a copy is given to the exporter.
- The cost of the letter of credit is usually paid by the importer.
- The exporter complies with the requirements of the letter of credit, and provides the specified documentation to a bank that will check to make sure that all the documentation is in order. This bank could be either the bank that issued the letter of credit or the confirming bank.
- If the documents are in order, the exporter will be paid under the terms of the letter of credit. In many cases, this involves a bill of exchange (see below).

The guarantee provided by the issuing bank in its letter of credit relates to compliance by the exporter with requirements relating to the documentation. The bank does not get involved in the details of the trading transaction itself.

- Even if the goods are shipped correctly, the bank will not guarantee payment if the documentation fails to meet the specifications in the letter of credit.
- If there is a dispute between the buyer and the importer about the actual shipment, the bank will honour its guarantee provided that the documentation was provided correctly and as specified in the letter of credit.

A bill of exchange

A bill of exchange is a method of arranging a payment. There are three parties to a bill of exchange:

- the drawer, who is the person who issues the bill
- the drawee, who is the person to whom the bill is addressed, and
- the payee, who is the person to whom payment should be made.

The drawer and the payee are often the same person. A bill of exchange might be a sight bill, which is payable immediately, but bills used for export finance are term bills, which are payable at a specified future date.

Payment by means of a bill of exchange is arranged as follows:

- The drawer issues a bill of exchange (or 'draws the bill on the drawee'). It might help to think of the bill at this stage as a 'You Owe Me'. It specifies that a sum of money must be paid by the drawee to the payee on a specified date.
- The drawee acknowledges the obligation to make the payment by signing the bill. The drawee is said to 'accept' the bill by signing it. In effect, an accepted bill is no longer a 'You Owe Me' from the drawer, but an 'I promise to pay' by the drawee.
- The accepted bill is returned to the drawer, who might hold it until maturity.
- When the bill reaches its maturity (the payment date specified), the drawer presents the bill for payment through the banking system.

A significant characteristic of bills of exchange is that:

- the drawee is given a period of credit before having to pay a term bill, but
- the drawer or payee can obtain payment earlier than the bill's maturity date, by means of discounting the bill.

When a bill is discounted, it is sold in the financial markets at a discount to face value. The size of the discount reflects the rate of interest that the buyer of the bill requires from holding the bill to maturity.

Export factoring

Export factoring is similar to ordinary factoring, with the exception that the factoring organisation agrees to factor the client's trade receivables for exports. The factor's services include administration of the receivables ledger and collecting payment, and providing factor finance.

In view of the problems that can arise with collecting payments from customers in other countries, the expertise of an export factor can be very helpful, particularly for small and medium-sized businesses with little experience in collecting foreign payments.

Forfaiting

Forfaiting can be a source of medium-term trade finance. It is particularly suitable for the financing of export transactions for which, due to the nature of the goods involved or the size of the transactions, payments are made over a period of several years. It has been used fairly widely in Europe, particularly in Switzerland and Germany where forfaiting originated.

An importer might want to buy capital goods, such as machinery or equipment, but needs finance for the purchase. The capital goods will be used to earn profits in future years, and the importer might want to use these future profits to provide the cash to pay for the goods.

In order to set up a forfaiting arrangement, the importer must be prepared to:

- pay some of the purchase price on delivery, and
- make the remaining payments at regular intervals over a period of several years.

In a forfaiting arrangement:

- The importer issues a number of promissory notes with payment dates at regular intervals. A promissory note is a promise to make a specified payment, and by issuing a series of promissory notes the importer is promising to make a series of payments at future dates, over a period of several years. (Instead of using promissory notes, the importer might be required to accept a series of term bills of exchange drawn on it by the exporter.)
- The importer must then find a bank that is prepared to guarantee the promissory notes. Guaranteeing a promissory note is called avalising the note. The avalised notes can be sold, like bank bills of exchange, at 'fine' rates of discount.
- The exporter's bank finds another bank that is willing to act as forfaiter. Some banks specialise in this type of finance. Forfaiting involves buying the avalised promissory notes at a discount to face value (or buying bills of exchange at a discount). The rate of discount at which the forfaiting bank buys the notes is specified as a fixed rate in the forfaiting agreement.
- The exporter therefore receives immediate payment from the forfaiting bank for the notes that it has purchased.

- The forfaiting bank holds onto the notes, and at the appropriate payment dates presents them to the importer for payment.

The forfaiter buys the promissory notes without recourse to the exporter. The exporter has therefore obtained payment for the goods, without any risk of having to return the money if the importer fails to meet its payment obligations.

The forfaiter therefore accepts the risk of non-payment by the importer (failing to honour the promissory notes or bills of exchange).

The key features of forfaiting are therefore that:

- The importer obtains medium-term finance for much of the purchase cost of the goods.
- The exporter receives immediate payment.
- The credit risk is accepted by the forfaiting bank, although this risk is reduced by the avalisation of the promissory notes by the avalising bank.

Forfaiting has been defined in CIMA's Official Terminology as follows: 'Forfaiting is the purchase of financial instruments such as bills of exchange … on a non-recourse basis by a forfaiter, who deducts interest (in the form of a discount) at an agreed rate for the period covered by the notes. The forfaiter assumes the responsibility for collecting the debts from the importer (buyer) who initially accepted the financial instrument drawn by the seller of the goods. Traditionally, forfaiting is fixed rate medium-term (one-to-five year) finance.'

4 Short-term investments

A business might have surplus cash for a period of time. Surplus cash is usually temporary and available for several weeks or months. Eventually it will be used to pay suppliers or settle other liabilities, invest in new non-current assets or pay a dividend.

Money in an operational bank account (a 'cheque account') earns no income, because banks do not pay interest to businesses for cash in their day-to-day accounts. If a business wishes to maximise its profits, it should consider using the cash to earn some return in the time when it is temporarily surplus to requirements.

Cash surpluses can be invested in a range of short-term interest-earning investments such as:

- Interest-bearing bank accounts
- Negotiable instruments
- Discount paper: the investment arithmetic
- Investing in short-dated government bonds
- Other short-term investments

Investment criteria

When a business has surplus cash to invest temporarily, it has to decide which investments to select from the different choices available. There are several criteria that should be considered when making these choices:

- maturity
- return
- risk
- liquidity
- diversification

More details

Maturity

A short-term investment might involve investing an amount of money for a specific period of time, and receiving interest and the payment of a principal amount at a specified future date (the 'maturity' of the investment). If the investment is cashed in or sold before maturity, there could be a risk of some loss of market value or some loss of interest.

The maturity of a short-term investment should ideally be no longer than the duration of the cash surplus. If the cash is needed before the investment reaches maturity, the investment will have to be 'cashed in' early, with some risk of loss of capital value or interest.

Return

With short-term investments, return is the interest yield on the investment. Some investments offer a higher yield than others.

Risk

Some investments are more risky than others. Risk refers to the possibility that the investment might fall in value, or that there might be some doubt about the eventual payment of interest or repayment of investment principal. As a general rule, higher-risk investments have to offer a higher return in order to attract investors.

For example, suppose that two banks offer high-interest savings accounts to businesses, for which there is a minimum notice period of two weeks for withdrawal of funds. Bank A might be a major bank with a 'triple-A' credit rating, and Bank B might be a regional bank in a developing country. To attract investors, Bank B would have to offer a higher interest rate on its savings accounts than Bank A, because the perceived risk for investors in an investment in Bank B would be much higher.Investing in equities is high risk. The value of equities depends on the profitability and future prospects of the company, and share prices also rise or fall more generally in line with broader movements in the stock market. Since share prices can fall by a large amount in a short period of time, equities are generally regarded as an unsuitable form of short-term investment.

Investing in equities is high risk. The value of equities depends on the profitability and future prospects of the company, and share prices also rise or fall more generally in line with broader movements in the stock market. Since share prices can fall by a large amount in a short period of time, equities are generally regarded as an unsuitable form of short-term investment.

Short-term investments should usually be preferred to longer-dated investments, because the risk of a fall in market value is less. Prudent companies should also avoid high-risk investments such as equities, and should look for short-term investments that will keep the value of the investment secure.

Liquidity

Liquidity refers to the ease with which an investment can be 'cashed in' quickly, without any significant loss of value or interest. All short-term investments are less liquid than cash in an operational bank account (cheque account), but some are more liquid than others. For example, many savings accounts or deposit accounts are reasonably liquid, and a depositor can often withdraw cash immediately for the loss of only several days' interest.

In contrast, works of art such as paintings might be a profitable long-term investment, but they are very illiquid as short-term investments. Paintings cannot be sold quickly without a significant risk of having to sell at below true market value.

Diversification

There is a general rule that investors should not 'put all their eggs in one basket'. They should perhaps diversify by investing in a range of different investments. In this way, if some investments perform badly, the investor is not exposed to significant losses, because the other investments in the portfolio should perform better.
However, diversification is less essential for investing short-term cash surpluses than for investing long-term in equities and bonds.

Interest-bearing bank accounts

These can fall into two categories:

- deposit accounts
- money market deposits

Deposit accounts

- Some deposit accounts are 'instant access' accounts, which allow the investor to withdraw the money without notice and without loss of interest. The interest rate is usually low on these accounts, and they are used when the investor wants to earn some interest on surplus cash, but places great importance on instant liquidity.
- Some deposit accounts or savings accounts allow the investor to withdraw funds without notice, but the investor will suffer some loss of interest. For example, a deposit account might require a notice of withdrawal of at least seven days, but the investor might be permitted to withdraw the funds without notice with a penalty of seven days' lost interest.
- In some cases, an investor might be unable to withdraw funds from the account without giving a minimum notice period.

Money market deposits

Money market deposits are amounts of money deposited through a bank in the money markets. These are the financial markets for short-term borrowing and lending. The money markets are used largely by banks and other financial institutions, for depositing and lending funds. Banks can deposit short-term funds with other banks, or borrow short-term from other banks in the inter-bank market.

Interest yields in the inter-bank market are often reasonably attractive, and it is now quite common for companies with large temporary cash surpluses to arrange with their bank to have the money deposited in the money markets (interbank market) or at money market interest rates.

Money invested in a money market deposit cannot be withdrawn until the deposit matures. It is therefore important that money should not be invested for a period longer than the investor's expected cash surplus. Money market deposits can be for very short periods of time, as little as one day, or for as long as several months (and even up to one year). However, very short-term deposits should be large amounts of money, so that the interest earned justifies the effort of making the deposits.

Effective annual interest yield

Interest on bank deposits accumulates on the principal sum invested. Interest is added at specified regular intervals, such as every month, every three months, every six months or annually. The frequency of adding interest affects the actual interest yield on the investment.

Example 1

A company has $1,000,000 to invest for 12 months.

The choices available are:

- a deposit account offering interest at 10% per year, with interest calculated quarterly
- a deposit account offering interest at 10.25% per year, with interest added annually.

Calculate which deposit provides the best return.

Interest earned

You might be required to calculate the amount of interest earned on a deposit or savings account within a particular period of time. If you are given the effective annual yield (or if you are given an 'annual yield' with no further information), the interest calculation is simply:

$$\text{Interest} = \text{Amount deposited} \times \text{Interest rate} \times \frac{\text{Number of days' interest earned}}{\text{Annual day count}}$$

The annual day count is the number of days in the year, for interest calculation purposes. This might seem unusual, since a year has either 365 or 366 days. However, in the financial markets, there are special conventions for the number of days in a year. Whereas interest on sterling is calculated on the assumption of a 365-day year, interest on the US dollar in the money markets is calculated on the assumption of 360 days in the year

Negotiable instruments

Negotiable instruments are financial instruments that may be obtained as investments. A key feature of negotiable instruments is that title passes when the instrument is handed from one person to another. They are 'bearer instruments', and ownership does not have to be recorded in a register of owners. This means that a negotiable instrument can easily be sold by one person to another.

Examples of negotiable instruments are:

- banknotes
- bearer bonds
- Certificates of Deposit
- bills of exchange
- Treasury bills.

The most important negotiable instruments as short-term investments are Certificates of Deposit and Treasury bills, and possibly also bills of exchange (particularly bank bills of high quality banks).

More details

Certificate of Deposit

A Certificate of Deposit or CD is a negotiable instrument that provides evidence of a short-term deposit with a bank with a fixed term and earning a specified amount of interest. The maturity of the deposit is usually 90 days or less, but can be longer. The amount deposited is at least US$100,000 (or its equivalent in other currencies), but usually larger.

The holder of the CD at maturity has the right to take the deposit with interest. The CD holder presents the CD at maturity to a recognised bank, which will then present the instrument to the bank holding the deposit, and arrange for the withdrawal of the deposit with interest.

Until maturity, the money is 'locked up' with the bank, and cannot be withdrawn.

When an organisation has a temporary cash surplus, it might arrange with its bank to place the money in a fixed term deposit account, and for the bank to issue a CD. The CD will state the identity of the bank, the amount deposited, the maturity date of the deposit and the interest that will accumulate.

- The organisation can hold the CD until maturity and then claim the money.
- Alternatively, if it needs cash before the deposit matures, it can sell the CD. There is an active secondary market in Certificates of Deposit, and a company can arrange for its bank to sell a CD on its behalf.

Another company with a short-term cash surplus could either arrange its own Certificate of Deposit or purchase an existing CD in the secondary market.

Investment yield on CDs

Since Certificates of Deposit are negotiable instruments, they are more attractive investments than money market deposits from the point of view of liquidity. A CD holder can sell the CD to obtain funds quickly, whereas a money market deposit cannot be withdrawn until maturity. Yields on CDs are therefore slightly lower than interest yields on money market deposits.

Bills of exchange

Bills of exchange have been described in an earlier chapter, In the context of export finance, although they have a broader use and are not restricted to export finance arrangements.

The significance of bills of exchange as a short-term investment is that they are negotiable instruments. There is an active money market for bills of exchange (which might be called the discount market) and investors can buy bills. The market is particularly active in bills of exchange that are payable by top-quality banks: in the UK these are sometimes called 'eligible bank bills'.

The buyer of a bill of exchange obtains the right to receive payment of the bill when it matures. A bill of exchange is usually an undertaking to pay a fixed sum of money at maturity, with no interest. An investor in a bill will therefore buy the bill at a discount to face value. Bills of exchange are therefore examples of discount paper.

Although it is possible to buy bills of exchange that have been accepted (and so are payable) by trading companies, investors place more value in bank bills. These are bills of exchange that have been accepted by a bank, and are payable by the bank. If the bank has a high credit status, the risk of investing in its bills is very low.

Yields on bills vary according to the credit risk associated with the bill, and an investor will be prepared to pay more for a top-quality bank bill than for a trade bill with much higher credit risk.

Treasury bills

Treasury bills are negotiable instruments issued by the government, with a maturity of less than one year. In practice, most Treasury bills have a maturity of three months (91 days). Treasury bills are used by a government to finance short-term cash requirements, and in countries such as the US and the UK, Treasury bills are issued at regular intervals when investors are invited to apply to buy bills in the new issue.

Since Treasury bills are debts of the government, they have a high credit quality, risk is low, and yields for investors are therefore also lower than for many other short-term investments. Treasury bills issued by a government and denominated in the domestic currency should be risk-free. For example, US Treasury bills are risk-free investments, because there is no doubt that the US government will redeem the debt at maturity.

Treasury bills are redeemable at face value. For example, the US government will redeem a 91-day $1,000 Treasury bill for $1,000 91 days after its issue. Since the bills are redeemable at par, investors pay less than face value to buy them. Like bills of exchange, Treasury bills are examples of discount paper.

Although yields on Treasury bills are relatively low, they can be attractive short-term investments because of their risk-free nature and their liquidity. There is a large and active secondary market in Treasury bills, such as US Treasury bills in the US and UK government Treasury bills in the UK.

Calculations

The amount of discount on a bill can be calculated as follows:

$D = R \times F \times T/Y$

where:

D = the amount of the discount
R = the rate of discount or discount yield, expressed as a proportion (for example, 6% = 0.06)
F = the face value of the bill: this will be paid to the bill holder at maturity
T = time, measured as the number of days in the interest period
Y = the days in a standard year (applying the appropriate 'day count convention' for the number of days in a year)

The issue price of a discount interest instrument such as a Treasury bill or bill of exchange is its face value less the discount:

Price = F – D

The discount explained

Whereas some investments such as bank deposit accounts and money market deposits earn interest on a capital sum invested, other instruments are issued at a discount to face value, and investors earn their return from the difference between the discount price on purchase and the par redemption value at maturity.The mathematics of discount paper returns are slightly different from the calculation of interest-yielding investments.

When a financial instrument is quoted on a discount interest basis, it is redeemed at maturity at its face value, and issued at a discount to face value. For example, a 91-day Treasury bill for $1,000 might be issued at $998.25 and redeemed at $1,000. The difference between the issue price and the redemption value is the discount which represents the return that the investor will make by holding the bill until maturity. The size of this return can be measured as a discount interest rate.

Example 2

A US Treasury bill with a face value of $1,000 is issued at a 5% discount yield for 91 days. Calculate its issue price?

(There are 360 days in a year for interest purposes.)

Short-dated government bonds

Companies can invest temporary surplus cash in government bonds. If they do so:

- they will receive interest on the due payment dates
- they can liquidate their investment at any time by selling the bonds in the secondary market
- if the bonds are short-dated when purchased, they can hold the bonds to maturity and have them redeemed at par.

However, there is some price risk with bonds, particularly longer-dated bonds. If interest rates change in the market, the market value of bonds will rise or fall. Bond prices rise when interest rates fall, but prices fall when interest rates go up. The movement in price is greater for longer-dated bonds.

If a company invests a cash surplus in longer-dated bonds, it must therefore recognise that if interest rates go up, there will be some loss on the investment.

Government bonds

Treasury bills are government debt instruments with a maturity of less than one year when they are issued. Government bonds are longer-dated government debt instruments, with a maturity of several years, sometimes 20 years or longer, when they are issued.

Government bonds are issued by governments in order to borrow long-term, and they can be purchased by any investors, including private individuals and companies. Investors can buy government bonds when they are first issued. Alternatively, they can be purchased in the secondary market at any time up to maturity of the bonds. There is a very large and active secondary market for the bonds of some governments, such as:

- the 'Treasuries' market in the US for US government Treasury bonds and notes (a note is similar to a bond, but with a shorter maturity on issue), and
- the 'gilts' market in the UK. 'Gilts' is short for gilt-edged securities, which is a term used to describe Treasury Stock and other bonds issued by the UK government.

An attractive feature of government bonds issued by a national government is that they are risk-free when they are issued in the domestic bond market and denominated in the domestic currency. For example, UK gilt-edged securities denominated in sterling are risk-free, in the sense that there is no credit risk. It is absolutely certain that the UK government will pay the due interest on time and will redeem the bonds at maturity.

Investors with a temporary cash surplus wishing to invest in government bonds should ideally invest in short-dated bonds. These are bonds with only a short time remaining to maturity. However, they can invest instead in longer-dated bonds, which can be sold easily in the secondary market when cash is needed.

Characteristics

Government bonds and corporate bonds (bonds issued by companies) have many features in common

- **Face value.** Bonds have a face value or nominal value.
- **Coupon.** Interest is payable on bonds at regular intervals, such as every six months or every year. Interest is usually a fixed rate, although some bonds (floating rate notes or FRNs) pay a variable rate of interest. For example, if bonds have an 8% 'coupon' on which interest is payable every six months, interest will be paid at the rate of 4% (8%/2) on the face value of the bonds every six months.
- **Redemption date and redemption value.** Bonds are redeemable at maturity (unless they are 'perpetual bonds' or unless they are 'convertible' into another financial instrument). Bonds are usually redeemable at their face value ('at par').
- **Market value.** Bonds are not necessarily issued at par, although they are usually issued at close to their par value. Their market value will vary over time, between their issue and their redemption. However, if they are redeemable at par, their value will move towards par value as the redemption date approaches. For comparative purposes, the market prices of bonds are quoted relative to their par value of $100. For example, if bonds are priced at $102.50, this means that their current market price is $102.50 for every $100 face value of the bonds.

Calculations

The yield on a bond investment is usually measured as a **redemption yield**. The redemption yield can be calculated as the discounted annual rate of return (internal rate of return) at which the present value of the future interest payments and the redemption value of the bond at maturity are equal to the current market value of the bond.

More details

Although interest on bonds is shown as a coupon rate, the actual investment yield earned by investors in bonds is a different amount. There are two reasons for this:

- The market value of a bond is not the same as its face value. For example, suppose that a bond with a 4% coupon has a market value of $95.00. The coupon is 4%, but the interest yield is 4.21% (4/95.00).
- The market price of a bond is not the same as its eventual redemption value, which is usually at par, and the yield for the investor should also take into account the gain or the loss for the investor from holding the bond to maturity. For example, if a bond has a market price of $95.00 and is redeemable in four years at $100.00, the investor will gain $5.00 on the investment of $95.00 by holding the bond for four more years.

The yield on a bond investment is usually measured as a redemption yield. (Also known as the yield to maturity.) This is the yield that will be obtained from an investment in the bond at a price P, and holding the bond until maturity. The redemption yield is a combination of:

- the interest yield on the bond (the coupon as a percentage of the market price),
- plus an annualised return to maturity from the capital gain on redemption of the bond at par,
  100 – P, where P is less than 100, or
- minus an annualised negative return from the capital loss at redemption, P – 100, where P is higher than 100.

The redemption yield can be calculated as the discounted annual rate of return (internal rate of return) at which the present value of the future interest payments and the redemption value of the bond at maturity are equal to the current market value of the bond.

Investors are interested in the redemption yield from a bond, not the coupon yield.

Example 3

A bond with a coupon rate of 7% is redeemable in eight years' time for $100. Its current purchase price is $82. Calculate the percentage yield to maturity?

Other short-term investments

This chapter has described the short-term investments that are most commonly purchased or used by companies. There are other short-term investments such as:

- corporate bonds, and
- commercial paper (CP).

These are more likely to be purchased by investment institutions rather than by companies with a short-term cash surplus.

More details

Corporate bonds

Corporate bonds are bonds issued by a company. They are long-term investments, and so unsuitable for investing a short-term cash surplus, and they can also be a high risk investment. Bond prices fluctuate with movements in the general level of interest rates, and corporate bond values are also affected by the perceived credit risk of the company issuing the bonds.

Commercial paper (CP)

Commercial paper consists of short-dated negotiable debt instruments issued by a company, and sold by a bank managing the company's commercial paper programme. In practice, although CP is negotiable, it is generally purchased by large investment institutions and held to maturity. It is not normally regarded as a suitable type of short-term investment of cash surpluses by a trading company.

Chapter summary

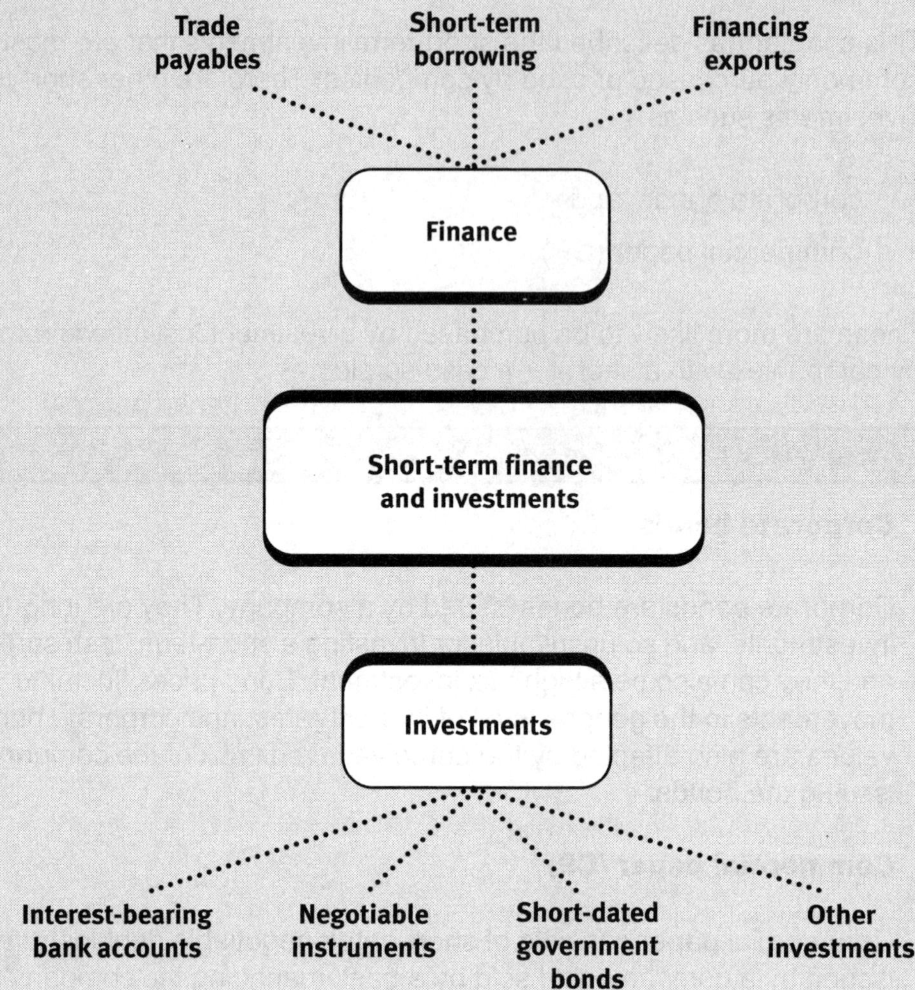

5 Practice questions

Test your understanding 1

Identify which of the following investments offers the highest effective annual interest yield:

A A deposit account paying interest at 5%, interest payable monthly

B A deposit account paying interest at 5.25%, interest payable every three months

C A deposit account paying interest at 5.4%, interest payable every six months

D A deposit account paying interest at 5.5%, interest payable annually

Test your understanding 2

On 1 April 20X4 a company placed $5 million on deposit at an interest rate of 6.25%. The deposit has a maturity date of 30 June 20X4.

Calculate the amount of cash that the company will receive on maturity of the deposit.

Test your understanding answers

Example 1

It might seem that the better investment is the deposit account offering 10.25%, but this is not the case.

When interest is quoted at 10% per year, payable quarterly, this means that the interest rate is 10%/4 = 2.5% each quarter. Interest is paid on the initial deposit plus the interest accumulated in previous quarters. In other words, interest is earned on the interest. The actual effective annual yield on an investment at 10% with interest paid quarterly is:

$[(1 + 2.5\%)^4 - 1] \times 100\%$
$= [(1.025)^4 - 1] \times 100\%$
$= [1.1038 - 1] \times 100\%$
$= 10.38\%.$

This is a higher effective annual yield than a deposit paying 10.25% annually.

Example 2

D = R x F x T/Y

where:

R = 5%
F = $1000
T = 91
Y = 360

D= 0.05 x 1000 x 91/360 = 12.64

P = F - D

= 1000 - 12.64

= $987.36

Example 3

To answer this question you will need to use the annuity factors and discount rates from the tables.

We need to assume two discount rates between which the required percentage is likely to fall. The yield to maturity will obviously be greater than 7% as the bond was purchased for less than its par value, so we will use rates of 10% and 12%:

t = 8; r = 10

(7 × 5.335) + (100 × 0.467) = 37.345 + 46.7 = $84.045

t = 8; r = 12
(7 × 4.968) + (100 × 0.404) = 34.776 + 40.4 + $75.176

By interpolation:

10% +(((84.045 – 82.0)/(84.045 – 75.176)) × 2) =

10% + (2.045/8.869 × 2) =

10% + 0.461 + 10.461% = **10.46%**

Test your understanding 1

The correct answer is **D.**

A

Interest at 5% per year, payable monthly means interest at 5%/12 = 0.4167% each month.

The effective annual yield is $[(1.004167)^{12} – 1]$ x 100% = 5.12%.

B

Interest at 5.25% per year, interest payable three-monthly means interest at 5.25%/4 = 1.3125% every three months.

The effective annual yield is $[(1.013125)^{4} – 1]$ x 100% = 5.35%.

C

Interest at 5.4% per year, interest payable six-monthly means interest at 5.4%/2 = 2.7% every six months.

The effective annual yield is $[(1.027)^{2} – 1]$ x 100% = 5.47%.

D

The effective annual yield on the deposit account paying interest annually is 5.5%.

Test your understanding 2

The interest on the deposit will be $5 million x 6.25% x 91/360 = $78,993.

At maturity the deposit will be $5 million + $78,993 = $5,078,993.

Index

Index